Blazing Cane

American Encounters / Global Interactions

A series edited by Gilbert M. Joseph and Emily S. Rosenberg

Blazing Cane

Sugar Communities,
Class, & State Formation
in Cuba, 1868–1959

Gillian McGillivray

Duke University Press
DURHAM & LONDON 2009

© 2009 Duke University Press
All rights reserved
Printed in the United States of America on acid-free paper ∞
Designed by Jennifer Hill
Typeset in Arno Pro by Achorn International, Inc.

Library of Congress Cataloging-in-Publication Data
appear on the last printed page of this book.

About the Series

This series aims to stimulate critical perspectives and fresh interpretive frameworks for scholarship on the history of the imposing global presence of the United States. Its primary concerns include the deployment and contestation of power, the construction and deconstruction of cultural and political borders, the fluid meanings of intercultural encounters, and the complex interplay between the global and the local. American Encounters seeks to strengthen dialogue and collaboration between historians of U.S. international relations and area studies specialists.

The series encourages scholarship based on multiarchival historical research. At the same time, it supports a recognition of the representational character of all stories about the past and promotes critical inquiry into issues of subjectivity and narrative. In the process, American Encounters strives to understand the context in which meanings related to nations, cultures, and political economy are continually produced, challenged, and reshaped.

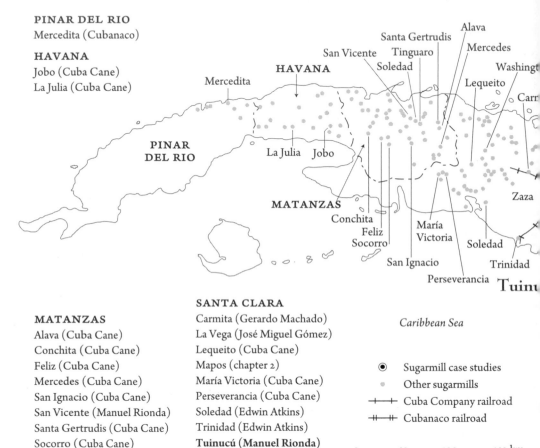

PINAR DEL RIO
Mercedita (Cubanaco)

HAVANA
Jobo (Cuba Cane)
La Julia (Cuba Cane)

MATANZAS
Alava (Cuba Cane)
Conchita (Cuba Cane)
Feliz (Cuba Cane)
Mercedes (Cuba Cane)
San Ignacio (Cuba Cane)
San Vicente (Manuel Rionda)
Santa Gertrudis (Cuba Cane)
Socorro (Cuba Cane)
Soledad (Cuba Cane)
Tinguaro (Cubanaco)

SANTA CLARA
Carmita (Gerardo Machado)
La Vega (José Miguel Gómez)
Lequeito (Cuba Cane)
Mapos (chapter 2)
María Victoria (Cuba Cane)
Perseverancia (Cuba Cane)
Soledad (Edwin Atkins)
Trinidad (Edwin Atkins)
Tuinucú (Manuel Rionda)
Washington (Manuel Rionda)
Zaza (chapter 2)

Caribbean Sea

◉ Sugarmill case studies
○ Other sugarmills
+―+ Cuba Company railroad
+‖―‖+ Cubanaco railroad

MAP 1   Cuba's 198 sugarmills, 1917. Alphabetical list (by province) identifies mills that are featured in this study; main case studies are in boldface. Drawn by Carolyn King, Geography Department, York University.

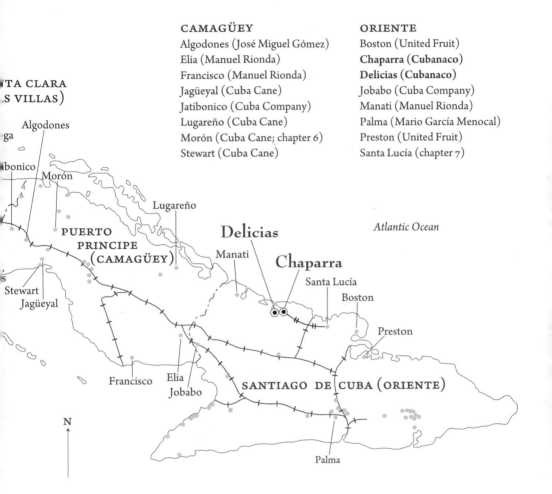

CAMAGÜEY
Algodones (José Miguel Gómez)
Elia (Manuel Rionda)
Francisco (Manuel Rionda)
Jagüeyal (Cuba Cane)
Jatibonico (Cuba Company)
Lugareño (Cuba Cane)
Morón (Cuba Cane; chapter 6)
Stewart (Cuba Cane)

ORIENTE
Boston (United Fruit)
Chaparra (Cubanaco)
Delicias (Cubanaco)
Jobabo (Cuba Company)
Manati (Manuel Rionda)
Palma (Mario García Menocal)
Preston (United Fruit)
Santa Lucía (chapter 7)

TA CLARA
S VILLAS)

Algodones

ga

bonico

Morón

Lugareño

**PUERTO
PRINCIPE
(CAMAGÜEY)**

Delicias

Manati

Chaparra

Santa Lucía

Boston

Preston

Atlantic Ocean

s

Stewart

Jagüeyal

Francisco   Elia
            Jobabo

SANTIAGO DE CUBA (ORIENTE)

N

Palma

Contents

Preface & Acknowledgments

When a ragged army of leftist guerrillas rode into the streets of Havana in revolutionary triumph in January 1959, U.S. diplomats turned their attention southward. Cuba, after all, was only ninety miles from Florida's coast. The boom in U.S. Latin American studies programs in the 1960s can be traced to the Cold War domino theory that the rest of the continent might follow Cuba into the communist camp. Academics from across the political spectrum pondered why revolution had triumphed and what made Cuba different from the rest of Latin America. Relying predominantly on U.S. diplomatic records, many emphasized the imperialism that began with the U.S. intervention in 1898 separating Cuba from Spain and ended with its so-called puppet dictator Fulgencio Batista in the 1950s. Today, as the U.S. embarks on "freedom and democracy building" projects in the Middle East and the State Department's Commission for Assistance to a Free Cuba promises to do the same when the Castro brothers' rule ends, it makes sense to weigh the historical impact of the United States on republican Cuba (1902–59) and to evaluate its relationship to revolution. That is one of this book's goals.

The Spanish colonial system's extensive bureaucracy generated reams of paperwork, which partially explains the depth of historical research on colonial Cuba. In contrast, republican Cuban archival sources are challenging

to access and difficult to use. Cuba's early-twentieth-century archival documents are as mixed up as mid-nineteenth-century documents in other parts
of Latin America, because archives reflect the difficult process of building
and organizing new states. (Cuba did not become a nation until 1902, in
contrast to most other Latin American colonies, which achieved independence in the 1820s.) Only historians have the luxury of time to plow through
unsorted documents in series with titles such as "Donated Files" or "Special Files," versus, say, "Department of Finance" or "Department of Labor."
This laborious research is the only way to accomplish the second of this
book's goals: to identify the nuts and bolts of republican Cuban state formation (where "state" is understood to include political, judicial, and military
institutions).

In the late 1960s and the 1970s, J. O'Connor, Eric Wolf, and Jorge
Domínguez published less-U.S.-centric analyses of the Cuban Republic
that argued that Fidel Castro was able to break the deadlock between the
various sectors of society represented in Batista's corporatist state—particularly between landowner associations and labor unions. How this corporatist state came to be remained unclear. What much of the historiography
lacked—and what this book contributes—is more serious attention to the
mass participation and important political zigzags between left and right
that took place between 1898 and 1959, in particular the changes surrounding the 1925 elections, the 1933 Revolution, the Second World War, and the
Cold War.

Cuban historians on and off the island—including Luis Aguilar, Olga
Cabrera, Alejandro de la Fuente, Alejandro García, Gladys Marel García-
Pérez, Jorge Ibarra, Jorge Renato, Lionel Soto, José Tabares del Real, and
Oscar Zanetti—have paid closer attention to the changing domestic politics and economics of the republic. Many researchers today are looking at
how the Spanish, Caribbean, and Asian immigrant experience changed over
the course of the twentieth century. Recent books by historians including
Alejandra Bronfman, Lillian Guerra, Aline Helg, Louis Pérez Jr., Rebecca
Scott, Lynn Stoner, Jean Stubbs, and Robert Whitney have also placed a
refreshing focus on culture, particularly gender, race, and nationalist ideology (*Cubanidad*) in early-twentieth-century Cuba. Their sources include
newspapers, writings by Cuban and Afro-Cuban students and intellectuals,
and Cuban archival data, which they have used with remarkable success.
All of these studies—and others too numerous to mention in this brief

overview—represent a significant step that moves Cuban historiography beyond the obsession with U.S. power, shifting the focus from Washington to residents in Havana, Cienfuegos, and other Cuban locations.

This book takes a different approach from much of Cuban historiography primarily because I am what David Collier and Ruth Berins Collier call a "lumper" rather than a "splitter." I recognize national and regional differences, but I try to see patterns within the Western Hemisphere. My first exposure to Latin American history came by way of John Tutino, James Brennan, and Peter Klarén, historians of Mexico and South America. Bill Beezley's monthlong seminar where I met my husband James Cypher was only one among many forums on Mexican history that I have attended since 1998, thanks to Tutino's and Beezley's influence. I have become rather obsessed with Latin American populism—with the anti-imperialist coloring it adds to the typical populist mix of idealizing "the common people" over the elites and the "producers" of wealth over the capitalists—thanks to Brennan and Klarén. For several years now, I have been reading U.S. and Latin American history more broadly to teach surveys on Latin America and the Americas. In consequence, this book's third goal is to ask not what was exceptional about Cuba, but what it shared with the Americas surrounding it.

Teaching has given me an overwhelming desire to try to write a book that can bring something new to the study of Cuba while at the same time synthesizing other research in a way that is accessible to newcomers. Mexican history inspired me to approach Cuba through regional case studies and led me to see that Cuban revolutionary *caudillos* (military strongmen and political bosses) claimed national power through regional networks built during the war of 1895–98, just as northern Mexican caudillos took control through Mexico's 1910 Revolution. Comparative readings on the impact of the Great Depression and the smaller agricultural depressions that preceded it led me to see that Cuba was one among many nations in which nationalism and populism emerged tentatively in the 1920s and more pervasively in the 1930s in response to the dominant gospel of modernity, progress, and free trade that reigned across the Americas from the 1880s to the 1920s. A Latin American Studies Association panel organized by Barry Carr, César Ayala, and Aldo Lauria-Santiago reinforced my conviction that we need to pay attention to what middle sectors did in the stereotypical "banana (or coffee, or sugar) republics" falsely assumed to have only rich landowners and poor, landless workers. The medium-size coffee or cane farmers were often the ones to push through nationalist and popular reforms during the economic swings of the 1920s and 1930s. Their associational and political movements were more subtle than the worker strikes and revolutions that followed in the 1930s, but they are at least as important to understanding social and nationalist reforms.

This book argues that revolutionary caudillo networks formed in Cuba in 1895–98 and middling farmer and working classes formed in the 1920s and 1930s, respectively, influenced both local day-to-day Cuban politics and national state building. Cuba experienced revolutionary caudillo and populist rule as well its better-known dictatorships and revolutions. It analyzes why shifts from caudillos to populists to dictators and revolution occurred. At the broadest level, it explores what we can learn about the meaning of "democracy" by looking at worker and farmer mobilization under caudillos, populists, and dictators.

Some of these themes have been addressed in other studies, but they have tended to emphasize Cuban difference and to carve up the colonial and republican periods into pieces (usually 1868–98, 1898–1933, and 1933–59). This initial periodization was necessary to get at Cuba's incredible complexities of region, class, and race. *Blazing Cane* builds on these important studies to provide a narrative that covers the whole of the revolutionary and republican periods (1868–1959). Highlighting the interaction between local and national history makes it clear that Cuban cane farmers and sugar workers, together with other activists, pushed the Cuban government to move from exclusive to inclusive politics and back again. Over the course of the twentieth century, Cuba began with a shallow democracy best defined as *caudillismo* and then shifted back and forth between more inclusive populism, exclusive dictatorship, and full-scale revolution in 1933 and 1959. Individuals went from looking "up" to their bosses who connected them to the government, to looking "beside" to their fellow workers, fellow farmers, or fellow mill owners, organizing horizontally into more powerful classes that could then make demands on the government.

The relationship between popular mobilization and state formation that creates zigzags from exclusive to inclusive political systems is recognized for other Latin American nations in studies by the likes of Gilbert Joseph and Daniel Nugent on Mexico; Daniel James on Argentina; and John French, Barbara Weinstein, and Joel Wolfe on Brazil but generally denied to the stereotypical "dictatorship" states of Nicaragua, the Dominican Republic, and Cuba. A Nicaraguan exception to this rule that inspired my own methods and approach is Jeffrey Gould's *To Lead as Equals*. Richard Lee Turits and Lauren Derby are also re-conceptualizing the Dominican Republic's Trujillo regime. State formation theory emphasizes that Latin American states express the relationships between local, regional, and national agents as they interact with international political and economic realities. Large political and economic events like wars, booms, or busts can change these relationships abruptly. National politics can only be understood by looking both outside the nation to the influence of foreign politicians and capitalists and inside the nation to the actions of municipal, provincial, and national leaders, as well as to the lower and middle sectors of society who seek to support, challenge, or overthrow them. Following E. P. Thompson's work on Britain, Lizabeth Cohen's on the United States, Thomas Klubock's on Chile, and Greg Grandin's on Guatemala, I trace how lower and middle sectors of society overlooked their differences to join together and define themselves as a "class" (in this case, "sugar workers" and "cane farmers").

This book builds a narrative of nineteenth- and twentieth-century Cuba by contrasting the development of two sugar communities from the 1860s through the 1950s. Most studies written on Cuba's republican era are national, not local; they have outlined important social, political, and economic changes, but the local processes and outcomes of these changes remain little analyzed, especially for areas outside Havana, Santiago de Cuba, and Cienfuegos. We can only build "the national" by layering "the local," as the historian Rebecca Scott has emphasized: the close study of individuals and social networks at the local level allows us to better understand larger mechanisms and interactions. This book joins the very few other analyses that focus on single Cuban communities, but it offers a broader time frame and scope by contrasting the development of two communities from colonialism through the first two-thirds of the twentieth century. Case studies of sugarmills make important building blocks for colonial and republican Cuban politics because sugarmills transformed the island's countryside and served as a base for political networking, class formation, and revolutionary mobilization.[1] By examining closely the radical changes in the relationships and responsibilities linking workers, cane farmers, and sugarmill owners with the state, I offer a new picture of how Cubans lived and worked and of how the colonial, and then Cuban, state operated from 1868 to 1959.

Previous historians have developed useful conceptual shorthand that divides Cuba into two regions. The West was the center of national power, closely tied to Spain, sugar, and slavery in the colonial era and negotiations with U.S. power in the twentieth century. The mountainous East was home to runaway slaves, bandits, subsistence peasants, and rebellion in the colonial era, and it became the site of U.S. imperialism and rebellions against U.S. power in the twentieth century. My research has led me to adjust the model, emphasizing that there were subregions within each region that resembled the other and giving more space to the central province that straddled the two regions (called "Las Villas" in the colonial era and then "Santa Clara" in the republican years).

The triumph or failure of revolutionary struggles depended largely on the capture of the central region of Las Villas / Santa Clara. That center served as the base from which to conquer Havana. By 1920, sugar had spread almost entirely across the island, making Cuba an extreme case of the single-crop export economy,[2] but sugar communities had sprung up across the colony in an uneven pattern beginning in the western provinces of Havana and Matanzas and only gradually spreading to the East and Center.[3] Until the mid-eighteenth century, the western provinces of Havana and Matanzas produced about 85 percent of the sugar on the island, while central Las Villas produced most of the rest. Through the 1850s and 1860s, Las Villas's share increased to 30 percent. The two regions' sugar production leveled off at about 40 percent each from 1900 through 1908, at which point the eastern provinces of Oriente and Camagüey started to claim a larger share of production.

Eastern production rose as a select group of mills built in the region during and after the U.S. occupation of 1899–1902 began to hit their stride. Chaparra, the grandest sugarmill in the world in the early twentieth century, was the first of a new type of plantation in Cuba. Established in Puerto Padre, Oriente, the mill was characterized by large-scale U.S. investment, ultramodern machinery, massive landholdings, and an integrated system of production that included ports, railroads, and easy access to food, work animals, and sugarcane. Sugar baron Manuel Rionda's Francisco sugarmill began to produce shortly after Chaparra, alongside the United Fruit Company's Boston and Preston mills, among others (see map 1, above).

Ramiro Guerra's *Sugar and Society in the Caribbean*, first published in 1927, argued that these super-plantations of the East threatened social and political stability on the island. He advocated that the more stable "Cuban" system of the West should be applied to the more "American" East. Guerra's regional contrast influenced policymakers at the time, and many analysts have built upon it since (most recently Oscar Zanetti, Alan Dye, and César Ayala). Fascinated by Guerra's argument, I initially chose Chaparra and Tuinucú in order to establish a contrast between North American and Cuban systems of production. According to the construct, Chaparra, being in the East, would be the largest and most "American" mill in early-twentieth-century Cuba, while Tuinucú, being closer to the West, would be decidedly "Cuban." (I was unable to find a mill in the West proper that had not changed owners, thereby dispersing source material, during the 1868–1959 period.) On closer examination, I had to put Guerra's construct aside because at least during the first twenty years of the century, both mills appeared to be quintessentially "Cuban American" in that they combined attributes from both worlds. Moreover, closer study revealed that workers and cane farmers in the foreign enclaves of the East ended up organizing and winning more demands than those of the West precisely because of the rising nationalist context in which Ramiro Guerra wrote *Sugar and Society*.

Although a number of studies focusing on U.S. imperialism in Cuba have sought to identify the number of "American" versus "Cuban" mills on the island (beginning with Leland Jenks's 1928 *Our Cuban Colony* and continuing through Jorge Ibarra's and Oscar Pino Santos's studies), I believe that this quest blinds us to the complex realities of corporations. It is extremely difficult to unravel a sugarmill's "nationality." For example, Tuinucú was owned predominantly by Spaniards, but it was incorporated in the United States. Manuel Rionda, a Spanish subject, studied in the United States from a young age and lived in New York, while much of his family was based in Matanzas, Cuba. He made some decisions regarding Tuinucú from his New York office, but other Rionda family members lived in Cuba and administered the mill directly on a day-to-day basis from the 1880s through the 1940s. Manuel himself would claim to be Cuban in one context, Spanish in the next, and American in a third. After so many years of residence, at what point does one cease to be "Spanish" and become "American" or "Cuban"? If part of the capital is North American but the corporation has offices in both Havana and New York, should we consider the mill "American," "Spanish," or "Cuban"?

Equally complex, Chaparra was set up and administered by a Cuban, General Mario García Menocal, but Texas Congressman Robert Hawley and Hawley's group of New York–based sugar capitalists funded and incorporated the company in the United States. Menocal's identity is similar to that of Manuel Rionda (minus the Spanish nationality) in that he spent much of his life studying in the United States and embraced many things American. He graduated from Cornell University with an engineering degree shortly before the 1895 insurgency began. Although he ran Chaparra in close conjunction with the American directors, as general manager of the Chaparra mill Menocal doled out cane farms to Cuban generals, officers, and family members.

When my research did not fit Guerra's model, I shifted my objective to using the Tuinucú mill in the relatively old central region and the Chaparra mill in the eastern "frontier" to gain a broad understanding of island-wide change from the colonial through the republican eras and to study the impact that sugar communities had on the state. (The eastern "frontier" region hosted little large-scale industry but was home to many squatters and small to medium-size farms producing tobacco, cattle, cane, and other products.) Since the Tuinucú estate began producing sugar early in the colonial era, and Chaparra did not enter the scene until 1895, my initial focus is mostly on Tuinucú in the central province of Las Villas. Chaparra enters the study later but becomes the central focus for the discussion of the republican era because it was significantly larger and its inhabitants achieved more political power than Tuinucú's. Chaparra's first administrator, Mario García Menocal, became Cuba's president from 1913 to 1921, and Puerto Padre's significant cane farmer and worker associations of the 1920s, 1930s, and 1940s were among the vanguard pushing through laws to protect cane farmers and workers in those same decades.

Though less prominent in the republican era, Tuinucú serves as a useful comparison that sometimes mimics and sometimes diverges from its much larger counterpart to the east. Overall, the comparison and contrast of the two communities make it possible to explore how the local—specific individuals, enterprises, and regions—interacted with power changes at the national and international levels. We see how the communities were affected by global processes such as changes in the international sugar economy, wars, nationalism, and depression, and how they in turn sought to use and shape the national responses to these processes.

Before continuing, I want to alert the reader to a few of the most important people, places, and sources for this story. The sugar baron Manuel Rionda organized a U.S. corporation to purchase the Tuinucú estate in 1893. Tuinucú's U.S. base proved important because it allowed the stockholders to sue the United States for damages perpetrated during Cuba's third war for independence from 1895 to 1898. (On signing the Treaty of Paris at the end of the Spanish–American War, the United States made itself responsible for property claims against the Spanish government.) My analysis of the 1895–98 Revolution in the Sancti Spiritus region builds on evidence from this legal case and Rionda family correspondence contained in the University of Florida's Braga Brothers Collection. Though often contradictory, the testimonies of planters, cane farmers, workers, Cuban insurgents, and Spanish soldiers confirm the importance of central Cuba and provide an exceptionally detailed description of the state of contested power in that region in the 1890s.

Documents from the Braga Brothers Collection in Florida and the Cuban-American Sugar Mills Collection at the provincial archives of Las Tunas provide the scaffolding for chapters 4 to 8 on the Cuban Republic. The former was donated by the Braga–Rionda family and contains correspondence, production data, and maps relating to the Czarnikow–Rionda Company, one of North America's largest importers of sugar and molasses. The records deal with its affiliated companies in Cuba and the United States, including cane farms, storage facilities, a sugar refinery, alcohol distilleries, cattle ranches, and sugarmills, Tuinucú among them. Manuel Rionda was very hands on, demanding detailed contact from each mill manager and company president; the records therefore provide a rich source on Tuinucú and the other Rionda mills.

Especially during the years surrounding the First World War (roughly 1914–20), Rionda played a very important role nationally as organizer of the largest ever sugar conglomerate on the island, the Cuba Cane Sugar Company. Muriel McAvoy, who was extremely helpful throughout my research and writing, documents this side of the Rionda story in *Sugar Baron: Manuel Rionda and the Fortunes of Pre-Castro Cuba*. Rionda's association with this larger conglomerate helps to stretch *Blazing Cane*'s coverage beyond two mill case studies. During that same period, Rionda served as a sugar broker and negotiator for President Mario García Menocal, a second central character who helps this book bridge the local–national gap.

Menocal was a revolutionary caudillo, then the general manager of the
Chaparra sugarmill, and then the president of Cuba from 1912 to 1921.

Rionda's close friend Robert Bradley Hawley also served as an important
negotiator for Menocal during the First World War. He owned the second
large conglomerate at the time, the Cuban-American Sugar Company (Cubanaco). At its peak, Cubanaco owned two refineries (one in Matanzas and
one in Louisiana) and six sugarmills, including Chaparra and its neighbor
Delicias in Puerto Padre. Cubanaco's annual production capacity was over
300,000 tons of raw sugar and 150,000 tons of refined sugar. The corporation also owned mechanical workshops; electricity, power, and ice plants;
and large storage, communication, and transportation facilities (over 2,000
miles of telephone lines and railroad tracks for public and private service).
When the Cuban revolutionary government nationalized Chaparra and
Delicias in July 1960, all company records were to be destroyed to make
space and clear the imperial record, so to speak. Thank goodness one
worker, José Collazo, decided to preserve as many documents as possible
in an abandoned scale house at Chaparra. His family donated the material
to the provincial archives of Las Tunas, where Marina Pichs Brito, Antonio
Oliva, and other dedicated archivists have created a well-organized and professional place to research, despite the lack of resources.

Newspaper and magazine clippings and Eva Canel's and Carlos Marti's
travel diaries, along with documents from the national and provincial archives of Cuba, the United States, and Great Britain, helped me sketch out
the 1900–20 period that is less well documented in the Braga and Cubanaco
collections. Also, in 1959 and shortly thereafter, Cuban sugar workers had
the foresight to understand the importance of the historic worker struggles
that they had lived through. "Historical Committees" formed at each mill
to write short histories of the mills, and I found some of these precious
histories in provincial libraries and archives and in the "kitchen archives"
of former sugar workers.

Oral history and worker histories highlight the humble counterparts to
the patrons, matrons, and middlemen and women in this study. You will see
the likes of Agustín Valdivia, Melanio Hernández, Eduardo Bertot, Jesús
Menéndez, Rita Díaz, and Ester Villa standing up to Manuel and Isidora
Rionda, Oliver and Elena Doty, Mariana Sava and Mario García Menocal, Robert Bradley Hawley, and R. B. Wood. I found their stories through
Eladio Santiago, Arquímedes Valdivia, Omar Villafruela, Rita Díaz, Tomás

González, Ester Villa, Victor Marrero, and Jose Abreu, who let me interview them and showed me their own notes from Tuinucú and Chaparra histories. While early-twentieth-century everyday life at the mills is extremely difficult to reconstruct, the Rionda family correspondence and the days and days of interviews with old-timers that Eladio and Victor shared with me made it possible to imagine life during what Eladio calls the "Golden Age" from 1900 to 1920 and during the more turbulent years thereafter. Where relevant, I also cite the testimonials of sugar workers from other mills on the island to fill out the human side of the story. Although they may be tinted with nostalgia in some areas and exaggerated by anti-American bias in others, these reminiscences offer irreplaceable insights into the lives of the workers. Their words can touch us in ways that the contemporary historian cannot.

The Cubans mentioned here are only a few of the many to whom I owe a huge intellectual debt. Between the time I wrote my dissertation proposal (on sugar workers in the 1933 Revolution) and the time I began my research, Robert Whitney published an important book, *State and Revolution in Cuba: Mass Mobilization and Political Change, 1920–1940*. I am extremely grateful to Bob, Barry Carr, Marc McLeod, César Ayala, Muriel McAvoy, Lillian Guerra, and Rebecca Scott, among other Cubanists, for helping me identify sources and potential areas for research when I was casting around for ideas between 1998 and 2000.

James Cypher, whom Eladio Santiago so beautifully named my "fiel compañero," fed me, copied lists of names and numbers for me, and was my home in Gainesville, Florida; Bloomington, Indiana; Washington, D.C.; and across the island of Cuba. Since then, he has become an incredible father to our four- and six-year-old bundles of joy, Charles and Justine, and has cooked and provided for the family to let me finish this book. I also thank my mother, Helen, for her editing; my father, Donald; my grandmothers, Helen Weider and Sheila McGillivray; and my brothers and in-laws for being so supportive along the way. José Abreu, Domingo Corvea, Fe Iglesias, Jorge Giovannetti, Rafael Soler, Olga Portuondo, Reinaldo Román, Michael Zeuske, and Jorge Renato Ibarra all shared their work with me and pointed me in the right direction. Franklin Knight, Berarda Salabarria, Luis Frades, and Carmen Valdes did the *"trámites"* to get me permission to do the research at archives and libraries across Cuba; and Oscar Zanetti, Amparo Hernández Denis, Omar Villafruela, Victor Marrero, and Belkys Quesada helped me to do follow-up research in Las Tunas in September 2005. The archivists in Gainesville, Las Tunas, Sancti Spiritus, Havana, Santa Clara, Holguín, Santiago de Cuba, London, Boston, and Washington helped me find documents to look at and—in the Cuban provinces—places to stay.

Carl Van Ness went way beyond the call of duty, sending me photographs and maps that the University of Florida's George A. Smathers Libraries, Department of Special and Area Studies Collections, allowed me to use for this book. Omar Everleny Pérez and his friend Elpidio Rodriguez Alvarez in Havana offered valuable assistance in reproducing the bulk of the book's photographs. Everleny's aunt, Daisy Villanueva, and her family and friends in Sancti Spiritus let me watch the Brazilian soap opera (*El Rey del Ganado*) that helped me survive the seemingly endless televised roundtable discussions on the Elian González saga during my dissertation research in 2000.

Mike Socolow showed me the ropes at Georgetown University, an extremely supportive institution from start to finish. I cannot praise John Tutino and Alison Games enough for their time and effort at getting me through the program and getting me jobs and funding. Financial support came from Georgetown (Graduate Fellowship and Glassman Award for Best Dissertation in the Humanities), the Social Sciences and Humanities Research Council of Canada, the University of Florida (Library Travel Grant), the Coordinating Council of Women Historians (Ida B. Wells Dissertation Grant), Brock University's Humanities Research Institute, and the Office of the Principal at Glendon College, York University.

Thanks to Louis Pérez Jr., to Greenwood Press, and to the *Journal of Caribbean History* for permission to reprint the parts of chapters 2, 6, and 7 that appeared in "Revolution in the Cuban Countryside: The Blazing Cane of Las Villas, 1895–1898," *Cuban Studies* 38 (2007): 50–81; "Reading Revolution from Below: Cuba, 1933," in *Daily Lives of Civilians in Wartime Latin America: From the Wars of Independence to the Central American Civil Wars,* edited by Pedro Santoni (Westport, Conn.: Greenwood Press, 2008); and " 'Dear President Machado': Colono Nationalism in Cuba's Turbulent 1920s and 1930s," *Journal of Caribbean History* 37, 1 (2003): 79–109.

I am grateful to three of my undergraduate professors at Dalhousie: Stephen Brooke, for making me fall in love with history; John Kirk, for getting me interested in Cuba; and Judith Fingard, for warning me against "belabored writing" in my first thesis. And I thank all the other young Cubanists who are making important contributions to the field and who have influenced my work in many ways: Bob Whitney, Marc McLeod, Frank Guridy, Ricardo Quiza, Maikel Fariñas, Reinaldo Román, Michele Reid, Matt Childs, John-Marshall Klein, David Sartorius, Kym Morrison, Rosann Santos, Alejandra Bronfman, Lillian Guerra, Mariel Iglesias, Michelle Chase, Alan Dye, and Manuel Barcia, among others.

My Latin American survey students and graduate students struggled through earlier versions of *Blazing Cane* to graciously point out when I assumed too much knowledge and when I delved into too much detail. I thank them for their time and have done my best to address their suggestions alongside the more specialized ones that Duke University Press's two readers, Alejandro de la Fuente and William French, generously provided. Essential input on how to make this a better manuscript came from John Tutino, Alison Games, Thomas Klubock, Franklin Knight, William Taylor, and Margaret Chowning. Anne Rubenstein, James Cypher, Derek Williams, Michael Lima, Peter Blanchard, Catherine LeGrand, Stephen Palmer, and others in the Toronto Area Latin American Research Group offered advice on parts of the text, as did members of the History Departments at Brock University and York University and the editors Cy Strom and Susan Deeks, for which I am very grateful. I benefited greatly from the support of Valerie Millholland, Miriam Angress, and Mark Mastromarino of Duke University Press.

In the end, Bob Whitney's book and Barry Carr's articles on sugar workers in Cuba's 1933 Revolution forced me to become more ambitious in time and scope. Thanks to them, this book aims to describe the process of class organization among sugar workers, cane farmers, and sugarmill owners that dominated the Cuban countryside from Cuba's first war for independence in 1868 all the way through to the 1959 Revolution. It seeks to identify the political openings and blockages related to international events that these groups used to construct and change the Cuban state at the local and national levels. I hope the book demonstrates that we can understand national change only by paying attention to international context and local agency.

Chronology of Major Political Events

1934 . . . . . Fulgencio Batista led military coup to install President Carlos Mendieta

1935 . . . . .General strike; Carlos Mendieta resigned

1936 . . . . Miguel Mariano Gómez elected president, then deposed by Batista

1939 . . . . . . .Communist CTC founded to replace CNOC; FNOA to replace SNOIA

1940 . . . . Cuban Constitution passed; Batista elected president

1944 . . . . Ramón Grau San Martín of the Auténtico Party elected president

1947 . . . . . U.S. Truman Doctrine introduced; communists jailed, exiled, and killed

1948 . . . . Carlos Prío Socarrás of the Auténtico Party elected president

1951 . . . . Eduardo Chibás (leader of the Ortodoxo Party) committed suicide

1952 . . . . Batista led military coup and took power

1953 . . . . Fidel Castro attacked military barracks in Santiago

1956 . . . . Castro's M-26–7 guerrillas established a base in Sierra Maestra in East

1958 . . . . . . M-26–7 conquered Santa Clara in December, pushing Batista into exile

1959 . . . . .General strike allowed Fidel Castro's M-26–7 to take power

See the glossary on pages 345–48 for explanation of acronyms used in the book.

Introduction

Ay Miranda, tiene caña quemada	*Alas, Miranda has blazing cane*
Palmarito tiene caña quemada	*Palmarito has blazing cane*
Santa Lucía tiene caña quemada	*Santa Lucía has blazing cane*
Qué es lo que pasa en mi Cuba	*What is happening in my Cuba*
Que ya no se vende caña	*That cane is now hardly being sold*
Yo me muero para que su precio suba	*I'm dying for the price to go up*
Que le pasa al Buen Vecino	*What is happening to the Good Neighbor*
Que me compra poca caña	*He is buying very little cane from me*
Le grito al Buen Vecino	*I'm shouting to the Good Neighbor*
"Tienes que aumentar la cuota"	*"You need to raise the quota"*

Lorenzo Hierrezuelo and his Duo Los Compadres composed this song sometime around 1930, when the siren of the Miranda sugarmill near Santiago de Cuba signaled that one of its cane fields was on fire. The song's refrain offers a litany of sugarmill names—Miranda, San Antonio, and Jatibonico, among others—all suffering from outbreaks of cane fires. As the recording's liner notes explain, these fires could mean many different things.[1] The history of late-colonial and republican-era Cuba is inextricably linked to the history of sugar (and cane fires) because sugar constituted 75 percent of all Cuban exports from the late eighteenth century throughout much of the twentieth. Large sectors of the Cuban population depended on sugar for their livelihood, including workers, cane farmers, merchants, sugarmill owners, and the colonial and national politicians who lived off customs duties. Economic depression did not always usher in cane fires, strikes, or revolutions, and economic growth did not always equal peace. Nevertheless, we need to keep in mind two broad cycles to understand Cuban history. One was economic, the booms and busts of the international sugar market. The other was agricultural, the timing of the sugar harvest.

The Cuban economy peaked during and after World War One (specifically in the years around 1917–21) when cane sugar's main competitor,

European beet sugar, virtually disappeared from the world market. Until the 1920s, the sugar harvest lasted roughly half the year, but over the course of that decade, as beet sugar returned to the market and Europeans embraced protectionism, Cuban politicians and sugarmill owners cut the harvest down to two intense months of production. They allocated tight quotas to each farmer and sugarmill in hopes of curbing the world supply and increasing the price of sugar. Other nations simply poured more beet and cane sugar into the world market, resulting in Cuba's long periods of economic stagnation and unemployment each year, dubbed "the dead time," from the 1920s onward. Workers, cane farmers, mill owners, and politicians battled over how much cane to produce; how often to weed, cut, and replant it; and how much it should cost. The status quo of ten months of unemployment for a vast majority of Cubans—and the cane fires lit in reaction to this status quo—served as backdrop to both the 1933 and 1959 revolutions.

Hierrezuelo's song presents the perspective of an important social group largely ignored in historical analyses of Cuba: the cane farmers, or *colonos*.[2] The colono that Hierrezuelo represents in this song was likely a small farmer growing and tending cane with his family to sell to the nearest sugarmill. Colonos could also be comfortable middle-class owners or renters of medium-size plots of land. A few were large landowners who rented out their land to *subcolonos*. Fidel and Raul Castro's father, for example, amassed enough profits managing a work crew in the boom years to become a large landowner in the 1920s.[3] In Hierrezuelo's day, the colonos were reading and hearing about the "Good Neighbor" policy of the United States through the press and the new mass medium of radio, but they did not see their local patrons (the sugarmill owners) or their national and international patrons (Cuban, U.S., and British politicians) demanding more cane, or paying more for it.

Cane fires could harm people, animals, cane carts, or buildings, and burned cane lost all of its sucrose unless it was processed within twenty-four hours. If a heavy rain fell during or after the fire, the mud might render it impossible for bulls to move the heavy carts full of cane from cane farm (*colonia*) to mill on time. It invariably cost more to replant burned fields than it would have cost had they been left fallow or harvested less hastily. The replanting issue was especially relevant for older colonias: Sugarmill owners preferred to leave these fields fallow most of the time, asking cane farmers to cut and replant only once every four years.

By torching an old colonia's cane, a cane farmer or worker could force the sugarmill owner to mill inferior, burned cane rather than lose it entirely, thus diverting cane carts and extra workers from the higher-yielding colonias originally scheduled for harvest. Some colonos took to setting their own fields on fire to force the mills to grind more cane than their quotas allowed. This colono strategy was so widely used that the owners of one of this book's case studies, the Chaparra sugarmill, had to abolish the special treatment of burned cane fields in the early 1930s.[4] Colonos at the Tuinucú sugarmill—the second case study—used the same approach (see map 1 for case-study locations). Manager Oliver Doty wrote to the owner Manuel Rionda in January 1928: "The colonos are sending in so much cane that we find it necessary to grind at full speed. If we reduce our rate of grinding I am afraid we will have cane fires."[5] The liner notes to Hierrezuelo's song mention these motives and another that did not come out in more formal sources: A farmer could burn his or her cane to collect insurance.[6]

Workers, too, resorted to arson. Masters at lighting the fires clandestinely, they might wire a firebrand to a snake's tail or light the oil-soaked fur of a large rat and then let the snake or rat dash in agony through the cane fields.[7] This was only one of the many tricks described in this book. It created jobs to burn cane that would otherwise be left standing until sugar brought a better price. The burned cane had to be cut and hauled to the mill, and the fields needed to be cleared and replanted during the dead season leading up to the next harvest. Sometimes workers opted to burn cane for other reasons. Cutting sugarcane was a brutal task that required great dexterity. The worker had to stoop below the base of the cane stalk (where there was the most sugar content), cut it with a single powerful stroke of the machete that sent it flying into the air, and then strip each stalk of its leaves.[8] Experienced cutters could slash the leaves as a stalk fell to the ground, but even then they had to take the time to lift the stalk again, cut it in half, and leave it in a pile to be loaded into carts, weighed, and brought to the mill. Workers were paid by the task, and they could cut more cane in a shorter amount of time if it was burned. In 1906, according to a U.S. observer, "an ordinary laborer working from three in the morning until eleven" could make as high as $3.60 per day cutting burned cane, in contrast to the $1.80 to $2.50 per day he or she would make normally.[9]

Another motivation for burning the fields was to improve working conditions. Although ashes made the work hot and grimy in the sweltering heat, this was preferable to cutting through a field infested with the *aroma* or *pica pica* climbing weed that itched and burned the skin on contact.[10] Fortunately, the weed was not common, and Cuba did not have poisonous snakes or other dangers that explain the consistent practice of burning before cutting in Australia or Mexico. The Cuban government actually adopted the Australian system of controlled burning for a brief era after the 1959 Revolution to try to improve cane cutters' productivity levels.[11]

Political repression became a new factor leading to arson in the later years of the 1920s and the early 1930s. Workers and revolutionaries set fires as a means of committing sabotage because President Gerardo Machado's more repressive approach to rule after his fraudulent reelection in 1928 left few other options. Political dissidents used the same strategy against Fulgencio Batista's regime in the late 1930s and again in the 1950s, and anti-Castro exiles dropped fire bombs into cane fields from airplanes departing from Miami after 1959. Workers and revolutionaries on other sugar islands in the Caribbean and in Hawaii also used cane fires to protest against colonialism and elite rule and to create jobs in times of economic depression.[12]

The burning of cane fields was a sign of internal labor negotiations during times of peace and also a dominant form of political civil warfare during the revolutions and rebellions of Cuba's nineteenth century and twentieth. What made the cane burnings of 1868–79, 1895–98, 1933, and 1957–59 "revolutionary" was the fact that they were instigated by leaders who aimed to destroy the social and political system sustained by the sugar economy. In contrast, leaders of the 1906, 1912, and 1917 "rebellions" threatened to burn cane only if their demands for political reform were not met. Burning cane functioned as a means of imposing the colonos' or workers' will over mill owners, as a means of protest, and as a text that sugarmill owners and politicians had to read in order to understand what goal colonos, workers, or revolutionaries were trying to achieve, depending on the historical context. It will therefore serve as a recurrent theme, assuming particular importance during the revolutions of 1868 and 1959 that frame this study.

Although Cuba's revolutions have received a great deal of attention and they constitute an important focus of this book, my larger aim is to offer a synopsis of the development of the social classes linked to sugar and their contribution to the formation and transformation of the Cuban state from the first Cuban Revolution for Independence in 1868 through the Cuban

Revolution of 1959 that brought Fidel Castro to power. Classes and states are neither structures nor categories but things that in fact happen in human relationships.[13] By watching men and women over a long enough historical period, we can perceive the formation of patterns in their relationships, their ideas, and their institutions; we can see people begin to think and organize themselves as individuals joining those next to them to form classes that build states as opposed to being linked only vertically and tangentially as individuals to local and national political bosses.

Previous studies of Cuba have focused a great deal of attention on the impact of U.S. power on Cuban development. The impact is undeniable, but it should not blind us to specifically Cuban class- and state-formation patterns and to the many parallels with the rest of Latin America. Cuban dependence on sugar, slavery, and colonial rule made the nineteenth-century island significantly different from the rest of the hemisphere (with the notable exception of Brazil), and Cubans' embrace of universal manhood suffrage in 1902 made it unique, but the way that economics and politics functioned in Cuba from 1900 through 1950 was similar to the way they functioned in other Latin American countries. Just recently, the editor of *The Second Conquest of Latin America: Coffee, Henequen, and Oil during the Export Boom, 1900–1930*, ventured to argue that Cuba's economic development was consistent with that of much of Latin America. The common features were European and North American capitalist investments in export commodities and related infrastructure. The export boom's roots lay in the European and North American demand for Latin American raw materials and consumer goods during the second phase of the Industrial Revolution.[14] Latin America's receptiveness lay in the elites' belief that exports would pave the way to progress and modernity.[15]

Blazing Cane's focus is more political. It argues that Cuba moved through three successive systems of negotiation between the state, capitalists, and the popular classes defined as "the colonial compact" (1780–1902), "the patrons' compact" (1902–32), and "the populist compact" (1933–52). The term "compact" rather than "contract" applies because these were unstated agreements on how to keep the peace day to day; they were "patterns in relationships" that established the boundaries of acceptable behavior that all parties recognized.[16] In the first and second periods (1780–1932), sugarmill owners and cane farmers controlled individual workers as best they could and agreed to be ruled by the colonial power or the Cuban president as long as they could continue to make profits. In the third period (1933–52), workers, farmers, and sugarmill owners forged what we would today call "lobby groups," effectively creating a more class-based system of rule for the Cuban state. Each compact lasted for a relatively long period of time— especially the colonial one—and the second two compacts ended with dictatorships and then revolutions that ushered in new compacts.[17]

Caudillos were usually war heroes from the provinces who became heads of political parties such as the Conservative Party and the Liberal Party.[18] In most of Latin America, these two parties fought over the relationship between church and state, but in Cuba ideological differences between the two (or more) political parties were slight. A wide network of personal and business relationships extended from the caudillo and his war companions to individuals throughout the nation to make up the ruling or opposition party. When in power, the caudillo, acting as *patron*, would dole out jobs, contracts, and favors to party members and supporters ("clients") in exchange for their political support. Politicians in the United States engaged in similar bribery (called "pork-barrel politics") during the same period. At the local level, estate owners linked to the Conservative Party or the Liberal Party would also rule over workers and their families through a system of patronage whereby they would provide certain benefits and favors in exchange for labor and votes. In Cuba's case, sugarmill owners and cane farmers were the capitalists who practiced this patronage, but elsewhere in the United States and Latin America they might be the owners of company towns surrounding automobile plants, textile mills, or cotton, coffee, or banana plantations. Regional and national caudillos balanced the demands of capitalists for profits with the needs of the lower- and middle-class members of their political clientele groups for jobs and income.

Chapters 1 through 5 of this book show that in Cuba many such clientele groups, including the liberals at Tuinucú and the conservatives at Chaparra, were rooted in the nineteenth-century wars for independence and grew within twentieth-century sugar and cattle-ranching communities. Foreign and domestic capitalists used patronage, or what might be termed "capitalist welfare," at the local level to maintain peace in their communities—providing health care, housing, and education benefits to loyal friends and employees in exchange for labor and profits.[19] Cuba in this important era of economic growth shared many characteristics with other American nations, including the rulers' obsession with progress and modernity at all costs.

Chapters 6 through 8 show that the patrons' compact between caudillos, capitalists, and workers survived only until the 1920s and 1930s, when economic depression hit the Americas, creating the conditions for a new era of populist, nationalist rule. Populism across the Americas had two main ideological components. One elevated the moral virtue of "the common people (*populus*)" over the political elite, while the other elevated "producers" or "labor" over capitalists as the source of progress.[20] Latin Americans often critiqued the United States, as well, adding nationalism to the populist mix. This was because Americans constituted many of the biggest capitalist investors in Latin America, and U.S. Marines occupied Latin American countries repeatedly during the early twentieth century to protect these capitalist interests. When national economies wavered in the 1920s and then crashed in the 1930s, Latin Americans blamed U.S. capitalists and their domestic elite allies. Workers, farmers, and professionals began to unite and call themselves working or middle "classes." They lobbied the state for protection as a group because their patrons' Depression-era cutbacks had failed them as individuals. Populist parties led by military men or civilians appealed to these new self-defined classes through slogans, symbols, and (less consistently) reformist laws that included protection for national industries, farmers, and labor.

Latin American sociologists and leftist political scientists of the 1960s and 1970s depicted populism in very negative terms; they described demagogic charismatic leaders and ruthless union bureaucracies ruling over naïve, manipulated masses who were not yet class-conscious enough to carry out an authentic social revolution.[21] According to these analyses, populists incorporated more people into the political system but disempowered them at the same time by stripping them of any autonomy they may have had through worker or community organizations. Recent scholarship on populists of the mid-twentieth century presents a more nuanced vision of these movements by exploring diverse communities within the "masses" to emphasize how and why many chose to engage with populists as a way to be included in the system of rule.[22]

This book makes a comparatively positive assessment of populism. During the middle decades of the twentieth century, between roughly 1930 and 1970, humble people in North, Central, and South America chiseled rights and more social-democratic systems of rule for their nations by organizing and acting together as classes or in radical political groups that might be labeled "Socialist," "Christian Democratic," "Populist," "Social Democratic," or any combination of the above. Beginning in 1947, the Cold War policies of anticommunism in the United States and Latin America allowed many conservative Latin American elites and armies to crush these more socially oriented forms of democracy. They replaced them with either flat-out dictatorships or much more superficial forms of individualistic "political" democracies.

The textbook example of this argument is the 1944–54 Revolution that Guatemalan elites and soldiers crushed with the help of the U.S. Central Intelligence Agency. Other examples include the shifts from inclusive populist to exclusive military rule under Getúlio Vargas in Brazil (1930–45), Rafael Leonidas Trujillo and others in the Dominican Republic (1930–61), the Somoza family and others in Nicaragua (1936–79), and Juan Perón in Argentina (1946–55). The final chapter of this book describes the case of Cuba under Fulgencio Batista and others from 1933 through 1959. The populist eras of rule should not be idealized, since they frequently included corruption, inefficiency, and military infiltration into society. Yet they should be recognized as times when more people had a stake in their nations. Working and middle-class groups or parties could claim more as "citizens," and many at least fleetingly gained more dignity, rights, and economic power.

Workers, farmers, professionals, and other groups in Cuba, like their counterparts elsewhere in Latin America, used the international context to push the system of rule from a dictatorship to a more populist body politic. Populist reforms became especially pronounced during the Second World War era, when Britain, the Soviet Union, and the United States allied against fascist Germany and Italy. Communists and socialists across the Americas temporarily won the freedom to organize and demand a stronger social role for the state, including reforms for women, workers, and the unemployed. This era was Latin America's Democratic Spring: Whereas only five out of twenty Latin American republics could be considered democracies in 1944 (Mexico, Uruguay, Chile, Costa Rica, and Colombia), by 1946 only five of the fifteen dictatorships remained (Paraguay, El Salvador, Honduras, Nicaragua, and the Dominican Republic).[23] When Cubans rallied against Spain's Francisco Franco in 1937, they were in fact critiquing the dictatorial aspects of Fulgencio Batista's rule at home. Batista, like other populist leaders, responded to the challenge by becoming less repressive and more reform-oriented. He and the rulers who followed him were the consummate populists, negotiating with Cuban lobby groups through a combination of co-optation and coercion (inclusion and force). Although many sources on the 1952–59 Batista regime are not yet accessible, it appears that the rulers broke the populist compact in the late 1950s by using too much military force and favoritism for individuals and not enough political inclusion for organized groups such as workers' unions and associations of cane farmers, industrialists, professionals, and mill owners.

Chapters 6 through 8 trace these national changes at the local level, as well, where mill owners and managers overestimated the number of cutbacks workers and cane farmers were willing to accept. By looking at sugar communities during the national strike waves of 1923–25 and the revolution of 1932–35, it becomes evident that cane farmers and workers first contested and then rejected the patronage system. When the fragility of patronage and "capitalist welfare" became exposed in the context of agricultural depression in the 1920s and 1930s, workers and colonos in Cuba, like their lower- and middle-class counterparts across the Western Hemisphere, demanded more formal, lasting "state welfare" reforms. During these economically volatile nationalist decades, the class-based mobilizations of first cane farmers (described in chapter 6), then workers (described in chapter 7), pushed Cuban presidents to replace the client-based patronage politics with class-based populist politics and legislation that more directly confronted foreign capitalist interests in the 1930s and 1940s.

Attention to the changes in these decades reveals another large pattern that finds parallels across the Americas. The Cuban labor legislation of the 1930s described in chapters 7 and 8, like the Democratic Party's New Deal in the United States or Carlos Ibañez's 1931 labor code in Chile, sought a way to contain the popular revolutionary anger and demands for socioeconomic justice arising out of the Great Depression through conservative reform. Cuba's 1933 Revolution began with the overthrow of the dictator Gerardo Machado, passed through a period called "one hundred days of reform" under Professor Grau San Martín, and then ended with a Liberal Party presidency buttressed by Fulgencio Batista's military might. The new president did not reverse the reforms passed during the one hundred days, but labor legislation was written and enforced in such a way as to give as much control as possible to the government. This in itself was an important change, for if we conceive of the relationship between mill owners, cane farmers, and workers as a triangle in which "the state" rarely intervened from 1898 to 1933 (with the exception of occasional coercion when the army was sent in to reinforce private security forces), 1933 signified the arrival of the state as mediator between mill owners and cane farmers, mill owners and workers, and even cane farmers and workers. The populist compact meant that the state had to negotiate with lobby groups from each sector of society, including national associations of mill owners, cane farmers, workers, and industrialists.

Chapter 8 shows that workers at first rejected the reforms, but again as in the United States and Chile they opted to work from within and push the reforms further as the 1930s wore on. At the expense of autonomy (independence) from the state, workers were able to win substantial gains during the Second World War Popular Front era. Class-based representative politics remained strong until 1947, when U.S. Cold War policy pushed first the Auténtico Party (in power from 1944 to 1952), and then Fulgencio Batista (after his 1952 military coup), to ban Communist labor leadership. The Auténtico Party, created by Ramón Grau San Martín as an "institutionalized" version of the 1933 Revolution, introduced a highly insidious form of populism that divided labor unions from within and undermined some of the power workers had accumulated. The Batista "dictatorship" of 1952–58 maintained many of the constructions of the populist compact, officially dealing with workers through the Auténtico Confederation of Cuban Workers (CTC), cane farmers through the Association of Colonos, and mill owners through the Association of Mill Owners. However, these institutions, like the Cuban Institute of Stabilization for the Sugar Industry (ICAE) that the populist state created in the 1930s to control and stabilize sugar production and prices, became completely self-serving tools through which only a favored few "friends of Batista" gained millions by speculating at the expense of the nation's sugar industry. Here, sugar serves as but one example of a larger problem: Batista's regime alienated increasingly large segments of the population through rampant corruption, favoritism, and repression in the context of economic stagnation and high unemployment born of the island's monocrop economy.

Blazing Cane's epilogue argues that we need further research into the Cold War period before we can accept the dominant version of the 1959 Revolution that attributes its success to guerrilla leaders in the mountains and radical students and professionals in the cities, acting in the context of Cuba's supposed lack of a middle class.[24] This book documents the colonos' history of protest and political participation throughout the twentieth century, showing that it is simply incorrect to assert that there was no Cuban middle class. Colono demands were strongly represented in Castro's famous "History Will Absolve Me" speech in 1953. Likewise, given the workers' record of protest and political participation also described in this book, it would be surprising indeed to find them as quiescent in the 1950s as many studies would have us believe. While it is true that organized labor at the time was under the leadership of government-controlled associations and unions, interviews and anecdotal evidence suggest that workers did in fact protest and support the revolution outside their official unions.[25]

The extensive cane burnings of the late 1950s, like those of 1895, were an attack on the political, social, and economic systems that underwrote sugar production in colonial and republican-era Cuba. Revolutionaries did not necessarily want to abolish sugar production from the island, but they did not agree with a status quo that prioritized sugar above all else. Participants in the sugar economy, colonos and workers, wanted a larger share of the profits, and the middle classes—students, industrialists, and professionals—wanted a more diverse national economy. Overall, those who fought in the revolutions wanted greater access to political and economic power on the island. Upon the triumph of the 1959 Revolution, workers forced the government to carry out extensive land reform and to nationalize sugarmills by doing what they wanted rather than what reformist leaders told them to do.[26] As was the case in 1868, to which we will now turn, popular actions preceded, and made essential, the reforms that followed.

The Colonial Compact, 1500–1895

Let the flames that destroy the fortunes and furrow the sugar regions with their fire and ruins be our beacon of liberty! . . . If the destruction of the cane fields does not suffice, we will carry the torch to the towns, villages, and cities. . . . It is better for the cause of human liberty . . . better for the children of our children that Cuba be free, even if we have to burn all vestiges of civilization. . . . Spanish authority will not be tolerated.

CARLOS MANUEL DE CÉSPEDES, cited in
Ibarra Cuesta, *Ideología mambisa*, 90

1 The Cuban revolutionary Carlos Manuel de Céspedes made this historic statement embracing the burning-torch policy in October 1869, one year after his call to arms in eastern Cuba that opened the island's first war for independence. By gathering his slaves together in 1868, telling them they were all free, and inviting them to fight alongside him as citizens for a new Cuban nation, Céspedes and his revolutionary allies brought an unprecedented fervor of nationalist politics to the sugarmill communities. Revolutionaries burned cane fields before towns, villages, and cities because they saw sugar and slavery as the chains that linked Cuba to the Spanish Crown. Focusing on the uneven development that sugar brought to the island, this chapter explains why Cubans did not declare such a war until some forty years after the bulk of Spanish America had won its independence, and why most residents of western Cuba rejected independence. The wealth that sugar and slavery generated for sugarmill owners and merchants in western Cuba led them to try to keep politics and the French Revolution's rhetoric of "liberty, equality, and fraternity" out of their communities to maintain a secure and racially segregated labor force. These western merchants and mill owners had plenty of loyalist reinforcements from the 1820s

onward: Spanish troops and civilians flocked to western Cuba after mainland Spanish Americans became independent.[1]

Western planters benefited most from a sort of "colonial compact" with
Spain whereby the planters agreed to colonial rule in exchange for Spain's
military and legal protection of slavery and sugar production. The farther
one moved from the merchants and capital in the West (primarily the provinces of Havana and Matanzas), the less one could benefit from colonialism; thus, central and eastern planters were the first mill owners willing to
contest the compact. The refusal of most western mill owners to join the
revolution, combined with class and ethnic differences within Cuban revolutionary ranks, undermined Cubans' first attempts to gain freedom from
Spain—the Ten Years' War (1868–78) and the Little War (1879).

Nevertheless, the wars did prompt Spaniards and Cubans to renegotiate
the compact, allowing some fifteen more years of colonial rule during which
important social transformations took place on the island. Slaves finally
gained full emancipation in 1886, some sixty years after their counterparts
elsewhere in Latin America.[2] Cuban sugarmill owners were financially devastated by the years of revolution and feared labor shortages, so they rented
or sold their land to cane farmers. Some fell to the status of cane farmers
themselves. These colonos would become one of Cuba's most influential
(but least analyzed) social classes, assuming national prominence from
the 1920s onward.[3] The colonos were sandwiched between the mill owners and the wage workers and constituted a varied lot from sharecroppers
who rented land—to small landowners—to large absentee landowners.
Despite the creation of the colono system, sugarmill owners faced repeated
challenges to their livelihood under Spain's incoherent rule: The tug-of-war
between liberals and conservatives in Madrid drastically affected political
and economic realities in Cuba. When combined with the great upheavals
in the world sugar market that climaxed with the economic crisis of 1894,
this rule pushed more Cubans to support a renewed struggle for independence in 1895.

The Tuinucú estate in the jurisdiction of Sancti Spíritus within the colonial province of Las Villas serves as an ideal lens through which to view
Cuba's colonial origins, transitions, and regional differences. Tuinucú was
founded early in the colonial era; it went through many of the transitions
that other parts of the island experienced; and it lies near the geographic

center of the island, thereby offering a perspective on change in both East and West. Moreover, Cuba's central region became the strategic focus in the independence struggles because the Spaniards understood that only by conquering Las Villas could the insurgents move on to Havana. Tuinucú stood in the eye of the storm during the nineteenth-century wars for independence.

LANDHOLDING, THE SUGAR REVOLUTION, AND THE MAKING OF THE COLONIAL COMPACT

The Tuinucú estate is adjacent to the town of Sancti Spiritus, one of the earliest Spanish settlements in Cuba. In 1514, Diego Velázquez founded that town on an indigenous village located on the banks of the river Tuinucú. The native population declined rapidly due to a combination of Spanish aggression, enslavement, and disease that dislocated and undermined indigenous systems of production.[4] As the indigenous population dwindled and the search for gold in the area proved fruitless, many Spaniards left for Mexico. The remaining residents focused primarily on providing beasts of burden and food for larger towns in the Center and West of the island.

To motivate Spaniards to settle and farm the land, town councils across the island decided to grant local residents circular estates defined as a specific number of leagues emanating from a central marker, usually a tree or a rock, in exchange for a small fee. The land between the circles remained crown land, and the Spanish king also remained the official owner of the estates. The estates were eventually subdivided among offspring, sharecroppers, squatters, and outsiders apt at bribing local authorities.

Trees fall, rocks move, and circles are hard to trace in nature; therefore, the original land grants over time led to great confusion. By 1577, the town council of Sancti Spiritus had allocated land to twenty estates. Many of these original estates became towns and cities after the mid-eighteenth century, but prior to that, the jurisdiction of Sancti Spiritus remained predominantly rural, and its inhabitants engaged in only rustic production. Most of the region's plots, including the estate that would later become the Tuinucú sugarmill, began as pig farms and only later expanded into other produce.[5]

Sugarcane began to dominate western Cuba when the English occupied Havana in 1763. The market for slaves in the English sugar islands was saturated, and English slave traders needed new buyers. During the mere ten months of occupation, merchant vessels brought some four thousand slaves to Cuba, contributing a tremendous stimulus to a process already under way.[6] Influenced by the 1763 boom and the growth of the international sugar market, Charles III (reigned 1759–88) instituted a series of reforms that eventually contributed to the consolidation of land and power on the reconquered Spanish island. One of the most important changes was the 1776 Regulation of Free Trade between Spain and the Indies that authorized minor ports to conduct free trade directly with Spain and with neutral and allied countries.[7] In the late eighteenth century and early nineteenth, colonial residents also gained a certain degree of freedom to legislate and trade as they wished, because the French Revolution and the Napoleonic Wars diverted Spain's attention away from the colonies.[8] Residents pushed through changes in land tenure that permitted outright ownership of vast areas of former crown land. By 1815 residents had gained the right to parcel, sell, sublet, and use their estates without legal intervention. They also won permission to cut down the expansive hardwood forests previously reserved for constructing Spanish ships.[9] Investors felled the magnificent trees to make way for sugarcane.

Rich Europeans' demand for sweets was seemingly insatiable, and sugar and slavery crossed the Atlantic Ocean together.[10] Residents of Cuba thus convinced the Spanish Crown to pass legislation in 1789 allowing foreigners and Spaniards to sell as many slaves as they wished. Eighteenth-century mill owners perceived slavery as the best labor regime to produce sugar for three main reasons. First, it was the regime used across the Americas that had started with Portuguese islands in the Atlantic and then moved to Brazil and the Caribbean basin. Second, Cuba's large tracts of uncultivated land gave workers many options besides the thankless work of cutting and hauling cane and processing it in the hot, dangerous mills. Finally, planters believed that only slavery guaranteed the stability and harsh discipline necessary to produce sugar profitably. The harsh discipline was necessary because time was of the essence: Large amounts of cane needed to be cut and hauled when the proportion of sucrose in the juice was highest. The juice, in turn, had to be extracted within twenty-four to seventy-two hours to prevent spoilage.[11]

Thanks to the changes in land tenure and free trade in slaves, residents of Cuba created vast plantations based on an expensive, but stable, enslaved labor force. Shortly after the British occupation of Havana, revolutions in the Americas expanded the market for Cuban sugar. The American Revolution transferred British North America's demand for sugar and molasses from the British sugar islands to Cuba. The Haitian Revolution (1791–1804) removed Cuba's main competitor and brought a number of expert French producers to the country. Immigration and travel contributed to the dissemination of advanced technology. From the 1830s onward, particularly in the western region of the island, plantation owners built railroads to provide access to larger numbers of cane fields, and they replaced ox-driven mills with steam-powered ones to grind more cane, faster. These technological advances combined to make Cuba the world leader in cane sugar production—and the first Latin American country to build railroads. Production expanded rapidly. In 1760, Cuba had about 120 sugarmills, and by 1827, the number was up to 1,000. By 1855, the island produced almost one third of the world's sugar.[12]

Much of this sugar expansion took place in Havana and the adjacent jurisdiction of Matanzas; however, a Las Villas region just south of Tuinucú called Trinidad experienced its own unique sugar and slave boom between 1790 and 1860. Trinidad planters continuously expanded their holdings of slaves and land. They also purchased machinery to make their mills more efficient. The problem was that these more efficient mills demanded more cane, and the valley's land, already planted and replanted in cane, became increasingly depleted.[13] The mill owners knew that they needed to invest capital to keep up with new developments in the European beet-sugar industry, but investments made little sense on plantations facing dwindling cane supplies. Whereas earlier in the sugar-and-slavery cycle, the search for more profitable (virgin) sugar lands had moved the center of sugar production from one colony to another, in Cuba's case, the colony was large enough to allow a simple shift to other regions of the island.[14]

Planters migrated from Trinidad northward to Sancti Spiritus and westward to Cienfuegos armed with their capital, slaves, and expertise. This migration of planters, slaves, and capital accelerated in 1857, when European beet sugar flooded the world market, provoking a crash in world sugar prices. That same year, Don Francisco del Valle of Trinidad petitioned for permission to build a railroad linking Tuinucú to the municipal capital of Sancti Spiritus and to the nearest port, Tunas del Zaza.[15] When Valle inaugurated the railroad in 1863, new towns, sugar plantations, and cane fields accelerated the destruction of the forests of Sancti Spiritus.[16] Tuinucú was one of many properties modernized by Trinidad-based capital. On 10 April 1861, Justo German Cantero put up the plantation (including livestock and 155 slaves) as a guarantee to Trinidad's Lleonci and Company in exchange for a loan to develop the sugarmill.[17]

Sugar and slavery transformed Cuba from Spain's gateway to the Americas into an important source of wealth, but this wealth came at a price. Competition for resources on the island intensified as the population increased from approximately 174,000 inhabitants in 1770 to 1.4 million in 1860. More African slaves entered Cuba in one hundred years (roughly 750,000 between 1763 and 1862) than the total number of slaves brought to North America during its two hundred and fifty year slave regime (approximately 560,000).[18] The boom in sugar and slavery fostered more rigid class and racial divisions on the island.[19]

Planters feared the type of social revolution developing in the Americas and other parts of the world during the same era. The Spanish Crown shared these fears: After the wars for independence triumphed in mainland Spanish America (1808–24), Spain wanted desperately to keep Cuba, one of its most lucrative remaining colonies. An implicit colonial compact thus developed whereby planters agreed to remain a colony of Spain in exchange for the king's promise to protect the institution of slavery. On the ground, this meant allowing planters to rule their sugar and coffee plantations largely as they wished and providing Spanish soldiers and jails to help control the slaves who escaped or committed crimes. On paper, it meant keeping the slave trade legal despite growing European and American opposition. Plantation owners in Cuba chose colonialism and slavery over independence to protect racial hierarchies and their sugar fortunes.

CONSPIRACIES, FLIGHT, AND "FREE" LABOR: UNDERMINING THE COMPACT FROM BELOW

Spanish soldiers and legislation aimed to protect slavery, but many other forces attacked the institution from without and within. British naval blockades closed off access to Africa after Britain abolished the slave trade in 1807, driving up the price of slaves. Abolitionists, free Afro-Cubans, mulattos, and white liberal Cubans enlisted slaves directly in their struggles against the

Cuban elite and their Spanish allies, as in the 1843–44 Escalera conspiracy allegedly initiated by the English abolitionist David Turnbull.[20]

Slaves found inspiration to rebel without outside assistance through the examples of Haiti and the Spanish–American revolutions that abolished slavery.[21] While Cuban planters rarely had to face large-scale rebellions, they did have to deal with smaller ones. For example, in 1838 a group of slaves from the Sancti Spiritus region escaped to the dense mountains in the Zaza plantation, where they built forts and created a large runaway community. The Spanish authorities captured the leader of the slave runaways in June, then stripped him and his followers of their machetes before jailing some and killing others. Trinidad also witnessed a slave rebellion in 1838, about which a local historian noted: "Such rebellions occurred frequently given the large groups of slaves in the important region."[22]

On 24 March 1863, the foreman Luciano Bravo reported that fifteen blacks had run away from the Tuinucú sugarmill, then the property of Don José Font y Surís, in three or four groups. Bravo gathered a group of employees to find and detain them.[23] Running away was a common form of resistance against slaveowners. On a small scale, it functioned as a sort of steam valve to relieve conflict between slave and master or overseer without seriously challenging the institution of slavery.[24] When slave flight reached larger proportions, though, the effect on slaveholding was significant.

The number of runaway slaves in Sancti Spiritus increased along with the sugarmills' expanding production between 1850 and 1870. This was most likely due to the fact that fewer slaves were having to handle a larger workload.[25] Steam-powered mills had a much higher production capacity than those driven by oxen; therefore, slaves had to work longer than the already brutal sixteen hours a day to cut, haul, and process cane. Slaves surely resented these voracious new mills.[26]

Planters responded to increasing resistance among slaves by importing labor-saving technology that European beet-sugar producers had developed. They also adopted a variety of new labor systems. They hired white, free black, and mulatto workers; they rented slaves; and in the 1870s, they got permission to employ prison labor. Another increasingly common strategy was to contract laborers from Mexico, China, and Europe.

In 1859 the Tuinucú mill employed 158 black, 26 Chinese, and 12 white workers.[27] Only three years later, the number of Chinese had increased to

56.[28] Between 1847 and 1874, approximately 125,000 Chinese entered the island as indentured workers.[29] Instead of their bodies, planters bought and sold these Asian workers' contracts. According to most eight-year contracts, workers had to agree to work up to twelve hours per day and be "subject to the order and discipline existing in the workplace" in exchange for room, board, and a small monthly wage. On signing, workers formally relinquished their right to bargain or protest these conditions. (The wage was far lower than free workers' wages or the cost of renting slaves.) In practice, this allowed planters to treat their indentured workers in much the same way that they treated their slaves. But contract workers did not think of themselves as slaves, and many submitted formal complaints to their consulates or contract overseers. Like slaves, indentured workers often chose to run away. Flight did not always end in freedom: Colonial authorities jailed workers and slaves alike in prisons or "runaway" compounds across the island, charging them with sabotage, fleeing, or refusing to work.[30]

The mixed forms of plantation labor undermined the slave system from within by breaking slaves' isolation on the plantations.[31] Planters and their colonial protectors knew the importance of isolation. After the 1843–44 Escalera conspiracy, the captain-general ordered foremen and administrators to prohibit free blacks and mulattos from entering plantations and to detain those found "loitering" nearby. He also ordered them to allow only white workers to fulfill tasks outside the plantation in order to avoid contact between slaves and the black and mulatto peasantry.[32] When planters opted to abandon this rigid segregation for the sake of an expanded workforce, free, indentured, and rented workers became at one and the same time visible alternatives, sources of information, and potential allies for the slaves. A slave woman might join a Chinese man to seek freedom for their child, or a free black worker might encourage and assist a member of his or her family to purchase freedom, flee, or rebel.[33] The social isolation and racial lines so rigidly enforced under slavery began to blur.

Reformers also attacked slavery as an institution, especially from the 1860s onward. Some Cubans demanded an end to the contraband slave trade, arguing that the trade was enriching Spanish merchants to the detriment of Cuban planters and that the new infusions of Africans were making the island racially "unbalanced."[34] The conclusion of the U.S. Civil War in 1865 left Cuba and Brazil the only major slave societies in the Americas.

Although still not willing to abandon slavery altogether for fear of losing its Cuban planter allies, the Spanish government passed the "Law for the Suppression and Punishment of the Slave Trade" on 9 July 1866.[35] This law weakened the colonial compact; shortly thereafter, small Cuban planters and professionals attacked the compact directly when they initiated the island's first large-scale insurrection for independence.

CONTESTING THE COMPACT:
THE TEN YEARS' WAR AND THE LITTLE WAR

In 1868, a small number of prominent eastern Cubans resolved to take up arms. They believed that only this measure could end Cuba's subservience to Spain and give them control over the island's economy and politics. These leaders "imagined" a national community, a Cuba free from Spanish rule.[36] They emancipated their slaves and for the first time openly introduced politics into their mill communities.[37] On 10 October, Carlos Manuel de Céspedes, the owner of a small eastern sugar plantation, told his assembled slaves: "You are as free as I am." He then invited these new "citizens" to help him "conquer liberty and independence" for Cuba.[38]

To understand Cuba's first wide-scale insurrection for independence, we must look back to the 1857 economic crisis. The crisis taught planters a clear lesson: To compete with the European beet sugar flooding the world market and pushing the commodity's price down, they had to make sugar more efficiently. In the context of rising labor costs, this meant borrowing ever larger quantities of capital from Spanish banks and merchants to staff and mechanize their plantations. The already scarce capital available to Cubans became even scarcer; interest rates soared; and large numbers of planters lost savings and property to their Spanish creditors. Part of the problem stemmed from the lending system on the island: Planters had to pledge their plantations as collateral to secure credits and loans. By the early 1860s, planters had mortgaged a vast majority of sugar properties.[39] Among them was Font y Surís, who mortgaged the Tuinucú sugarmill in 1867, presumably to gain credit to modernize it.[40]

Cuban planters demanded a renegotiation of the colonial compact to address these extreme economic conditions. In 1866, the Spanish government responded by organizing a commission to consider labor, trade, and tax reforms. Elections were held on the island to choose Cuba's delegates. The debates surrounding the reform process inspired confidence across the island that the commission would convince Spain to give more political power to Cubans and reduce the abhorred customs duties.[41] But when conservatives overthrew the liberals in Spain, the reform process in Cuba froze. The conservative Spanish regime not only precluded any hope for reform on the island, it also imposed new restraints on Cuban liberty. In 1867, Spain increased military authority on the island, censored newspapers, and exiled opponents.[42] Meanwhile, the price of sugar crashed. Almost all of the leading banks in the country suspended payments, and at this dire economic moment, the Spanish government decided to impose a new direct tax on incomes, real estate, and businesses.[43]

The economic crisis hit the eastern part of the island much harder than the West. Even at the best of times, the two eastern provinces of Camagüey and Oriente were far less developed than the four "western" ones (Pinar del Rio, Havana, Matanzas, and Las Villas). Although colonial statistics grouped the central province of Las Villas with "the West," it actually lay in the middle of the country both geographically and economically. It was in transition, with Sancti Spiritus (including Tuinucú) and Cienfuegos on the rise and Trinidad past its peak. Historically, the mountainous eastern region of Cuba had functioned as the island's frontier, providing refuge for runaway slave communities, black and white squatters, smugglers, bandits, and enterprising Cuban farmers and merchants. Eastern planters, when able to borrow capital at all, paid an interest rate two and a half times higher than western planters, who tended to have closer economic and social ties with Spaniards.[44] This meant that sugarmills in the East were neither able to make the critical transition from ox-powered mills to steam nor able to purchase as many slaves as western planters.[45] The sugarmills that made it through the 1857 crisis in the two eastern provinces generated average profits three times lower than those on the rest of the island.[46] All told, more than 90 percent of total agricultural production came from the four "western" provinces.[47]

These figures only hint at some of the profound regional differences related to sugar that explain the 1868 insurrection's failure. Racial tensions also played a crucial role. Careful statistical research shows that the planters who joined the insurrection tended to come from eastern regions where whites formed a majority, followed closely by free blacks. Less than 8.5 percent of the total population was enslaved in these regions, where small-and medium-sized farmers raised products other than cane. In contrast, planters did not join the struggle against Spain if they came from almost any of the western jurisdictions and certain pockets of the East such as Guantánamo, where slaves accounted for almost half of the population and a majority of inhabitants lived on sugar plantations.[48] Simply put: Where sugar and slavery dominated, the colonial compact remained firm. Although planters from slave regions were frustrated with Spain, they were not willing to risk an armed rebellion that might disrupt the social, economic, and racial status quo.

When revolutionaries destroy capitalist property, this clearly indicates their aim to overthrow the established order. We may therefore measure the "revolutionary" nature of Cuba's insurrections by asking how insurgents treated slaves, fields, and factories. Céspedes and his elite colleagues initially tried their best to recruit planters on both sides of the island by emphasizing the movement's nationalist aims and limiting comments on slavery. In fact, the self-named "revolutionaries" began their struggle with the moderate goal of replacing Spanish rulers with Cubans while maintaining the overall socioeconomic order. Their initial call to arms promised to protect private property and advocated a gradual process of slave emancipation to be introduced after their triumph with compensation for slave owners. Céspedes promised freedom only to those slaves who fought in the separatist army. He insisted that the separatist army would only admit slaves "donated" by patriotic masters or slaves whose masters' allegiance lay with the enemy.

Two weeks after the insurrection began, Cuba's Spanish captain-general observed that he had no doubt the instigators conceived of something limited, but "the fact is that shortly after declaring war, they began to burn sugarmills and take the slaves as free people, in effect rais[ing] the issue of the social question and arous[ing] with their conduct the spirit of people of color."[49] Still hoping to gain planter allies, Céspedes tried to arrest this tendency by decreeing in November that the rebel administration would judge and sentence to death any rebel found guilty of stealing slaves or property from peaceful citizens or farms.[50] His efforts were to no avail. Throughout the insurgent regions, slaves filled the separatist ranks in large numbers as they deserted their owners or found themselves captured by insurgents during raids.[51]

Over the course of the first war of independence, later dubbed the "Ten Years' War," Céspedes and his fellow leaders changed their goals and means repeatedly. When a majority of mill owners opted to place their money and arms behind Spain rather than join the separatists, the separatist platform began a rapid shift to the left. The insurrection itself engaged in a spiraling process whereby the military leaders expanded their program to incorporate more insurgents, then these popular participants pushed the program further until the stated goals of the insurrection became truly revolutionary. In October 1869, one year after the rebellion began, the destruction of sugarcane fields became a part of the mainstream program with Céspedes's burning-torch policy. Just over a year later, in December 1870, the revolutionary government added the abolition of slavery to the separatist program.[52]

After Céspedes embraced this more radical strategy to destroy the base of Spanish wealth and support, some of the leaders in the revolution's official political arm initiated his removal from leadership. Two interlinked questions separated Céspedes from more conservative reformers: whether or not to burn the enemy's private property and free their slaves, and whether or not to invade the Center and West of the island.[53] The more radical revolutionaries who favored the destruction, abolition, and invasion policies tended to come from areas where non-landowners constituted the majority of insurgents. The more humble insurgent army that formed in those regions was far more inclined to push for a complete reversal of the socioeconomic order.[54]

A list of political prisoners executed between 1870 and 1872 suggests that the insurgents in the Sancti Spiritus region were mostly from the lower and middle sectors of society. There were twenty-two field workers; three students; two journalists; two teachers; one merchant; one landowner; one bookkeeper; two potters; one machinist; one coach driver; and one maker of machetes.[55] Memoirs and local histories indicate that most planters in the region stayed loyal to Spain, while professionals and workers, including large numbers of slaves and Chinese contract workers, joined the insurgency.[56]

The insurrection reached Sancti Spiritus as early as 6 February 1869, when five revolutionary leaders simultaneously declared their armies' adherence to the revolution. Planters in Sancti Spiritus joined their counterparts across the island to contribute a voluntary tax on their land to help Spain arm defense forces for the specific purposes of protecting mills and catching runaway slaves.[57] Many Sancti Spiritus planters also took defense into their own hands by contracting and arming guards for their mills and fields. Tuinucú's owner, for example, got permission to arm thirty men with rifles and ammunition in 1874.[58]

These efforts at defense crumbled when the Dominican-born insurgent leader Máximo Gómez and Serafín Sánchez, born in Sancti Spiritus, invaded the region in 1875.[59] A Spanish report in 1876 indicates that only five of the jurisdiction's forty-three sugarmills remained. Of these five, two had lost slaves and suffered considerable damage to their cane fields. Insurgents had destroyed the remaining thirty-eight, "for the most part even their factories." The mill owners who did manage to protect their factories from fire nevertheless had to abandon production because the cane fields were being invaded and burned.[60] Tuinucú was not among the sugarmills that survived ruin. It stopped milling at some point during the war and would not resume production until 1881.[61]

The insurgents destroyed the fields and plantations near Sancti Spiritus and managed to dominate the rural and mountainous regions during the Ten Years' War,[62] but they experienced great difficulty trying to control rival chiefs and bandits. A communiqué to the provisional revolutionary government written in June 1870 declared: "First, no one obeys anyone; second, with respect to banditry, it will not end until there are enough forces to be able to shoot all those who do not behave."[63] Despite these challenges, insurrectionary forces continued to expand in regions such as Sancti Spiritus and Santiago (Oriente) through the early 1870s. In contrast, they decreased remarkably quickly in the eastern province of Camagüey. Many leaders there opted to accept bribes and disarm between 1870 and 1878. They fell prey to their own racial fears and to Spain's exaggerated racial portrayal of the conflict as black against white and barbarity against civilization.[64] The same patron–client relations that they had used to rapidly expand insurrectionary ranks in 1868, incorporating their own slaves, workers, employees, and godchildren, allowed them to quickly demobilize in 1870.

General Máximo Gómez and General Antonio Maceo, a mulatto who suffered racism and Spanish chauvinism while growing up in the eastern province of Oriente, did not share the Camagüeyans' fears. These two generals led insurgent columns through rural Oriente, burning cane fields, destroying coffee plantations, and liberating slaves during the summers of 1870 and 1871. Gómez wanted the fearless Maceo—nicknamed "the Bronze Titan"—to lead similar invasions through the West, but the revolutionary government did not support the plan. Again, some of the political leaders' reticence can be traced to racial prejudice. At the time, Spanish and revolutionary sources alike were spreading rumors that Maceo wanted to impose the rule of blacks and mulattos. Consequently, the revolutionary government placed the Dominican Gómez, rather than the Cuban Maceo, at the helm of the invasion to conquer the central province of Las Villas in January 1875.[65]

The Spanish fortification surrounding Sancti Spiritus made it impossible for insurgents to attack the city, but local leaders including the mulatto General Serafín Sánchez and Francisco Carrillo joined Gómez in his ride through the countryside. They torched cane fields and liberated slaves across the province of Las Villas, burning the fields of eighty-seven sugarmills in forty-six days.[66] The successes in Las Villas demonstrated the revolutionaries' capacity to attack the sugar and slave regime of the Center and West, which made Gómez and other generals want to forge on to Matanzas and Havana.[67]

The conservative leadership prevailed in the end. Relegated to only half the island—the poorer half, at that—the insurrection began to crumble. The revolutionaries had little access to food and shelter and less access to weapons, and their eastern base was materially devastated by war. Moreover, many of the separatists' rich Cuban exile allies in the United States shifted their support to the annexationists, who advocated joining the United States, or to the autonomists, who pushed for negotiation with Spain. Some of the insurrection's original leaders had been killed, and others were abandoning the revolution for Spanish peace. According to the efficient Spanish propaganda of the era, anarchy and chaos reigned, sinking the morale of the troops and their families. When Spanish Army Commander Arsenio Martínez entered the scene in November 1876, joining an army that had reached nearly one hundred thousand, he was able to wage a strong campaign against the insurgents by promising pardons, land, animals, and money in exchange for their surrender.[68]

MAP 2   Cuba, 1898. Spanish General Arsenio Martínez completed a north–south trench in Puerto
Principe (Camagüey) to help keep insurgents on the east side of the island. Spanish
General Valeriano Weyler used the same strategy during the 1895–98 war, reinforcing the
old trench and adding a second one west of the city of Havana to isolate insurgents in
Pinar del Río. Drawn by Carolyn King, Geography Department, York University.

Recognizing the strategic importance of Las Villas, the province that
straddled the East-West socio-economic divide, Martínez divided it into
twenty-seven small districts and allocated one battalion to each district.
His plan was to crush rebellion in those districts, complete a well-manned
trench across the island from shore to shore protecting this pacified Center
(and West) from the East, and then begin a march eastward to isolate revolutionaries there. Roughly twenty-five miles long, the trench had a railroad
track equipped with armor-clad cars as well as forts and barbed-wire fencing
(see map 2). Many have argued that the trench and march eastward, combined with regional differences, racial tensions, and the domino effect of
insurgent surrenders, signified the death toll for the island's first revolution
for independence.[69]

In 1878 the civilian leaders of the revolution opted to renegotiate, rather
than break, the colonial compact with Spain, despite Gómez's assurances
that "what the bullet and the machete cannot accomplish, the climate will."[70]
Gómez and other leaders believed that marching Spanish soldiers would
soon either lose morale from the heat, exhaustion, and ambush that characterized the tropical guerrilla warfare or die of yellow fever. Spanish victory
was not a fait accompli when the revolution's political leadership agreed to

disarm for "peace," but local military leaders such as Maceo, Sánchez, and Gómez did not have enough power to override the 1868 revolution's political leaders.

A few insurgents, including Ramón Leocadio Bonachea in Sancti Spiritus, refused to put down their arms until overwhelming odds forced them to flee the island in April 1879.[71] These leaders refused to accept a peace that conceded none of their goals. The Pact of Zanjón granted legal freedom only to the slaves and Chinese contract workers who had fought in the insurrection. Spain gave a mere 3 percent of the population—those who paid over twenty-five pesos of land tax—the right to elect deputies to the Spanish court and provincial and municipal assemblies.

Many elite Cubans joined the newly legalized Autonomist Party that served to distract them from separatist goals during the next seventeen years. Less-privileged Cubans launched the so-called Little War on 26 August 1879 in the East, with the clear aim of ending slavery as well as colonialism. The new insurgent ranks included professionals and artisans, overseers and administrators, and large numbers of unemployed whites, blacks, and mulattos.[72]

Slaves figured prominently in the ranks. Spain's Moret Law, passed in 1870 to counter slaves' attraction to the separatist camp, promised freedom to elders and to slave children after a period of subsidized work for their parents' master. Neither Moret nor the Pact of Zanjón offered working-age slaves who had remained neutral any promise of freedom. They must have been outraged at their exclusion, especially since Spain granted freedom to slaves who had fought for the Cuban enemy. Some slaves sabotaged their plantations from within. Official reports from the East complained of slaves' "passive resistance to work" and "refus[al] to obey their owners and overseers." They also described slaves setting fire to cane fields, chanting, "No freedom, no cane!"[73] Other slaves took advantage of the disorder to escape their plantations and form independent communities. Many who had been freed through their participation in the first war also joined the second war to fight for complete abolition and independence.

Non-whites played a larger role in the Little War than they had in the previous conflict. This profile helps explain the second revolution's more radical platform. It also explains the revolution's rapid undoing, for Spain easily convinced the exiled political leadership and white Cubans that the war presented too much of a threat to the social order. The civilian leaders' racial fear and most western Cubans' refusal to join the insurrection helped Spain defeat the second war for independence in less than a year.[74] Ultimately, the Ten Years' War and the Little War did not achieve independence because the leadership opted to renegotiate the colonial compact to preserve Cuba's socio-racial order.

CENTRALIZING MILLS AND THE
BIRTH OF THE COLONO CLASS

Eastern and central sugar planters suffered much more from the first two wars for independence than their western counterparts. Whereas in 1868 the West's Havana and Matanzas produced roughly 62 percent of the island's sugar, Las Villas produced 29 percent, and Oriente and Camagüey produced 9 percent, in 1878, production in Havana and Matanzas had increased to roughly 77 percent; in Las Villas, it had declined to 21 percent; and in Camagüey and Oriente, it had fallen to 2 percent.[75] Most cane fields and many factories in the East and Center fell victim to the revolutionaries' burning torches, either in retaliation for their owners' loyalty to Spain or simply because they were symbols of Spanish colonialism. The revolutionaries and their Spanish enemies did extensive damage to nearly all of the plantations in the eastern provinces of Camagüey and Oriente.

In contrast, the mills in the western provinces of Pinar del Rio, Havana, and Matanzas made it through the conflicts practically unscathed, and many were actually able to increase their production through improved technology immediately following the war. Thanks to these improvements, Cuba recovered overall sugar production, providing almost 16 percent of the world's sugar supply in 1878 and 23 percent in 1879.[76] The province of Las Villas stood in the middle of Cuba in more ways than one: Parts of the province seem to have shared the West's good fortune, whereas other parts, including Sancti Spiritus, were subjected to the burning torch. Tuinucú's Font y Surís, whose machinery and cane lands were already mortgaged before the war, had to go into greater debt to replant fields and repair machinery destroyed by the torch.

Repairing was not enough. To compete on the international market, planters had to produce sugar more efficiently by modernizing their mills.

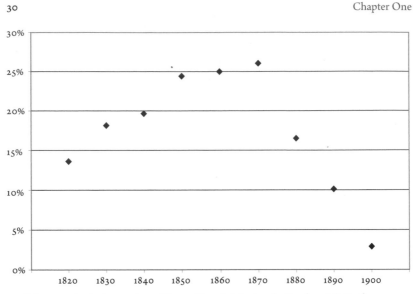

1   Cuban sugar's actual percentage of the world market, by decade. Based on statistics from
    Moreno Fraginals, *El ingenio*, 3:35–38.

Sugar in 1878 sold for half of its 1868 price.[77] Several factors led to the decline
in world sugar prices. Other Caribbean and Latin American countries had
flooded the market with sugar to make up for Cuban scarcity during the Ten
Years' War, and they continued to produce during the peace. Technological
advances and protectionism continued to help European countries produce
more beet sugar at lower costs (beets were ready to be converted into sugar
after only five months of cultivation, whereas sugar took fifteen months).[78]
Steamships made it faster and easier for all of these competitors to move
sugar to consumption markets.

A final significant factor concerns the large U.S. market. By 1880, the
United States absorbed over 80 percent of Cuba's sugar exports; therefore,
the U.S. tariff on imported sugar had a strong impact on Cuban production.
In the 1880s, North American refiners united into a sugar trust that significantly reduced the prices for raw sugar and virtually destroyed the market
for refined sugar. Cuban mills had to produce sugar cheaply or perish. The
number of mills grinding dropped from more than one thousand in 1877 to
about four hundred by 1894, and Cuba's proportion of the world market declined from 1880 through 1900.[79] Figure 1 illustrates how dramatically Cuba's
position in the world sugar market changed.

To deal with increased world competition, sugar production in Cuba divided into two sectors—one industrial, and the other agricultural. Following the Ten Years' War, planters with the most capital focused on the industrial side of production to create more efficient sugarmills. These mills needed far more cane than those that had preceded them, but without slaves or excess capital, buying and cultivating ever larger expanses of cane land was not viable. Mill owners thus devised a system whereby they could either buy cane from colonos who owned their land or rent out plots of land to subcolonos who would work as sharecroppers. The colonos would plant and tend the cane, then receive either money or sugar in exchange for the cane they delivered to the mill. The rate of exchange—cane for sugar, or cane for cash—was often highly contested. It varied greatly across time and region and was agreed on by written or oral contract.[80]

Several factors made it possible for mill owners to buy cane from ever larger expanses of colono lands. These included a drop in the price of steel to build railroads, the invention of narrow-gauge railways to take cane directly from field to mill, and the opening of public railroads to transport cane in 1881.[81] The colonos were an extremely varied lot: Cuban and foreign; large, medium, and small; tenant or landowner; and usually male but sometimes female. The one commonality among colonos was that they were predominantly white.[82] A large number of Cuban landowners, especially from the central and eastern regions of the island, were ruined by the Ten Years' War and became colonos. Some small landowners situated near large sugarmills also switched from raising cattle or cultivating tobacco to cultivating cane.

Many of the more than fifty-four thousand Spaniards who migrated to Cuba between 1882 and 1890 became colonos, as well (others manned commissary stores or did menial work).[83] Spanish immigration was promoted as part of an official government and planter policy to "whiten" Cuba's racial makeup. Brazil and Argentina adopted similar policies, recruiting larger numbers because the governments provided more funding. Government officials were influenced by European and North American scientists such as Herbert Spencer, who applied Charles Darwin's "survival of the fittest" concept to human beings, suggesting that peoples of the white "race" were superior to black or indigenous peoples.[84] At Tuinucú, at least two Spaniards established new colonias on previously uncultivated lands in the year

1880. Both men had come as soldiers in the Spanish Army during the Ten Years' War.[85] More colonias spread around the mill thereafter. By 1887, colonos cultivated 30–40 percent of the cane ground in sugarmills across the island.[86]

The decision to modernize and divide plantations into sugarmills and colonias was not motivated purely by economics. The Little War had succeeded in at least one realm—it convinced the Spanish government that slavery had to be abolished. In 1880, Spain extended the tutelage system to all slaves, not just children, as in the Moret Law of 1870. The master still had the right to their labor, but in return he or she was required to feed and clothe the former slave. Families could no longer be separated; domestic servants could not be sent to the countryside; and laborers age eighteen and over were entitled to a monthly stipend. This system was allegedly designed to "prepare" the slaves for complete freedom, which was to come in 1888. In fact, it was a delaying tactic designed by the planters to ease the transition from slave to wage labor. Many slaves managed to use the tutelage laws to free themselves before the complete abolition of Cuban slavery, pushing complete abolition forward two years, to 1886.[87]

The demise of slavery and the changes taking place in the international sugar market created a competitive selection process for sugarmills in Cuba from 1878 through 1895. Some planters, most from the central and western regions and a much smaller number from the East, survived and industrialized their plantations with savings generated earlier through sugar, slavery, and tobacco commerce. Some even managed to increase their savings through speculation and lending during the crises of the 1860s and 1870s. Fortunate planters protected and modernized their mills through alliances with Spanish or American capital, the latter being most common in Cienfuegos, in the southwestern Las Villas region.[88] The less fortunate planters lost their mills through bitter legal struggles, as was the case for Tuinucú's Font y Surís.

Although Font y Surís had mortgaged Tuinucú in 1867, he managed to hold on to it through the Ten Years' War, and in 1880 he began to add steam power to the mill and boilers. In 1883, unable to continue modernizing the mill on his own, Font y Surís rented his mill to Agustín Goicochea for a period of ten harvests. Goicochea paid $5,000 in gold to rent a number of machines. When he could not make payments in 1885, the merchant who lent Goicochea the machines repossessed them. The merchant's wife

2   Manuel Rionda. Manuel, his brother
    Francisco, and Edwin Atkins were
    among the first to establish and
    modernize mills in Cuba through
    U.S.-based corporations funded by
    European, North American, and
    Cuban capitalists in the late nineteenth
    century and early twentieth. Braga
    Brothers Collection, University of
    Florida, Gainesville.

made a pact with the Matanzas merchant Joaquín Rionda y Polledo to take away not only the machines belonging to her deceased husband but also those that Goicochea had purchased earlier.[89] Another merchant initiated judicial proceedings against Tuinucú's owner José Font y Surís that same year.[90]

Tuinucú played a significant role in the local economy, so these proceedings attracted a lot of attention. In January 1886, a Cienfuegos newspaper condemned Font y Surís for stopping the sugarmill's harvest, stating that he was "seriously damaging" the commerce of the city of Sancti Spiritus. Font y Surís's lawyer responded that the planter did not want to stop grinding, but he was forced to do so when judicial administrators unjustly took over the mill and appointed an administrator to run it.[91] The Tuinucú estate was put up for auction on 29 September 1886. When nobody bid, the court named a merchant to administer it to pay Font y Surís's debts. The merchant was thus able to wrest the whole estate out of Font y Surís's hands. Joaquín Rionda bought the estate, mortgages and all, at a public auction for the sum of $55,970 in gold on 7 September 1888.[92]

Joaquín Rionda and his brother Francisco Rionda initially purchased Tuinucú's machinery to transfer it to another mill in Matanzas. However, when they saw how good the lands adjoining the mill were, they decided to purchase them—in all, about 2,500 acres.[93] Joaquín Rionda died the next year, at thirty-nine. According to the family narrative, he had "dined and wined too well" and drowned "while attempting to ford the Tuinucú River on horseback."[94] His brother Francisco took over management of the still indebted mill. In 1891, a third Rionda brother named Manuel, director of a sugar merchant house in New York City, purchased the estate. That same year, Manuel Rionda began to organize a U.S. corporation for the express purpose of purchasing and improving the mill (see figure 2, above).

PRELUDE TO REVOLUTION: 1891–95

Manuel Rionda's timing was excellent. In 1891, Spain signed the Foster-Cánovas Treaty with the United States granting raw sugar duty-free entrance into the United States in exchange for lower import tariffs on a wide variety of U.S. goods. Sugar production increased from about 636,000 tons in 1890 to about 808,000 tons in 1891, reaching 1 million tons for the first time in 1893.[95] The U.S. corporation called the Central Tuinucú Sugarcane Manufacturing Company purchased the Tuinucú estate during the economic boom, in 1893.

"American" corporations, many with a mix of Spanish, Cuban, and American stockholders, purchased several other mills during this period, reflecting the other side of the boom. Cuba's dependence on the United States expanded alongside sugar production, making the island more vulnerable to the U.S. tariff. By 1894, the U.S. market was absorbing 91 percent of Cuban sugar exports.[96] Moreover, sugar became even more dominant in the Cuban economy as cheap imports from the U.S. eliminated other Cuban products. This included food. During the three-year boom, farmers planted cane where foodstuffs once grew, and merchants on the island switched from European to U.S. food suppliers.

The Foster–Canóvas Treaty lifted the Cuban economy for a brief moment, but when it expired in 1894, sugar profits came crashing down again. The United States was reeling from a domestic economic panic in 1893. To protect the small U.S. sugar industry, the Wilson–Gorman Act of 1894 imposed heavy new tariffs on sugar imports (see table 1). Spain responded with higher tariff barriers, hurting Cubans even more by rapidly increasing the price of the U.S. imports on which Cubans had grown dependent.

TABLE 1   Food prices before and after the U.S. Wilson-Gorman Act

PRODUCT	1893–1894	1894–1895
Wheat	$0.30 per 100 kilos	$ 3.95 per 100 kilos
Flour	$ 1.00 per 100 kilos	$4.75 per 100 kilos
Corn	$0.25 per 100 kilos	$ 3.95 per 100 kilos
Meal	$0.25 per 100 kilos	$4.75 per 100 kilos

Source: Ramon O. Williams to Assistant Secretary of State Edwin F. Uhl, 3 January 1895, Dispatches/Havana, cited in Pérez, *Cuba between Empires*, 32–33.

As tariffs and prices for consumer goods skyrocketed, tariffs on capital imports such as material for iron bridges, steel rails, tools, and machinery also increased from zero to between fifteen and sixty dollars per ton.[97] These new tariffs devastated the Cuban economy and society. Hunger and unemployment became widespread as hundreds of stores, colonias, and sugar-mills shut down. When the bust came, the nearly half-million Spaniards who had moved to Cuba during the boom years pushed even more Cubans into unemployment and destitution.[98] More than fifty thousand cane cutters, mill hands, and tobacco workers wandered from town to town looking for work as day laborers.[99]

During the fifteen-year period since the Little War's failure in 1880, patriot leaders had worked to mobilize economic and strategic support for another revolution. Until the crisis in 1895, few Cubans were receptive. Their lack of enthusiasm stemmed from fear of another drawn-out war and temporary satisfaction among the elite with the booming economy. Liberal Governor-General Antonio Maura passed initiatives between 1892 and 1895 that also hindered revolutionary mobilization. He expanded suffrage by lowering the qualification for voting from twenty-five pesos to five. He initiated new public works projects, and—most important—he promised Autonomist Party rule.

Spain's promise to grant autonomy was nothing new. This potential avenue to independence, combined with fear of social revolution, had motivated upper-class leaders to end the revolutions in 1878 and 1879. Spanish rule was convenient for Cuban sugar planters when they needed Spanish soldiers to contain potential social revolutions in the 1860s and 1870s and to oversee the transitions from slavery to free labor and the modernization of sugarmills. By the 1890s, the colonial compact had been severely compromised: Slavery no longer existed, and Cuban planters increasingly sought capital from the United States rather than Spain. When Spain isolated Cuba from the United States by raising tariffs to match U.S. protectionism, the island was literally squeezed out of prosperity by a battle between empires. This pushed Cubans of all social classes to seek an end to Spanish rule, but few agreed on what should replace colonialism. One issue was particularly central to the debate: the role sugar should play in Cuba's future. This debate became highly visible on cane fields across the island during Cuba's final war for independence.

Revolutionary Destruction of the
Colonial Compact, 1895–98

2 On Tuesday, 9 April 1895, insurgents began to torch the cane on Máximo Cisneros's colonia near Tuinucú. Cisneros got on his horse and rode to an elevated spot where there was an unmanned Spanish fort from the Ten Years' War. From there, he could see plainly that ten or twelve men were riding through the fields, setting fire to the cane with torches made of palm leaves. He returned immediately to the Tuinucú mill town to inform Francisco Rionda of the fire. Rionda asked the Spanish commander there to send out soldiers to protect the cane, and Cisneros himself told the officer: "Let us go, I will join you with my men." The men he was referring to were the roughly thirty laborers who had been helping Cisneros tend his colonia's crop. The officer replied that he and his soldiers "would not go anywhere to put out fires."[1]

This anecdote is one among many of the stories of destruction at Tuinucú in 1895–98. The evidence presented in this chapter highlights two key strategies that guaranteed revolutionary triumph in both 1898 and 1959: the invasion of the central region, and the destruction of cane and other capitalist property. The chapter gets closer to understanding what rural Cubans did during the revolution and, by extension, what mattered to them. From the perspective of the elite, revolutions mean chaos and ruin. From the perspective of poor residents, they may signify the opportunity to live without masters and to eke out an autonomous existence, at least momentarily.[2] Tuinucú's owner labeled his estate a "republic of anarchy" during the war, but his letters describe country residents settling on land, growing food, and creating makeshift mills to make cane into sugar (to sell to insurgents or Spanish soldiers).

When Cuba's third war for independence started in 1895, the center of the island, particularly the province of Las Villas, became a highly contested region. It was strategically important because it produced 40 percent of the island's sugar and because it lay between the revolutionary East and the Spanish-loyalist West. The 1868 and 1879 wars had proven that revolutionary success depended largely on the capture of Las Villas, the base from which to conquer Havana. The veteran networks forged there during the wars for independence served as springboards to national power for Liberal Party leaders in early-twentieth-century Cuba (see chapters 3–6).[3] Revolutionaries shifted operations to Las Villas early in the struggle to overcome the regional isolation experienced during the first wars for independence. Spanish forces responded in kind, meeting mobilization with mobilization and later, destruction with destruction.

Revolutionaries and Spanish soldiers had to decide whether to burn or protect cane and buildings, a highly charged issue in terms of both strategy and ideology. Spanish policy initially prioritized protection of the sugar industry to demonstrate to the world that everything in Cuba was "business as usual," and that the revolutionaries were a small minority. But as Cisneros's account reveals, this policy was not always adhered to on the ground.[4] After Spanish General Valeriano Weyler arrived, Spanish policy began to shift, eventually advocating destruction to remove revolutionaries' sources of food and support from the sugar communities across the island.

The civilian leaders of the revolution worried that burning cane might alienate anticolonial planters and keep U.S. politicians from recognizing Cubans as legal belligerents (a status that would allow them to purchase arms from the United States legally). Military revolutionaries like veteran General Máximo Gómez considered destruction essential to prove that Spanish rule was bankrupt and to divert workers' attention away from the harvest and toward the revolution. These leaders set the cane ablaze to destroy a social and economic system built on racism and inequality. The fissures between civilian and military visions of revolution witnessed on the ground became the basis for division and the infiltration of U.S. power after the marines landed in April 1898.

In a broader context, Cuba's 1895–98 war for independence can be considered the first of Latin America's twentieth-century social revolutions. As during the Mexican Revolution of 1910 or the Nicaraguan Revolution of 1979, humble revolutionary combatants sought to destroy property and overthrow the government so they could create something completely new. In contrast, many of their leaders merely aimed for political reform. The mobilized masses usually managed to push through some radical post-revolutionary reforms, especially in the cases of Cuba, Mexico, and Nicaragua. During the war itself, Cuban revolutionaries embraced a few quintessentially "modern" strategies that other Latin American revolutionaries would also use. For example, guerrillas attacked new means of communication and transportation such as telegraph wires and railroads and extorted money from U.S.-based corporations. On the Spanish side, General Weyler introduced extensive concentration camps—with the aim of removing support from guerrilla revolutionaries in the countryside—a strategy that would soon be mimicked by other armies. U.S. newspapers and politicians justified intervention in response to Weyler's policy, but the next chapter will show that many Americans had ulterior motives. U.S. power cast a shadow over Cuba in 1898, just as it would over much of Latin America in the twentieth century.

BUILDING THE REVOLUTIONARY ARMY

In 1895, economic depression and political frustration combined to create an ideal climate for revolution. Exiled leaders were ready to return to the island. The journalist José Martí had managed to unite civilian and military patriots in the Revolutionary Party of Cuba (PRC) that he established in New York City in 1892 to organize and raise funds for a new independence struggle. Unity did not come easily: The same tension between civilian and military leadership that had marked the first wars for independence reemerged. Having studied the military caudillos that ruled mainland Spanish America after their wars for independence, Martí did not want to ally with Máximo Gómez unless he would agree to a *Cuba Libre* (Free Cuba) under civilian rule. This caused a split between the two leaders in 1884, but when exile after exile sought—and failed—to land expeditions and spark revolution in Cuba, Gómez agreed to join Martí in the PRC.

During the 1880s and 1890s, the patriots gathered funds and supporters among Cuban exiles in Jamaica, Mexico, and other locations in Europe and the Americas.[5] Serafín Sánchez and Francisco Carrillo of Sancti Spiritus organized in the Dominican Republic and Florida. Cuban tobacco workers in Florida provided the greatest financial backing for the revolution, giving the movement more of a lower- and middle-class financial base than the two previous movements for independence and thus more freedom to demand radical change. As of 1893, veterans and new revolutionaries also began to recruit, raise money, and establish PRC committees across Cuba. Gerardo Castellanos Leonard constituted one such committee in Sancti Spiritus on 12 August 1893 under orders from José Martí.[6]

A great variety of Cubans joined the revolutionary ranks. Women played significant roles in organizing and fundraising, founding almost a quarter of the clubs that supported the PRC from Cuba and from exile.[7] Women often trekked across the island with their spouses, brothers, and fathers in guerrilla bands. They provided food for the family and sometimes engaged in combat, as well. At least twenty-five women achieved the rank of colonel or captain during the 1895–98 Revolution.

The group that the historian Rosalie Schwartz has labeled "patriot-brigands" made a significant contribution to the revolution, specifically in the provinces of Havana, Matanzas, and Las Villas. The Spanish down-played their political goals by calling them "bandits." Governors pursued them with zeal, especially when the escalation of kidnappings and extortion in the early 1890s seriously undermined Spanish military authority in the countryside. Manuel García, for example, managed to elude Spanish capture through communication networks and civilian allies that would later serve revolutionaries during the insurrection of 1895 to 1898.[8]

The patriot-brigands practiced extortion in the name of revolution, demanding protection money from cane farmers and mill owners. Some small farmers made contributions to the patriot-brigands willingly to support the revolution, but most paid out of fear that a few burning torches would completely destroy their investments.[9] Revolutionaries had used the tactic in the Ten Years' War, but not on such a large scale. During the interwar period, farmers with large cane fields considered the payments for protection "an operating expense against sugar profits."[10] The practice continued well into the twentieth century, and Tuinucú's owners faced it in the 1890s and beyond.[11] In 1893, Martí and the PRC demonstrated just how important they considered the support of the patriot-brigand Manuel García when they appointed him one of the six members of the internal command team.

By designating the mulatto journalist Juan Gualberto Gómez coordinator of the independence movement in Cuba, the PRC courted another large segment of society: Cubans of color. Gómez had excellent organizational skills, a remarkable ability to persuade, and connections to thousands of potential revolutionaries as leader of a central committee that represented approximately one hundred black and mulatto associations from across the island.[12] Gualberto Gómez, Martí, and other PRC leaders incorporated Cubans of color into the revolution symbolically, as well. The veteran mulatto general Antonio Maceo argued that Cuba would be a nation with "no whites nor blacks, but only Cubans."[13] PRC leaders hoped that this argument would at one and the same time attract more Cubans of color and prevent white Cubans from fearing this larger presence. Drawing lessons from the failures of 1878 and 1879, Martí proclaimed that powerful men invented "textbook races" merely to divide anticolonial struggles and to justify expansion and empire.[14] Raceless nationalism was a remarkable concept in the late-nineteenth-century Atlantic world. It contributed great ideological strength to the revolutionary movement and left an enduring legacy.[15]

Manuel García and Juan Gualberto Gómez were the only non-veterans in the central command group on the island, which points to another fundamental PRC strategy: to incorporate leaders and soldiers of all classes and races from the earlier wars for independence. Other veteran leaders included the mulatto Serafín Sánchez and Francisco Carrillo from Las Villas, Guillermón Moncada (a black carpenter, natural son of a free black), Bartolomé Masó (a wealthy white planter of Spanish origin), and Salvador Cisneros Betancourt (the Marquis of Santa Lucía, a sixty-seven year-old white aristocrat).[16]

The PRC's strategy to recruit soldiers based on the loyalties forged during the two earlier struggles for independence was successful in the East and Center of the island, where the revolution had been strong. Newspaper accounts, war diaries, and army enlistment rolls help identify the regional makeup of the PRC's military wing, the Liberation Army. Blacks and mulattos made up a majority of military forces in Oriente. Family ties, labor relationships, and friendships encouraged many to join. Others rebelled against racism and inequality. Peasants fought for land, and caudillos fought for political power. Residents of the East in general hoped to gain more control of their region.[17] Revolutionaries in neighboring Camagüey were lighter-skinned and came from higher social classes, as was the case for that region during the Ten Years' War. Most chieftains in the western province of Matanzas were also white professionals or estate owners, some of whom brought their workers with them. Overall, at least half of the insurgents were Cubans of color, and most were rural peasants.[18] The fact that most insurgents were small farmers rather than landless day laborers explains their outrage at Spanish land taxes and their willingness to destroy the sugar industry (not their direct employer but, in their eyes, a blight on the peasant economy).[19]

Revolutionary forces in Las Villas included large landowning cattle ranchers as well as merchants, doctors, carpenters, day laborers, and Afro-Cuban bandits from the mountains of Trinidad.[20] Many Las Villas officials from the Ten Years' War joined with their clienteles of seventy-five to one hundred and fifty men, as did other chiefs with smaller numbers. Extended families constituted another important network for revolutionary forces in Las Villas.[21] The Menéndez Alvarez clan were ancestors of the powerful sugar worker leader Jesús Menéndez (popularly baptized "the General of the Cane" in the 1940s). Doroteo Menéndez, son of a freed slave from the Ivory Coast, fought with his wife, Felicia Alvarez, in the Ten Years' War and achieved the rank of commander. After the war, Menéndez and Alvarez settled in a municipality of Las Villas, establishing an agricultural commune with other family members. When the new war began in 1895, the entire family gathered and agreed to head for the forests of the province's north coast to join the revolutionaries. Five of Jesús Menéndez's uncles and two of his cousins fought, along with his father. Jesús's father, barely a youth, won the rank of captain after invading the West.[22]

That Menéndez and the soldiers he fought with did have to invade the West was not a foregone conclusion. Determined to avoid the regional pitfalls that had plagued the earlier movements, Martí and the PRC placed special emphasis on that region. On the first night of Carnival, 24 February 1895, when revolutionaries sounded the call to arms in the East, a simultaneous call rang out from Matanzas in the West. Spanish forces killed the leader in Matanzas and incarcerated his counterpart in Havana within the first week. Left without leaders, western brigands and separatists demobilized.[23] But the movement continued in the East. It picked up considerable momentum in April when Martí, Maceo, and Gómez arrived on the island.[24] The timing was ideal: Their arrival coincided with the ending of the 1895 sugar harvest on most of the mills in the island, adding unemployed sugar workers to the revolution's potential recruits.[25]

In April 1895, most sugar planters in the Center and West remained confident that the movement would fail. Three main assumptions born of historical experience inspired the planters' confidence. All three rested on the certainty that sugar would remain the primary force in the Cuban economy. The first assumption was that Spain could confine and put down revolutions in the East. The second, that planters could pay off revolutionaries—just as they paid off bandits during times of peace—for protection against burning of field or factory. The third, if revolutionaries could not be bought, Spanish military forces would protect the plantations, as they had done from 1868 through 1880. All three assumptions proved false, and in the end most plantation owners (like the colono Máximo Cisneros) ended up watching in disbelief as their property turned into ashes.

ASSUMPTION ONE: THE REVOLUTION WILL STAY IN THE EAST

Confident that Tuinucú was safely out of revolution's way, Francisco Rionda paid $3,000 advance rent for a thirteen-year term for an adjacent colonia beginning in the inauspicious month of April 1895. Just over a year later, he pleaded with the colonia's administrator to waive the 1896 rent. He explained that he had spent thousands of dollars preparing and planting cane fields because he believed that the revolutionary movement, immediately suppressed in Matanzas, would not last long. "All the planters expected without any doubt whatever that it would have the same end," he said. "But unfortunately, men of this jurisdiction who had remained at their labors began to fall away from peaceful pursuits, and in the first days of July [1895] this jurisdiction was also in agitation . . . up to the point that the insurgents ruled the workmen of this district [and] all the work had to be abandoned. . . . An unexpected force opposed itself with an iron hand to the better purposes of the planter."[26]

The insurgency's rapid shift westward to central Las Villas likely stemmed from Spanish tactics based on the same regional assumption. When Arsenio Martínez Campos (the Spanish hero of 1878) returned to Cuba in April 1895, he concentrated Spanish forces in the East, placing his headquarters at Santiago. He left a much smaller military force in central Cuba, leading astute revolutionaries to shift operations from Oriente and Camagüey to Las Villas.

By June 1895, the insurrection was very strong in the central district of Sancti Spíritus, with some four hundred armed insurgents.[27] Generals Carlos Roloff, Serafín Sánchez, and José María Rodríguez joined these men in July with about one hundred and fifty more revolutionaries, landing at a coconut grove on the south coast of Sancti Spíritus. During the summer and fall, the insurrectionary forces fanned out across the district. At the end of November, Máximo Gómez and Antonio Maceo met just east of the Zaza River, and their brigades joined the already large numbers of insurgents in Las Villas. Some of them moved west to Santa Clara, and others settled in mountainous regions near Zaza, Trinidad, and Tuinucú.[28]

Manuel Rionda recalled that Sancti Spíritus had been quiet during a visit he made in March 1895, but when he returned in December the Cubans were roving around in groups, interrupting transportation and inspecting travelers. Manuel's memoirs vividly depict the level of mobilization in the area. On arriving at the port of Tunas de Zaza, he and his wife learned that the Cubans had blown up the railroad bridges between Tunas and Sancti Spíritus. Once the bridges were repaired, Cubans simply switched strategies, shooting at the moving train. The Riondas made it to Sancti Spíritus safely, but then they had to continue by carriage from the town to the sugarmill. Manuel's brother Francisco led the way on his horse. About fifteen minutes after passing a column of one hundred Spanish soldiers, Francisco saw two armed Cubans approach the carriage at a full gallop from the woods beside the road. He put spurs to horse and ordered the carriage driver to hurry, but the Cubans caught up. After examining a little black bag, which they thought contained correspondence for the Spanish army, the revolutionaries let the Riondas continue on their way.[29]

A report in the British *Daily Graphic* dated 23 November 1895 confirmed the strength of the movement in Sancti Spíritus. Its author, young Winston Churchill, described the thirty miles of railroad from Tunas de Zaza to Sancti Spíritus (see map 2, on page 27) as "the most dangerous and disturbed in the whole island." The line ran through thick forest, very close to the mountains occupied by insurgents. The city of Sancti Spiritus was "a forsaken place," plagued by smallpox and yellow fever. It was full of soldiers, but fifteen thousand to twenty thousand insurgents dominated all of the mountainous country to the southwest. Only large columns of troops could pass freely through the outposts surrounding the city.

Churchill witnessed an incident that showed the unusual concentration of revolutionary forces in Las Villas. A group of insurgents commanded by Máximo Gómez opened fire on a fort protecting the Tunas-Sancti Spiritus railroad tracks. Gómez drew the Spanish soldiers' attention by shooting at them from a hill about five hundred yards away, and then two other groups of Cubans attacked the Spaniards from opposite flanks. A fourth group of about one hundred Cubans destroyed the fort's gate. The fifty-soldier Spanish garrison surrendered promptly, and the Cubans let them go after taking their arms and ammunition.[30]

Spanish Infantry Captain Eugenio Pérez de Lema testified that in his judgment, Sancti Spiritus "was the zone in which there was the most insurrection."[31] Engagements were very frequent, as were deliberate blockages of the roads by different kinds of obstacles. Both prevented or slowed the march of the Spanish troops. Rionda's correspondence indicates that the insurgents had enough force to bar neutral residents from moving between Tuinucú and Sancti Spiritus without explicit permission.[32]

Spanish Officer Antonio Chies Gómez commented that "as a general rule the attitude of the country people in that jurisdiction was more favorable to the insurrection than to the Spanish cause." The people furnished the "revolutionary element" with news and clothing, which they "took out surreptitiously" from the towns garrisoned by Spanish troops.[33] Letters from Francisco and other Rionda family members relate that General Weyler particularly resented Sancti Spiritus because of its many revolutionary sympathizers; in Cienfuegos and Matanzas, Weyler appeared to be more at ease. The larger numbers of Spanish settlers in areas west of Sancti Spiritus help to explain this difference.

The best testimony to the strength of the revolution's movement westward is the fact that when the Liberation Army ordered Tuinucú and the other mills in the East and Center not to begin grinding in December and January, as was customary, the mills had to obey. The 1895–96 harvest was virtually paralyzed. Within less than a year, Maceo, Gómez and their "Army of Invasion" had arrived farther west than the combatants of the Ten Years' War. They landed in Matanzas in December 1895, paused at a Havana suburb in early January, and then invaded Cuba's westernmost province (Pinar del Rio) on 22 January 1896.[34]

It was at this same historical moment that General Weyler, the man who earned the nickname "the Butcher," replaced Martínez Campos as governor-general of Cuba. He radically changed Spanish strategy to reflect the new regional reality, adding a new "trench" between Pinar del Rio and Havana to the one his predecessor had established between Camagüey and Las Villas (see map 2, on page 27). He also clamped down on autonomists, eliminating the politically moderate alternative to revolution, and brought great numbers of Spanish soldiers to the island.

ASSUMPTION TWO: WE CAN PAY FOR PROTECTION

With revolutionaries concentrating in the Center and invading the West, planters could not afford to put all of their trust in Weyler. Many therefore tried to protect their estates by padding revolutionaries' pockets, offering money to both insurgent generals and PRC leaders in exile.

As with the first insurrections, whether to burn or not to burn was a central strategic question.[35] On 28 April 1895, shortly after arriving on the island, José Martí promised that revolutionaries would respect "all properties that respect us" and destroy "only those that serve or habitually support the enemy."[36] In Oriente, Antonio Maceo and his brother José independently set up payment schedules with several landlords to permit planting and harvesting. Like many other Cuban patriots, they felt that it was better to collect money for weapons and supplies than to destroy sugarmills and cane.[37]

A circular issued to all owners of sugarmills in November 1895 indicates that Sancti Spiritus insurgents followed the same policy as the Maceos. Of particular interest is the circular's combination of a threat to property with formal language and official payment remittance information (to a U.S.-based treasurer). The format likely aimed to differentiate revolutionary practice from banditry:

> I impose upon you as security for the work of your property the sum of 4,000 dollars, Spanish Gold; such sum to be paid within one month from the date of this circular and no delay will be granted. The payment will be

made as follows: You will remit 2,000 dollars to the Treasurer of the Delegation of the Revolutionary Party of New York, Dr. Benjamin Guerra, 192 West St., New York, forwarding the proper receipt for the same, and you will deliver to me 2,000 within the specified period.

The circular went on to request that its recipient "send by the bearer of this and as soon as possible—10 rifles and 2,000 cartridges, 1,000 for carbines and 1,000 for rifles," deducting the price of these from the total owed. "Do not forget that there will be no delay allowed in the payment," it ended, "and that the safety of your buildings depends upon your fulfillment of these requirements. Yours with the highest consideration, Chief of Brigade."[38]

Francisco Rionda's relations with the insurgents are difficult to ascertain. Spanish Colonel Hilario Santander Rodríguez reported that Francisco tried negotiating with one of Máximo Gómez's representatives for permission to cut cane, but they could not agree on the sum.[39] Infantry Captain Eugenio Pérez de Lema testified that he could "almost assert that Mr. Rionda held frequent intercourse with the insurgent bands [operating] in that zone and furnished them with supplies and news, as it was a rare thing for the Spanish troops to pass by that place without being fired upon by said bands."[40] Just what Pérez meant by "almost assert" and why he assumed it was Rionda and not the workers or colonos who passed on this information remain open to question. Officer Chies Gómez was slightly more hesitant. When asked whether Rionda had cooperated with insurgents, he stated that he knew "nothing more than what public rumor said about all the proprietors of sugar estates in Sancti Spiritus, charging them with having communication with the leaders, prefects and managers of the revolution in order that they might be permitted to carry on their estate operations necessary to gather the crop without disturbance, through payments."[41]

The colono Máximo Cisneros testified that Francisco had sent a letter to the insurgent leader Serafín Sánchez requesting permission to grind. Apparently, Sánchez sent word that he did not object but asked Rionda to consult with a local leader, Dr. Santiago García Cañizares, before proceeding. When asked specifically how much money he or Rionda had contributed to the insurgents, Cisneros replied: "There was no reason for anything to be given—if they had permitted us to grind, something might have been given." The revolutionaries would only allow Rionda to grind cane if he "brought a ship load of war materiel for them."[42]

Francisco never mentions paying off insurgents directly in his correspondence with his brother Manuel or with Tuinucú's President Juan M. Ceballos. (Both resided in New York throughout most of the war.) The closest he comes is a rather vague reference in a letter to Ceballos dated 25 December 1897. At that date, close to one hundred Spanish soldiers were residing at Tuinucú, and Francisco was hoping to grind what cane remained from the previous year's crop. Francisco asked Ceballos to have someone "write a letter to our friend Carrillo [presumably General Francisco Carrillo, the Liberation Army representative for Las Villas], encouraging him to take an interest in making sure the plantation is not harmed."[43]

A time came when planters across the island no longer had the option to pay off revolutionaries in exchange for permission to grind. The tension between civilian and military leaders over whether to grant permission to grind in exchange for cash and ammunition was intimately linked to the recurring insurrectionary question of whether to destroy or not to destroy. Martí, the Maceos, and Sánchez at first did not oppose giving permission in exchange for money. Máximo Gómez, The Liberation Army's general in chief, preferred to paralyze the sugar economy through destruction. As the revolution intensified in the Center and East of the island, the revolutionary army began to embrace Gómez's strategy. The goal was to end economic activity to recruit more worker-soldiers, demonstrate revolutionary strength, and discredit Spain in elite-Cuban and international opinion.

Gómez had to defend his position repeatedly to Tomás Estrada Palma, the man who replaced Martí as head of the PRC in New York City after Martí died in combat in 1895. Planters in exile pleaded with Estrada Palma to permit them to grind in order to collect funds "patriotically" for the revolution, but when he communicated such requests to Gómez, the general stood firm. In words reminiscent of those stated twenty-eight years earlier by Céspedes, Gómez wrote to Estrada Palma: "The harvest . . . causes us great damage. . . . Work implies peace, and in Cuba we must not permit work. When a people embark on a war for their emancipation, they must not be permitted to think [of] anything other than the war. . . . The chains of Cuba have been forged by its own riches, and it is necessary to put an end to this in order to finish soon."[44]

Gómez's statement reveals two of his revolutionary goals. The first was to destroy the riches that generated social and economic inequalities on the island. During the Liberation Army's westward trek, Gómez was shocked by colonos' and workers' living conditions. Many had no schools or health care and lived in poverty and hunger. An 1890 newspaper article noted that some mill owners still locked workers' barracks at night, a carry-over from the era of slavery, along with the brutal work hours from 4 A.M. to 6 P.M.[45] Gómez envisioned a post-independence Cuba with a new class of small independent farmers that would "achieve independence and dignity" from the fruit of their labor on land that they owned.[46] Thus, he passed a land decree on July 1896 declaring that "all lands acquired by the Cuban Republic either by conquest or confiscation . . . shall be divided among the defenders of the Cuban Republic against Spain, and each shall receive a portion corresponding to the services rendered, as shall be provided by the first Cuban congress."[47]

The second goal was to paralyze the harvest so that Cuban workers and farmers would abandon what little they had to join the Liberation Army and struggle for a more equal nation. As early as July 1895, Gómez had threatened planters, farmers, and ranchers that their estates would be destroyed and their owners tried for treason if they did not discontinue work and suspend trade with towns occupied by enemy forces.[48] His army's "Instructions to Cubans," issued in October 1895, ordered revolutionaries to stop the gathering and grinding of cane by all possible means. Suggestions included sending squads of four or five to burn all that lay within reach; terrorizing those who were cutting cane by carting it away; cutting off the heads of two or three men in every place where the cutting was in progress; and destroying the buildings on the estate by burning them, if possible, or blowing them up. The circular even provided suggestions on how to blow up factories: Ask for work in the boiler house and, "when opportunity offers, throw the stick of dynamite into the furnace in operation." Or hollow out a thick cane stalk, then fill it with dynamite and place it on a loaded cart on its way to the sugarmill: "It will be thrown out among the rest so that upon arriving at the sugarmill it will explode."[49]

Gómez issued another circular one month later aimed specifically at sugar workers: "Any worker assisting the operation of the sugar factories will be considered an enemy of his country . . . and will be executed."[50] This raises the questions of who joined the revolution, why, and when. These are very difficult questions to unravel, given the scarcity of materials that address the matter directly and the myriad contingencies one might propose to explain workers' actions.[51] The evidence from Tuinucú is tentative. The colono foreman Máximo Cisneros stated: "I used to go out to look after my fields and would meet [insurgents]. Many of them were workmen who had been with me before."[52] But when the commissioner enquired further, asking, "The workmen and laborers were very much in sympathy with the Insurgents, were they not?" Cisneros replied rather ambiguously: "Yes, they used to get along well together—some, others not."[53]

Few people kill or risk death for even the most inspirational revolutionary programs. Cuban leaders understood this and knew that only by disrupting the daily routines of the majority could they mobilize more Cubans.[54] Gómez certainly believed that many tied to the sugar industry would not join unless the sugar harvest was paralyzed, and certain events strengthen this theory. We have already seen that the wealth generated by sugar and slavery kept many from fighting during the first two wars for independence, and that the third war did not look very hopeful until the 1894 bust. Planters and landowning colonos had the obvious motivation to grind to pay off debts and make profits. Workers and colono sharecroppers needed the wages. Many had to support their families for the entire year with the little they earned during the six or seven months of harvest.[55]

Colonos and workers stopped working at Tuinucú only after local insurgents demonstrated that their threat of execution was serious; they killed a worker taking tiles from the estate's tile factory to the mill. A majority of Tuinucú workers again slighted the revolution's calls for solidarity in the spring of 1896, when they returned to plant and tend the fields. Francisco Rionda's son José testified that about one hundred and fifty workers were at the plantation on 8 April, where normally there would be about two hundred and fifty.[56] They left only after insurgents burned the fields surrounding their work residence, taking away the work and frightening them off the estate.[57] A similar pattern emerged on the national scale. On 30 January 1896, the *Willett and Gray* news from Havana read: "Amongst the causes interfering with the crop, the difficulties planters have to contend with to find laborers willing to work on sugar plantations must be mentioned in first place, since the insurgents pitilessly hang, shoot, or behead all those caught by them working in such factories."[58]

By January 1896 the revolutionary strategy was working. Only a few plantations in Pinar del Rio, Havana, and western Matanzas were able to start grinding. In the Center and East, none of the mills save three or four in

Oriente were able to harvest cane.[59] In response to the propaganda war being waged in the press—Spain and the PRC competing with false victory news—*Willett and Gray* commented on January 16: "The fact of only 3,260 tons receipts for the week, against 19,173 tons for the corresponding week last year, and 30,000 tons the previous year, tells the story of the desperate condition of the island."[60] From a sugar crop of roughly 1 million tons in 1895, Cuba's total fell by 70 percent in one year.[61] Tuinucú produced only two hundred bags of sugar in 1895–96, versus 31,000 bags in 1894–95.[62]

ASSUMPTION THREE: SPANISH FORCES WILL PROTECT THE FIELDS

When the insurgents proved that they could effectively prohibit grinding in January 1896, Spain's General Weyler responded with a series of extremely harsh decrees.[63] He shifted troops from the sugar estates, where Martínez Campos had placed them, to active combat units. He used them to protect communication and transportation systems instead of sugarcane. With this act, Weyler went against Cuban planters' third assumption—namely, that Spanish soldiers would protect their fields and factories. Weyler authorized planters to hire and arm private guards at their own expense, and many did so to protect their plantations from further damage. Few opted to grind because they were afraid of revolutionary retaliation.[64]

Weyler's "re-concentration" decrees in 1896 and 1897 ordering the rural population to move to Spanish-controlled fortified towns affected plantations even further.[65] Revolutionaries had set the precedent in 1895 of relocating or killing civilians who would not join them, but they lacked the numbers (and inclination) to regularly enforce this policy. At the best of times, only some forty thousand Cuban revolutionaries stood against one hundred fifty thousand Spanish soldiers and sixty thousand Cuban loyalists. *Pacíficos* (neutral civilians) outnumbered Cubans who joined either side. Revolutionaries wanted pacíficos to concentrate in guerrilla camps in the countryside because their small everyday acts—such as farming and selling food to Spanish-dominated cities, putting out fires, and policing the streets—buttressed Spanish rule. Weyler saw pacíficos as providers of food, supplies, and military intelligence to the revolutionaries (Cuban women were particularly talented at sneaking supplies and notes about Spanish troop locations out of the cities and into insurgent camps in their long turn-of-the-century dresses).[66] Weyler's decrees affected far more civilians than did revolutionary concentration because he had both the will and the way to carry it out. Spanish forces lacked the money, food, and medical knowledge to protect the half-million civilians herded into these crowded concentration camps from starvation and disease. Epidemics and starvation killed more than one hundred thousand.[67]

Weyler's extreme measures hurt the Spanish Government both economically and politically. Insurgent attacks on sugarmills combined with re-concentration meant no sugar production, and thus no taxes for the colonial government. Europeans and Americans censured Spain for the dire conditions in the camps. Re-concentration of this scale, intensity, and efficiency was unprecedented, and it generated a public outcry abroad in defense of Cuban human rights.[68]

The Spanish government became extremely concerned that the U.S. might recognize Cuba to be in a state of war and thereby grant the insurgents belligerency status (and thus the legal right to import arms). To prove that there was no "state of war" and at the same time address some of the international criticism, Weyler softened his policies briefly in March 1896. That month, the Spanish generals in command at Sancti Spiritus, Camagüey, and Santiago de Cuba received notice that they were authorized to postpone re-concentration in the jurisdiction. The first re-concentration order, they were advised, was "not intended to refer to the large industrial and agricultural establishments employing a great number of hands. . . . Such establishments should endeavor by all means to keep at work and the necessary protection should be afforded them."[69]

In March and April 1896 the Tuinucú plantation became caught in the middle of Spain's efforts to prove that Cuba's sugar industry was safe and the insurgents' strategy to paralyze production. On 1 March, desperate to recover some of the expenses from planting the previous year's crop, Francisco started the harvest at Tuinucú. Eight days later, the insurgent leader Santiago García Cañizares sent an emissary bearing a formal note to Francisco that read: "You will accompany the bearer to this place. In case you do not comply with my request you will be responsible for the serious consequences."[70] At around 9:30 A.M., Francisco went to a colono's house on the boundary of the estate, where Cañizares was staying with about two hundred and fifty or three hundred men. According to the colono Máximo Cisneros, who was present at the meeting, Cañizares asked Francisco why he was grinding despite revolutionary orders to stop. He replied that he had obtained permission from other insurgent chiefs to do it. Cañizares responded that "such permissions were not in order, as Articles 17 and 21 of the Rules of the Insurgents were against any grinding." (Note the insurgents' effort to come across as legitimate rulers, not bandits.) Francisco suggested that the Tuinucú estate should be permitted to grind because it was an American company, and the United States was certainly going to grant belligerency status to the insurgents. Cañizares responded that when this status was granted, he would permit the estate to grind. Francisco stopped the grinding immediately. Even the cane that had already been cut was not hauled to the mill because the insurgents threatened to "cut down anybody that worked in the fields."[71]

A month later, on 7 April 1896, Francisco received a letter from Spanish Captain Antonio Chies asking him to confer with General Pin in Sancti Spiritus.[72] At that afternoon's meeting, Pin asked him why his sugar estate was not grinding. Francisco replied that he was afraid that insurgents would burn the cane fields and damage the buildings, recounting his meeting with Cañizares. Pin promised to build two additional forts on the sugar estate and—at least according to Francisco, his son José, and the colono Ramon Ferrer—Pin ordered him to start grinding again.[73] The next day, Colonel Santander arrived at the plantation with some two hundred and fifty men, who began to construct the forts with the help of some Tuinucú employees. They made a square barricade out of cane wagons, placed one on top of the other like blocks of masonry, and filled them with earth, leaving loopholes through which the guns of the soldiers could be fired.[74]

In an August 1896 protest against the Spanish government, Francisco described what transpired next: "On April 8, I received a private letter, signed by José Miguel Gómez . . . in which I was told that if the construction of the . . . additional forts was carried out, he would immediately order the destruction by fire of all the property belonging to the 'Central Tuinucú Sugarcane Manufacturing Company.' "[75] (José Miguel Gómez, whom Francisco described as "an acquaintance of mine before the troubles," took over as insurgent leader in the district of Sancti Spiritus after Serafín Sánchez's death; he would become governor of the Province of Santa Clara in 1901, lead a Liberal Party revolt in 1906, and win the presidency from 1909 to 1912.) Rionda showed Gómez's letter to the Spanish officers in command and asked them to stop, but the troops continued to erect the forts.

The very next day, insurgents began to torch the cane on Máximo Cisneros's cane farm at Tuinucú. As mentioned in this chapter's opening anecdote, Cisneros told the Spanish officer that he could help him and his men protect the fields, but the officer refused to combat the fires.[76] Spanish forces were willing to protect the mill town, but not the fields. Francisco's son reported, "[Almost] every night the insurgents used to approach from the hills and fire volleys [at] the troops encamped at the mill town," and the Spanish forces "simply fired back from the town."[77]

This raises the question whether Spanish forces actively decided not to protect cane fields or were simply incapable of doing so. The question is debated at length in the Spanish Treaty Claims Commission Case, and it is of interest because it reveals whether Spanish policy abandoned, did everything possible, or made only small efforts to protect Cuban sugar plantations in the context of revolutionary insurgency. The carpenter Juan Echevarne of Tuinucú reported that a group of eight men fired the cane fields at three different places at midday on 9 April, then resumed firing on 10, 11, 12, and 16 April, with the result that nearly all of the cane fields were destroyed; this despite the presence of two hundred and fifty to three hundred Spanish soldiers and five hundred to six hundred more who arrived on 16 April. Echevarne went to the house where the Spanish soldiers were staying and asked the captain to take his soldiers out to stop the fire, but the captain apparently replied, "Let it burn."

When the defense tried to make the case that there was nothing the Spaniards could have done, Echevarne responded: "their mission was to go there and protect the place so that we could grind, and the fact of the matter is that in consequence of their coming, the fields were set fire to and they did not go out to defend or protect the place." When questioned exactly how they could have put out the fires, Echevarne replied: "Fire is surrounded by people, and cane is cut away from in front of the fire. . . . [A] counter-fire is started. . . . The two fires come together, and the fire is ended." He explained that there were workers there who had the tools to cut the cane and stop the fires, if only the soldiers would accompany them outside the mill town to protect them while they did so. This the soldiers refused to do.[78]

Military witness after witness among the Spanish denied that there was a fire at all, blamed the colonos for lighting it (to save the cost of cutting the cane), or claimed that Spanish soldiers were so "daring" that they surely rushed to extinguish all fires.[79] The Spanish defense team argued that it was impossible to protect all of the fields because they were too vast; protecting the buildings in the mill town was a more feasible priority. An American soldier with extensive experience defending sugar plantations elsewhere looked over the fields and mill town of Tuinucú to help them make their case. He testified that it would have taken five hundred to eight hundred men to protect all of the cane, buildings, and machinery on the plantation during wartime (manning the forts and forming a roving column to make sure no insurgents could enter and set fires at night).[80]

The claimant countered with the statement of the retired Spanish officer Ramon Ferrer that he and a much smaller force had been able to protect the mill and even allow its workers to cut, haul, and grind, during the entire Ten Years' War.[81] As we know from chapter 1, this was not the case: Tuinucú did suffer stoppages and damage during the war. Moreover, revolutionaries and Spaniards had a much stronger presence in the center of the island in the 1890s than they did in the 1870s, and both sides embraced the strategy of destruction to a greater extent than their predecessors in 1868.

Whether Spanish forces could have actually stopped the insurgents from setting fires at Tuinucú in April 1896 remains open to debate. One of the insurgents who participated in the burning of Tuinucú cane that April commented that it only took him and his comrades-in-arms "some ten minutes" because the fire spread so quickly in the fields.[82] The same defense team brought up a powerful argument in a similar case against Spain for alleged negligence (the Mapos sugarmill case). They pointed out that Spanish forces could not possibly guard against a particular form of burning cane used by the insurgents: A few men would slip into the cane fields at night and scatter balls of phosphorus covered with wax. The next day, the sun would melt the wax and light the phosphorus on fire while the arsonists rested safely back at their base.[83]

The insurgents at Tuinucú did not have to use phosphorus and wax in April because the Spanish soldiers allowed them to ride freely through the cane fields. Nevertheless, the existence of such methods suggests that the fields might have been torched even if the Spanish troops had practiced what the claimant defined as "due diligence" by attacking the revolutionaries. The testimony of another insurgent indicates that Tuinucú could only have avoided the torch had the Spanish general not insisted—or Francisco not decided, depending on whom you believe—to grind. "I burned the cane on Tuinucú," the merchant and local insurgent José Antonio Jimenez y Cañizares stated explicitly, "because grinding was forbidden, and it was understood that [Tuinucú intended] to grind."[84]

Most of the Spanish soldiers left soon after the fire, allegedly because Francisco had negotiated with the insurgents (an ironic accusation given that insurgents had just destroyed his sugarmill's cane). A small force remained on the plantation until August 1896, when they destroyed the forts and left the mill town completely unguarded. The Spanish soldier Ramon Sobrino testified that the commanding chief in Sancti Spiritus sent him and one hundred mounted men to accompany Francisco and his family back to Sancti Spiritus after the burning of the cane.[85] According to José Rionda, Francisco first went to Sancti Spiritus with Máximo Cisneros to recruit workers and colonos to cut and process some of the burned cane, but the workers refused to go to the plantation out of fear of the insurgents and knowledge that the Spanish would not, or could not, protect them. "Seeing that he could not grind the cane that had been burned," José testified, "my father returned with my mother, brothers, and sister to Sancti Spiritus." They left Sancti Spiritus for the United States in August 1896.[86]

The Braga–Rionda family narrative, written some eighty years later, depicts an especially colorful version of the events that transpired in March and April 1896. It shows how family memory transformed Francisco into Tuinucú's "beloved patriarch" and a Spaniard loyal to his country. Although the testimony and evidence cited here surely provide a historical reconstruction that is closer to actual events, the family narrative accurately communicates the essence of Francisco Rionda's experience: He was caught between Spanish demands to grind and Cuban demands to halt the harvest:

> [Spanish forces ordered all mill owners] to grind on pain of death. The rebels, to disrupt the economy, ordered all . . . to shut down on pain of death. Pancho [Francisco] was a loyal Spaniard. It also suited him to grind as late in the year as possible and so turn cane into money in the bank. Tuinucú continued to grind until one night a rebel chief took Pancho . . . to the woods. This chief was known never to return a prisoner alive. Elena and the children considered Pancho as good as dead. There were heart-rending final farewells. But he was popular with the workmen, and when he arrived at the rebel camp, the men, led by one big Negro,

began to chant, "Viva Don Pancho." He was freed and returned to his family. Pancho was a frightened man and prudent. He ordered Tuinucú to stop grinding.

The next morning, seeing no smoke from Tuinucú's chimneys, the commanding officer at Sancti Spiritus sent for Pancho. They were on friendly terms, and the officer regretted that he [had to] order Pancho to be shot as a traitor to Spain. As a last gesture of loyalty, Pancho gave valuable information about rebel encampments and about traitors within the Spanish ranks. Grateful for [the] excuse to stay the execution, the officer ordered Pancho to Tuinucú and to prepare to leave Cuba immediately with his family. . . . At the sight of him in sound health, the family dried their untimely tears and prepared to celebrate—until Pancho told them of their banishment. . . . Pancho and Elena, their six children, the ex-slave Concha la Negra, [Pancho's sister] Isidora, and her maid, Teofila, took what valuables they could carry and rode under Spanish military escort to the port of Tunas on the south coast. There they hired a fishing boat [to] Savannah, Georgia.[87]

REVOLUTION IN THE COUNTRYSIDE: THE TUINUCÚ "REPUBLIC OF ANARCHY," 1896–1898

The self-defined campesino (country laborer or peasant) Manuel Ferrer moved into the Rionda family dwelling with his wife and nine children to watch over the estate in exchange for a monthly stipend. He and Máximo Cisneros, who also remained at the estate, both testified that only a few workers and colonos lived in the houses in or near the mill town after Francisco's departure. Ferrer and Cisneros described Tuinucú as a free-for-all during the half-year between August 1896, when Spanish forces abandoned Tuinucú, and February 1897, when Weyler returned to Sancti Spiritus. Spanish columns repeatedly passed through the plantation on their way from Sancti Spiritus to nearby towns, camping overnight and sometimes longer. Among other things, the Spaniards and their insurgent enemies ate many of the animals, destroyed parts of the machinery, and used construction lumber and furniture for firewood. They also destroyed papers and books, removed goods from the commissary store, and destroyed fences to allow the free passage of troops.[88]

Unable to afford living as exiles in the United States, and eager to resettle at their Tuinucú home, Francisco and his family returned to Sancti Spiritus in January 1897. Francisco wrote detailed letters to his brother Manuel in New York that month and the next that offer a glimpse of life on the plantation during the revolution. He described Tuinucú as a "Republic of Anarchy" where soldiers and insurgents tramped, taking clothing, furniture, and machinery to sell or make explosives with. Insurgent, pacífico, and Spaniard alike ate most of the plantation's animals. Francisco complained that without fences, the more than thirty thousand cows ranging free in the jurisdiction of Sancti Spiritus ate and trampled large amounts of cane. Meanwhile, the neutral residents and insurgents (some former workers or small colonos) living rent-free in houses belonging to the sugarmill, also used Tuinucú's cane. According to Ferrer, who had to sneak from the plantation to Sancti Spiritus to deliver the news, neutral residents on the estate had built forty makeshift cane-grinding mills.[89] Francisco was perhaps speculating in rage when he stated that they "cut the cane carelessly, picking the best of the lot, then giving or selling their 'harvest' to the rebels with whom they sympathized."[90] Although Francisco does not mention other crops, residents likely survived in 1897 on the same things Francisco mentions them doing at Tuinucú the following year: cultivating corn and yams and raising chickens and pigs.[91]

In response to such anarchy in the countryside, Weyler ordered troops to re-concentrate once again. Francisco reported on 12 February 1897 that Weyler was expected to arrive with twelve thousand infantrymen and fifteen mounted squadrons that day or the next. As soon as they marched through an area, they would declare it "pacified," then authorize grinding there. "Continuing the farce," the Spaniards published reforms in an effort to demoralize the revolutionary movement. Francisco wrote a letter three days later telling how General Luque, who was in charge of the Sancti Spiritus jurisdiction, had secured verbal permission from Weyler to allow many of the February 1896 reconcentrados to return to the countryside because of the sickness and hygiene problems in Sancti Spiritus. The columns passing through Tuinucú did not bother the residents (despite their obvious rebel sympathies) because they were "General Luque's group." But "Crazy Weyler and his troops surely did not remember the verbal promise, and when they entered. . . . You should have seen the outrages [committed by] the troops, the laments, and the seas of families pouring into the city." Many neutral residents went straight to Francisco, telling him that they had not come to see him earlier because the revolutionaries did not permit it.[92]

Francisco and the Rionda women wrote letters to Manuel describing the great numbers of soldiers and reconcentrados in Sancti Spiritus and the illness and hunger afflicting the town from February through June 1897, when the family once again took refuge in the United States. These letters constitute a rich window into life in a re-concentrated town. Francisco's daughter Elena Rionda described Spanish soldiers running through the streets and holding a dance to celebrate the death of Antonio Maceo. Her mother's and aunts' letters expressed concern about all of the disease and destruction surrounding them.[93] Yellow fever and dysentery killed soldiers and civilians in large numbers. The population in the entire municipality of Sancti Spiritus (including Tuinucú) declined from 29,278 inhabitants in 1887 to 25,709 in 1899. The fact that 76 percent of the 3,569 people who died were in the capital city suggests that re-concentration was largely to blame.[94] The province of Santa Clara was particularly hard hit because it was the war's front line in 1897; it lay in a deadly zone in between the Spanish-controlled West and the revolutionary East. Spanish forces re-concentrated 140,000 people in the province as a whole, and more than 52,997 died.[95]

When Francisco returned to the island in late 1898, he raged against the cumulative effects of the inhumane re-concentration: "It is the most shameless mistake and the greatest advantage Spain could give to the enemy. . . . Spanish forces should find a way to make sugarmill owners give shelter to these reconcentrados, to provide for them until they are able to grow a few things; in effect, to do what I have done at Tuinucú, where there are 300 living off the land and costing me nothing."[96] It is unclear exactly who these neutral residents were and when he allowed them to move to Tuinucú. The fact that residents went to him for help in February 1896 and that he allowed them to live at Tuinucú rent-free at some point thereafter lends credence to the family narrative's claim that he was considered a relatively "good" patriarch.

In February 1897 Weyler's troops ruthlessly destroyed the family huts and makeshift sugarmills of poor country folk. They even cut tiny tobacco, cane, and vegetable plants off at their roots. This kind of repression, though tragic, may not have completely destroyed many planters' assumption that Spain would at least try to protect their fields and factories. But it shocked Cubans and foreigners alike when the troops made a direct attack on Spain's most obvious allies by adopting a deliberate strategy of destroying capitalist property, burning cane fields and buildings in February 1897 to keep neutral residents and insurgents from using them for food or shelter. One Spanish captain, when asked directly whether General Weyler's orders were to destroy property in the line of march, replied: "I do not know that they had orders or not, but they were burning on their line of march."[97]

The question of nationality came up repeatedly in the face of destruction in the Sancti Spiritus district. Francisco wrote to Manuel that Spanish colonos believed Spanish troops were harder on their buildings than on Tuinucú's because the colonos could not protest to the American government as the Tuinucú corporation had done. "According to all these theories," Francisco mused, "it will soon be better to be Chinese than Spanish."[98] Tuinucú's lawyer tried to make the opposite case—that the Spanish troops were harder on Tuinucú specifically because it was owned by an American corporation. To support this argument, the lawyer cited Manuel Ferrer's experience as guide to General Carlos Ruiz's column.

Ferrer testified that when he saw Spanish guerrillas setting fire to several fields and buildings at Tuinucú, he told the lieutenant beside him that the property belonged to an American citizen, "because it was said that the troops respected American citizenship." When the lieutenant replied that he "did not care," Ferrer maneuvered to the center of the column to tell General Ruiz the same, but the general replied, "with sternness, that General Weyler had given orders to destroy everything." In contrast, when the column arrived at the Zaza estate, owned by a Spaniard named Zulueta, no fields were burned, and "the officer in command of the vanguard gave orders to the soldiers that they should not light any cigarettes while marching across the cane fields."[99]

Ferrer's testimony underscores the challenges of pinpointing perpetrator and motive for a cane fire. We can read Ferrer's testimony in several ways. The "it was said" indicates that the Spanish troops may indeed have tried to protect American property as a general rule. This would certainly fit in with Spain's overall policy to keep the United States from granting Cubans belligerency status. The cigarette instruction could be read as an officer learning from his troop's mistakes: Maybe Tuinucú's fields were set aflame by a carelessly discarded cigarette butt. Another possibility is that the Spanish troops targeted Tuinucú specifically because they had heard about Francisco's protest to the U.S. State Department or because they believed that Francisco sympathized with the enemy. The latter motive is not far-fetched. Other studies of the 1895 insurrection have emphasized the increasing alienation between Spanish military personnel and the Spanish residents of the island as more and more soldiers fell ill while the residents they were fighting for played both sides.[100]

By 1898 alienation, illness, and debt had taken a significant toll on the Spanish forces. On the other side, the Cubans had lost the united front that José Martí had worked so hard to forge between military and civilian, Cuban and exile, separatist and autonomist, and humble and wealthy "imagined citizens" of an independent Cuban Republic. Revolutionary movements always combine diverse disaffected social groups. Unity can be easily destroyed by sticky questions such as what should replace the old regime.[101] Generals like Máximo Gómez, Antonio Maceo, and Serafín Sánchez wanted the revolution to accomplish a certain social leveling through land distribution, racial equality, regional distribution, and economic diversification. Afro-Cuban participants, at least according to the army surgeon Manuel Arbelo, "imagined a state of things founded on social equality, on the supremacy of military men, of the *guapos* [the 'brave' or 'strong' men], without the distinctions that forcibly impose themselves in any society."[102] It should be noted that even this more egalitarian vision excluded a large number of Cubans from the idealized Cuban nation; the rhetoric did not incorporate the guapa women who sustained and fought alongside male revolutionaries or the vast number of pacíficos.[103]

The Cuban elite at home and abroad were as terrified of a redistributive revolution from below as they were distressed by Weyler's destructive reaction from above. Revolutionary insurrection, combined with Spanish military policy under Weyler, had annihilated the colonial pact with Spain by 1898, leading sugar planters to seek protection elsewhere. The few who had ever supported a Cuba Libre joined other Cuban and resident Spanish elites to demand U.S. intervention instead. In June 1896, nearly one hundred planters, industrialists, and lawyers petitioned President Grover Cleveland to intervene and resolve the crisis. Such demands became increasingly common as the war progressed.[104] When the American government answered this call, U.S. agents and their Cuban allies tried to place many of the revolution's demands for leveling on the back burner, squeezing things Cuban out of the equation. Cuba's third war for independence became "the Spanish–American War."[105]

United States' intervention ensured that sugar would remain a dominant force in the island's economy. This condemned Cubans to virtual dependence on one product—subject to extreme fluctuations on the U.S. and world markets—and from six to ten months of very high unemployment every year between the harvests. Foreign capital pushed railroads and a new type of sugar enclave community to Cuba's East. This spread sugarcane (and the potential for revolutionary reactions against it) across the entire island. Over the course of the first twenty years of the republic, Oriente and Camagüey took the place of Havana and Matanzas as the largest sugar producers of the island.[106] The former province of Las Villas—renamed "Santa Clara" on independence—remained the island's most productive single province from 1901 through 1921, producing roughly 40 percent of the total crop in the early years of the republic and being surpassed by both Camagüey and Oriente only in 1922.[107] The site of major battles from 1895 through 1898, the central province was home to many of the strongest caudillo-clientele groups on the island.[108]

The Tuinucú sugarmill recovered from the destruction of 1895–98 because the Riondas had access to the foreign capital necessary to repair damage and build powerful enough mills to compete on the world market. In contrast, many Cubans and Spaniards fell to the status of cane farmers or managers for foreign owners. Foreign capital squeezed Cubans out of property and resources, but U.S. annexationists were unable to squeeze them out of political power. A new constitution and elections created space for limited yet meaningful Cuban political participation, and in 1906, mostly Las Villas veterans and Afro-Cubans demanded political inclusion through José Miguel Gómez's Liberal Party rebellion.

U.S. Power and Cuban Middlemen, 1898–1917

3 On 18 September 1906 the Trinidad Sugar Company manager Harry Garnett warned British officials that a Liberal Party rebellion, sparked by fraudulent elections, seriously threatened property on the island. Cuba's first president, Tomás Estrada Palma, had already accumulated over $500,000 in his first term and was attempting to prevent the Liberal Party from assuming its rightful place in power. He had improved on "every trick known to American elections," stuffing ballots and preventing liberals from going to the polls.[1] Garnett blamed Sir William Van Horne for introducing Cubans to bribes in exchange for concessions. (Van Horne's Cuba Company railroad cut through the center of the island—right by the Tuinucú sugarmill—to finally link East to West; a few extra dollars bought him the public land to build two adjacent sugarmills and a lucrative shipping port.)[2] The Liberation Army veterans united in José Miguel Gómez's Liberal Party wanted fair elections to stop Estrada Palma's graft, and they knew about the 1902 U.S. Platt Amendment to the Cuban Constitution granting U.S. forces the right to intervene to maintain a "stable Government adequately protecting life, property, and individual liberty."[3] Foreign capitalists and politicians worried that insurgents might put two and two together and try to hasten intervention by beginning "to burn the sugarcane and destroy property

commencing . . . with that of foreigners."[4] The U.S. Secretary of War William H. Taft feared that, "unless we assure peace, some $200,000,000 of American property may go up in smoke in less than ten days."[5]

Liberals wrote to U.S. diplomats asking them to force new elections, and British diplomats wrote asking them to protect foreign properties. Two facts explain why: the U.S. occupation from 1898 to 1902 increased U.S. capitalists' stake in maintaining order, and the Platt Amendment identified the U.S. government as the final arbiter of Cuban national power. The U.S. Military Government's so-called concessions and reforms of 1899–1902 reallocated land and resources mostly to U.S. and other foreign capitalists, not to Cuba's liberators. U.S.–Cuban treaties locked Cuba into economic dependence on one country and one product, as U.S. capital (and Van Horne's railroad) spread sugarcane to Cuba's relatively undeveloped central and eastern frontiers. Most studies on the Cuban Republic acknowledge that U.S. policy squeezed Cubans out of property and resources, imposed limits on Cuba's sovereignty, and reversed many of the revolution's goals. The first two sections in this chapter leave the local sugarmill community to analyze at the national level how U.S. forces achieved this—a shocking feat, given the extreme level of Cuban revolutionary mobilization that we saw in chapter 2.

Without sufficient capital to buy or maintain land and resources, most Cuban elites were reduced to playing the role of middlemen and service providers for foreign bosses, serving as lawyers, managers, foremen, and politicians. The U.S. military administration gave Liberation Army veterans a small stipend, but it was rarely enough to purchase land. Caudillo war heroes and elites became go-betweens for U.S. politicians and capitalists in hopes of ushering in peace, progress, and modernity—in the form of foreign investment, technology, and export agriculture—rather than the great social and economic leveling that the wars for independence promised. The fascination with progress in the early twentieth century helps explain the bizarre fact that foreign investors (including Americans, Britons, Spaniards, and Canadians) infiltrated the island after nearly thirty years of Cuban nationalist revolutionary struggle. Latin American leaders elsewhere embraced export agriculture and the fixings of modernity during the same era. U.S.- and European-influenced architecture, wide avenues, telegraph wires, and streetlights spread through the Western Hemisphere. What made Cuba unique was the extreme concentration in a single export commodity that could be grown in every province of the country; most other Latin American countries had at least two regions, perhaps a banana zone on the coast and a coffee zone in the mountains. The sugarmill communities dotted all the way across Cuba (see map 1, on pages vi–vii) were like "islands of modernity," imitating the architecture and technology of America's and Europe's larger cities.[6]

United States' capitalists dominated the new nation's economy and forced the Platt Amendment into the constitution (by threatening not to leave unless it was added), but U.S. politicians were unable to contain the "popular" in Cuban political democracy. Cubans insisted on universal manhood suffrage in their constitution of 1902, rejecting U.S. pressure to include landholding requirements. The revolution's mass-mobilization had created overwhelming pressure for independence, racial equality, and access to political power. U.S. rhetoric promised these same things, with the possible exception of racial equality. By allowing U.S. corporations to flood Cuba with direct investments instead of offering credit to Cuban entrepreneurs, U.S. policy left few avenues for capital accumulation open to Cubans. The journalist Miguel de Carrión wrote in 1921 that politics had become Cuba's only industry, "stronger than the sugar industry, which is no longer ours, more lucrative than the railroads, which are managed by foreigners [and] safer than the banks, maritime transportation and commercial trade, which also do not belong to us."[7]

Cuba's president could rise above the middleman status to become a patron doling out jobs, contracts, and cash benefits to family, friends, and party members. His "largesse" would filter down to even the most menial positions, such as street sweepers, garbage collectors, and postmen, via the men he appointed as provincial governors, municipal mayors, and army and police chiefs. Elections sparked insurrections because so much was at stake: the power to distribute jobs, as well as the opportunity to make a fortune.[8]

Presidential elections thus added to Cuba's economic and agricultural cycles—the booms and busts of the international sugar market and the yearly harvest schedule—a four-year political cycle. The rebellions surrounding the 1906, 1912, and 1917 elections were all Cuban efforts to use U.S. power and the Platt Amendment to fulfill the promise of democracy: political participation for all Cubans.[9] Liberal caudillos and Afro-Cubans threatened sugar companies and other foreign properties as a way to draw U.S. attention, but they rarely followed through, which is what made these rebellions rather than revolutions. The caudillos accepted sugar and foreign investment as Cuba's economic base, and sought not to destroy it but, rather, to use the threat of destruction as a way to gain power.[10]

The broader context shows that most new nations start out with periods of violent debate over issues such as state autonomy versus federal centralization or church versus state power. The United States faced such rebellions in the 1780s and 1790s, and Spanish American caudillos battled over these issues through the nineteenth century. U.S. politicians thought they could preclude such disputes in Cuba with the Platt Amendment, but they simply inserted U.S. power into the mix. From 1898 through 1906, U.S. officials pushed upper-class Cuban exiles into political power at the national level, squeezing out many military leaders, along with the revolutionary principles that they defended. Yet in the meantime, veterans such as José Miguel Gómez, Evaristo Estenoz, Pedro Ivonnet, and Mario García Menocal began to build strong clienteles and to forge political alliances at the local and regional levels. In 1906, 1912, and 1917, they used these networks to claim what they considered their "rightful share" at the national level.[11] These Liberation Army veterans deliberately threatened and staged disorder in hopes that U.S. intervention would win them their demands for racial, political, and social equality.

The generals who had struggled for independence managed to gain power and become Cuba's presidents from 1908 through 1933 via a caudillo-patron pattern similar to that in the rest of Latin America. In Cuba, as in those other nations, wars for independence ushered in periods of rule by caudillos, nicknamed "generals and doctors," capable of claiming national power by mobilizing their clientele into voter booths or insurgent armies.[12] This chapter's final section presents an explanation of why only the 1906 Liberal rebellion triumphed, not the 1912 struggle for Afro-Cuban rights or José Miguel Gómez's 1917 Liberal rebellion. In short, racial prejudice remained tenacious among Cuban and U.S. politicians. Cuba's third president, Mario García Menocal (1913–21), was José Miguel Gómez's nemesis. He built a Conservative Party network at the Chaparra sugarmill in eastern Cuba (this book's second case study and the largest sugarmill in early-twentieth-century Cuba) and became the perfect U.S. ally—an authoritarian leader whose troops were able to repress the 1917 rebellion without U.S. aid.

DIVIDING THE REVOLUTION:
U.S. INTERVENTION, 1898–1899

Mario García Menocal, José Miguel Gómez, and a select few other major-
generals were leading the Liberation Army in April 1898 when the United
States declared war against Spain and organized a naval blockade to cut off
supplies. Between April 1898 and March 1899, President William McKinley
sent some forty-five thousand American servicemen to occupy Cuba for an
undefined period of time. This was the first of a series of twentieth-century
U.S. interventions in Latin America supposedly to help flailing nations free
themselves from tyranny and establish democracies. In fact, interventions
occurred wherever revolutionaries threatened foreign interests and U.S.
capitalists had enough investments at stake to force their government to
buttress dependent elite regimes.[13] U.S. forces intervened thirty-four times
in nine Latin American countries between 1898 and 1934. Good Neighbor
policies from the 1930s onward prompted instead non-recognition of radical
governments and behind-the-scenes maneuvering for more U.S.-friendly
regimes.[14]

The most common characteristic of these interventions (beginning with
Cuba) was the U.S. administrations' need to portray them as motivated by
humanitarian generosity when what really drove them was U.S. capitalists'
desire for new markets. By the late nineteenth century, many U.S. industrialists were ready to export goods, to import and process primary resources,
or to set up export industries abroad. These industrialists lobbied the U.S.
government to lower import tariffs. In direct contrast, many U.S. agricultural producers continued to depend almost entirely on protectionist tariffs.
Sugar had one group in each camp: U.S. sugar refiners and brokers wanted
lower tariffs for importing raw sugar from abroad, while most producers
of beet sugar in the western United States and cane sugar in the south-
ern United States wanted higher tariffs. At least until the First World War,
most Americans preferred to think of their nation as a protected agrarian
country magnanimously helping new Latin American republics establish
themselves.

Within this framework, one can understand the contradiction between
what U.S. politicians said they were doing and what they actually did in
Cuba and the rest of Latin America. The hypocrisy began with the myth that

U.S. forces invaded Cuba to help the Cubans win freedom from Spain. The actual goal was to preclude a social and racial revolution ("another Haiti") and to create a new, dependent, and politically moderate Cuba safe for U.S. capital.[15] Differences arose over whether Cuba should be a nation, a protectorate, or a U.S. state, but most agreed that it should be dependent.[16] The myth and rhetoric mattered because they created a space, however limited, within which Cubans could push for more political power, democracy, and independence.

On the Cuban side, José Martí had hoped to establish a Cuban nation free from the sort of violent caudillo rule that plagued many of the new Latin American republics after they gained independence in the 1820s. That is why he refused to join General Máximo Gómez until the general agreed to submit to civilian rule. In his prolific writings, Martí cautioned against both caudillo rule and American imperialism. His vision was to build revolutionary institutions that would struggle together to establish a democratic and socially just Cuba. He helped build three institutions: the Revolutionary Party of Cuba (PRC) to organize and raise funds in exile; the Liberation Army to fight on the island; and the Provisional Constitutional Government to coordinate military activities and rule the areas conquered by the Liberation Army. As we saw in chapter 2, conflicts arose among and between the patriot leaders in exile, the constitutional government, and the liberators fighting on the island. The three revolutionary institutions nevertheless maintained a minimal level of cooperation throughout the war. Martí bridged the civil–military gap when he landed on Cuban shores, shouldered a rifle, mounted a horse, and rode into the hills with his comrades-in-arms in May 1895. This action, combined with Martí's insightful writings, have made Martí Cuba's national martyr. But Martí was one of the few to support all three revolutionary institutions, and the "myth of Martí" was not strong enough to unite civilian, exile, and military Cubans once U.S. occupation began in 1898.[17]

When the U.S. military intervened, U.S. officials undermined all three revolutionary institutions by exploiting the disagreements among Cubans over whether the revolution should bring redistribution and political independence or merely the latter.[18] U.S. officials negotiated with patriot leaders in exile such as Tomás Estrada Palma whenever possible. These leaders were on the whole lighter-skinned, wealthier, more conservative, and more positively disposed toward the United States than the civilian and military leaders on the island. Moreover, because U.S. policy rested on non-recognition of the Cuban belligerents, U.S. officials preferred to avoid overt alliances with either the revolution's Liberation Army or its provisional government.

To win the war against Spain and "pacify" the island, U.S. forces were forced to engage in a certain level of coordination with the Liberation Army. U.S. commanders dealt with individual generals strictly one-on-one. Their most prominent ally was Major-General Calixto García, who occupied a beachhead in eastern Cuba with thousands of Cuban soldiers on 20 June 1898 to allow fifteen thousand U.S. soldiers to land.[19] Spanish forces surrendered the second largest city on the island, Santiago de Cuba, on 16 July due to the relentless siege of Cuban and American forces combined, but Cuban soldiers were excluded from the victory parade. García resigned in protest, telling Commander-in-Chief Máximo Gómez that he no longer agreed with the Cuban government's promise to cooperate with U.S. forces.[20]

Warships of the U.S. Navy bombarded Tunas de Zaza, the port south of Sancti Spiritus and Tuinucú, on 30 June and 2, 15, and 26 July in order to land without Cuban assistance. Máximo Gómez and his soldiers were camped at a nearby sugarmill, and José Miguel Gómez was at another Las Villas sugarmill with his forces. Either squadron could have easily made it to the small fishing village to spare its destruction and protect the U.S. landing. The U.S soldiers' landing and subsequent occupation of the town of Sancti Spiritus irked Cuban revolutionaries, as did the sight of U.S. soldiers replacing the Spanish flag with the Stars and Stripes.[21]

After signing the Spanish–American truce on 12 August 1898, U.S. politicians sought to improve Cuban–American relations. A U.S. general invited García and his soldiers to parade through the streets of Santiago on 23 September 1898. A few days later, García told a correspondent from the *New York Herald* that "there is no government in Cuba of Cubans. I do not recognize any government on this island, save that of the United States."[22] Convinced by official promises that U.S. soldiers would leave as soon as Cubans disarmed and established an orderly government, García helped U.S. officials distribute jobs and rations and encouraged his followers to disarm. By November 1898, fully one quarter of the Liberation Army in the East had disbanded.[23] The strongest revolutionary institution therefore began to pose less of a threat to U.S. rule.

García's statement undermined Cuba's constitutional government symbolically while U.S. power undermined it economically. By usurping the island's administration and using it to distribute rations, jobs, and money, U.S. occupying forces deprived the constitutional government of the legitimacy and power to build its own administration. The devastated postwar economy forced many revolutionaries to negotiate with Americans in order to survive. U.S. forces thus coerced Cubans from all political positions—autonomists (who had wanted political power within the Spanish empire), separatists (who had wanted full independence), and annexationists (who wanted to join the United States)—to engage and cooperate with U.S. power.[24]

Better days seemed at hand for separatists when the Liberation Army selected its own delegates to the constitutional government, creating a more popular Cuban Assembly in October 1898. The assembly appointed a commission to go to Washington to identify U.S. intentions and secure a loan to help war veterans make the adjustment to civilian life. The U.S. administration was careful to meet the commission, which was headed by García, not as representatives of a government but as individuals. President McKinley offered funds as an outright gift rather than a loan, since the latter might suggest tacit recognition of the representatives as legal spokesmen for the island. García accepted the $3 million that McKinley offered, but the rest of the commission refused, considering it insufficient. McKinley took advantage of the split in the commission and insisted that another offer would not be made.[25]

On 11 December García died of pneumonia. That same month Estrada Palma declared the work of the PRC done, closing the central office and subsidiary clubs across Cuba and abroad. The first revolutionary institution created by Martí thus disappeared completely, leaving only the assembly and the Liberation Army.[26] The commission returned to Cuba in December without money and with little faith in U.S. intentions to "give" Cuba its freedom anytime soon.

Four months later U.S. agents and their chosen successor to García, Máximo Gómez, dissolved the remaining two revolutionary institutions with a single blow. McKinley made private arrangements with Gómez in February 1899 to distribute the $3 million and disband the Liberation Army. U.S. officials declared that Gómez would be considered the only representative authorized to speak for the Liberation Army, and just to make things absolutely clear, they added: "The so-called Assembly or any part of it will not receive recognition by this Government under any conditions whatever."[27] The assembly protested by dismissing Gómez from his position as commander-in-chief, but the popular reaction against this dismissal was so strong that on 4 April 1899 the assembly disbanded the army and dissolved itself. The assembly gave Gómez and U.S. Military Governor John R. Brooke a list of Liberation Army soldiers and officers to distribute the money to.[28]

Thus began the era of the patrons' compact. Each soldier received $75—not land, as Liberation Army leaders had hoped—and by the end of the summer the Liberation Army had been disarmed and paid.[29] The distribution of this pay, like the distribution of an additional sum of more than $57 million in 1903,[30] provided a privileged group of individuals the opportunity to reward friends and strengthen clientele groups. They made the lists of veterans, gave them paper titles for their participation in the war, and distributed the money to them once it arrived. Among those making the lists was the mulatto lieutenant (and former poet) Martín Morúa Delgado, who would soon play an important role as one of the token blacks in José Miguel Gómez's Liberal Party.

The veterans did not get land, nor did they get all of the money. In 1903 speculation abounded over whether a $35 million loan from U.S. banks would be secured to pay Cuban veterans. A series of lending agencies sprang up that bought up veterans' titles for a quarter of their value or less. "The agencies," Rafael Martínez Ortiz explained, "spread the word to veterans and their families that the titles were worthless pieces of paper."[31] The Liberation Army veteran Eduardo Guzmán y Macías fronted one such agency in Las Villas. The investors behind the agency were predominantly Spanish, Basque, or Catalan merchants, but since a veteran headed it and veterans needed the loans from it, the agency did very well. These same veterans were willing to take up arms under their caudillo patron Guzmán during the 1906 Liberal Party rebellion. Guzmán was an essential middleman: His extensive clientele network forged through bonds of friendship and trust on the battlefield led the merchants to hire him. Through him, the veterans had access to funds before they were officially distributed, even if they got less than they were entitled to.[32]

Eduardo Guzmán was a local patron and middleman. He had national counterparts—Tomás Estrada Palma, Calixto García, and Máximo Gómez—who served as indispensable mediators, allowing the U.S. imperialist administration to undermine the three revolutionary institutions. Estrada Palma was passionately committed to the struggle against Spain, but he was also a naturalized American citizen who had lived much of his life on U.S. soil. He was very positively disposed toward U.S. institutions, and from the beginning, he was on the more conservative side of the PRC: Recall, for example, the disagreements between Estrada Palma and Máximo Gómez over how to deal with sugar properties and over the importance of belligerency status. With these characteristics in mind, the former exile's cooperative attitude toward U.S. agents is not so surprising. In contrast, García and Gómez were committed separatists who fought all three wars for independence on Cuban soil. These prominent leaders' actions, like those of Guzmán and his clients, can only be understood as negotiations within unequal relations of power.

Four concrete factors explain this relationship. The first, mentioned earlier, was division within the ranks, which made Cubans vulnerable to appeals from U.S. agents to one-up their separatist, annexationist, or autonomist competitors. The second was the high level of unemployment, starvation, and isolation on the island and the fact that U.S. agents controlled access to the jobs and the treasury. Even high Cuban officials were unable to feed and clothe their families. Cuban generals feared that their soldiers might turn to brigandage, thereby providing the United States with an excuse to occupy and annex the island permanently—the U.S. pledged to protect life and property in Cuba, the Philippines, Puerto Rico and Guam in the 1898 Treaty of Paris that ended the Spanish–American War. This factor relates closely to the third, the Philippine insurrection, which began on 6 February 1899. U.S. forces brutally repressed revolutionaries, even resurrecting Weyler's re-concentration strategy. This served as a demonstration of what lay ahead if Cuba's Liberation Army tried to mobilize against U.S. forces. Exhausted by three years of war, Cuban generals chose to put their faith in the U.S. promise of neutrality to avoid further death and destruction.

The final factor was the joint resolution that the U.S. Congress passed before intervention began. The resolution's "Teller Amendment" declared that the United States had no intention "to exercise sovereignty, jurisdiction, or control over said island except for pacification thereof," and promised "to leave the government and control of the island to its people" once pacification was accomplished.[33] García, Gómez, and Estrada Palma had to believe that U.S. forces would keep their promise and leave once the army disbanded and Cubans established a government.

UNDOING THE REVOLUTION:
U.S. OCCUPATION, 1899–1902

The contrast between what U.S. politicians promised to do in the Teller Amendment and what they actually did in Cuba reflects the push-and-pull of competing forces within U.S. politics—namely, the imperialists who favored building an overseas empire versus the idealists who wanted to protect domestic agriculture and remain an honorable republic.[34] With Cuba's army disbanded and municipal governments established, U.S. forces should have left the island. Instead, U.S. imperialists managed to push through a military occupation beginning on 1 January 1899, with no stated ending date. The imperialist faction included Republican President McKinley, Senator Henry Cabot Lodge, General Leonard Wood, and future president Theodore Roosevelt, who had led "Rough Rider" soldiers against Spanish forces in Cuba in 1898.

With the revolutionary institutions out of the way, to a degree self-effaced, these American expansionists began to deliberately ignore and reverse the revolution's most hallowed principles. By most accounts, Leonard Wood, Cuba's second U.S. military governor-general, did far more damage to the country than his predecessor, John R. Brooke (January 1899–December 1899).[35] On the positive side, both governors used the capital generated through the Cuban Treasury and Customs to initiate significant improvements across the island in sanitation (to combat yellow fever) and infrastructure. However, these improvements benefited U.S. and Spanish soldiers and investors on the island more than Cubans, at least in the short term. Foreigners were the primary victims of yellow fever; Cubans could not live in the barracks constructed for American forces; and very few Cubans made it through the revolution with the investment capital needed to take advantage of new infrastructure.

The ambiance in cities like Sancti Spiritus quickly shifted from jubilation over the end of the war to resentment of U.S. occupation. Cubans clashed with Americans over Cuban women's honor, among other things. Prostitution increased in Sancti Spiritus during the occupation, likely because of the desperate postwar economic situation, but disrespectful U.S. soldiers provided an easy scapegoat.[36] Sancti Spiritus residents remembered the six companies of volunteers that had arrived from Tennessee on 12 December 1898 committing "immoral acts" in plain public view, trying to violate Cuban women in their homes, wandering the streets drunk, and disrespecting all "as though they were conquerors rather than the allies they hypocritically claimed to be."[37]

Racial attitudes constituted another significant point of tension during the U.S. occupation. The Sancti Spiritus police chief Raimundo Sánchez—brother of the important mulatto leader Serafín Sánchez, who was killed during the war—had to respond to Wood's inquiry on 3 April 1900 requesting the numbers of white, colored, Cuban, and foreign prostitutes registered in the city. Many Cubans complained about this U.S. tendency to categorize people as "black," "brown," or "white," and they protested against the "whites only" signs posted in stores and restaurants across the island during the occupation. Although it would be incorrect to assert that the United States brought racism to Cuba, American policy did reinforce racist tendencies that flew in the face of the Cuban triumph in drawing together Cubans of all races to fight against colonialism during the 1895–98 Revolution.[38] For the most part, U.S. officials tried to turn around the equalizing effects and goals of the revolution, as when Wood excluded nonwhites from the Havana Police Force under its first director, Mario García Menocal.

Wood's policies and style of rule also undermined other democratic and equalizing principles of the revolution. His authoritarian attitude led him to promote pliable political candidates at the municipal and national levels. Brooke had allowed revolutionary leaders to play important political roles as mayors and governors. For example, he permitted Santiago García Cañizares to become mayor of Sancti Spiritus and José Miguel Gómez to become governor of Las Villas (the insurgent doctor Santiago García had threatened Tuinucú with retaliation for grinding in March 1896, as had José Miguel Gómez in August). In contrast, Wood removed anyone too eager to stand on revolutionary principles.

In September 1899 Mayor García Cañizares complained about the behavior of the U.S. military officials assigned to Sancti Spiritus. They would give the mayor's office permission to purchase and sign contracts for medicine, food, and public works, and then refuse to provide payment for the expenses. "They disregard municipal laws, and with this behavior they foment bad perceptions of our administration, which is being compared to the bad Spanish one. The people believe that despite the promises, there is no law beyond the whims of American officials."[39] It comes as little surprise that, over the course of Wood's tenure as governor-general (December 1899–December 1901), he had the vocal García Cañizares removed.[40]

Nothing seems to have irked Cubans on the island more than the fact that Wood helped place in public office former autonomists, pacíficos, and exiles rather than separatist members of the Liberation Army. At the municipal level, these men won their positions through Cuba's first "free" elections in 1900, but the U.S. military administration severely limited suffrage. To vote, one had to be a Cuban male older than twenty-one, literate, and an owner of property worth $250 or to have served honorably in the Liberation Army prior to 18 July 1898. Two-thirds of all Cuban males were thus excluded from the vote.[41] To ensure that the conservative candidates he liked would win, Wood also set the precedent of placing more members from the Conservative Party (called the "Moderate Party" at the time) in the electoral college than its opposition, a tactic repeated in 1905 and 1916 by conservatives seeking to remain in office.

SUGAR, RAILROADS, AND "RECIPROCITY"

Wood and his like-minded allies reversed revolutionary principles and sought to promote annexation through educational and electoral policy. They also believed that once Cubans acquired a taste for things American, they would chose to become a part of the United States. Governor Wood spent millions of Cuban Treasury dollars to lobby for a U.S.–Cuba reciprocity treaty that would lower the U.S. tariff for importing Cuban raw sugar in exchange for lower Cuban tariffs on a vast array of U.S. goods.

The Reciprocity Treaty seriously affected Cubans' ability to diversify and industrialize their economy. Cheap U.S. goods flooded the Cuban market, unfettered by the sort of protectionist tariffs that had allowed U.S. industries to develop over the course of the nineteenth century.[42] Nascent Cuban industries could not yet mass-produce things like soap and shoes, so they could not compete with U.S. products. Even within sugar production, Cubans were discouraged from industrializing because the treaty offered low tariffs only on raw, not refined, sugar. In consequence, a system of sugar production developed that was most favorable to U.S. capitalists. Americans

secured access to cheap raw sugar either by producing it themselves in Cuba
or by offering credit to Cuban producers in exchange for a monopoly on
their product. Americans then processed this sugar in their own refineries
(most of them in the United States) and sold the final product at a much
higher price to U.S. consumers. Protectionists from beet-sugar states and
idealist (anti-imperialist) congressmen tried to oppose reciprocity, as they
had opposed intervention and occupation, but to no avail.[43]

Between January 1899 and May 1902 a series of military-government
policies led to the transfer of vast amounts of land—and much of the sugar
industry—to citizens of the United States, England, and Canada. U.S. policy
also kept Cubans from taking over the significant land and resources that
Spaniards had accumulated under the colonial regime, prohibiting Cubans
from exiling Spaniards and taking their land, as other Latin Americans had
done upon gaining independence. Wood's Military Order 139 got rid of the
moratorium on debts that had protected landowners and industrialists in
Cuba from losing their property during the first two years of recovery from
the war for independence. As of 1 June 1901, all classes of creditors were allowed to claim mortgaged properties. The military government provided
neither credit nor banks to help Cuban farmers and plantation owners re-
cuperate. Of the 574 mills that produced sugar in 1894, only 29 could make
the minimal amount of twenty thousand bags after the war.[44] Cash, not land,
was distributed to Liberation Army soldiers. Finally, Civil Order 62 undermined the communal estate land-tenure system that continued to dominate
in the Center and East.[45] Civil Order 62 allowed any plaintiff to hire an attorney and commission a judicial survey to fix the boundaries of a tract
of crown land. A court-appointed tribunal met to examine all communal
landowners' ownership deeds, determined their legitimacy, and then issued
new deeds of titled ownership.

Landowners needed basic literacy skills to defend their land, and they
needed money to pay lawyers, land surveyors, and the occasional corrupt
judge or official. Many land documents had been destroyed during the
wars; others were taken to Spain by colonial officials fleeing the island. All
of these factors made the system favor rich, politically connected individuals or syndicates capable of fabricating and legitimating new land titles.[46]
Foreign investors and speculators, predominantly American, bought up
large amounts of territory from Cubans (including veterans) desperate for
money to live on.

Some thirteen thousand foreigners paid more than $50 million to acquire land titles on the island between 1899 and 1905.[47] Among these was the title for a plot of virgin soil on the southern coast of Camagüey that Francisco Rionda had purchased shortly before his death in November 1898. Manuel Rionda gathered a group of investors from Philadelphia to purchase and develop the Francisco Sugar Company as a large enclave plantation with its own sugarmill, railroad, port, and commissary stores. Francisco was the first such U.S.- and European-funded enclave, but it was soon dwarfed by the Chaparra sugarmill on the northern coast of Oriente, established by former Texas Congressman Robert Hawley and some prominent New York-based sugar refiners. Hawley had three times the capital available to Rionda.

The Chaparra Sugar Company purchased 66,000 acres of land surrounding the bay of Puerto Padre, where it constructed Chaparra in 1899.[48] The largest mill ever built in Cuba at the time, Chaparra contributed 10 percent of Cuba's harvest even in its initial 1899–1900 crop.[49] Robert Hawley's group also purchased the only remaining sugar refinery and the 7,000 acre Tinguaro estate in Matanzas, and it took over the Mercedita mill in Pinar del Rio. United Fruit interests followed suit in 1901, purchasing 240,000 acres surrounding Nipe Bay in northern Oriente.[50] The two leaders who dominated Cuba in the twentieth century, Fulgencio Batista and Fidel Castro, were both born near the United Fruit enclave, Batista as son of a cane cutter and Castro as son of a colono.[51]

In the Sancti Spiritus region, foreign corporations owned some seven-eights of the land by 1905.[52] Because the Tuinucú corporation had a lot of reconstruction to do—buildings and machines to repair and fields to replant—it could not purchase new land. However, the corporation's annual report on the crop of 1901–1902 indicates that the sugarmill was able to lease 900 acres of fertile land under very good terms because Tuinucú stockholders were also the largest stockholders of the U.S. real-estate company that leased the 900 acres.[53] Manuel Rionda also acquired the Francisco, San Vicente, Washington, Elia, and Manatí sugarmills and organized the Cuba Cane Sugar Corporation, which controlled seventeen mills by 1916 (see map 1, pages vi–vii). In all, by 1902 companies incorporated in the United States owned 55 of the 223 sugarmills operating that year, claiming roughly 40 percent of the island's total sugar production.[54]

With U.S. capitalists flooding the administration with requests for cheap land and resource concessions, Senator Joseph B. Foraker of Ohio proposed an amendment forbidding U.S. officials from granting "franchises or concessions of any kind whatever" in Cuba for the duration of the American occupation.[55] The Foraker Amendment passed with support from antiimperialists and senators from beet-sugar-producing states, anxious to protect their industry from the duty-free sugar sure to flood U.S. markets if Cuba became a state or protectorate.[56] Wood consistently found ways around the amendment, all the while setting negative precedents—disobeying the regulations, going back to colonial laws to override new ones, and taking bribes in exchange for concessions and contracts. Wood's policies permitted wide-scale U.S. takeovers of sugarmills, public utilities, mines, and other resources.

The Foraker Amendment temporarily blocked Van Horne's crosscountry railroad project. But the promoters mounted a massive propaganda campaign about the benefits such a railroad would bring, integrating the island and developing neglected regions. This helped the company push landowners to cede land for the railroad and towns. The Cuba Company eventually acquired 300,000 acres of land on which to construct 350 miles of railroad and organize the Jatibonico (Camagüey) and Jobabo (Oriente) sugarmills (see map 1, pages vi–vii.)[57] The railroad had to traverse rivers, public roads, and state land, as well, and the Foraker Amendment tied the provisional government's hands. To get around the rules, Washington officials gave Governor Wood permission to grant "revocable licenses" authorizing railroads to cross public property. Van Horne staged dramatic shows to allow Wood to justify these licenses: The officials of the Cuba Company halted work and laid off workers any time they came close to public property, claiming that they lacked authorization. The town halls, workers, and merchants wired piles of telegrams to Wood, requesting that permission be granted to the company, allowing him to grant the licenses "in response to the people's will."[58]

Before leaving Cuba, U.S. officials imposed the Platt Amendment on the Cuban Constitution, a legal instrument that would shore up these "revocable" licenses and ensure that all of the concessions made during the occupation would be protected under the new Cuban Republic.[59] Tuinucú's annual report for 1924 summarized how Van Horne's railroad expanded sugar production to central and eastern Cuba. Before the railroad began running in 1902, Tuinucú had had to haul sugar by ox cart over six miles to Sancti Spiritus, from whence it was loaded onto trains and transferred to the port of Tunas de Zaza. The railroad enabled Tuinucú to increase annual sugar production from roughly 30,000 bags before 1895 to 277,000 bags in 1919. Tuinucú was one of very few inland sugar plantations (far from the Atlantic or Caribbean coast) in 1902, and it was one of the first plantations to haul sugar over the Cuba Company's railroad to the company's Oriente seaport, Antilla. There were no plantations in the entire province of Camagüey, save one or two on the north and south coasts. "The total production in eastern Cuba in 1902 was only 160,000 tons," the report concluded, "against 2,200,000 tons this year. There is no parallel to such progress in so short a time anywhere."[60] Map 1 (see pages vi–vii) demonstrates the large number of mills clustered along Van Horne's cross-country railroad, the dense concentration of smaller mills in the older sugar-producing regions of Havana and Matanzas, and the giant mills constructed on the eastern coasts in the early twentieth century.

Civil Order 62 for the division and sale of communal estates, the Platt Amendment to the Cuban Constitution, and the Cuba Company railroad development constitute three key symbols of what U.S. intervention brought to Cuba: mediated independence and mediated development. Order 62 and the railroad opened up the Center and East of the island, and many mills began to spring up along the railroad lines. Evidence of this can still be seen today when traveling across Cuba's East by rail, especially in the flat, rich lands between Camagüey and Las Tunas. First one sees the sugar towers, then the rows of wooden houses reminiscent of towns in the American West, then the railroad station—all evidence of past glory. These mills symbolized "development" and "progress," but owners purposely spaced them apart so that each could be its own enclave. The greater the distance between mills, the harder it was for colonos to get a good deal on their cane by threatening to sell it elsewhere. The same applied to workers wanting to bargain for higher wages.

Unlike Van Horne's railroad in Canada, which made its money by promoting a clientele (small farmer pioneers in the central and western provinces), the cross-country railroad in Cuba made its money the way money had been made in Cuba since 1760—through sugar company enclaves. These enclaves varied from their colonial predecessors: They hired workers instead of slaves, and most purchased cane from tenant or independent colonos rather than growing it directly on company land. They found new means to achieve significant growth, profits, and "social harmony" during the first two decades of the twentieth century. The next chapters detail these methods at the Chaparra Sugar Company, erected on the north coast of Oriente, and at the rebuilt and expanded Tuinucú in Sancti Spiritus. Before turning to Mario García Menocal's construction of Chaparra and Manuel Rionda's reconstruction of Tuinucú, a sketch of the national political negotiations that took place around them must first be established.

VETERANS CLAIM THEIR RIGHTS:
THE REBELLIONS OF 1906, 1912, AND 1917

Although the 1906, 1912, and 1917 movements have been called "revolutions," the term is misleading. None of the rebellions aimed to overthrow Cuba's political-economic system. Liberals and Cubans of color merely sought fair access to political and economic power within the existing system. Until the economic crash of 1920–21, few Cubans openly questioned whether foreign investment and sugar production represented an acceptable base to Cuban economic life. The 1906, 1912, and 1917 rebellions were essentially negotiations with incumbent Cuban regimes and U.S. power; they threatened capitalist property but only selectively committed real damage. Images of burning cane from the nineteenth-century wars for independence certainly remained a powerful memory, and rebels and bandits used the threat of the torch to extort money and political power from plantation owners and politicians. Overall, though, from 1899 through 1931 the burning of cane became much less a grand-scale political strategy and more a small-scale or "everyday form" of negotiation between worker, cane farmer, bandit, and mill owner.[61]

This was clearly communicated in U.S. Captain J. A. Ryan's report on cane fires in Santa Clara dated December 1906, which placed "Burning by Disaffected Persons for Political Reasons" second to last of eight reasons for cane fires. "The talk heard in the cafés in the vicinity of sugar estates," Ryan observed, "would lead one to believe that one of the means employed by these revolutionists to spread terror through the land is a threat to burn sugarcane . . . but up to the present time, in the vicinity of Santa Clara Province, it is believed that no sugarcane has been destroyed by disaffected persons."[62] Ryan suggested that it was much more common for an accident such as a lit cigarette stub thrown by a passerby or sparks from a train to cause these fires than for workers or cane farmers to light the fires intentionally. His report's conclusion indicated that cane fires were not as big a threat as planters and politicians were making them out to be. "I have found, as a rule, that the Spaniards who have been in this country for some time fear no burning of cane and say that there is little danger of loss to be anticipated," he wrote. This contrasted with the Cuban, American, and English owners who "desire very much to have troops in the vicinity of their estates, but cannot give good reasons why they should be there."[63] In other words, Spanish mill owners figured out faster than their counterparts that rebels did not intend to carry out their threats to property.

In August 1906 General José Miguel Gómez and the liberals staged a rebellion to make U.S. mediators listen to their calls for fair elections; the large number of Afro-Cubans also demanded access to economic and political power and an end to racial discrimination. The liberals succeeded in wresting political power from their conservative opponents, Tomás Estrada Palma's Moderate Party, after the 1906 rebellion—Gómez won the 1908 elections held under the second U.S. military occupation from 1906 to 1909. The same tactics failed when Afro-Cubans tried them against the liberals in 1912, and the liberals tried them a second time against their conservative opponents in 1917. This section explores why the 1917 movement and the racial protest of 1912 that preceded it were so much less successful than the 1906 rebellion. After 1906 Cuban rebels thought that they had figured out how to use U.S. power. But U.S. policy shifted according to domestic and international political demands, and the Cuban rebels' timing was less propitious than that of their predecessors in 1906. The rebellions of 1906, 1912, and 1917 were driven by a combination of race, class, regional, and political demands, but the explicit racial dimensions of the 1912 and 1917 rebellions made elite Cubans and U.S. politicians less responsive. Persistent racism pushed great numbers of Cubans of color to join all three rebellions; they were largely excluded from access to decent jobs and political positions.

All three rebellions shared the same means and forms of mobilization: Veteran caudillos led small groups of rebels who threatened to damage property if ignored. The most notable aspect of the 1906 rebellion was its geographical and racial profile: White Cubans and Afro-Cubans fought together under the banner of the Liberal Party for the cause of democracy and the "redemption" of the 1895–98 revolution. They did so mostly in the Center and West of the island, in sharp contrast to the nineteenth-century struggles that were strongest in the East. According to the British ambassador, 90 percent of the rebels were Afro-Cubans (a high ratio considering that only 32 percent of the island's population was Afro-Cuban).[64] Afro-Cubans also helped José Miguel Gómez win the presidency in 1908 against conservative candidate Mario García Menocal.

Las Villas—renamed Santa Clara in 1902—functioned as a springboard to national power for two main reasons. First, it was the province with the largest and most modern sugar plantations. Second, the most important campaigns during the latter part of the 1895–98 War for Independence took place there, and the region's insurgent leader, José Miguel Gómez, built a cross-racial network there that formed the core of his bid for presidency at the head of the Liberal Party in 1906 and 1908.[65] The Las Villas municipality of Sancti Spiritus was home to large numbers of independence fighters, and José Miguel Gómez, who was born there, fought most of his battles in the area.

An astute caudillo and presidential candidate, Gómez used nationalist rhetoric, introduced popular policies, and armed some of his followers at the local and provincial level. As governor of Santa Clara in 1902–1905, Gómez allowed cockfights despite Estrada Palma's ban and permitted Afro-Cuban recreation and mutual aid societies to thrive in his province (conservative governors in other provinces banned them). This explains why when the liberals lost, most Afro-Cubans in the province mobilized to support the 1906 Liberal rebellion—up to 85 percent of the insurgents in Santa Clara were black.[66] Gómez also issued a large number of arms permits to liberal farmers in the Sancti Spiritus region before the conservative party (then called the "Moderates") replaced him in 1905. The man who supervised the numerous colonos and workers weighing their sugarcane to sell to Tuinucú reported that "nearly all of the farmers in the district were so armed, fortified with [Gómez's] permits."[67]

Sancti Spiritus residents clearly favored Gómez over the Moderate Party's candidate Mario García Menocal. When Menocal staged a parade in Sancti Spiritus with his conservative running mates during the presidential campaign of 1908, he made the strategic error of allowing someone to carry the Spanish flag. Many former Spanish autonomists belonged to the Moderate Party, alongside the conservative Cuban caudillos and their followers. As Menocal's column passed through the town's central plaza, a group of liberals threw bricks and stones at them, attempting to pull or knock them from their horses. The flag bearer was actually stabbed and shot to death.[68]

When Gómez won the presidency in 1908, he gave jobs and positions in the Constitutional Army almost exclusively to white liberals. This led a group of Afro-Cubans to organize the Independent Party of Color (PIC) in 1908 to promote Afro-Cuban integration into society and government ranks.[69] The Liberal Party responded with the Morúa Law prohibiting political parties based on racial distinctions; this excluded the PIC from participation in the national elections held in November 1912. Morúa, the most powerful Cuban of color in Gómez's party, justified the bill by arguing that a black party would generate a white party and thus contribute to racial conflict on the island.[70] The Morúa Law's real goal was to remove Gómez's caudillo competitors, the PIC leaders Evaristo Estenoz and Pedro Ivonnet. The former had been a lieutenant in the Liberation Army and the latter, a colonel; both previously had belonged to Gómez's Liberal Party.

Since the PIC formed during the second U.S. occupation from 1906 to 1909, its leaders first approached U.S. representatives to help them abrogate the law and regain party status. When that did not work, they did on 20 May 1912 what liberal insurgents had done in 1906: staged a protest and threatened to damage property to force the president's hand. A British vice-consul in Oriente reported on 9 July 1912: "In the first days of the rising all the sugar estates in this district received letters from Estenoz . . . in which the destruction of the estate was threatened unless arms and ammunition were furnished them within 72 hours." But subsequent events indicated that "there was never any intention on the part of the Negroes to destroy properties on which most of them depended for a living," except as a last resort or as the means to bring about American intervention if the government did not repeal the Morúa Law.[71]

The PIC movement, like the multiracial veterans' movement that preceded it in 1911–12, made demands for access to jobs and other opportunities on the basis of the contributions its members had made to Cuba's struggles for independence. The chief of the revolutionary forces, Colonel Ivonnet, addressed long letters to the British official Stephen Leech and other ambassadors in Cuba, explaining that the movement arose "owing to the bad treatment which blacks have received and the absence of political equality." The letters clearly stated that the rebellion was not directed against the white race; it was a struggle for freedom, equality, and liberty.[72]

Government forces, their U.S. allies, and many Cuban citizens—including veterans of the War of Independence—reacted violently to the protest.

Cuban and U.S. journalists labeled it a "race war." The liberal administration, the new Constitutional Army, volunteers from western Cuba, and U.S. Marines violently repressed non-white Cubans across the island, whether they were members of the PIC or not. In Oriente many peasants and workers of color were re-concentrated in a strategy reminiscent of Weyler's brutal repression in the 1890s.[73] Even the conservative caudillo Menocal offered to mobilize three thousand volunteers to put down the rebellion (his offer was made to U.S. forces, not directly to his rival, Gómez).[74] Fortunately for Menocal, nobody took him up on it, so he was able to enter the presidency in 1912 unscathed by the reputation for racist intolerance and brutality that plagued Gómez and the liberals after the massacre.

In February 1917 the liberals staged another rebellion against Menocal's electoral fraud using the same kind of rhetoric and tactics as the 1906 and 1912 protest movements. The former president José Miguel Gómez and three other Liberation Army veterans who would become presidents participated in the rebellion: Alfredo Zayas (1921–25), Gerardo Machado (1925–33), and Carlos Mendieta (1934–35). Their timing could not have been worse. The United States was on the verge of sending troops to fight in the First World War and had little desire to intervene directly in the Caribbean. More important, the U.S. Ambassador William Gonzales was convinced that Menocal was the pro-United States "law and order" man for the presidency. As with the rebellion of 1912, government forces were able to stamp out the rebellion in the West with a little help from U.S. Marines, but it continued in the East for longer. Near the end of March, rebels had partially destroyed sugarmills and looted villages in and near the Cuba Company's Jobabo sugarmill in Oriente. Government troops shot some twenty black residents, including several British subjects, at Jobabo without a trial and barbarously killed two Jamaicans at the nearby Elia sugarmill.[75] Despite the lack of evidence that British West Indians were joining the Cuban rebellion, it seemed government troops felt that "black outsiders" were to blame for the ills of the island.[76]

On 3 May 1917 a British official sent a report describing the rebellion in Oriente Province as "extremely serious." Some five thousand to fifteen thousand well-armed rebels practically controlled the country districts, declaring that if Mario García Menocal took the inaugural oath on May 20, warfare would "commence in earnest with total destruction of all property." The British official speculated that Afro-Cubans in particular wanted revenge for the five thousand killed during the 1912 rebellion. Residents of Oriente Province, in general, were anti-American.[77]

We can presume that the anti-American feelings reflected the frustration with a U.S. policy that called for free and fair elections in principle but turned a blind eye in practice, as long as the president committing the fraud could repress rebels and protect U.S. interests. The liberals targeted U.S. interests directly to undercut Menocal's image as a strongman. A U.S. resident in Cuba reported, "General Blas Masó has told us to get away from our homes and properties, if we wish to avoid getting killed; he has begun the destruction of our colonies for this reason: 'You will holl[er] loudest and we will destroy until your holl[er]ing will be heard in Washington, and force intervention. . . . We are only fighting now with the torch, terrorizing and organizing. But if Menocal does not step out May 20, we will fight and kill."[78]

The liberals backed down from their threats when the United States announced that the rebels were "enemies of the United States" since they were attacking an industry that was fundamental to the war effort in Europe. The United States was willing to intervene in 1906 but not in 1917 because the international context was fundamentally different. Also, Mario García Menocal was very different from Tomás Estrada Palma. Whereas Estrada Palma was a civilian who called for U.S. intervention apparently without hesitation, Menocal was a general capable of mobilizing Liberation Army allies and their clienteles to fight against the liberals. Menocal was as much a caudillo as José Miguel Gómez, but he used different tactics. Gómez employed popular anti-U.S. rhetoric to build his power base primarily among disaffected social groups in the cities, including Cuban and Spanish industrialists, unemployed veterans of all races, and veteran cattle ranchers in the countryside. In contrast, the conservative Menocal appealed to foreign diplomats, capitalists, and employed Cubans—all of whom wanted peace and stability—by constructing his image as an incorruptible veteran committed to building a progressive, capitalist Cuba. The stable and prosperous sugar communities that flourished from 1900 to 1920 served as the base of this vision. The next chapter will describe the construction and reconstruction of two of these mills, and document the conservative patron caudillo Menocal's rise to power via the clientele and the reputation he built at the Chaparra Sugar Company.

The Patrons' Compact: "Peace," "Progress," and General Menocal, 1899–1919

4 The early twentieth century was an era of frequent political turmoil in Cuba, when rebellions surrounded every national election and sugarcane was the most threatened property on the rebels' agenda. Yet paradoxically, a vast majority of sugar communities on the island remained stable enough to produce ever-larger amounts of sugar. Table 2 demonstrates the increase in sugar production on the island overall, and at Chaparra and Tuinucú in particular, during the period between 1902 and 1919.[1] For the sugarmills, this period can be seen as the patrons' era of "peace" and "progress" because, on the whole, many owners were able to maintain a semblance of social peace and at the same time reap profits ranging from modest to spectacular.

Chapter 3 showed how U.S. politicians managed to compromise Cuban political independence. The two sugarmill case studies in this chapter and the next describe how foreign capitalists and their Cuban middlemen established economic control over much of the island's rural population in the early twentieth century. They explore day-to-day life at the Chaparra and Tuinucú mills to determine how planters managed to keep the peace necessary to extract such high profits. Cubans' fascination with progress and modernity played an important role, as did the methods of social control

TABLE 2   Sugar production, in metric tons, 1902–1919

YEAR	TUINUCÚ	CHAPARRA	CUBA
1902	N/A	128,594	876,027
1903	32,500	119,168	1,028,205
1904	35,000	239,521	1,078,706
1905	43,200	230,415	1,209,882
1906	56,721	257,547	1,259,350
1907	67,210	335,321	1,478,515
1908	71,917	251,585	995,373
1909	82,644	482,428	1,563,628
1910	92,545	531,049	1,868,913
1911	71,550	453,660	1,534,607
1912	106,306	436,591	1,968,840
1913	153,436	475,362	2,515,103
1914	173,063	616,179	2,622,036
1915	178,000	517,210	2,693,210
1916	164,526	613,454	3,124,277
1917	183,582	602,639	3,145,348
1918	228,043	513,746	3,598,489
1919	227,463	550,895	4,180,621

Source: Moreno Fraginals, *El ingenio*, 3:38–39; Muriel McAvoy's statistics compiled from *Moody's* and *Cuba Review*; *Agricultura y Zootecnia*, special edition, 1924.

that Robert Hawley, the Menocal military clique, and the Rionda family introduced at Chaparra and Tuinucú. The early-twentieth-century system of rule was both a patrons' and a matrons' compact: Presidents, sugarmill owners, and administrators needed their wives, daughters, and sisters to smooth relations with their subordinates.[2]

Tuinucú and Chaparra fit the larger national pattern in that the 1906, 1912, and 1917 rebellions had very little impact on their sugar production (see Table 2). Factors specific to local circumstance suggest why. Eladio Santiago, a former office employee at Tuinucú, recalls seeing evidence from the accounting department that Tuinucú paid off both liberal and conservative leaders in 1917 to leave the plantation alone.[3] The Riondas likely did the same in 1906 and 1912. In his report of 1906, mentioned earlier, Captain J. A. Ryan wrote that most administrators opted to pay protection fees quietly because they felt that sugar estates could not afford to have "small enemies."[4]

At Chaparra, the fact that the Moderate (later, Conservative) Party enlisted most of the veteran residents of the region explains in part the lack of liberal rebels in 1906 and 1917. The one liberal who was trying to start an insurrection in 1906 was bribed to stop in exchange for the title of assistant to the collector of customs at Puerto Padre.[5] In 1912, the fact that local Chaparra residents were predominantly white limited potential supporters for the Independent Party of Color movement. Cuba's 1899 census listed only 25 percent of the residents at Puerto Padre as "of color," the rest being white Cubans or recent immigrants from Spain.[6] Puerto Padre locals certainly constituted the bulk of the "3,000 volunteers" Menocal told U.S. diplomats he would be able to mobilize to "crush" the movement in 1912.[7]

General Menocal achieved social order at Chaparra partially through hierarchies and alliances imported from the war for independence. He and Manuel Rionda both also played the role of the "benevolent patron" at various times. At Tuinucú, we find two Rionda women—Isidora Rionda and her niece Elena Doty—smoothing out relations between worker and management through companionship and philanthropy, and patrons' wives and daughters played similar roles at Chaparra.

Yet these factors are mostly specific to Tuinucú and Chaparra. To understand the peace in mill communities across the island, we must analyze how mill owners got workers and colonos to agree to the patrons' compact. This was closely tied to how the patrons brought "progress" to their mills. Company files and clippings from local and national newspapers demonstrate that the owners of Chaparra, Tuinucú, and many other mills established industrialization, urbanization, and social-welfare projects that were an integral part of the early-twentieth-century concept of "progress." Historians have labeled similar projects in the Progressive-era United States "capitalist welfare." This was because capitalists provided the welfare, in contrast to the 1930s era, when governments began to establish nationwide programs.[8] These projects helped create more stable and prosperous sugarmills, and only they can explain the longevity of the patrons' compact. Although the scarcity of documents does not permit a year-by-year comparison of company expenses on salaries, bonuses, health care, and other benefits, it appears that the projects began with the very establishment of the mills. They grew especially rapidly during the high-profit years surrounding the First World War; contracted briefly during the crash of 1921–22; then began to grow again from 1923 until 1925. What happened between 1925 and 1928 varied greatly according to the mill, but as of 1929 all were feeling the Great Depression and cut the programs back significantly. The cutbacks undermined the bond between patrons and residents in their communities, ending the era of peace and progress.

The term "peace" here is used to establish a contrast with the open confrontation and rebellion elsewhere on the island; however, perfect harmony did not reign between workers, cane farmers and mill owners. Worker and colono resistance—including cane fires—made an appearance during these early years of the twentieth century, but popular resistance in the sugarmills became much more pronounced from the 1920s onward.

GENERAL MENOCAL'S FIEFDOM BEGINS
AT THE "GREAT CHAPARRA SUGARMILL"

Across the island, the wars for independence and U.S. occupation created economic space for a relatively new group, American capitalists and the Cuban heroes of independence who became their middlemen. In the East, these new patrons began to absorb and overshadow the older planter elite immediately after 1898, dominating municipal governments, appropriating land, and building sugarmill communities on the coasts or along the Cuba Company railroad line in Oriente and Camagüey. Chaparra is a perfect example—the first of a series of massive coastal plantations in eastern Cuba. It was quintessentially Cuban American in that a Cuban caudillo (Mario García Menocal) built the mill, and a group of American sugar capitalists (fronted by Texas Congressman Robert Hawley) funded it. The mill was equipped with the best machinery then available in the world, and the Chaparra Sugar Company purchased massive expanses of rich, virgin soil around it. Chaparra formed an enclave community that was practically self-sufficient, with an integrated system of production that included ports, railroads, and easy access to sugarcane, food, and beasts of burden.[9] An article in the *Louisiana Planter and Sugar Manufacturer* correctly predicted that the mill's "powerful and modern machinery . . . will cause in Cuba an industrial revolution by its novelty."[10] The same article lauded Chaparra's "extensive fields of cane . . . of great production and excellent cultivation; its extensive railroad, and its commodious port of Cascarero," concluding that "this

enormous planting is without precedent in the history of Cuba and probably in the entire world."[11]

Now let us turn to the central question of how Menocal and his American capitalist sponsors managed to establish the Chaparra mill and achieve
political, economic, and social domination in the Puerto Padre region of
Oriente. Chaparra was constructed on the ruins of a smaller mill by the
same name whose first harvest was in 1895 under the Spanish planter
Antonio Mahiques. According to newspaper and historical accounts,
Menocal signaled the potential of Puerto Padre to Robert Hawley. An engineer who had graduated from Cornell University, Menocal allegedly recognized the region's possibilities during his time in Las Tunas, where he
fought and won important battles against the Spaniards during the 1895–98
Revolution.[12] An alternative possibility is that the machinery salesman Juan
Clark was the point of contact. He wrote to Manuel Rionda between April
and October 1899 that both Hawley and Mahiques had approached him—
the first in search of sugar lands, and the second trying desperately to find
funds to rebuild his small Chaparra sugarmill.

Clark's observation regarding Hawley is indicative of the environment
created by Civil Orders 62 and 139: "I guess he wants to speculate, just like a
great many that come to this country and think they can buy a sugar estate
for a dollar."[13] In contrast, Clark spoke highly of Mahiques, wrote that he
considered Chaparra's land "the best on the island," and added, "On top of
that, all of the workers in that region are white, hardworking, and committed
to improving the locality."[14] Rionda was interested, but he had his hands full
raising funds for the recovery of Tuinucú and the building of the Francisco
mill. He was thus unable to find funding for Mahiques, who became one of
the many Spanish and Cuban sugar planters obliged to sell their mortgaged
plantations after the provisional government and other potential sources
refused them credit or aid.

Menocal was the indispensable Cuban agent who allowed Hawley and
his New York sugar partners to buy Mahiques's small mill and 66,000 acres
in the Puerto Padre region.[15] Another important ally was Francisco Plá,
owner of the San Manuel sugar plantation and most of the real estate in the
town of Puerto Padre.[16] Plá survived the revolution far better than Mahiques
because he was a first-generation Cuban who supported the patriots economically during the insurrection. He had also helped sabotage the town's

port, used by the Spanish military. (Puerto Padre was Cuba's first free port. It was liberated from Spain in May 1898.)[17] Company documents suggest that Plá was absorbed into Chaparra's elite: He became the largest colono. He was a plantation owner, as well, until 1909, when he sold his San Manuel mill, just next to Chaparra, to Menocal and the Cuban-American Sugar Company. It had been incorporated in New Jersey in 1906.[18]

According to local histories, Chaparra began to "swallow up" land in 1899, forcing hundreds of peasants to sell their land through complex judicial processes or, worse, expropriating land through legal and administrative trickery. "In this way," wrote Víctor Marrero, municipal historian of Las Tunas, "the locals went from being landowners to day laborers, squatters, or sharecroppers."[19] Documenting these allegations is extremely difficult for these early years.[20] Much of the land for Chaparra and Delicias was purchased between 1907 and 1909, after the passage of Decree 77 under the second U.S. Military Occupation (1906–9). The decree extended Order 62—which allowed the breaking up of crown land only—to all communal estates, prompting another round of rapid land transfers from poor, illiterate landholders to U.S. capitalists and real-estate companies across the island.

Chaparra's manager R. B. Wood blatantly admitted to New York headquarters in 1928 that the legal proceedings to divide up communal estates were "notoriously crooked—without exception."[21] The next year, another official spelled out the company's strategy clearly: "The estate will not be divided, unless this company guarantees the costs.... Even if the proceedings would be undertaken by outside holders, the landholders would have to be reputable residents of Puerto Padre, holding possession in the estate, and we would always be able to procure the nomination of at least two friendly owners, through whom the company's interests would be protected."[22]

What little remains of the company correspondence and government documents from these early years suggests that there was significant political and economic collusion between company officials and government representatives at the municipal and provincial levels. In one case, six councilors—five Chaparra colonos and one Chaparra doctor—proposed legislation lowering the tax the sugarmills paid on cane. When another councilor dared to accuse them of corruption, the colonos insisted that they were paid a set amount of sugar per pound of cane and that they would in no way benefit from increased profits on the company's part. None of the other councilors spoke up, so the regulation went through. It can only be presumed that the councilors did in fact get a little thank-you bonus from the company.[23]

Chaparra company archives and legal correspondence from later years provide copious evidence of patronage between company administrators and politicians. Chaparra offered access to health care and jobs for political-clientele members in exchange for a mutually rewarding placement of "pliable" judges, customs agents, and tax collectors at Puerto Padre. A 1932 letter from Manuel Machado y M. de Oca to General Manager R. B. Wood demonstrates this collusion: "I am happy to tell you that on the third of December, I became Chief of the Municipal Police force. . . . I simply want to let you know that you have at your disposal your friend as always. P.S. I forgot to thank you for your support in getting my brother Claudio to be named Secretary of the Court."[24]

When company officials were unable to secure what they wanted through political patronage, they could call on more forceful allies. The U.S. military administration from 1899 to 1902 linked Cuba's new Rural Guard directly to property owners. One official told his assistants to "obtain as many of the men as possible from those recommended by plantation owners, as it is for the protection of rural estates and maintenance of order in rural districts that this guard is being organized."[25] Many companies, including Chaparra, Tuinucú, and United Fruit, donated land to the Rural Guard to establish posts. In addition, Chaparra created its own private security force to monitor the lands and sugarmill.

Eva Canel, a Spanish visitor to Puerto Padre in 1916, remarked on the company control over residents:

> Individual will does not exist for anyone under the Chaparra Sugar Company's shadow; all speak in time (*al compás*) as if being led by a baton invisible to the outsider. . . . Nobody complains: all is good, all is going well. Only the foreigners who do trade with the Chaparra Commercial Department are willing to reveal the truth, but they do so mutely because, although they cannot be fired or dismissed like employees, they could have the doors to Chaparra and Delicias slammed on them. They spoke to me of whippings, deaths, and clandestine burials. . . . Everyone at Chaparra denied these stories, but is it because they are lies, or is it because the residents have a tacit pact to remain silent?[26]

PATRONAGE AND PROGRESS
BUTTRESS THE COMPACT

At this point, we must ask why the residents of Puerto Padre, so recently liberated from the Spanish yoke, agreed to submit to this control. A foreign company was entering their territory and using judicial, political, and military state power against them to control, employ, and eject them from their lands. First and foremost, the residents did not see foreigners. Mario García Menocal, the Las Tunas hero of independence, with his bride, Mariana Sava de Menocal; his brothers; and his fellow officers—all Cubans—contracted the labor, purchased the land, and camped out in dense forests to supervise some two thousand men clearing the land, planting the cane, and building the mill town and cane farms of Chaparra. Many workers had served directly under Menocal and the captains and generals he brought with him from the 1895–98 war. As general manager, Menocal named Cubans as chiefs of most of the departments, including those of engineering, railroads, land, and sanitation.[27] He also doled out cane farms to Cuban generals, captains, and each of his six brothers, creating a sort of Menocal fiefdom that carried over many of the hierarchies and clienteles developed during Cuba's nineteenth-century wars for independence.[28] (See figures 3 and 4.) Surely, Menocal achieved respect and social "order" in the community partly through these friendships and hierarchies.

Menocal was like Eduardo Guzmán y Macías but on a much larger scale. Guzmán, as described in chapter 3, played the role of local patron-middle-man in Santa Clara. He provided a limited number of fellow veterans access to credit and loans, and he allowed foreign capitalists to secure small profits via interest on these loans. Menocal provided hundreds of jobs and farmland ranging from humble to top rate for his family, friends, and local residents. At the same time, he served as an essential mediator who allowed the American owners of the Chaparra Sugar Company to gain access to labor, land, and extensive profits.

The prewar history of Puerto Padre also contributed to local residents' acceptance of capitalist penetration. Residents were no strangers to the economic and commercial advantages sugar production could bring. Puerto Padre had been a small fishing village until the 1860s, when the Spaniard José Plá Monje established the San Manuel sugarmill some seven kilometers from the port. Plá constructed a railway from San Manuel to the port

3   Major-General Mario García Menocal, Liberation Army, 1895–98. *Album de vistas del gran central Chaparra*, 1910, 15.

4   Chaparra's General Manager Mario García Menocal in the head office. Mario García Menocal is standing at the right; next to him is his brother Serafín Menocal. Ignacio Montalvo is behind Serafín, and Manuel Mesa is to his left. *Album de vistas del gran central Chaparra*, 1910, 17.

in 1879, increasing development across the region and making it lucrative through sugar production. Plá's San Manuel and Mahiques's Chaparra had, therefore, already brought a railroad and many jobs to Puerto Padre before the outbreak of revolution in 1895. The population of the municipality of Puerto Padre also increased significantly, by 65 percent between 1887 and 1899.[29] Juan Clark's letter to Rionda suggests that the locals were desperate for jobs and aid to rebuild the region so devastated by the 1895–98 insurrection. Chaparra certainly provided some satisfaction: By 1911, the sugarmill was reported to be the largest in the world, providing about three thousand day jobs and spending an average total of $2,450 a day on salaries during the harvest.[30]

The *Louisiana Planter and Sugar Manufacturer*'s laudatory article, cited earlier, was only one of many post-1898 sources pointing to Chaparra as a harbinger of employment and progress in the region. The book *The Grand Chaparra Sugarmill*, published in 1910, is full of eight-by-ten black-and-white photographs illustrating some of the "modern" fixings Chaparra brought to Puerto Padre: top-of-the-line sugar machinery, efficient port facilities directly linked to the private railroads, tree-lined avenues and gardens with decorative electric streetlights, a fancy railroad station and hotel (see figures 5–6), and sports facilities, including baseball and tennis courts and even a YMCA. The book's introduction boasted, "On the 15th of March, Chaparra turned out 5,556 sacks of sugar . . . , no other plantation in the world having ever produced three-quarters of this amount in one single day."[31]

Bohemia magazine featured Chaparra as the first mill in its 1923 series on "Cuba's Grandest Sugarmills." The tone of the article reveals the journalists' fascination with the efficiency and "modernity" that the mill embodied. They reflected on the "great agricultural and scientific progress our people have made," from the moment the journalists boarded the company trains that "ran on schedule with English exactitude" to when they saw the powerful iron hooks transferring bundles of cane from the bull carts to the company trains. They voiced their amazement at the sugar towers of the famous sugarmill, "of enormous proportions and reaching boldly upward, as if challenging infinity" (see figure 7).[32] As is clear from the pictures from 1910, the only aspect of sugar production not being done with the help of machinery was the cutting and loading of canes onto carts (figure 8). Machines transferred the cane to trains (figure 9), from the trains to the mills (figure 10); then it was crushed with steam mills (figure 11) and boiled

5   Chaparra train station. *Agricultura y Zootecnia*, special edition, 1924, 22.

6   Chaparra's Grand Hotel, owned by Colonel Manuel Lechuga. *Album de vistas del gran central
     Chaparra*, 1910, 60.

in huge vats (figure 12) before leaving in boats from Chaparra's private port (figure 13).

The *Bohemia* journalists also highlighted some more tangible benefits for Chaparra residents—benefits that made residents more likely to accept capitalist penetration. They described Chaparra's hospital, founded in 1902, as "one of the best in the Republic, after those of Havana." It included a radiography room and several operating rooms where noteworthy surgeries were performed, as in the case of a black man who was completely cured after having had his intestines perforated.[33] The authors do not state how much patients had to pay, and the only surviving company documentation on health care dates from 1928. At that point, the company routinely gave employees a 25–50 percent discount on hospital bills. Since the economy was then on a downswing and the company was cutting costs, employees likely got more of a discount in earlier years.[34] Most rural Cubans did not have any access to health care, so Chaparra's hospital and the doctors and dentists who serviced its mill town and colonias served to attract workers and colonos.

Less obvious benefits included housing, an employee cafeteria, a pharmacy, an aqueduct, and paved streets with street-cleaning crews on company pay (one such team is in figure 14).[35] The Spanish journalist Carlos Martí praised Chaparra as "a flourishing and prosperous population" with "comfortable and modern" housing complete with electricity and plumbing for drinking water and showers.[36] There were 262 wooden houses in the town of Chaparra and the adjacent Pueblo Viejo (Old Town) in 1912, and by 1923 there were an additional 387 houses, all new and made of brick.[37] Again, little documentation remains addressing who was given housing, who paid rent, and who received electricity. A Cuban sociologist's study asserts that only Americans and the higher-strata of Cuban employees (such as department chiefs, engineers, and office employees) received twenty-four-hour access to electricity at Chaparra, but no source is cited to back the claim.[38] The fact that one of the demands made by striking workers in 1933 was for the company to grant free housing and electricity suggests that workers' households may have had more access to these benefits prior to the Depression-era cutbacks of the 1930s.

Residents of Chaparra had access to leisure, religious, and social activities that their more rural counterparts could not enjoy. Privileged employees could read the local *El Eco de Chaparra* newspaper printed at the mill, as

7 Chaparra sugarmill, including towers. *Bohemia*, 10 June
1923, 13.

8 Field workers loading cut
cane onto an ox cart. *Album
de vistas del gran central
Chaparra*, 1910, 48.

9 Hoist moving cane from cart
to railroad car at Dr. Tomás
G. Menocal's colonia. *Album
de vistas del gran central
Chaparra*, 1910, 44.

10 Hoist moving cane from railroad car into the Chaparra sugarmill. *Album de vistas del gran central Chaparra*, 1910, 38.

11 Mill workers at one of the dynamos in Chaparra's electrical plant. *Album de vistas del gran central Chaparra*, 1910, 45.

12 Mill workers beside vacuum pans. *Album de vistas del gran central Chaparra*, 1910, 46.

13 Chaparra's shipping wharf at Cascarero, Chaparra Bay. *Album de vistas del gran central Chaparra*, 1910, 24.

14   Street-cleaning crews on their carts. *Album de vistas del gran central Chaparra*, 1910, 37.

well as other newspapers and magazines in the reading library of the Club Chaparra. The mill had three theaters, churches of various denominations, and several recreational clubs and mutual aid societies. Residents from any sector of society could become members of the popular Chaparra baseball team, which played against teams from other mills. British West Indians formed a cricket team that also competed with other mills.[39]

Public and private schools constituted perhaps the greatest benefits for workers and colonos. In 1910 Chaparra had ten schools (two public and eight private) spread throughout the town and colonias (the students and teachers from one of the public schools are in figure 15).[40] By 1923 the number of company schools at Chaparra and its sister mill Delicias had grown to thirty, with thirty-six teachers and an average daily attendance of one thousand four hundred students. In addition, there were eighteen public schools attended by an average eight hundred students per day. The mill town had two night schools for workers' children who were obliged to work during the day. The numbers suggest that boys had less access to schooling than girls, likely because jobs and apprenticeships at the mill went almost exclusively to boys and men (the only exception being the commercial department and the schools, where *señoritas* worked as attendants and teach-

15 Chaparra public-school students and teacher. The Chaparra Sugar Company paid for the school, which was located in Pueblo Viejo, the humble neighborhood next to the mill town where workers and their families lived. *Album de vistas del gran central Chaparra*, 1910, 63.

ers).[41] Again, there is no surviving documentation from the early years on how much the company spent on schools, but the data from 1927–28 indicates that the company spent an impressive $36,950 on directors, teachers, and janitors' salaries and $7,400 on materials for the schools.[42]

THE DARKER SIDE OF PROGRESS: SOCIAL CONTROL

It likely took very little time for the workers and the community to perceive the underbelly of these benefits—the extreme level of control the company had over residents' lives. Control and repression helped keep large-scale rebellions from developing at Chaparra. Workers could lose everything—their homes, their jobs, and all of their worldly possessions—if the company chose to target them. Menocal, general manager at Chaparra from 1899 to 1913, and his two former comrades-in-arms Colonel Ernesto Fonts (general manager in 1913–17) and Colonel Eugenio Molinet (general manager in 1917–25), regularly expelled workers from their jobs and their homes at Chaparra if they demanded improvements or tried to organize a labor movement. In October 1919, Manuel Rionda wrote that R. B. Hawley allowed "some unions amongst the workmen" at Chaparra and Delicias, but "no strikes occurred" because "whenever there are any disturbances, the instigators are sent off the property."[43] One such case, under Fonts Sterling's rule in 1914, made it to the pages of the national *Heraldo de Cuba* newspaper. After demanding a salary increase, a Spanish worker named Eloy Vázquez was forced to walk sixty-nine kilometers along the railroad until he left company territory, leaving all of his possessions behind. A Rural Guardsman escorted him off company land and then gave him the *Plan de Machete*—a beating with the side of his knife.[44] (Figure 16 shows the Rural Guardsmen's barracks at Chaparra.)

Geographical isolation bolstered company control in the region. The distance between Chaparra and other urban centers was significant, and workers could only use the railroad with permission from the company. The nearest urban center to Chaparra was another sugarmill town, San Manuel. It stood only ten kilometers away, but as mentioned earlier, there was a high level of cooperation between Chaparra and San Manuel's owner Francisco Plá. When the Cuban-American Sugar Company (Cubanaco) bought San Manuel in 1909 and changed its name to Delicias, the mills acquired the nickname "the greedy twins."[45] Puerto Padre was only twenty-two kilometers away, but as a U.S. military report dated 1907 put it, Puerto Padre was simply "the port for Chaparra and San Manuel Sugar Companies. . . . The town is supported by these companies." That same year, Puerto Padre had only two thousand residents while Chaparra had five thousand, and San Manuel had close to three thousand. The closest public railroad station from which passengers could travel east to Santiago or west to Havana was at Sabanazo, a full sixty-nine kilometers from Chaparra.[46]

Workers were not the only ones to suffer from isolation and company control. Independent merchants were not allowed to use company railroads without permission, and in the early years there were no public railroads or roads in the area to provide alternative means of transportation. Besides these challenges, merchants had to battle with the fact that the company paid workers with tokens that were accepted at face value only at company stores. Workers could exchange tokens for cash if a product they needed was unavailable at the company stores, but a certain "tax" was discounted for the transaction. The token system was outlawed with the Arteaga Act of 1909.

16 Rural Guard post at Chaparra. *Album de vistas del gran central Chaparra*, 1910, 49.

It nevertheless continued unofficially throughout the republican years.[47] In 1916, the Spanish visitor Eva Canel told an employee that Chaparra, of all mills, should not use the token system because President Menocal was associated with the mill.[48] The employee responded that the bank would change the tokens, and "nobody complained" because the mill was always solvent, in contrast to the situation at many smaller, less financially secure mills.[49]

The private railroads and tokens gave Chaparra and Delicias nearly monopolistic control over commerce in the region. The 1924 issue of *Agricultura y Zootecnia* that focused on Chaparra and Delicias considered this an advantage to local residents. They described the mills' commercial department as "the finest of its genre in the Republic" and praised the efficiency of its two hundred stores. The journalists pointed out that mill residents had access to specialized products not available to other residents of the island. They also argued that the fixed-price system used by the mill was better than the bargaining system used on the rest of the island.[50] Finally, the journalists proposed that, because the company produced its own meat, milk, and bread in such large quantities, it could provide these products to the consumer for less.[51]

Interviews with workers and common sense provide the flip side to these "pros" of the company store—dependence. In the 1920s, workers complained that the company was taking advantage of the lack of competition by charging too much for basic goods. According to an article published in the national newspaper *La Prensa* in June 1925, the combined retail sales of three Cubanaco mills (including Chaparra and Delicias) exceeded $2 million annually.[52] When workers could not afford goods, the company extended them credit. As time went by, it became clear that debt tied workers and cane farmers to the mill.

The company also controlled electricity. As of 1916 the Chaparra Electric Company provided power to all of the surrounding towns—Holguín, Las Tunas, Gibara, and Puerto Padre. Again, *Agricultura y Zootecnia* portrayed this as an advantage, stating that the wealthy company provided power to the region for less than any other source could have. But a look at local politics tells a different story. Holguín and Las Tunas consistently elected liberals, and their mayors pressured Chaparra again and again to provide power and electricity for more reasonable rates. Puerto Padre, by contrast, seemed to remain in the pockets of company officials; the mayors were usually colonos or former lawyers of the company. Like Menocal and his comrades-in-arms, they were conservatives from the time of Puerto Padre's establishment as a municipality in 1899 through the revolution of 1933. All cooperated to skim profits from the region's residents and consumers.

Through urban and social planning, the mill reinforced ethnic, racial, and occupational divisions among residents, instituting yet another dynamic that discouraged rebellion. Chaparra used immigrant workers from its inception, importing Spanish and Chinese laborers when national laws prohibited black immigrants.[53] Thanks to these new immigrants and internal migrations from Santa Clara and other provinces, Chaparra's population of permanent administrators, employees, and families grew from 1,038 inhabitants in 1899 to 4,069 in 1907.[54] In the 1910s and 1920s the company began paying government officials for permission to import large numbers of workers from other Caribbean islands. A visitor to the sugarmill in 1916 noted that men and women of all races and ethnicities wandered the streets of Chaparra, giving it a very cosmopolitan feel.[55] The Cuban poet Pablo Armando Fernández, who grew up in neighboring Delicias, described his community as "predominantly Spanish, with some Cuban families, thousands of immigrants from the Lesser Antilles, an abundance of Chinese, as

well as Syrians, Lebanese, Puerto Ricans, Dominicans, Venezuelans, Co-
lombians, and Mexicans."[56]

Cubanaco segregated workers from each other by allocating specific jobs
to each ethnic group. Until the 1930s, Spaniards tended to work in construction, on the railroads, and in the boiler rooms. Immigrants from the British,
French, and Dutch Caribbean islands tended to work in the fields, and the
Chinese worked in teams in the mill's centrifugal department. When Eva
Canel asked why one department had exclusively Chinese workers, she was
told that the work required patience and great care, skills for which the Chinese were "irreplaceable."[57]

Housing policies also segregated residents according to class and ethnicity. Chaparra housed mill workers of Spanish, Chinese, and British West
Indian origin in separate barracks or in separate ethnic neighborhoods of
the mill town, and many field workers lived outside the mill town altogether, dispersed among the barracks in the colonias. Whereas the barracks
for mill workers and the homes for the skilled employees were decent and
equipped with plumbing and electricity, Luis Merconchini, a former labor
leader in Delicias, described the field workers' barracks as "infernal." Apparently, those that Cubanaco built were slightly better than the colonos'
because they had wooden floors; however, all shared the characteristic of
being highly unsanitary.[58] Certain buildings such as the hotel, its restaurant, and the Club Chaparra were for "whites only." Upper-strata American
employees and administrators were thus grouped with upper-strata Cuban
employees (a sea of white faces in the photographs in the *Album de vistas* of
1910 and the 1924 issue of *Agricultura y Zootecnia*).

Canel commented on racism during her visit to Chaparra in 1916. She
was pleasantly surprised to find a mulatta named "Santa" running Chaparra's
new hotel with her longtime partner and companion, Vigil. Canel had met
the couple twenty-five years earlier when they had run a hotel in Matanzas.
Thanking Canel for her play, titled *La Mulata*, Santa told her: "We women
of color owe you so much. You were the first white woman to give us dignity
in Cuba." When Canel asked Santa why she had not married Vigil after such
a long time, Santa replied: "Why should I impose such a 'social nightmare'
on such a good man?" This response prompted Canel to comment that
many white women brought "sexual impurity" to their marriages, not hesi-
tating to throw this "nightmare" on their husbands, whereas "the modest
woman who has dedicated her life to a man since she was a child, helping

him with his work . . . that woman, because of the pigmentation of her skin, will not become a legitimate companion of the one who respects and loves her because the rest of society would make them feel ashamed."[59]

More institutionalized racism against Asians, blacks, and mulattos also played an important role in dividing Chaparra's residents. Chaparra's clearest example of this came every year at the end-of-harvest celebration, when the administrator draped a rope across the sugar-factory floor, and whites danced on one side while blacks, Asians, and mulattos danced on the other.[60] The photographs of office workers and skilled employees indicate that only light-skinned Cubans could join Chaparra's elite society. Finally, there is no subtlety in the letter the general manager of Chaparra wrote to the captain of his private security force on 6 February 1930: "My dear Sir, Please transfer the two colored guards that I will indicate to Mr. Peña away from Cayo Juan Claro, replacing them with two white ones. Sincerely, R. B. Wood."[61]

Religion forged another dividing line. Catholics, Protestants, Spiritists, Quakers, and followers of Afro-Cuban beliefs (Santeros), among others, practiced their religions in Chaparra homes and temples. One evangelical preacher expressed directly in a letter to Chaparra's general manager in 1939 the "pacifying" effect religion could have on workers: "Mill owners who have co-operated with us have expressed their satisfaction in the changes that have been brought about in the lives of many of their workers. They have declared it to be a decided advantage in that it produces a better, faithful, and more loyal employee."[62]

Other institutions such as schools and clubs reinforced class, race, and ethnic divisions. At the private schools, parents had to pay for uniforms, books, and scholastic materials: They were thus the nearly exclusive domain of American and well-positioned Cubans' children. (Again, these better-off Cubans tended to be white.) The public schools were the domain of lower-strata Cuban, Spanish, and Chinese children. The predominantly white Club Chaparra and Yacht Club functioned side by side with the mutual aid societies for Spaniards; a Sociedad de Color for non-white Cubans; a British West Indian association for immigrants from the Caribbean islands; at least two women's clubs; several Masonic lodges; and Spiritist societies.

While these clubs provided much needed spaces free of company control where residents of Chaparra could socialize, only the Masonic lodges and Spiritist societies seem to have really encouraged solidarity that cut across ethnic or class lines. Tomás González Romero and Ester Villa Nápoles, who belonged to the Sociedad de Color in these early years, remember the club refusing to admit poor blacks (including prostitutes) as members. The Sociedad men tried to exclude women from the club at one point, but their wives and daughters refused to be excluded. Much later, in the 1940s and 1950s, González urged a group of Chaparra mulattos not to leave the Sociedad de Color to form a separate mulatto Club Espuma. His calls for unity were ignored.[63]

With all of these factors in mind, we are better equipped to understand how managerial strategies discouraged large-scale mobilizations at Chaparra in 1906, 1912, and 1917. Private guards and Rural Guards stood ready to intervene at the will of the company. The benefits of employment at the mill provided incentives not to rebel. These same benefits gave the company a great deal of social, political, and physical control over its residents, making it difficult for them to rebel. Institutions established by the company or voluntarily formed by residents at the mill divided them from within. Finally, the administrators, department heads, cane farmers, and political appointees at Chaparra and Puerto Padre were part of a strong Conservative Party power base beginning with the Menocal family's founding of the mill through the administrations of Menocal's war companions from 1913 to 1925. Chaparra's chieftains were neither popular liberals nor members of the Independent Party of Color. There were therefore no natural leaders during the liberal revolts of 1906 and 1917 or during the PIC protest movement of 1912.

Elsewhere in Oriente and Camagüey, Liberal cane farmers burned cane fields to extort arms and funding for the liberal cause (under the threat of further destruction).[64] In March 1917, Manuel Rionda deplored the Liberal rebellion in a letter to his friend Albert Strauss: "The trouble started on November 2 when 'the powers that be' tried to change the results of the election. . . . Up to February 11 the sympathies were with the liberals; after that I, for one, left them, especially when they commenced to burn! . . . So far 'Francisco' and 'Elia' are the ones to have suffered the most of all the estates in Cuba. So perhaps I have more reason to be bitter, for instance, than Mr. Hawley of the Cuban-American Sugar Company, whose properties have been spared."[65] Tuinucú was spared, too, but before comparing the Tuinucú community to the picture we now have of Chaparra, it is essential to look at how Menocal's experience at Chaparra facilitated his rise to power and informed his approach to the "management" of the Cuban nation as president from 1913 to 1921.

THE FOREMAN OF CHAPARRA BRINGS "ORDER" TO THE NATION: 1913–1921

Planters' ability to extract profits increased enormously with the outbreak of the First World War and the concurrent rule of President Mario García Menocal (see table 3). This section shows that Menocal was U.S. capitalists' ideal middleman: He was able to win the presidency in 1913 based on his as yet untainted reputation as a general in the Liberation Army and his success as general manager of Chaparra and Delicias. Once in power he began with a few minimal "popular" measures, but during the First World War years, he consistently supported U.S. capitalists over Cuban industrialists, farmers, and workers. He enacted legislation favoring mill owners; the most important decrees legalized private sub-ports and allowed sugar companies to import temporary agricultural laborers from the "black" Caribbean. He also prohibited strikes and exiled labor leaders from the island, just as he had done at the Chaparra Sugar Company enclave.

TABLE 3   Sugar crop's value in millions of dollars and percentage of Cuban exports, 1913–1920

YEAR	VALUE ($ MILLIONS)	CUBAN EXPORTS (%)
1913	115.8	72
1914	163.4	77
1915	202.4	84
1916	308.5	85
1917	332.2	86
1918	347.1	85
1919	472.1	89
1920	1,016.8	92

Source: Pérez, Cuba, 225.

Menocal used his reputation from Chaparra as a springboard to national power during the 1912 presidential campaign. He won the support of middle- and upper-class Cubans (and Americans) by positioning himself as the polar opposite to the incumbent liberals, and his relationship with Chaparra was central to this campaign. Through Chaparra, he had become rich; therefore, many assumed that he was incorruptible and would not engage in the outrageous graft of his predecessor. As engineer and manager of one of the most advanced sugarmills on the island, he had also proved that Cubans could do everything that Americans could do, all the while building prosperity and maintaining social "order."

Nevertheless, to win the elections the conservatives had to appeal to the masses, and this is where Menocal's status as a man of the provinces and hero of independence came into play. In one important way, Menocal shared what had given José Miguel Gómez such broad initial popularity. The political cartoonist Massaguer said it all with his election-campaign image titled, "El Guajiro de Chaparra (The Peasant from Chaparra)." The cartoon shows a man dressed in white wearing a bandanna and straw hat running to a young Menocal, dressed in kind, with a machete hanging from his back pocket. The caption reads: "Now the peasants will have our president."[66]

Not only was Menocal a man of the countryside; he was also a heroic national veteran who was as yet untainted by political opportunism. During the 1906 rebellion, he had distinguished himself as a leader of the national veteran's association. He traveled to Havana to mediate so that the crisis could be resolved among Cubans and another U.S. occupation avoided.[67] His efforts failed because Estrada Palma would not negotiate, but that made Menocal even more of a hero after U.S. "intervention" turned into another three years of occupation and U.S. capitalist incursion. The veteran's network of clienteles allowed Menocal to ally with other conservative chieftains and ride to victory in Havana in 1912 with his like-minded comrades-in-arms. Major General Francisco Carrillo—whom we saw burning cane in chapter 1 and receiving Francisco Rionda's pleas for permission to grind at Tuinucú in chapter 2—was one such leader, with his clientele in Remedios, Santa Clara. Carrillo was Menocal's running mate in the 1917 elections. Many officials in Menocal's two administrations were drawn from the ranks of Chaparra's or Menocal's military brigade, including veterans from the Menocal family. His brother Fausto, who became a senator in Oriente during Menocal's first regime, was accused of donning a Rural Guard outfit to collect and destroy all of the liberal votes during Menocal's corrupt reelection in 1917.[68]

Another reason for voters to favor Menocal and the conservatives over the liberals was the broad popular resentment against liberal President Gómez for his extreme repression of Afro-Cubans in 1912. Few Cubans were aware that Menocal had volunteered to crush the rebellion, and since the liberals were in power at the time of the war, voters held them responsible for the violence. The British diplomat Stephen Leech reported on 5 June 1912 that General Menocal's visit to Havana the previous month had provoked "a remarkable and spontaneous outburst of popular enthusiasm and this, coupled with the general disgust with the present administration, augurs very favorably for his success at the forthcoming elections on the first of November."[69] The same report also mentions a final factor to explain Menocal's success: The liberals were divided from within, between the presidential candidate Dr. Alfredo Zayas and his competitor, General Asbert.[70] Menocal's electoral success in 1912 was due in part to the fact that two key liberal military leaders and their clienteles shifted their support to Menocal.[71]

Menocal promised to bring order and progress to the nation as he had to his plantation, but the larger task proved far more difficult. Early in his presidency, Menocal tried to co-opt workers by paying corruptible labor leaders and subsidizing a workers' congress. The Cuban Association for the Legal Protection of Work organized the sparsely attended conference in 1914 via Menocal's Justice Ministry's Commission of Social Affairs.[72] More often than not, though, he opted for repression over persuasion. In his messages to Congress, Menocal frequently referred to German Chancellor Otto von Bismarck and his authoritarian principles. He argued that the state should introduce minimal social reforms and should under no circumstances permit strikes or social agitation.[73]

Mariana Sava de Menocal, the president's wife, served as an important counterpart to the patriarchal head of state, softening the family's image with high-profile acts of charity.[74] Mariana was frequently photographed in society pages of newspapers and magazines handing out toys and candy to poor children. She also organized charitable activities on a larger scale, opening orphanages, girls' schools, and hospitals. Mariana sought to exemplify Catholic compassion and charity, inspired by Cuba's national saint the Copper Virgin of Charity.[75] She stopped short of organizing federally funded social programs, as Latin America's most famous first lady, Argentina's Eva Perón, would do in the 1940s. But she did take charity to a new level when she organized Cuban high-society women into Red Cross cadres packing medical supplies and knitting scarves and socks for the allied soldiers in Europe during the First World War.

The war and U.S. policy demands led Mariana's husband to take a more repressive approach to labor. In response to inflated wartime sugar prices, the Allies fixed the prices of Cuba's sugar crops in 1917–18 and 1918–19 at 4.6 cents and 5.5 cents per pound, respectively. The relatively high sugar prices and the expanded market for sugar allowed mill owners and colonos to enjoy greater profits, but the wartime inflation of food and shelter costs meant that benefits did not trickle down to workers.

Squeezed by the high cost of living and inspired by the European labor movement, workers across the island staged a series of strikes beginning with railroad workers in December 1916. Many of the Spanish and Cuban socialists and anarcho-syndicalists who led these strikes had been exposed to these ideologies in Europe or had come into contact with them through the books, pamphlets, and word of mouth circulating in Cuban cities via railroad workers, tobacco workers, and dock workers. Literacy rates were quite high in Cuba (61.6 percent of the population was literate in 1919),[76] and even workers who could not read might gain exposure to the ideas when anarchist magazines such as *Tierra* were read aloud in cigar-rolling factories or in smaller, informal gatherings at cafés or in workers' homes.[77]

To offer a crude definition of two very complex ideologies, both socialism and anarcho-syndicalism were opposed to a state run by capitalists. Socialists wanted to reform the state by letting workers run it, whereas anarcho-syndicalists wanted to get rid of the state altogether to allow grassroots workplace and community councils—called "soviets" after the 1905 and 1917 Russian revolutions—to run their own affairs. In 1917 these two tendencies were able to minimize their differences in Cuba, but the rivalry between the two schools of thought would drastically divide workers during the 1933 revolution.

The "labor aristocracy" of the sugar factories (the skilled mechanics and metalworkers) led the 1917 strikes at the mills. Because they were organized as "guilds" that would only admit members of the same craft or trade, they did not receive much support from other sectors such as field workers, rail workers, and dock workers.[78] This parallels a British official's take on the railroad workers' strike demanding a 30 percent salary increase: "Owing to the very large increase in the cost of living, one cannot but feel a certain amount of sympathy with the men, but labour associations are not organized here as they are in other countries and lack the strength obtained from co-operation."[79] Workers did not really start to unite across job sectors and regions until the early populism of the 1920s.

Although there may have been tensions and conflicts at Chaparra and Tuinucú during Cuba's heightened strike period of 1917–19, the written and oral histories record only one strike. Railroad workers at Delicias struck in 1918 to demand that the administration pay them overtime and reimburse them for food when work kept them away from the sugarmill at mealtime. The unsuccessful strike lasted less than twenty-four hours because the demands did not stretch beyond a small cadre of workers.[80]

Just as Chaparra did with its own "troublemakers," Menocal exiled Spanish labor leaders from 1917 through 1921, labeling them communist or anarcho-syndicalist agitators.[81] Their Cuban counterparts were jailed. The president announced in September 1917 that all foreigners fomenting strikes in sugarmills would be deported and that no strikes would be permitted during the world war.[82] In October 1917 the moderate Cuban labor leader Vicente Martínez wrote to his U.S. counterpart, Samuel Gompers, about Menocal's approach to a "peaceful and reasonable" strike among workers at several sugarmills in Matanzas, Las Villas, and Camagüey. "The planters," he reported, "had decided to cede some of the demands, but Menocal intervened—he is also a planter—and told them not to give in under any circumstances, because he would end the strike forcefully. Menocal suspended civilian guarantees, and told the planters that the U.S. Government had ordered him to prosecute any strike activists."[83]

Menocal sent the Rural Guard to repress the strikers, but the strikes spread nonetheless, along with demands for higher wages. A special edition of the *Gaceta Oficial* published a message from the president "to the people of Cuba" on 11 December 1918 that underscores the importance of Cuba's agricultural cycle. "It is a cause of serious concern for the country," Menocal noted, "that more or less general strikes are being staged frequently at just the time that the country needs to dedicate itself to the sugar harvest."[84] In response to worker mobilization, the government eventually had to legislate moderate wage increases for workers across the island. In 1918, sugar companies began to pay cane cutters $2 a day—up from $1.50 in 1917—and by 1920, rural wages averaged $4.62 a day.[85] The Cuba Cane Sugar Corporation, a conglomerate organized by Manuel Rionda that owned some sixteen mills on the island at the time, reported that wage rates were approximately 80 percent higher in 1918 than they had been in 1916.[86]

The pay increases of 1918 did not match inflation, and mill owners and colonos pushed wages down over the longer term by persuading President Menocal to allow the massive importation of "black" workers from other islands in the Caribbean for seasonal agricultural work ("whiter" Spanish and Asian immigrants had dominated in the earlier years of the republic).[87] The Cubans commonly grouped these immigrants into the category of "Ingleses" if they were from the British West Indies or "Haitianos" if they were from the French Caribbean. This Caribbean immigration began before Menocal. Between 1908 and 1911, 13,685 migrants entered, but more than half of the total migration for the years 1900 to 1930 occurred during the Menocal–First World War years of 1916–20: 75,871 immigrants out of a total 142,275.[88]

Cubanaco alone brought 22,058 workers through the ports of Havana, Santiago de Cuba, and Puerto Padre between 1917 and 1923.[89] The company opted for approximately 50 percent Ingleses during the greatest period of dependence on immigrant field labor, from 1917 through 1928. A racial and ethnic job hierarchy manifested itself at Puerto Padre whereby British West Indians came first, followed by Dutch Islanders, then Haitians and Asians. A Chinese worker complained in 1938 that the British West Indian immigrants from the 1920s were being allowed to stay despite the laws "nationalizing" labor, whereas Asian workers there since the company's foundation were being forced to leave. Hourly wages from that same year indicate that the Ingleses received the highest pay among non-white foreign nationals.[90] This may have been related to the fact that the British government offered more protection for its "colonials" than other countries did for their citizens. Many Ingleses had served overseas beside British nationals during the First World War, and this gave them the sense of entitlement to demand such protection from British officials. The Ingleses also tended to have higher education levels and shared the same language as the upper-level American administrators and engineers some of them cooked and cleaned for; both education and proximity to the English-speaking elite allowed them to demand better pay.[91]

Despite their privileged position within the non-white hierarchy, British West Indians at Chaparra and Delicias were more subordinate to the company than their counterparts at other mills on the island. The United Fruit Company and other large mills in eastern Cuba had to compete to recruit workers mostly from Jamaica and Haiti, but Chaparra and Delicias drew on its own exclusive pool of immigrants from other Caribbean islands, including Barbados, Granada, St. Vincent, Montserrat, Antigua, Dominica, St. Kitts, St. Thomas, St. Martin, and Curaçao. These immigrants did not have the same freedom of mobility or power in numbers that the large networks of Haitians and Jamaicans on the island shared. The latter often paid for their own passages to Cuba on the numerous boats traveling between the two large islands; they were thus free from prior contractual obligations to specific mills. Jamaicans also had access to diplomatic redress for abuse through British consuls specifically focused on Jamaican immigrants, and they could easily find transportation back home to their island. In contrast, Chaparra and Delicias had a great deal of control over "their" immigrants from the Lesser Antilles because only their ships picked up the immigrants directly from their islands, brought them straight to Puerto Padre, and returned them at the end of the harvest.[92]

Nevertheless, according to the mayor of Puerto Padre, Cubanaco enjoyed a better reputation among immigrants than Rionda's Manatí and other mills because it paid off tokens at the end of the season. Also, because the season at Chaparra and Delicias tended to be longer than elsewhere, and other mills did not pay to return their workers to the islands, many flocked to the Puerto Padre region at the end of their contracts elsewhere—as in July 1921, when Chaparra set up tents for migrant workers and provided charity health services for them.[93]

Immigrant field workers were willing to work for lower wages than Cubans in a few documented cases. For example, one group of Cubans attempted to prevent a group of Haitians from cutting cane at the Cuba Company's Jatibonico sugarmill when the Haitians accepted wages 20 percent below those demanded by the Cubans.[94] No such evidence has surfaced for Chaparra (where there were many immigrants from the islands) or from Tuinucú (where there were very few). Whether most immigrants worked for lower wages is unclear, but it stands to reason that the sheer number of immigrants served to increase the overall supply of agricultural workers in relation to demand, thus driving down wages. Beyond this obvious benefit to sugarmill owners, Menocal's administration and the companies backing it probably hoped that the Caribbean immigrants would deepen ethnic, language, and racial divisions among workers. We will see how this theory played out by exploring the experiences of some of the non-white immigrant workers at Chaparra and elsewhere in chapters 6 and 7.

Besides opening up immigration, Menocal passed other legislation in his years as president that allowed U.S. investors to continue to extract exceptional profits from the island. He did so as subtly as possible, and often under extreme pressure from U.S. capitalists and politicians. For example, on taking over from José Miguel Gómez in 1912 he cancelled a scandalous (and lucrative) concession Gómez had granted to a U.S. company to dredge the Havana harbor. The company protested to the U.S. State Department, and the State Department "encouraged" some U.S. bankers to tell Menocal that they would significantly cut the loan he had negotiated with them unless the U.S. dredging company was indemnified. U.S. Ambassador William E. Gonzales told Menocal to indemnify the company "even if he had to override all of the laws and institutions of the Republic." Menocal tried to get his allies in Congress to propose indemnification, but the congressmen kept breaking quorum. In the U.S. ambassador's opinion, they wanted to negotiate a price for their votes. Gonzales actually proposed giving $5,000 to each congressional member.

Gonzales may have been simply an unscrupulous foreign diplomat assuming that Cuban statesmen were corrupt. The diplomat, however, was one of the most well-informed people in Cuba. His proposal likely reflected a very accurate read on the internal mechanisms used to get things done in congress. Menocal, the clever middleman, eventually figured out the best way to give the ambassador what he wanted without destroying the president's personal prestige. He had Gonzales write him a note threatening intervention if the company was not reimbursed. As a result, on 24 July 1917, the company (which had started the venture with very little capital of its own) got to keep lands by the ocean worth somewhere between $4 million and $12 million.[95]

One of the most challenging issues President Menocal faced during his time in office was how to balance Cuban and U.S. needs surrounding railroads and ports. On 8 May 1915 he imposed mandatory reductions in railroad freight charges, a move that was extremely popular among Cuban farmers and mill owners who had to use the predominantly U.S.- and British-owned public railroads. But when the strikes in 1917 forced rail companies to increase wages, the rail companies pressured Menocal to remove the reductions (insisting that they needed more income to pay higher wages). Menocal, who was negotiating a loan from J. P. Morgan at the time, finally submitted to the foreign pressure, increasing freight rates by 20 percent. This came at a time when farmers and mill owners in Cuba were already struggling with inflated wartime prices for industrial supplies, including sugar bags and machinery. Overall, Cuban and Spanish farmers and mill owners suffered the most because they had no recourse but to use public railroads. Companies such as Chaparra and Francisco were not affected by these changes because they had their own railroads leading to their own private ports. Under the pretext that the war demanded special concessions to sugar production, Menocal actually authorized forty-seven "North American" plantations to load and export their sugar from the sixteen private ports on the island. Hawley's Cubanaco was among these, as were Rionda's Manatí and Francisco.[96]

The political and economic context of the First World War made it extremely difficult for Menocal to reconcile U.S. demands with what he perceived to be Cuba's primary need: peace and order for lucrative sugar production. He succeeded in two realms, as an authoritarian leader and as a businessman. Menocal used the military leadership capacity he had accrued as a veteran to contain the 1917 rebellion in February and the strike waves thereafter. The 1917 rebellion did not usher in three years of U.S. intervention, as had the 1906 movement, or a massacre, as had the movement of 1912. Instead, it was put down quickly, earning it the nickname Guerrita de febrero (Little War of February). While Menocal's regime did not completely crush the wartime strikes, the strikes did not escalate into a revolution, as would those of 1932–33. The 1917 rebellion failed in part because U.S. power supported Menocal (especially Ambassador Gonzales, who by then was Menocal's personal friend) and in part because Menocal had brothers and war comrades from the 1895 revolution willing to take up arms to defend his regime.

The evidence suggests that Menocal maintained a loyal middle-class following at Puerto Padre. Carlos Martí remarked in 1915, "One senses a profound affection for general Menocal in the whole Puerto Padre zone. He is remembered at every instant, and named at every moment."[97] Martí found a lot of residents expressing love and respect for Menocal, reminiscing about their childhood with him and praising him for the progress and development he brought to the region. However, we cannot assume that this love stretched to the people at the bottom of the socioeconomic spectrum, especially since all of Martí's quotations seem to come from colonos.

What speaks louder than Carlos Martí's words is the fact that Chaparra remained an island of quiet while the 1917 rebellion raged in almost all the other regions of Oriente. A British report dated 27 April 1917 stated, "The rebels spread over the province [of Oriente], in a short time controlling it all with the exception of Antilla and Manzanillo *and the district around Puerto Padre*."[98] This suggests that residents did have a special, perhaps nostalgic, connection with the caudillo. It helped that Menocal had left the mill in 1912, so the blame for day-to-day problems could be shifted to his successors—also former comrades-in-arms—Colonel Ernesto Fonts and Dr. Eugenio Molinet. The nostalgia factor is important; when stripped of it, Menocal became the oppressor. At Palma Soriano, the Oriente mill that Menocal purchased while he made his millions as president, "The rebels . . . destroyed the private sugarmill of General Menocal and burnt his cane."[99]

Menocal's authoritarian approach to labor and his concessions to U.S. capital cut him off from his veteran links to the working-class base. By the 1917 election campaign, his image had shifted from "campesino of Chaparra" to "foreman of Chaparra." A popular song that circulated across the island went, "Cut the cane / be nimble, be quick / Run, Menocal is coming / Cracking his whip."[100]

Menocal's system of rule at the local and national level shared certain fundamental characteristics, combining tentative and limited reform with authoritarianism. But after a few years in the presidential office, his authoritarian tendencies tended to override any commitment to nationalist or social reform. As did Gerardo Machado and Fulgencio Batista after him, Menocal, upon entering the national scene, seemed truly to believe he could make a better Cuba. But the challenges from popular groups below, and domestic and foreign capitalists and politicians above him, led Menocal to opt for the easiest short-term policy. He repressed the workers and negotiated between Cuban and foreign capitalist pressures as best he could. The next chapter considers the management strategies of Manuel Rionda, one of the most powerful "foreign" capitalists Menocal had to deal with during and after his term in office.

Patrons, Matrons, and Resistance,
1899–1959

5 The management strategies and overall social relations at Tuinucú
were generally softer versions of the system of rule at Chaparra. Both
Manuel Rionda and Mario García Menocal practiced nepotism, giving family members jobs or land for cane farms. Rionda groomed an army
of nephews and in-laws to run each of his sugarmills, including Tuinucú,
Francisco, San Vicente, Washington, Elia, and Manatí. He was particularly
attached to Tuinucú, the family's first sugarmill, dubbing it Heaven (*Cielo*)
in family correspondences. During the early republican years, many members of the Rionda family made Tuinucú their home, just as the Menocals
did Chaparra, and yet Tuinucú was so much smaller that its rulers could
afford to be more congenial. Tuinucú did not inherit, or require, the
same military-style discipline that Menocal's clique imposed at Chaparra.
Menocal sought to cement a tight upper-class family of managers and department chiefs through organizations such as the Club Chaparra and the
Yacht Club; the Riondas were able to extend the family atmosphere further
because only about six hundred people lived permanently at Tuinucú (versus Chaparra's four thousand).[1]

This chapter explores the parallels and differences between Tuinucú and
Chaparra and at the same time describes more managerial strategies for

peaceful rule during the era of the patrons' compact. Rionda and his kin mixed the traditional social system of patronage with aspects of the newer American capitalist system of rule that historians call Fordism.[2] Rionda wanted workers, cane farmers, and their families to see him and his family members as stern, but fair, patrons and matrons. At the same time, he aimed to impress Cuban and foreign capitalists alike with a harmonious, modern, and efficient mill town and factory. We must take with a grain of salt the pretenses behind patronage and Fordism—bosses might fancy themselves to be "good," but those below them may not share the sentiment. The last part of this chapter describes how workers sometimes ridiculed and other times resisted their patrons. The fact that the bosses wanted to be considered decent and modern nevertheless led them to introduce tangible benefits for workers and cane farmers, who quickly figured out how to "work the system" by making demands in terms that their superiors could not refuse. They thus solicited funds for small expenses such as outfits for the baseball team all the way through to large investments such as light and electricity for workers' homes.[3]

RACE, REGION, AND PATRONAGE

The Chaparra and Tuinucú communities' greatest contrasts lay in their ethnic makeup and location. For skilled engineering and managerial positions, Menocal hired mostly Cuban veterans and a few U.S. citizens. Rionda hired mostly U.S. citizens. This could be due, in part, to the fact that Cuban veterans in the province of Santa Clara preferred pursuits other than sugar, predominantly cattle ranching.[4] The Sancti Spiritus veteran Tello Sánchez tried to recruit Cubans to work at Tuinucú through Liberation Army networks as did his counterparts at Chaparra, but to no avail: He lost his job as the sugarmill's labor contractor in 1905.[5] Residents in the Tuinucú region in general had more mobility and access to alternative means of employment than those near Chaparra. Tobacco, for example, thrived in the area. A letter from Pedro Alonso in February 1913 warned that sugarmills such as Tuinucú would suffer a labor shortage if the prices for tobacco were high during the months of March and April: "Workers will leave the cane fields for the tobacco harvest even if they earn less, because they prefer to work from 6 A.M. to 4 P.M. instead of waking up at 2 A.M. to prepare and haul the cane carts." For this reason, Alonso advocated that the sugarmill pay more to workers and colonos to augment the number of workers in the cane fields of both colono and company: "Mills need cane, and if colonos are no longer able to pay workers to cut and haul, they will start to leave their cane in the fields."[6] (Cane could be left standing for about four years, at which point the sugar content would decline dramatically.)

Menocal was a Cuban veteran and engineer himself, and he evidently believed that Cubans were perfectly capable of running a modern sugarmill together with Americans. In contrast, Rionda hired only U.S. employees and family members (whom he micro-managed) for upper-management positions out of admiration for the American model of progress and industrialism that surrounded him in New York City. In a letter to a business colleague, he credited Tuinucú's higher yield of 72,000 bags in 1907–8 to the U.S. technicians he had just hired. "You can imagine how much all this pleases me," he wrote, "regaining the plantation and placing it into the ranks of one of the most prosperous ones in Cuba when ten years ago it was a mass of ruins. There is nothing in life so gratifying as to see one's work producing and turning out as one expected."[7]

For non-managerial positions, Menocal hired Cubans and immigrants from all over the world—including Spain and the United States. Rionda favored Spanish veterans and Spanish immigrants, particularly Galicians and Canary Islanders, over all others.[8] Spaniards constituted some 70 percent of Tuinucú's workforce in the first decade of the twentieth century and 60 percent from 1910 to 1920.[9] They became cane farmers, store clerks, railroad workers, construction workers, and cane cutters. Tuinucú was thus the prototype of an island-wide problem that nationals labeled *sobrinismo* (literally, "nephewism"). (See figure 17.) Spanish bosses gave the best positions to their relatives, leaving Cubans with the lowest-paying jobs or no jobs at all. Rionda explicitly stated in July 1916 that he wanted to keep all his mills in the family so that there would always be somewhere for his "boys"—nephews and in-laws—to make a living.[10]

Tuinucú residents recall a sort of "racial" discrimination between the foreigners (Spanish and American) who got the best jobs and the Cubans as a group.[11] This was true for the Cuban labor market as a whole in the early twentieth century, as one historian remarked: "Immigrant presence . . . was so prominent that it tended to obscure racial differences among [Cubans]. 'Race' was frequently understood as a line that separated Cuban and foreign

17   "Sobrinismo" Manuel Rionda's nephews on bicycles. From the left: Manolo Rionda Benja-
      min, Cosme de la Torriente y Peraza, José Rionda y de la Torriente, Leandro Rionda y de
      la Torriente, and Bernardo Braga Rionda. Braga Brothers Collection, University of Florida,
      Gainesville.

workers rather than native workers of different skin colors."[12] Tuinucú was
too small a community to separate "whites" from "others" in social spaces
such as the primary school and the park—as was done at Chaparra and in
other larger towns and cities on the island—but privileged white spaces
nevertheless existed including whites-only movie nights and dances at
Tuinucú.[13]

Rionda's Spanish brother-in-law Pedro Alvarez became chief administrator at Tuinucú in 1899, and Rionda's nephew José took the helm in 1906. A
letter Manuel wrote to José on 3 February 1906 reads like a training manual
on how to be a good patron:

> Your attention should *never* be drawn to *one* thing. . . . *You* must be in
> *everything*. You have new recruits but as you are to occupy that position
> for many years you must either *drill* them or change them. Commence by
> getting a new foreman and look around for a bookkeeper and then oth-
> ers will see the manager means to be *a manager* and not a little boy they
> have known in short pants. Let things go now . . . but in the idle season

18   The "super-patron" Manuel Rionda
     on horseback. Braga Brothers
     Collection, University of Florida,
     Gainesville.

commence to show your teeth—It is healthy to show temper once in a while. . . . Walk about and be sure my astral body is often around you.[14]

Manuel was the "super-patron" at Tuinucú (see figure 18); he and his wife would arrive at the mill around Christmas time, always with great pomp and circumstance, and remain for one to three months. The visit usually came just after the harvest's start, conveniently placing the super-patron near his workers. Former workers recall seeing Rionda and family arrive in a special train car loaded with trunks full of luxury goods for Manuel's family. The proud Spanish gentleman would walk to the mill office, jangling gold coins in his pockets to give to the children who ran to his side.[15]

The super-patron had a fancy private railway coach custom made in 1916. He installed heating in case the car needed be sent to the United States to bring visiting dignitaries to Cuba. "We should have the vestibules," he wrote his nephew Leandro, "for it is always well to be able to sit and watch the cane fields."[16] The memoirs of George Atkinson Braga, one of Manuel's grand-nephews, contains a hilarious anecdote from 1933, when Rionda decided that Braga should drive him from his home in New Jersey to Tuinucú in Manuel's old Rolls-Royce. "All went well on the new [Central Highway] until we arrived at the Tuinucú River," Braga recalls. "The bridge had not yet been completed and, in attempting to cross by the old ford, the Rolls got stuck and had to be pulled out by teams of oxen."[17] Braga's memoirs capture the combination of fear and respect that Rionda's nephews had for the old man, and Tuinucú residents probably shared a similar combination of emotions, but with a stronger dose of ridicule and resentment.

MODERNITY AND URBAN PLANNING

A sort of competition seems to have developed in early-twentieth-century Cuba over who could have the most beautiful and modern mill town and sugar factory. This competition was not limited to any one part of the island: While Edward Atkins created botanical gardens full of exotic flowers and trees at his Soledad mill near Cienfuegos, Menocal established Chaparra's wide tree-lined avenues, tennis courts, mansions, and parks in Oriente. Outraged at the primitive state of the workers' housing at Tuinucú, Manuel Rionda asked his nephew José to have them rebuilt "in neater style" in a letter dated January 1905. "The rooms that you saw there were provisionally made," his nephew replied defensively. "We had to build them in a day for we did not have place to put some of the employees."[18]

This exchange between José and Manuel was rare. It was Manuel's sister, known as Doña Isidora to the residents at Tuinucú and *madrina* (godmother) to family members, who ironed out the vast majority of urban-planning details at Tuinucú from 1899 through 1912. (Map 3 shows the Tuinucú sugarmill and mill town in 1917.) She reported in March 1902 that since the workers building the railroads were coming to eat at the company store, Tuinucú was starting to look like a little town.[19] The workers ate there, but upper-strata Spanish and American employees ate and slept in the Rionda home, reinforcing the "family" atmosphere. This was still the case as late as 1918, when Rionda wrote to his niece Elena: "I want to see if we cannot confine our home to ourselves and have all the [clerks] take their meals at the American Club, even though they sleep in the big house. You see the more people we have, the more we have to attend to and I want to know if we could not reduce our little family so that [my wife] could come down to her meals, not like last year when owing to the great crowd, she had to keep away."[20]

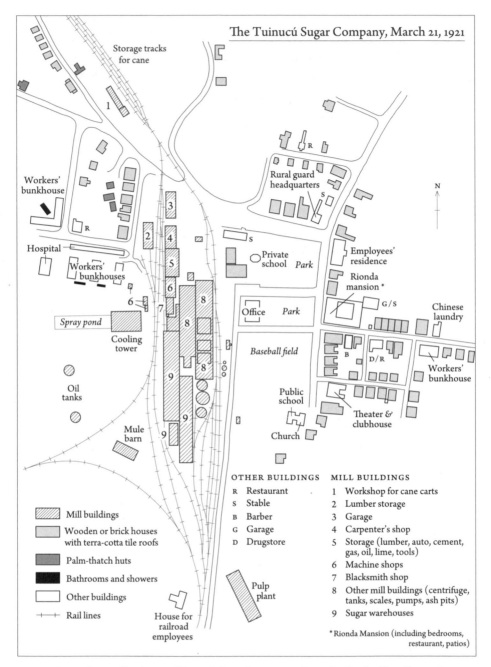

The Tuinucú Sugar Company, March 21, 1921

Storage tracks for cane

Rural guard headquarters

N

Workers' bunkhouse

Hospital

Workers' bunkhouses

Spray pond

Cooling tower

Oil tanks

Mule barn

1

3

2   4

5

6

8

7   8

9   8

9

9

R

R

S

Private school   Park

Office   Park

Baseball field

Public school

Church

R

S

Employees' residence

Rionda mansion *

G/S

Chinese laundry

B   D/R

Workers' bunkhouse

Theater & clubhouse

Pulp plant

House for railroad employees

Mill buildings

Wooden or brick houses with terra-cotta tile roofs

Palm-thatch huts

Bathrooms and showers

Other buildings

Rail lines

OTHER BUILDINGS

R   Restaurant
S   Stable
B   Barber
G   Garage
D   Drugstore

MILL BUILDINGS

1   Workshop for cane carts
2   Lumber storage
3   Garage
4   Carpenter's shop
5   Storage (lumber, auto, cement, gas, oil, lime, tools)
6   Machine shops
7   Blacksmith shop
8   Other mill buildings (centrifuge, tanks, scales, pumps, ash pits)
9   Sugar warehouses

* Rionda Mansion (including bedrooms, restaurant, patios)

MAP 3   Sugarmill and town of Tuinucú, Sancti Spiritus, 1921. Drawn by Carolyn King, Geography Department, York University.

19   Tuinucú train station. Braga Brothers Collection, University of Florida, Gainesville.

20   Tuinucú sugarmill and offices. Braga Brothers Collection, University of Florida, Gainesville.

Manuel Rionda's letters to Isidora and, after 1912, to his niece Elena
Doty offer long and rambling suggestions about how to make Tuinucú the
apple of his eye. Manuel wrote to Isidora in April 1906 that lumber for a
new hotel would soon arrive: "It's something of a luxury, but I want to see
my beloved Tuinucú bloom like a flower." He added that Tuinucú needed
a larger sugarhouse and more housing for workers, and for that reason
he would invest $60,000–$70,000 more, despite the overall slump in the
sugar economy that year. He was extremely pleased overall that Tuinucú
had the machinery to produce 80,000 bags the next year and had shed almost all of its debts. Rionda lamented that Francisco was not around to

see the mill's reconstruction and growth and vowed that as long as he was alive, he would make sure that Tuinucú was in a position to feed the Rionda family.[21]

Rionda's competitive side came through in a letter to Isidora in 1906: "The Hormiguero mill has a very beautiful train station. Try to make Tuinucú's as nice."[22] (Tuinucú's train station is pictured in figure 19; its sugarmill and offices in figure 20.) The same letter suggested that Tuinucú's carpenter build a new bathroom and attach a stable to the Rionda home. "The only payment I ask from Tuinucú for my work," he explained, "is to be able to live the good life with my family while I am there a few months each year. . . . I want good horses. . . . I also want a better road. . . . How are the trees? I really did not like those trees around the train station." He sent a machine for paving the roads and encouraged Isidora to lend it to colonos.[23] Manuel's sister Concepción wrote about the Rionda mansion in July 1915: "The living room is lovely and spacious, and this house really looks like a palace. What changes we old ladies have seen over the course of all these years! We are the ones who most appreciate the changes in our beloved Tuinucú, thanks to all of the difficulties you have passed through to make it into a little paradise."[24]

Beautifying their homes served not only to make managers like the Riondas (and the Menocals and Molinets at Chaparra) more comfortable; the big houses were a form of "public theater" to demonstrate to workers and cane farmers how much more wealth and power they held.[25] Colonos and upper-level employees also tried to make their homes as ostentatious as possible to emulate their superiors and differentiate themselves from their subordinates who lived in wooden barracks in town or straw huts in the countryside. Private mansions remained bigger than public buildings until President Gerardo Machado built the giant Capitolio (Capitol Building) in Havana in the 1920s, modeled after the U.S. White House, to symbolically show that the Cuban state was becoming more interventionist in the economy and in society at large. In the early twentieth century, "the state" let capitalist bosses pretty much do as they pleased in their factories and mill towns, intervening only occasionally in the form of repression, when they sent in the Rural Guard to reinforce private security forces. (Figures 21, 22, and 23 depict Rionda's, Menocal's, and Machado's architectural "public theater" of power.)

21 The Riondas' mansion at Tuinucú. Braga Brothers Collection, University of Florida, Gainesville.

22 The Menocals' mansion at Chaparra. *Album de vistas del gran central Chaparra,* 1910, 16.

23 President Gerardo Machado's Capitolio in Havana. Gerardo Machado built the Capitolio a few inches larger than its model, the U.S. White House, symbolically suggesting that the Cuban president would play a more assertive, nationalist role. Photograph by Elpidio Rodriguez Alvarez.

MATRONS, CHARITY, SOCIAL PROGRESS,
AND CONTROL

The histories of Chaparra and Delicias written by former workers emphasize the role that veteran patrons such as Menocal, Colonel Ernesto Fonts, and Colonel Eugenio Molinet played at the mills, but the patrons' wives, sisters, and daughters are less prominently featured. The caption under Caridad Cardenas de Molinet's photograph in the 1923 issue of *Bohemia* magazine reads: "Respectable and prestigious woman very much appreciated for her goodness."[26] The former worker Tomás González, when prompted to re-member women's roles at the mill, recalled two Molinet women giving out presents to children "mostly to win sympathy among the poorest families, who were the immense majority."[27] The same worker broke into an old song that began "Menocal for Chaparra, Marianita for *la Zona*" and explained that Mario García's wife, Mariana, used to offer assistance to prostitutes in the red-light district of Chaparra—where workers went for cockfights, alcohol, and sex. Menocal and Molinet women also gave the wood from old cane carts to workers when the company replaced them with metal carts. The former cart planks still line many of the rickety wooden floors in present-day homes in Chaparra's Pueblo Viejo, the humble workers' village next to the privileged employees' mill town.[28] Elite women likely did more charitable work than this, but very few details on the matrons' activities at Chaparra are recorded and remembered.

In contrast to this relative silence, a vast majority of the sources on Tuinucú—worker histories, press reports, business correspondence, and memoirs—mention Manuel's sister Isidora and his niece Elena (married to Oliver Doty, who became general manager in 1912). These women played significant roles getting Tuinucú up and running again after the 1898 war, and they helped smooth day-to-day social relations in the Tuinucú commu-nity. Overall, the charity of elite Catholic matrons such as Mariana Menocal and Isidora Rionda played an important role in softening rule at the national and local levels. Younger women like Elena Doty complemented this char-ity through a commitment to progress and gender-specific social reform in ways similar to early-twentieth-century reformers in rapidly growing cities in the United States, Argentina, and Brazil.[29]

Eladio Santiago has collected many anecdotes from old workers, employ-ees, and their families about Doña Isidora that provide a unique glimpse into social relations in the mill community. Isidora rode around Tuinucú in her carriage almost daily. If she saw a child outside during school hours, she would stop the carriage to ask the child why he or she was not at school. If the child lacked shoes or materials, she would buy them; if other challenges prevailed, she would visit the child's parents to talk about how they could address them together. Many of Santiago's interviewees mentioned that Isidora would invite residents of Tuinucú to her home, without regard for class or race. At least on one occasion, in the year 1934 or 1935, she also went against another elite woman's intentions to discriminate.

The discrimination incident offers a fascinating example of working-class Tuinucú residents practicing what one historian called "counter-theater." This consisted of jokes, actions, or anecdotes that ridiculed the patrons' "public theater," or demonstrations of wealth and power.[30] A Spanish society lady named Isidora Alvarez was organizing a dance, and one of her friends asked: "Why aren't the workers being invited?" Alvarez exclaimed: "Not that ash-covered mob!" Word quickly spread, and the workers organized a separate dance called "the ash ball" for the same day as the high-society gathering. Cuban men and women covered their faces in ash, dressed to the nines, and paraded through the streets bordering the park and the fancy homes, blasting horns and trumpets with a triumphant air. Isidora Rionda invited them into her home and told them that, if they wanted, they could all go to the Club House with her and have their own ball, which is exactly what they did.[31]

Some of the "ash ball" participants told Santiago that Isidora Rionda purchased their gowns, but others did not concur. This reminds us to be aware of the tricks that nostalgia can play on memories. Santiago's very label for the early twentieth century—Tuinucú's Golden Age—suggests this. At the time Santiago did most of his interviews, Cuba was going through its so-called special period. After the fall of the Berlin Wall in 1989, the island lost most of its socialist allies, and its economy crashed, leaving Cubans very little money to feed the population and maintain its infrastructure. Walking through the mill town with Santiago in January 2000, the sense of fading glory was palpable—the baseball field covered with weeds, the crumbling roads, and the decrepit buildings. Nevertheless, he and the other retired workers he had interviewed remembered the dark side of the Golden Age, as well.

Oral history can be usefully combined with company and public archives to steer a way through the past. The letters that have survived between

Isidora and her brother Manuel demonstrate that these elite siblings could be quite generous. Isidora often requested loans and gifts on behalf of Tuinucú residents. For example, in May 1914, she wrote: "I told poor Baltasar about the 500 pesos you are offering to lend him. His eyes filled with tears as he told me that he was very grateful and would pay you back as soon as possible."[32] A few years later, she requested cash to buy a sewing machine for the same man's daughters, since "the poor things" had to make their clothing by hand. "As your administrator of charity I am as eager to give to the poor as you are," she concluded.[33] Santiago's interviewees reported that during the economic crises of 1921 and 1929–34, Isidora distributed unlimited amounts of milk every day and portions of meat twice a week to the largest and most needy families. They also recall that she had the cane farms nearest to the mill planted with subsistence crops and that, "during the 1933 strike that lasted forty days, Isidora personally delivered the food that strikers and their families needed on a daily basis."[34] We will see from company documents cited in chapter 7 that Isidora and her sister Conchita were, indeed, poised to distribute $1,000 per week, as per Manuel's instructions, but a strike committee rejected the money and asked the sisters to leave the mill.

The former worker Arquímedes Valdivia (see figure 24) remarked that Isidora was an owner, but "she was very good, she was a Catholic who demonstrated her faith in practice."[35] Valdivia's father, a carpenter named Agustín, moved to Tuinucú in 1917 from Sancti Spíritus. There, he had been in close contact with Spanish anarcho-syndicalist organizers from the railroad and tobacco sectors. In 1925, he and a few other anarcho-syndicalists began to organize a union to incorporate workers from different departments of the sugarmill.[36] He was told to leave Tuinucú—his son does not know by whom—and thus had to move with his large family to Tunas de Zaza to work on boats. As his son tells it, "Doña Isidora went to see him there and told him he could come back if he left his ideas behind. He said, 'I respect you, and I appreciate your goodness in relation to my case, but I am not going to trick you, I am not going to change my ideas.'" Isidora made sure that he got his job back anyway. He and his family returned to the mill, and he resumed organizing workers.

Oliver Doty, general manager from 1912 through his death in 1942, is likewise remembered fondly for fraternizing with the workers at Tuinucú. Santiago's interviewees remember him risking his own health to person-

24   Eladio Santiago,
     Arquímedes
     Valdivia, and his
     grandson, Tuinucú,
     2000. Photograph
     by the author.

ally visit all of the sick workers when an influenza epidemic hit the mill in
1918.[37] Valdivia recalls that "Oliver would walk around the neighborhood
and say hi to people, no matter what rank, and he would chat with them
in their houses. . . . He was very humble."[38] Valdivia's father told him that
when the workers put forth their demands in the 1920s, Doty said: "If there
was one other mill that would do it first, we would agree to your demands,
but we cannot be the first."[39] In 1933, Doty went even further: Apparently,
he encouraged the Rural Guard to give union representatives permission
and tickets to go to Havana and present their demands to the corporate
headquarters.[40]

Santiago offers an acute analysis of the Tuinucú management strategy:
"There was a certain elasticity that I interpret as a way to keep the masses
drugged while at the same time dividing them. For example, if a worker
from the nearby central La Vega, or from the Camagüey Rionda mills like
Francisco or Elia told a Tuinucú worker that at their mills they had to do
this or that or they would be hit with clubs, the Tuinucú worker would say,
'At Tuinucú they don't do that to us.'"[41] The 1933 strike committee members
likely came to the same conclusion, which explains why they refused the
company's charity and asked Isidora to leave.

As to the question of physical repression, Valdivia and Santiago both
stated that Tuinucú managers kept the Rural Guard soldiers from abusing
the workers until the period "when Batista arrived" and the Rural Guard
began to assert its superiority over company officials.[42] Again, the size of the

mill is relevant: Whereas Chaparra was large enough that the Rural Guard soldiers or company security guards might not know the workers, the handful of soldiers and guards stationed at Tuinucú fraternized and lived among the workers.

Elena Doty played as important a role in smoothing relations at the mill as her husband and aunt. She started a Women's Club that held raffles and sold inexpensive clothing, aprons, flowers, and plants. Under her guidance, the club admitted the wives of day workers as well as salaried employees. Those who could read, write, and do arithmetic taught these skills to those who could not, and the club gave classes on sewing, embroidery, dressmaking, and "domestic economy." The "American" side of Tuinucú should be emphasized here: Elena's ideas on what a woman should do were certainly formed during her years living in the United States.[43]

Among other activities, the Women's Club organized contests for the best garden at Tuinucú. The reward was significant: A new home at the mill town. During the First World War inflationary period, when President Menocal demanded increased food production, the reward went to the resident who could cultivate the most fruits and vegetables (rather than flowers.) "Fine eggplants, cabbages, lettuce, peas, beans, peppers, and tomatoes" flourished during the October–May growing season at Tuinucú, and those who grew more than their families could consume sold the surplus for extra income. Manuel Rionda credited the women and children of Tuinucú for working the gardens.[44]

Elena took over the urban-planning details from Isidora in 1912, when the Doty family established themselves permanently in the community. She wrote to her uncle Manuel at length to make sure that the rapid urban growth of the mill from 1915 through 1920 was to his liking. Her letter of July 1915 reported that construction on the garden prizewinner's house had been started and the new slaughterhouse was almost finished. The old slaughterhouse site would be divided between the prizewinner's house and "the Chinamen" for vegetable gardens. At Tuinucú, as at other mill communities across the island, including Chaparra, Chinese families grew and sold vegetables and provided laundry services to mill residents, among other jobs and services.[45]

By 1917 Manuel was asking Elena about the Club House and the nearly complete schoolhouse. "Many years ago," he wrote, "when Tuinucú was the ugliest and dirtiest plantation in Cuba, I had sort of an idea that some day

I would have it one of the best, and as we are approaching that realization, it is natural that I should like to see done all those things. Although costing little, [they] tend to improve appearances greatly."[46] The following year, he suggested that the ground be cleared and leveled for a park. "That part of the property could be utilized to greater advantage in having the people congregate and walk about there under the trees," he wrote. "Perhaps you will think I am becoming romantically inclined, but I have always thought many of the beauties of Tuinucú were not appreciated by the people because they could not be reached."[47] The First World War years of high sugar prices were just the time for this sort of "romantic inclination," since the Tuinucú Sugar Company had plenty of profits to dispose of.

It was during this booming era that the company decided to recognize Elena's contribution to the Tuinucú community. A company memorandum dated 17 June 1919 reads:

> Whereas the social conditions prevailing at our plantation are of the highest order, the relations between employer and employee being most cordial; whereas the general feeling of content that prevails amongst the employees of the Company has tended greatly toward the success of the factory this year; whereas the very desirable social condition is due in major part to the efforts of Mrs. Elena R. Doty in fostering good feeling amongst the employees, and to her energy displayed in the development of the school work at the estate and in her other work for the betterment of all, it is unanimously RESOLVED that the President hereby is authorized to use the sum of [$——] in any manner which he may consider most appropriate as a recognition of the Company's appreciation of Mrs. Elena F. Doty's part in bringing about the existing pleasant social relations at Tuinucú.[48]

Besides spending money on charity, beautification, and recognition of "faithful" employees, Rionda made some very large expenditures to establish one of the island's first radio stations, an important symbol of progress and modernity. The Tuinucú Radio Station, started in early 1923, was a great source of pride for Manuel. The radio technician Frank Jones received letters from across the United States, Canada, and the Caribbean applauding the music and broadcasts, and Manuel Rionda was always pleased when friends told him that they had heard Spanish or Cuban music on a Tuinucú broadcast in North America.

Jones raised Tuinucú's profile significantly in April 1925 when he spent
more than $3,000 to increase the transmitter from 100 to 500 watts. He used
an additional $600 of his own personal funds to advertise the station, mak-
ing phonograph records and piano player rolls of a song called "Tune in
Tuinucú." Hundreds of orchestras all over Canada and the United States
received his sheet music, and "at least 20 of the big broadcasting stations"
played "Tune in Tuinucú" on numerous occasions.[49] Manuel was very en-
thusiastic at first, but he became concerned that Jones was neglecting his
department (he was head electrician). The super-patron also scolded his
employee for spending so much at a time when sugar prices were beginning to decline again: "With these low sugar prices we should not only
economize for the sake of economy, but also as an example to our employees. . . . With the $3,588 expended by you we could have built 4 small
houses."[50]

The Rionda clan's contributions in charity, employment, and progress
did not go unnoticed. A *Heraldo de Cuba* article dated 14 February 1925
on sanitation in sugarmill towns contained the subheading, "Tuinucú Is a
Model Sugarmill." Dr. López Silvero, a special investigator for the national
Sanitation Department, described the mill as a model in its class, with
worker and employee housing that "boasts magnificent sanitary conditions," street-cleaning gangs, and an emergency room equipped to handle
required care. He lamented that all mill owners did not imitate the Tuinucú
owners' laudable conduct.[51]

On 13 December 1924 a woman from Tuinucú who described herself as
"the loving wife of an honorable mechanic" wrote a letter to "Milliken" of
El Mundo responding to his column about the inferior living conditions of
workers in sugarmill communities across the island:

> You are absolutely right to emphasize that homelessness is the worst fate
> a poor person could possibly face. Humble and hardworking Cuban la-
> borers have a right to demand improvements for themselves and their
> families, to avoid death in miserable, dirty shacks. But you should also
> know that there are some hidden spots on the island where workers live
> relatively happy and satisfied. Here, in the Central Tuinucú . . . workers
> live quite comfortably in clean and well-ventilated homes. . . . While it is
> true that the workers' pay is not high, we have free, clean housing, pure
> water, and electricity year-round and healthy and noble activities that lift

our spirits and make us raise our eyes to heaven in gratitude. If you get the chance to come to this little corner of the island you will see that I am only telling the half of how well-off we workers are here . . . and that is why no one has ever joined or is thinking of staging a strike, because it would be very unjust for those who have a tranquil home where the worker can return to relative happiness after all the hard work. Here, I end my brief account in support of [an] administration that is truly democratic in its willingness to allow its workers relative well-being, making their lives pleasant.

Milliken advised other mill owners to read the letter. He then prophesized that when all of those who produced Cuba's millions of tons of sugar had safe roofs over their heads, like the workers of Tuinucú, there would be no worker conflicts at the mills because "life would not be so bitter for those who produce something so sweet."[52]

On 18 April 1927, Ricardo Bianchi proposed a motion to the Municipal Council of Sancti Spiritus that it recognize the contributions the Rionda family had made to the region. He suggested changing the name of a major street in Sancti Spiritus to Avenida de Rionda. The motion was unanimously supported, but Manuel asked that the street be named Avenida Tuinucú instead, because he preferred not to have the Rionda name "on any train station, building, or street."[53] Although Bianchi evidently aimed to flatter the Riondas more than anything else, his letter is useful because it summarizes some of their contributions. He thanked the "altruistic Sra. Elena Rionda de Doty" and the "venerable matron Doña Isidora Rionda" for their contributions to the poor within and outside Tuinucú's boundaries. Doña Isidora handed out blankets and jackets to protect the poor from the "glacial winter winds." The company gave workers' widows 40–50 pesos a month and celebrated holidays "with sympathetic camaraderie" among all of the workers, from the richest to the most humble, regardless of race or nationality. The Rionda family paid for the school, the hospital, the workers' homes, the recreation society, the park, and the post office. These, Bianchi said, "are all philanthropic works that elevate the population that was founded around this model sugarmill, which contributes greatly to the municipal treasury." The letter concluded: "He who arrives at Tuinucú to ask for help will find relief, to ask for bread will be fed, and all with a discreet smile. At Tuinucú, one breathes healthy air, of quiet and well-being, satisfied under the safeguard of the venerable matron Doña Isidora Rionda and the efficient help of all who assist her in her pious works."[54]

Bianchi expressed what other local residents certainly shared: an appreciation for the sugarmill that brought jobs and development to the region after the destruction of the nineteenth-century wars. Tuinucú's annual report for 1901–2 stated that "the disposition and discipline of the labor force have enabled us to make a great saving [in the cost of production]." That year, the mill spent $7,300 on day laborers' pay and $1,400 on salaries for office employees.[55] By 1923 Oliver Doty was proposing to give a total of $23,400 in bonuses to the workers and employees at the mill in addition to ninety-eight bags of sugar for employees with families who lived on the plantation.[56] Manuel Rionda told Doty to increase the bonuses to $31,000, commenting, "If we do not pay bonuses now that we are making money, we ought to be ashamed of ourselves for having reduced the salaries of our men in the hard times. You will always find me willing to reward in some substantial way—during the years of prosperity—the services of good, faithful, efficient employees."[57]

The "years of prosperity" clause is crucial; raises and bonuses would be eliminated in the lean years. Moreover, extreme inequality reigned between the salaries paid to the skilled employees and the modest wages paid to temporary day laborers. In 1922, Doty made roughly $20 a day all year long. During the three to six months of harvest, his superintendent Earl Hine made about $27 a day, and the top mechanic, Miguel López, made $10 a day. In contrast, regular mechanics averaged only $2.50 a day, and their assistants averaged $1.25; electricians averaged $3.00, and their assistants averaged $1.30; carpenters averaged $2.25, and construction workers, gardeners, and other workers in the mill town got from $1.10 to $3.10 a day.[58]

Although the letter from the worker's wife to El Mundo suggested that free housing and electricity made up for low wages, benefits at Tuinucú came with systems of control similar to those at Chaparra. During the negotiations surrounding the first general strike at Tuinucú in 1933, a labor minister reported: "The company says that it has always provided year-round housing, light, and water to its long-time workers and employees with families. It will continue to do so, but reserves the right to have families removed from the mill town if the company deems that they constitute a harmful or subversive element by their disorderly habits or customs."[59] Agustín Valdivia's experience is a case in point. Isidora was eventually able to help him and his family return to the mill, but the trauma of losing one's job and being forced to move elsewhere cannot be overstated.

This was especially true when the worker had a large family to support. Thomas Miller Klubock found that mining companies in Chile introduced programs to encourage marriage precisely to tie workers to the company and discourage them from risking their family homes.[60] By allocating houses to workers with families, managers at Tuinucú and Chaparra may in fact have encouraged male workers to marry and settle at the mill town. A more stable workforce had more to lose. This would be especially useful in the case of skilled mill or railroad workers, who were harder to train.

Manuel Rionda wanted to keep the mill town's housing limited to a select and controlled few. When Isidora asked him to give the Spanish store clerk Rafael Colunga and his new wife, Leonor, permission to build a home at Tuinucú, Manuel wrote: "I am willing for the Company to build it as a recompense for long, faithful services from Leonor, but at the Company's expense and as the Company's property. I do not like the idea of others owning houses in the mill town. It might be disagreeable some day, and we better not look for trouble."[61] Manuel had other reasons to limit the number of houses at the mill: Beyond one hundred, the "neighborhood" of Sancti Spiritus would become a "town" according to Cuban law. The town would be entitled to a mayor, and residents would have to pay higher taxes. The Cuban-American Sugar Company was wealthy enough—and the Cuban General Menocal "legitimate" enough—to co-opt the local administration at Puerto Padre; the Spanish Riondas and American Dotys might have had a harder time. The last thing Manuel Rionda wanted was to have to compete with a parallel system of municipal authority at "his" Tuinucú.

THE QUIET RESISTANCE TO THE PATRONS' RULE

Mill owners and managers borrowed from several traditions to establish social peace at their mills. These included patronage and philanthropy (bosses cultivating the image of themselves as "generous benefactors" to keep their dependents subdued); progressivism and Fordism (establishing limited social benefits that served as a form of social control); and time-honored repression (beatings or exile from the mill town). What the owners perceived as "charity" or calculated acts of appeasement, the workers and colonos likely considered rights.[62] The relationship of mill owners and managers such as Robert Hawley, the Menocals, and the Riondas to the colonos and workers of Chaparra and Tuinucú was profoundly ambiguous and always contingent on the mill owners' performance. Salaries, wages, and bonuses for workers and employees fluctuated drastically with the price of sugar, and residents' tolerance for control had limits.[63] Although no general strikes erupted at Chaparra or Tuinucú before 1925, smaller-scale negotiations took place daily between administrators, workers, and colonos.[64]

A rather casual aside in a letter from José Rionda to his uncle Manuel in 1911 suggests that small strikes were quite pervasive during these early years. "The strike of electric workers at Washington [sugarmill] is nothing; here it is rare to have a year without a small strike among the men who unload cane at the mill, or workers in the centrifuge department, etc. Last year we had to dismiss twenty-five such workers in one shot. . . . You are right to say that those classes of workers are annoying."[65] These strikes evidently suffered from the same problem as the 1917 strikes discussed earlier: They were limited to one group of workers within the larger mill community. The workers did not have the strength and support from other workers to win their demands or to protect themselves. The company was thus able to force them to leave their jobs and their homes.

The colono equivalent to strikes was to refuse to plant or sell cane. They used this tactic in 1905 when Tuinucú needed more cane to feed its higher-capacity machinery. Manager Pedro Alonso found farmers along the Cuba Company rail lines united in their stance to plant and sell cane to Tuinucú only if the mill would agree to pick up the cane at its own railroad sidings and pay the relatively high rate of 5 arrobas of sugar per 100 arrobas of cane.[66] Alonso reported to Rionda that the farmers eventually started planting cane but promised to sell only to "the best shepherd" in the area. Rionda penciled in "Sir William," indicating that the biggest competition for cane was William Van Horne's Jatibonico mill, east of Tuinucú along Van Horne's Cuba Company rail line.[67]

Field workers on Tuinucú's land also used the expanding mill's increased need for cane to demand their own terms. In April 1905 Alonso wrote that he needed one hundred men for various tasks during the whole month of May, but he could only get sixty men and he had to pay them "the salaries that they want" to clear and clean the cane fields.[68] The salaries ranged from $1.20 to $1.50 a day.

The cane fire was another strategy that colonos and field workers used on occasion to sell more cane, get more work, or improve working conditions. José advised Manuel Rionda on 9 February 1911 that a cane fire had begun at about 1:30 P.M. at the Caja de Agua colonia the previous day, but luckily, only three *cañaverales* burned (approximately 1.25 million pounds of cane), and they were able to redirect carts and workers from other colonias to cut and harvest the cane within two or three days. José was sure that the fire was intentional because it had started in the center of the cane field where no cuts had been made and where the most damage could be done because of the direction the wind was blowing.[69] Accidental fires were caused by a passerby's discarded cigarette butt or sparks from a train; in both cases, the fire would start beside the road or railroad, not in the center of the field. It had to have been a worker or the colono who set the Caja de Agua fields on fire.

In February 1918 the *Louisiana Planter and Sugar Manufacturer* stated that it was "not at all uncommon" for Cuban colonos to set their own fields on fire, "especially when labor is scarce," because the mill would transfer personnel and carts to try to harvest and grind the cane immediately before it lost all its sucrose.[70] The motivation to burn was high for the workers, as well, because burned cane fields signified more work and more pay—more work because colonos and mill owners usually opted to cut burned fields even if they had not intended to harvest them that particular year; faster work, because the fires took away the weeds and leaves that the workers otherwise would have to cut through.[71] Government agencies (Cuban and foreign), mill owners, and planters collected statistics and reports on cane fires only sporadically, so it is not possible to state conclusively when and how often this kind of "everyday" form of cane fire took place. Nevertheless, diplomatic, company, and newspaper archives suggest that there was an increase in cane fires during the 1920s and 1930s for reasons addressed in chapters 6 through 8.

Arson was risky. If a worker was caught lighting a cane fire, he would certainly lose his job; he would also be put in jail or made to pay a substantial fine. The novel *The Cockpit* by James Gould Cozzens, written after the author spent a year teaching English at Tuinucú, tells the story of a field manager who shot a worker because the foreman thought he saw the man holding a match by a colonia cane fire. The manager and foreman hid the body because the foreman was not absolutely sure he had seen the match.

The fact that they hid the body because they were not sure suggests that had they been sure, the shooting would have been publicly recognized as justified.[72] Ursinio Rojas wrote in his memoirs about life at the Tacajó sugarmill in the 1920s and 1930s: "If there was a cane fire, the guards made workers put it out and then detained anyone considered 'suspicious' and all who had matches in their pockets."[73]

Sabotage constituted another high-profile form of resistance. In April 1902, Silvestre Rionda reported to his half-brother Manuel: "Someone threw a one-inch nail into the mill the day before yesterday, at 5:00 in the morning, damaging the millstone in various places. We have not been able to determine who did it."[74] Manuel wrote to Isidora at the end of the 1906–1907 harvest that he feared there was a "bad person" at Tuinucú who was "throwing sugar into the ditch." "I am beginning to suspect that someone wanting to hurt me has placed a traitor at the mill," he confided.[75] As the 1907–1908 harvest approached, Manuel hired more Americans to work at Tuinucú and warned all his nephews to "keep an eye out for unfaithful employees."[76] His use of the word "unfaithful" underscores his conviction that the mill community was like a family to which all had to be loyal. Since the intricate machinery of the mills made them highly vulnerable to sabotage, companies tried to bar anyone but workers from entering the factories; as late as March 1937, Chaparra's general manager complained about the dangers of *chiquillos* (workers' little children) carrying packets and coffee to the men working their shifts.[77]

Without putting themselves or their jobs in danger, colonos and workers could engage in more subtle negotiations. For example, to cut corners, colonos could plant the shoots from one season's harvest to grow cane the next (instead of buying new seeds) or they could skimp on the number of workers they hired to weed their fields. When the Great Depression hit in 1929, colonos at Tuinucú refused to buy seed from the company. Instead they planted new fields and replanted old with their own, "infected" seeds.[78] In the end, the company had to give seed to the colonos, which cost it more than $13,000. A similar negotiation took place surrounding the colonos' neglect of the fields that same year. The company ended up forgiving a lot of debt and lending a lot more money to colonos because field inspectors found that the rented colonias needed more attention to be kept in shape for future harvests.[79]

After months of exhausting work in the hot, stinking, noisy mills, workers insisted on stopping during holidays such as Christmas and Easter. Company letters from December and April were invariably filled with complaints of production slowdowns. Mill owners eventually added unofficial worker holidays to the harvest schedule. On 6 April 1903 Pedro Alonso wrote to Manuel that the weather was perfect for milling, but the holiday parties were throwing everything off. "It will be impossible to mill until April 15," he grumbled, "because the workers will surely refuse to cut before April 13."[80]

Lateness or absenteeism on what bosses sarcastically labeled "Saint Monday" (after late-night partying on Sunday) was less faithfully practiced in Cuban mill towns than elsewhere because mill jobs were highly coveted for the social benefits and salaries—albeit minimal and varying—that they offered.[81] During the early years of the twentieth century and a few of the wartime years (e.g., 1917–19 and 1941–45) the demand for mill workers seems to have outstripped supply, but most seasons, men hoping for jobs would form long lines outside the main offices or gates of each mill. Ursinio Rojas described how, when the bell rang once after six hours, workers would flood out of the mill to make room for their replacements, who raced in before the door closed again because if a worker was late, he would lose six hours' pay.[82]

Workers used petty thievery and trickery as subtle forms of resistance to company rule. Chaparra cane weighers' reports are filled with complaints about the sticks that field workers interspersed within the cane so that their cuttings would weigh more and they could get more pay. Company police files indicate that workers regularly cut down trees from outlying forests on company land without permission, and they stole planks, iron objects, and paint to use to build or fix homes. They also stole telephone cable to tie up the animals that they kept in their backyards to provide food during the dead season or extra income year-round. Such animals included pigs, chickens, goats, and fighting cocks.[83]

The workers' small-scale animal husbandry and construction of their own homes constituted assertions of autonomy against company control. Workers built houses without permission, squatted in older houses or unoccupied cabins, or exceeded the maximum number of people allowed in official homes. One letter from a Chaparra employee to General Manager R. B. Wood reveals how closely monitored employee housing was. The author, the employee Manuel Fernández Pupo of the central office, had been asked to leave his room in the employee residence despite the fact that he never fell short in "moral behavior" or "made an attempt to hurt the interests of the company." He named several witnesses who could testify that he needed the residence and slept there every night. During the day he went to do the cleaning "because, as you know, those of us without work during the dead season must clean the floors and make our beds." He added that on moving into the room, he personally repaired the doors, windows, latches, and closets. The final paragraph of his letter reveals the real reason he was probably being asked to leave: "They may have informed you that I have a house, which is true; but it is also true that my house is very small for our twelve family members and it is therefore completely impossible for me to stay with them. Because of this, I hope that you will be benevolent and just in allowing me to stay in the employee residence or in the old hotel; and I promise that I will be the first to keep order and decency."[84]

The author's mentions of "moral behavior" and "cleanliness" reveal that the company shared the obsession with cleanliness and health that other progressives across the Americas espoused.[85] Cleanliness provided an excuse for the company to seek a monopoly over provision of food and housing at the mill. The company police would chase after and arrest any "outsider" found trying to smuggle in and sell meat to the mill community, and they drew up lists of people who violated "sanitary dispositions" by keeping animals in backyards or on roofs in the mill town and Pueblo Viejo. Not surprisingly, well-paid employees in the mill town committed fewer such violations than workers in Pueblo Viejo. For the Pueblo Viejo's more humble families, the animals constituted a source of security.[86]

Despite the mill owners' efforts at control, itinerant vendors would flood the mill towns on paydays to collect debts and tempt workers with food and consumer goods, cockfights, dances, concerts, alcohol, and sex. Ursinio Rojas mentions that these activities continued throughout the Depression era; the quantities were simply smaller, and the prices were cheaper. Three cigarettes would be sold for a cent instead of a case for a dollar, and the same applied to other divisible items, such as one banana or lemon (versus a dozen).[87] Not all of the vendors were outsiders. Some were residents of the mill trying to eke out an existence on their own or to supplement family incomes. This aspect of life at Chaparra is not well documented, but there are hints that workers' wives (as well as Asian and Caribbean immigrants) grew fruit and vegetables to sell, did laundry for employees, and set up makeshift cafeterias to sell snacks and drinks to mill residents. Such activities provided alternative means of support for the sellers and a way around company control for the purchasers. As such, these "informal" activities were extremely important.

Examples of subtle means of resistance in the form of "counter-theater" against the power holders abound (such as the Tuinucú workers' "ash ball"). In one such case, a worker purposely provoked the administrator at Tuinucú most obsessed with cleanliness—*Míster* Hine. After cleaning their workspace meticulously, just the way Hine demanded, the workers decided to smudge some oil on the railing exactly where Hine would grab it when he entered to inspect. When Hine touched the oil and yelped in disgust at the black on his hands, the workers broke down and laughed until their eyes watered.[88] At Chaparra, employees undermined the ultimate symbol of patrons' power—General Menocal's former chalet—by regularly taking prostitutes from Puerto Padre there when the lights were off.[89] Counter-theater offers a useful explanation for the fact that one of the first things workers did at Chaparra and Tuinucú upon the triumph of the 1959 Revolution was to completely burn down Menocal's and Rionda's chalets. But we need to see what happened during the decades that intervened between the two mills' "Golden Eras" and the 1959 Revolution before we can understand this violent rejection.

During the first two decades of the twentieth century, Cuban sugar community managers and their American corporate sponsors embarked on large-scale urbanization and social-welfare projects that created stable and prosperous initial eras for the Chaparra and Tuinucú communities. Sugarmill owners in the East, West, and Center practiced common managerial strategies combining elements of patronage, progressivism, and repression to control workers and colonos. But these projects expanded and contracted along with the sugar prices, and when the economy crashed in 1921, regional differences became more prominent. This was at least in part because Cubans themselves (mostly colonos, but also journalists and authors such as Ramiro Guerra y Sánchez) began to emphasize the predominance of large U.S.-owned sugarmill enclaves in the East versus smaller mills in the West that purchased cane from independent Cuban cane farmers. An ecological factor also explains the growth of the "East versus West" paradigm. Colonos in the East received a smaller percentage of sugar than colonos in the

West for every 100 arroba unit of cane that they sold to a mill. In the early twentieth century, colonos in the East were harvesting virgin land and could therefore get more than 100 arroba units of cane from the same quantity of land as their counterparts in the older cane lands of the West and Center. By the 1920s, the quality of the land in the East was probably leveling off with that of the West, thereby justifying the eastern colonos' demands for the same percentage as their western and central counterparts. Beginning with a narrative of the seismic economic and political changes arising out of the First World War, the remainder of this study focuses on how cane farmers first, and then workers, sought to forge solidarity to win benefits from mill owners and from the Cuban state at Puerto Padre, Tuinucú, and elsewhere on the island between 1919 and 1959.

6 In the early 1920s, economic conditions drove desperate workers to torch cane fields with increasing frequency.[1] The cane fires of 1921 and 1922 reflected broader tensions in Cuba's political, social, and economic system. During the era of sustained expansion of the Cuban sugar industry from 1900 to 1920, what was good for U.S. investors was generally good for Cuban sugar interests. Foreign holdings outstripped Cuban ones, but the island's share of the world sugar market grew enough to produce profits for all. Cuban intellectuals tended to see the U.S. presence as a positive force and blamed social and political problems on Cuban "decadence" and "cultural decline."[2] This changed when sugar prices plummeted in 1921 and U.S. policy exacerbated the crisis by raising the tariff on Cuban sugar. American capitalists fared significantly better than their Cuban counterparts, upsetting Cubans even more.[3] Cuban nationalism therefore fused with anti-imperialism among Cuban intellectuals, colonos, and workers alike. Authors and journalists began to speak of the "alienation" of Cuban land and the "proletarianization" of Cuban producers.[4]

Liberal President Gerardo Machado, who earned the title "dictator" in the 1930s, acted more like a populist during his 1924 presidential campaign and first year in power. He tapped into popular sentiment, promising protection for Cuban industry, roads, schools, and other benefits for the Cuban population. The 1924–25 elections represented Cuba's first shift from a system of rule based on caudillos and patrons to a more nationalist, interventionist state. Instead of caudillos distributing favors only to their political clients, this was the promise of national, social reform for humble and fortunate Cubans alike, regardless of party affiliation. A similar shift took place at the local level. Colonos, railroad, sugar, and dock workers across the island, unsatisfied with the patronage that gave them benefits only at the whim of their bosses and encouraged by the nationalist tone of the elections, demanded more lasting social benefits and a larger share of the sugar economy from the state.

Colonos responded to Machado's populist rhetoric by positioning themselves as Cuba's wronged middle-class yeomanry—the middle-class farmers that U.S. President Thomas Jefferson had once claimed would create a stable democratic society in North America. Especially at the large eastern sugarmills such as Chaparra and Francisco, Cuban colonos organized and sought Machado's assistance to negotiate with the large foreign sugar companies that purchased their cane. When Chaparra and Delicias colonos went on strike in 1925, Machado sought their support by serving as mediator between colono and company. These and other colonos won some battles with individual companies and also pushed Machado to introduce limited state reforms that benefited cane farmers across the island. For example, when prices started to decline in late 1925 because of overproduction of sugar worldwide and Machado decided to curb the Cuban supply, he assigned specific cane quotas to protect each colono.

The workers also used the electoral opening. The 1924–25 strike wave taught workers that the best way to counter the power of the patrons was to forge solidarity across occupational, ethnic, and class barriers. The National Confederation of Cuban Workers (CNOC)—one of the most important tools workers used to forge this solidarity—was formed in 1925, as was the Communist Party of Cuba (PCC), which would provide many of the most active and disciplined leaders of the incipient sugar workers' movement.[5] Rather than passing nationalist reforms as he did for colonos, Machado's regime brutally repressed workers after his inauguration in May 1925. In other words, colonos escaped the state's shift back to exclusion, but workers did not.

The political and economic climate of the early 1920s and the presidential elections of 1924 created a "populist moment" for colonos and workers to demand benefits from capitalists and the state while the sugar economy was on the upswing. The nationalist movements of the 1920s prepared cane farmers and workers to win more benefits during two other periods of political opening: the revolution of 1933, a moment of extreme economic depression, and the period of roughly 1939–45, when the Second World War increased both sugar prices and popular rights. Colonos were most successful when they maintained a united front of small-, medium-, and large-sized farmers and recruited national support through other sectors of the community and the media. The nationalistic climate of the 1920s made it easier for colonos at the foreign-owned eastern mills to win demands. Workers won the most benefits when leaders such as Enrique Varona, Eduardo Bertot, and Armando de la Pera united railroad, dock, cane-field, and sugar-factory workers, as well as the farmers and merchants of the surrounding region. The agricultural cycle affected both worker and colono movements: Strikes by colonos and railroad, dock, and sugar workers tended to be most effective when staged during the fall months (before) or the winter months (during) Cuba's sugar-harvest season.[6]

In the fall and winter of 1921 and 1922 Oliver Doty and Manuel Rionda exchanged a series of letters about cane burnings and colono policy at Tuinucú that reveal the complex relationships between workers, colonos, and managers in the context of low sugar prices. We need to understand these relationships to comprehend the rebellions and protests that are the subject of this chapter. During the late 1910s, Tuinucú used bonuses as incentives to reward colonos who did a thorough job of plowing and replanting their fields. Colonos were not eligible for these bonuses if their cane had been burned, because the company did not want to encourage cane fires.[7] In March 1921, though, the bonuses were not enough to motivate the colonos. Despite what Doty described as an "unusually high number" of burned cane fields, most colonos were opting not to tend their fields. They had borrowed only $5,000—against $32,000 the previous year—for cultivation and replanting and had prepared very little land. When colonos chose not to plow and replant their fields, workers had no jobs. This explains Doty's conclusion that the fires had been set "almost entirely" by field labor to try to force colonos to hire them for harvesting and replanting.

"In view of the special conditions this year," Doty told his uncle, "that is, the comparatively low price of cane compared with the price of production, and also the large amount of cane which has been burned, [we should make] an exception to our rule and help the colonos cultivate their fields which have been burned accidentally."[8] Manuel Rionda granted his request, authorizing additional bonuses of $20,000. The colonos desperately needed the cash, as Doty reported in August 1921 that "all owe considerable amounts of money to their workmen for work done."[9] Over the following months, Rionda granted Doty's requests not to collect colonos' rent, to stop charging interest, and to guarantee a fixed minimum price for cane. If the price of sugar quoted in Havana or Cienfuegos increased, the company would credit the colonos the extra at the end of the year, but if it decreased, their accounts would not be deducted. "We want our colonos to feel that we wish to share in all their difficulties and bear a good portion of their losses," Rionda explained. "I think our plan of having the colonos run our fate is better [even though] that may mean a heavy loss to us if we base the price on expected high prices for sugar and we do not get them."[10] Doty concurred: "If we wish to have any cane to speak of next year it is necessary to instill a certain amount of enthusiasm among our colonos and this is quite impossible with the present prices as quoted in Havana and Cienfuegos. To my mind it is far better for the company to lose $15,000 or $20,000 than to have our colonos lose money and stop cultivation. This latter would cost us far more in the long run."[11] The manager and the owner of Tuinucú were not alone. Many mill owners had the foresight to forgive debts and try to help their colonos out in the immediate aftermath of the 1921 sugar-price crash.

Such concessions helped Tuinucú and other small to medium-size mills across the island weather the turbulent 1920s with a lot of cane fires but no major strikes among workers and colonos. This was not the case for larger mills, especially the ones in the East, such as Chaparra, that had foreign owners, Cuban colonos, and a mix of Cuban and foreign workers. When the 1921 crisis hit, many colonos stopped tending their fields, and field workers consequently lost their jobs. Companies simultaneously cut back on salaries, wages, and bonuses, pushing factory workers and employees into the growing realm of the discontented and unemployed. Workers at sugarmills in the East began to organize and protest at the same time as colonos, but each "class" did so independently; there was a gap between the worker and colono movements. This chapter reflects the gap by moving from workers to colonos and back again in order to stay true to the contemporary developments and the relationships between worker activism, colono organization, and the state's responses to both.

FROM PATRONAGE TO POPULISM, 1914–1924

From 1914 through 1920, Cuba's economy gradually improved as the average price per pound of raw sugar in New York tripled from 2.15 cents in 1913 to 6.35 cents in early 1919. The price rose because the war increased the demand for sugar, destroyed European beet sugar, and prompted U.S. politicians to lower the tariff on Cuban imports. Cuban and foreign capitalists expanded existing mills and constructed some twenty-five new mills on the island, total production shooting up from 2.6 million tons in 1915 to 4 million in 1919.[12] Cane replaced other crops and Cuba began to import more of its food from abroad.

The island's economy grew, but the growth took a very specific form: Cubans and foreigners established most of the new sugarmills in the Center and East following the enclave principle set by Hawley's Chaparra and Rionda's Francisco. Whenever possible, the sugar corporations built their own ports and railroads to service the mill so they could export sugar and import all the products they needed, largely free of taxes and state legislation. Menocal legalized sixteen sub-ports that serviced forty-seven "North American" plantations during his term in office.[13] As at Chaparra and Delicias, owners of enclave sugarmills established near-monopolies over the supply and sale of food and goods. They frustrated independent merchants and farmers by refusing to allow "outsiders" to use the railroads or sell their products in mill and colonia commissary stores. They paid in tokens to be used exclusively at these stores (or exchanged for cash, at a loss).[14] Many mills also became the sole providers of utilities to the surrounding towns and cities of their region.

The new enclave mills of the East brought jobs and prosperity to sparsely populated regions, attracting new migrants from elsewhere on the island as well as immigrants from abroad. At least initially, residents enjoyed great potential for upward mobility. A lighter-skinned Cuban or Spanish father might become a colono, his daughter a clerk at the company store, and his wife and sons field hands on the colonia. As time passed, many colonos moved on to become merchants, municipal employees, and even mayors.

Their sons might become skilled factory or office employees at the sugar-mill, dock, railroad, or electricity plant—or all of the above at different points in their careers. All but the highest-paid employees needed to supplement their incomes during the so-called dead season by seeking temporary jobs. Families supplemented their incomes by fishing, hunting, or cultivating food in family or friends' colonias or in kitchen gardens adjacent to the family home. Some had to travel farther afield, seeking temporary work at coffee, rice, or tobacco plantations or in Cuba's growing cities.

From 1900 to 1920 Oriente's enclave sugarmills remained more or less peaceful, and the Cuban media praised them as harbingers of progress and modernity. Their socially explosive, nationalist potential only became apparent in 1921, when residents of the enclave communities decided that they should demand better conditions. The fluid nature of work and the common experience of enclave capitalism created the conditions for an oppositional movement against the company that united local residents across occupational, class, race, and ethnic lines. Such movements occurred both during depressions (as in 1921 and 1933) and during eras of growing prosperity (as in 1925 and 1941).[15]

Cuban and Cuban American producers rejoiced when the United States and Britain lifted price controls in late 1919 and the price of sugar skyrocketed to an all-time high of 22.5 cents per pound. However, so many Cuban producers held their sugar in hopes of even higher prices that sugar from Java, the Philippines, Mauritius, and elsewhere flooded the market, pushing prices back down.[16] This sugar, coupled with Cuba's remaining surplus from the 1919–20 crop, continued to push down prices in 1921 so that the commodity's average price that year was only 3.43 cents.[17] Many Cuban planters and colonos who had secured loans to buy or expand during the high 1919 and 1920 "Dance of the Millions" prices lost land and mills to their predominantly North American creditors. Between 1919 and 1920, almost one quarter of the 198 mills on the island changed hands. In 1921, most of these exchanges went temporarily to Canadian and U.S. banks because of bank foreclosures.[18]

Cuban nationalist resentment increased as the islanders watched foreign-owned banks take over property and mills while over-extended Cuban banks went bankrupt. Menocal declared a temporary bank moratorium in October 1920, but 334 branches of 19 Cuban banks went under in the 1920–21 crisis. They did not have access to the emergency funds available to American and Canadian banks.[19] North American sugar plantations also survived the crisis better than Cubans chiefly because of better access to credit, vertical integration, and economies of scale. At this dire economic moment, U.S. producers of cane sugar in Hawaii, Puerto Rico, and the Philippines and beet sugar on the mainland pushed through an "emergency tariff increase" on Cuban sugar exports to the United States.[20] The Cuban intellectual Herminio Portell Vilá assessed the effect of such protectionism in a language that eloquently reflects Cuban nationalist sentiment: "A difference of half a cent in the tariff . . . represents the difference between a national tragedy in which everything is cut, from the nation's budget to the . . . alms handed to a beggar, and a so-called state of prosperity, whose benefits never reach the people as a whole or profit Cuba as a nation."[21]

Meanwhile, in the political realm Cubans had yet another reason to be angry about U.S. power. The economic crisis of 1920–21 coincided with a political crisis on the island: the violently contested election campaign between José Miguel Gómez and his nemesis, the liberal lawyer Alfredo Zayas.[22] The conservative caudillo Mario García Menocal supported Zayas in exchange for his promise to give him back the presidency in 1925. He used the same coercive means to get Zayas elected in November 1920 as he had used to reelect himself in November 1916—stuffing ballots, taking away liberals' voting cards, placing pro-administration "military supervisors" at the polls, and so on.[23] The liberals threatened to start a "revolution" in 1921, as they had in 1906 and 1917, to protest electoral fraud. U.S. politicians responded to the crisis by sending Special Representative Enoch Crowder with orders to impose a sweeping reorganization on the Cuban government. This included the replacement of members of Zayas's cabinet and drastic cutbacks in the nation's budget, all under the auspices of Article 2 of the Platt Amendment. This blatant political intervention, combined with the budget cutbacks, undermined the Cuban political system that was already openly allied to U.S. authority.[24]

As the economic crisis prompted by sugar became linked in popular lore to U.S. policy and Cuban political corruption, many Cubans began to organize against the mono-economic body politic forged by the Platt Amendment and the Reciprocity Treaty on the nominally "free" island.[25] Given the increasing disparities between Cuban- and American-owned companies and banks, elite Cubans, colonos, and workers began to call for nationalist protection. One immediate effect of this anti-foreign sentiment was the forced deportation of Haitian and Jamaican laborers after the sugar harvest of 1921. All the same, big sugarmills in the East continued to import Caribbean labor on a smaller scale through the 1920s out of fear that a contraction in the labor supply would lead to higher wages.

Growing nationalism explains why sugar workers at the foreign-owned Narcisa and Victoria sugarmills in northern Santa Clara won popular support when they declared a strike in November 1923 to demand better salaries and immediate payment of four months' worth of late salaries.[26] The Rural Guard occupied the sugarmills and arrested the union leaders, but the strike continued. The few independent commercial establishments in the area closed in solidarity. In the end, the company agreed to pay workers every two weeks, increase their salaries by 15–30 cents a day, and give the detained workers their jobs back. The importance of community solidarity should be noted, as should the timing: It was November, the month before the sugar harvest was to begin.

Nationalist coalitions grew in urban Cuba, as well, influencing Havana politicians and giving the 1924 elections a populist hue that was not present in earlier Cuban elections. Julio Antonio Mella formed the University Students' Federation (FEU), the Anti-Imperialist League of Cuba, and the José Martí Popular University for workers. The intellectuals Rubén Martínez Villena and Juan Marinello led protests against administrative corruption and advocated Cuban intellectual regeneration. A group called the Veterans and Patriots movement that included veterans, colonos, women, professionals, and Afro-Cubans made similar demands. The movement lost momentum due to a combination of repression, co-optation, and moderate recovery in the national economy on the one side and support for Zayas from U.S. policy and the Cuban military on the other.[27] However, General Gerardo Machado absorbed much of the movement's rhetoric into his campaign for presidency in the November 1924 elections.

Previous election campaigns included certain vague promises to "the people," but they were small in contrast to those made in 1924. As we have seen, power passed largely from one president to the next through the caudillo–clientele, coup, and reelection patterns familiar to other Latin American nations. Machado's campaign promised something different: "water, roads, and schools." In contrast to the caudilloesque conservative campaign showing General Menocal on horseback, the liberals depicted Machado among the masses with the slogan "on foot, with the people."[28]

WORKERS USE THE POPULIST MOMENT: 1924–1925

Case studies from Mexico, Brazil, Nicaragua, and elsewhere have demonstrated that in populist political systems, workers and farmers get increased leverage around election time.[29] Oscar Zanetti's and Alejandro García's discussion of Cuban railroad workers proves this to be the case for that sector in 1924–25, and the case of Cuban workers and cane farmers at Puerto Padre demonstrate the same for Cuba's sugar sector. The nationalist tone of the elections inspired workers and colonos across the island to make demands. The liberals responded with a combination of populist co-optation and repression. Elections would not be held until November 1924, but as early as January 1924, Machado's supporters maneuvered to make the future presidential candidate look like a fair mediator between labor and capital. This strategy became especially pronounced during the period between November 1924 (when Machado was elected) and May 1925 (when he took power). This populist moment gave workers the space to organize and make demands on a larger scale than ever before. Many responded by forging unity across social and regional divisions.

The railroad workers were among the first to organize nationally, creating the Railroad Workers' Brotherhood in February 1924. Tobacco, railroad, dock, and sugar workers had to overcome the tradition of specific occupational guilds (that divided each sector from within since colonial times) before further national unions could be forged. Companies often tried to exploit these divisions. For example, when the Repair Shop Union and the Brotherhood of Engineers, Stokers, and Telegraph Operators declared a joint strike and called on workers in other divisions of the U.S.-owned Cuba Railroad Company to join them in mid-December 1923, the company "viewed the strike as a test of strength . . . and expected to obtain substantial advantages from it" by making concessions to the Brotherhood in exchange for their breaking with the more radical Repair Shop Union.[30]

The workers managed to maintain solidarity in this case, prompting Camagüey's liberal caudillo and Governor Rogerio Zayas-Bazán to send a mediator: presidential candidate Gerardo Machado. Machado met with the owners' representatives in Havana to draw up a formula that drastically reduced most of the workers' demands. He then met with two railroad leaders in Havana before proceeding to Camagüey. Company correspondence states that Machado "spent a great deal of time" making sure that the two

leaders (Abelardo Adán and Juan Arévalo) would support the reduced demands. The latter were apparently "eager" to end the strike because "they
personally [were] out of money and [gave] the impression that the Brotherhood [was] also short of cash." The railroad leaders opted to cooperate with
the capitalists, signing on to Machado's formula.[31]

Machado posed as an "impartial judge" when he arrived in Camagüey on
2 January, going through the motions of what Zanetti and García describe as
a "planned farce" meticulously. He advised the workers to change their tune,
told them of Adán's and Arévalo's decision, and made them believe that
their cause was lost. He then proposed to offer the minimal reforms that
the company's representatives had told him they were willing to concede.
Two days later, just in time for the sugar harvest, President Zayas was able
to announce jubilantly that the conflict was over. The authors conclude that
"many railroad workers went back to work thinking that the little they had
gained was due to the 'good offices' of Gerardo Machado."[32]

Perhaps we should give the workers more credit. They may have seen
through the farce but opted to take limited concessions over no concessions
in light of their Havana leaders' decision and the company's usual intransigence. One concrete conclusion that we can draw from the episode is that
politicians believed it necessary to portray themselves as impartial mediators. This was a change from the more openly repressive second regime of
Menocal (1917–21), and it reflected the growing importance of nationalism
and populism in Cuban politics of the 1920s.

Other worker strikes demonstrate the importance of solidarity and political and agricultural timing. In a region on the north coast of Camagüey
dominated in the early 1920s by sugar and railroad companies, a labor leader
named Enrique Varona set the important precedent of uniting railroad
workers (of the Ferrocarril del Norte), sugar workers (in the mills served
by the Ferrocarril), and stevedores (at the Ferrocarril's Puerto Tarafa) in
a single cross-sector organization called the Unión de Morón. Like other
important leaders who emerged in the 1930s and 1940s, Varona believed
in forging a broad oppositional movement because he had experience as a
worker in several different sectors before becoming a labor leader. Born in
the tobacco-dominated province of Pinar del Rio, he worked for some time
as a cigar maker, which is likely where he acquired his anarcho-syndicalist
convictions. He then took a job at the Patria sugarmill in Morón as a stoker

before moving up to the position of engineer. In 1920, he took an engineering position at the Ferrocarril del Norte de Cuba.[33]

Varona's Unión de Morón was so impressive because through it, sugar workers were able to unite with dock and railway workers. The latter had managed to organize more fully than sugar workers in the late nineteenth century and early twentieth because they tended to have longer-term employment than their counterparts in sugar. As mentioned earlier, when the spring sugar harvest ended, all but the most highly paid sugar workers routinely sought temporary employment or farming opportunities elsewhere. They returned to the mill only in the late fall to prepare for the next harvest. Organizing workers in the cane fields and creating unity between field and factory was especially challenging after 1917. This was due to the infusion of temporary agricultural workers from across the Caribbean, which added linguistic and ethnic barriers to the extant class and occupational differences. Moreover, during and after the strikes of 1917 and 1918, company armed forces and the Cuban Rural Guard increased the level of surveillance over sugar workers in factory and fields.[34]

In September 1924 the Union de Morón railroad workers boycotted freight from the sugarmills they serviced when the sugar companies refused to pay in cash rather than tokens and refused to recognize their workers as members of the union. The sugar companies convinced the military supervisor of Camagüey to have Varona and other leaders arrested on 15 October. The union responded that it would call a strike unless its leaders were released within seventy-two hours. Concerned about the inconvenience a railroad strike would create for the presidential election, the secretary of the interior and governor, Zayas-Bazán, freed Varona and his supporters.[35] Railroad workers went on strike regardless to protest the fact that the army was forcing striking sugar workers to leave their homes and jobs at the sugarmills. Stevedores and day laborers at Puerto Tarafa declared a solidarity strike, rendering the economic paralysis complete. The timing was ideal for the workers: The general election drew near, and preparations for the next sugarcane harvest became ever more pressing. On 28 October the strike ended well for the workers. The sugar companies agreed to all of their demands.

The successful strike inspired sugar workers at other mills in Camagüey to demand the same concessions, backed by the new Provincial Trade Union

of Camagüeyan Workers that Enrique Varona had created in recognition of
the strategic importance of sugar workers. Several trade-union organizations in the province of Oriente supported the strike, including the Railroad
Brotherhoods of Guantánamo and Santiago de Cuba.[36] Apparently, they
recognized the logic of cross-sector organization (strength in numbers), as
well as the timely political and agricultural moment for making demands.
When army troops failed to break the movement, the government prevailed
on the companies to consider the workers' demands. The strike ended in the
workers' favor, on the eve of the 1924–25 sugar harvest.[37]

As these movements were developing in Camagüey, workers and cane
farmers at Chaparra and Delicias also began to organize. It is not surprising
that Puerto Padre was home to the first powerful local colono association
as well as the first self-identified "sugar" union to incorporate dock and mill
workers, with very close ties to the Railroad Brotherhood of Puerto Padre.[38]
Puerto Padre constituted one of the most extreme cases of "enclave control."
Cubanaco, the owner of Chaparra, Delicias, and several other mills and refineries in Cuba and the United States, provided all of the light and power
to the surrounding cities and towns, including Holguín, Las Tunas, Gibara,
and Puerto Padre. It owned the private port called Cayo Juan Claro and
controlled all of the railroads in the Puerto Padre region, giving the mills'
massive commercial departments a near-monopoly over the sale of goods
in the mill towns and colonias. A report from 1921 stated that Chaparra and
Delicias, "which are operated as a single unit, form the largest sugar estate
in the world." By 1931 Chaparra comprised 260,000 acres of land; Delicias
comprised 130,000 acres. Combined, the two mills were capable of producing 1.8 million bags of sugar per year.[39]

Cubanaco's regional domination allowed the corporation to give colono
sharecroppers a smaller share of sugar profits and to pay lower wages to
workers. The U.S. consul of the Antilla district reported in May 1922 that
labor costs on the large north-coast enclave estates—including Chaparra
and Delicias, the United Fruit Company mills farther east, and the Riondas' Manatí Sugar Company farther west—were 40 percent lower than
elsewhere on the island.[40] Since colonos were the first to protest these inequalities at Puerto Padre in 1924, and they did so as a "class," this chapter
now turns to a broader discussion of Cuban colonos and how they fit into
early-twentieth-century Cuban society.

THE MAKING OF THE COLONO CLASS

Ramiro Guerra's *Sugar and Society in the Antilles*, perhaps the most influential example of Cuban nationalist literature in the 1920s, argued that Cuba's colonos were the equivalent to America's yeoman, the rural middle-class base that could ensure the sociopolitical stability of the nation. He argued that the *colonato* (colono system) needed protection from administration cane—the system whereby large American corporations purchased all the land, then produced cane directly using company workers. His nationalist argument was strengthened by the fact that many of these workers were not Cubans but foreign immigrants from the Caribbean.

Since the publication of *Sugar and Society*, several studies have used aggregate national statistics from 1910 through 1940 to demonstrate that Guerra's prophesy about the disappearance of the colono was inaccurate but that Guerra was correct to assert that the "sugarmill colono" (tenant colono) of the East was becoming more common than the "independent colono" (land-owning colono) of the West.[41] Based on the same statistics, these studies add that colonos won more benefits than any other sector of Cuban society after the 1933 Revolution. Such national-level statistics and conclusions lead to a series of questions that can only be answered at the local level. How did colonos—tenant and independent alike—at Chaparra, Tuinucú, and elsewhere on the island manage to get so much out of the 1933 Revolution? As we will see in chapter 7, they were not in the front lines bombing buildings, shooting politicians, or occupying mills and taking mill owners hostage. The soldiers of the revolution were students and field and factory workers. As one observer noted during the revolution, "The colonos are standing by, smoking their pipes while they wait to see what they can get out of the revolution."[42]

The rest of this chapter and the next demonstrate that the colono triumphs of the 1930s came out of the successful nationalistic campaign they began in the 1920s, Guerra's book being the most prominent and lasting reflection of this campaign. The chapter seeks to define who the so-called sugarmill colonos were; how they thought of themselves; and how they interacted with the company, the workers, the community, and the nation. In the 1920s and 1930s, colonos at Chaparra and Delicias adopted nationalist language and what one might call "anti-imperialist enclave politics." They portrayed themselves as both the downtrodden Cuban farmers of the nation and (collectively) the largest employers of Cuban labor, worthy of support from the Cuban president so they could guarantee the stability of Cuban society. A brief recap of the colonato is necessary here to sketch out colono–management relations before the conflictive 1920s.

The colonato emerged in the late nineteenth century, when the Cuban sugar industry divided into industrial sugarmills surrounded by agrarian colonias. This was in response to post-emancipation shortages of labor, shortages of capital brought on by Spanish fiscal policy, damage by the wars for independence, and the planters' need to modernize production to compete with cheap European beet sugar.[43] Colonos grew cane on their own land or on land rented from the sugarmill, which they then cut, hauled, and sold to the mill in exchange for cash or a specified percentage of raw sugar. When sugar prices increased between 1891 and 1894 under the favorable reciprocity treaty with the United States, some colonos began to organize to demand a larger percentage of sugar.[44] The third independence war largely paralyzed sugar production on the island, essentially stopping colono–planter negotiations on the mills from 1895 to 1898.

Perhaps in response to the threat of colono organization, at least a few mills in central and western Cuba opted to produce more sugar without colonos when postwar reconstruction began. For example, the Rionda family decided to cultivate much of the land surrounding Tuinucú directly rather than renew colono contracts.[45] Francisco Rionda's son Manolo wrote to his uncle Manuel in February 1905: "*Cheap* cane has been the secret of our success at Tuinucú and we ought to always be independent of *outside* colonos."[46] Tuinucú, like most other mills in the Center and West, was nevertheless forced to buy at least some cane from landowning colonos because the company had neither the capital nor the workers to buy, clear, and cultivate enough land to supply the large sugarmill.

Mill owners sought to design colono contracts that were as inflexible as possible, tying colonos to a specific rate of return in exchange for their cane during an eight- to ten-year period. Colonos could threaten to sell their cane to another mill when the time came to renegotiate their contracts. For the mill owner, the loss of a colonia could be serious since it also meant a loss of the railroad links and bridges built to transfer cane from that colonia to the sugarmill. Moreover, cane carts or trains often had to pass through one colonia to get to another. If one colonia left the mill, the company might have to set up new railroad sidings and bridges around that colonia's outer edge to get cane from the remaining colonias.

To establish a stark contrast between East and West, Ramiro Guerra emphasized the competitive advantage that access to public railroads and proximity to other mills gave to independent colonos in the West and Center of Cuba. This competitive advantage was undeniable, but we should not see the West and Center as a monolithic whole; there were pockets that looked more like "the East" in the Center and West, and vice versa. Moreover, the strategies that mill owners of the West and Center used to counter competition must be recognized. Some companies in these regions used a sort of "debt peonage" strategy to tie colonos to the mill. A study of the San Vicente mill in Matanzas provides explicit evidence of this strategy. "With the sugarmill's capital resources, which in general were superior to those of any colono," the study reads, "agreements with cane farmers were best arranged when they were low on money. . . . [The Manager] considered 'locking the colono in,' or 'trancarlo,' along with 'amarrar,' 'tying up,' as part of the special politics of dealing with colonos."[47]

To minimize competition for cane and labor with other mills, Tuinucú among other companies pressured the Cuba Railroad Company not to allow new mills access to the central railroad. In January 1905 Tuinucú's president, Joseph I. C. Clarke, wrote to the Cuba Company about rumors "in the neighborhood of Tuinucú" that the railroad company's new Herradura estate would seek part of its cane supply from colonos around Tuinucú. "You can readily understand that such a rumor—even if unfounded—since our mill has already begun grinding, is likely to give rise to complications with the colonos at a time when their cooperation is essential." He asked that the railroad company "kindly set the rumor at rest . . . looking back upon Tuinucú's friendly relations with the Cuba Company."[48] Such communications between mill owners and managers were common, for the best way to preclude competition was for all to agree not to buy from the others' colonos.

When the price of sugar began to increase after the outbreak of the First World War, word spread that a veteran named Hanibal de Mesa might establish a sugarmill near Tuinucú. This time, Manuel Rionda contacted the Cuba Company to protest. He received a confidential letter that reads:

While we should welcome any new legitimate sugar enterprise to our lines and give it just as fair and liberal treatment as is accorded to every other mill in our territory, we should be guilty of little short of a crime in giving special facilities to any attempt to . . . take away the cane on which our existing mills are dependent, the loss of which cane they could not possibly provide against before the coming grinding season. . . . We cannot give any assistance to anybody in a scheme [that] is apparently intended by means of a makeshift mill to make a raid on the cane [that] has all along been ground by the existing mills.[49]

The letter did end by saying that if de Mesa's mill intended to commence the following year, the company could not object because that would give the present mills time to make contingency plans for cane.

The Tuinucú corporation adopted another strategy to combat competition: Its owners bought up as much land as they could to keep independent colonos or other mills from buying it. This was most pronounced during the First World War boom years of 1915–19, when the mill made massive expenditures on land through new purchases and leases. Rionda evidently hoped that Tuinucú could achieve enclave-like landholdings in the West as Manatí and Francisco had in the East. When Rionda suggested to Doty that the mill offer the same conditions to Tuinucú colonos that colonos received at the Francisco mill in eastern Cuba, Doty responded: "The fact [is] that Tuinucú is in a competition zone, and the price paid by us to colonos who accept such a plan would necessarily vary greatly with that paid by other factories [to] colonos, thereby creating some discontent."[50]

As Doty's remark suggests, cane cultivation in the East differed from that in the West and Center. Particularly during the U.S. occupations from 1899 to 1902 and 1906 to 1909, wealthy U.S. corporations appropriated immense acreage to build mills, railroads, and ports, precluding the chance of competition from the start. Some corporations, especially the United Fruit Company (UFCO) in Banes, Oriente, opted to forgo the colono system almost entirely. Most of the cane for UFCO's Boston and Preston sugarmills was tended directly by company workers: this was the so-called administration system.[51] Other corporations used administration for some fields but rented the bulk of their lands to tenant colonos (called sugarmill colonos or controlled colonos) in exchange for a percentage of the cane grown on the company lots. Most of the corporations in eastern Cuba also adopted a third system of land tenure whereby they gave independent colonias to prominent Cubans in exchange for political favors and access to their labor clienteles. This last practice varied from very occasional in the case of the United Fruit Company to very common in the cases of the Chaparra, Delicias, Manatí, and Francisco mills in Oriente and Camagüey.

The nationalist literature of the 1920s and more recent analyses of the colonato have tended to ignore these politically powerful independent colonos of the East, instead emphasizing the "exploitative" administration cane system and the "feudal" tenant colonias. In this vein, Alan Dye's recent study echoes Ramiro Guerra's argument that colonos in the West were able to demand more sugar or cash in exchange for their cane because they had access to railroads; they could therefore threaten, bargain, and sell to competing mills in the same vicinity. Both Dye and Guerra posit that U.S. corporations established sugarmills in the East to avoid independent colonos like those of the West.[52]

While these authors are correct to assert that as a general rule individual colonos of the West had more power than those of the East, increased attention to the political clout of colonos as a group reveal that colonos of the eastern enclaves were able to organize, threaten to withhold cane supplies, gain political support, and win demands from mills on numerous occasions. Nationalism in the 1920s made this especially true at the eastern mills owned by "foreigners."[53] In some cases, independent colonos served as a vanguard to unite all of the colonos (tenant and independent), forging power through solidarity. In other cases, tenant colonos united on their own, organized colono associations and won better returns from the company. They used the threat of non-cooperation, garnered support from the local community, waged campaigns in the press, and appealed directly to the provincial governors and the president.

In contrast to the small colonos who cultivated their cane with family labor, large and medium-size colonos hired managers and laborers and sometimes even divided and rented their lands to subcolonos. Many of these larger colonos were high officials from the Liberation Army of 1895–98 who had accumulated enough cash during and after the first two periods of U.S. occupation (1899–1902 and 1906–9) to buy land for raising cane and other products. As we saw in previous chapters, some "Generals" and "Doctors" became high-level administrators, lawyers, labor brokers, and politicians; others became colono landowners or cattle ranchers.

Particularly during the war years from 1914 through 1920 increasing numbers of Cubans amassed enough capital to become sugarmill owners and colonos, some by investing their capital made through political graft, others by switching from cattle to cane, and still others through inheritance. The colonos of Chaparra managed to raise $8 million in 1920 to build a new mill in Oriente called "Yaguanabos," but apparently the 1920s crash cut the project short.[54] All in all, in the early 1920s Cuban sugar interests, including colonos, represented a significant economic class closely tied to (or coinciding with) the Cuban political class and often at odds with U.S. interests on the island.[55]

To cite just a few examples of prominent Cuban planter politicians: José Miguel Gómez owned the La Vega and Algodones sugarmills. Mario García Menocal owned the Palma and Santa Marta sugarmills, co-owned the Pilar sugarmill, sat on the board of directors of Cubanaco, and was a large colono of Chaparra. General Gerardo Machado, who was Cuban president from 1925 to 1933 and governor of Santa Clara earlier in the century, began as a colono, then bought the Carmita sugarmill. General Francisco Carrillo, who was a senator, then the governor of Santa Clara, and then vice-president of Cuba from 1921 through 1925, owned the Reforma sugarmill.[56] These veterans and a few more of their comrades-in-arms made it to the status of plantation owners, but many more became large colonos.[57] Nearly one hundred such *Libertador-Terratenientes* (liberator landlords) can be identified by cross-listing the names of officials from the Liberation Army with the names of large colonos found in publications of the era.[58]

Large colonos and plantation owners from the ranks of the Liberation Army constituted the rural power base for the island's political parties, at least from 1909, when the veteran leader José Miguel Gómez became president of the nation. By the 1920s and 1930s this group had amassed enough power to demand more from the mills that bought their cane and to influence national-level politics significantly.[59] They managed to get Machado to partially shield Cuban interests during the economic crises of the era and to permanently embed protectionism and favoritism for Cuban colonos into state policy.

Chaparra and Delicias provide a vivid demonstration of colono–veteran power in early-twentieth-century rural Cuba. While 1920s nationalists such as Ramiro Guerra grouped the mills with the United Fruit Company and

Rionda properties as perfect examples of U.S. imperialism in Cuba, we have seen that Cuban agency was vital to the early establishment and management of the mills. The way statistics were collected prior to the 1930s makes it difficult to define the breakdown of cane production between tenant, independent, and administration cane at Chaparra. A 1902 report from the secretary of agriculture suggests that Menocal initially distributed a great many tenant colonias and a few outright independent ones.[60] Chaparra and Delicias ground no cane at all from independent colonias in 1913–14; the vast majority of cane came from tenant colonos.[61] In 1926 Chaparra ground 1.5 million arrobas of independent cane, but the much larger total of 55.8 million arrobas came from tenant and administration lands.[62] The year 1930 is the first in which specific numbers are provided for each category. Colono cane continued to dominate over administration cane at Chaparra. Tenants provided 95 percent; independents provided 3 percent; and administration cane provided only 2 percent.[63]

Chaparra and Delicias adopted far more "Cuban" cultivation systems than the United Fruit Company plantations next to them. A similar argument might be made for Rionda's nearby Francisco and Manatí mills, the first initially administrated by Menocal's father Gabriel, and the second by the Havana millionaire Marqués Eduardo Díaz de Ulzurrún. The four largest sugarmills in the province had cultivation strategies that were polar opposites. Chaparra and Delicias purchased 93 percent of their cane from 1,169 colonos, while the United Fruit Company's Boston and Preston mills bought only 12 percent of their cane from a grand total of 154 colonos (the rest was produced by administration). For the entire province of Oriente in 1937, colono cane accounted for 61 percent of the total, versus administration's 39 percent.[64]

Case studies and the totals from 1937 demonstrate that "American-owned" mills did not necessarily flock to the East to avoid the colono system. The number of mills using administration versus colono cane varied significantly according to time and place. Changes from policies that favored colono cane to those that favored administration cane and vice versa seem to have been related to the preferences of the directors and administrators, colono organization (or lack thereof), and government legislation. But in the end, many eastern companies opted to give up some control over cane production to shift the burdens of dealing with field labor and the vagaries of weather to tenant or independent colonos.[65]

In 1913 Manuel Rionda very explicitly expressed the benefits of the colonato in reference to the Francisco mill. He wrote that the cost of labor was much higher than it was ten years earlier, which rendered the "labor question" very difficult. Francisco had far too many fields to tend all by administration, and the existing colono system was better in any case because it was the colono rather than the company that ran the risks of fires, death of cattle, loss of crops, and many other problems. "The colono system, while having its disadvantages," he concluded, "has many advantages, amongst which the most important one is that the Manager does not have to deal with the many details of the cultivation, nor the annoying ones of dealing with the labor, thus leaving the Manager free to give his entire attention to the factory, railroad, shipments and many other branches of the business, all of them more than sufficient to keep him very busy."

Given all of these factors, Rionda's "inclinations" were to make some concessions to the colonos at Francisco: to guarantee the colono a $2.25 minimum and remove the 10 cent railroad freight charge per 100 arrobas of cane. Rionda added, "If the colonos are not stimulated and have no hope for the future, their cane fields will suffer sooner or later, their production will decrease, [and] the quantity of cane for the mills will be decreased year by year." Such an outcome would force the company to either take over cultivation or suffer from a cane supply smaller than the capacity of the factory. The experienced mill owner observed: "It is not well to be surrounded by men striving for a living and hardly getting it. Men must be well remunerated. If not, disorder sets in. . . . The colonos should be given some additional share of the increased earnings of the Company by its increase of capacity from 100,000 bags to 300,000 bags. The colono did not contribute with money toward this increase of capacity, yet the Company, by now being larger, has become more dependent on the colonos." Finally, Manuel referred to the "troubles" at other mills in Oriente because of their lack of attention to their colonos: "We have seen what happened to Niquero and San Antonio. They pressed the colonos, but they lost more than the colonos in the end. I believe in anticipating advances to all employees, rather than [being] forced to give them. The colono is nothing but an employee after all."[66]

Rionda's mention of Niquero and San Antonio is important: It indicates how colono activism in one region, even at one mill, could affect mill owners' and managers' approaches to their colonos at other mills, whether in the East, West, or Center. Paradoxically, it seems that in the 1920s many colonos in the West and Center, who held more bargaining power than their eastern counterparts historically, benefited from the mobilizations of colonos in the East. The same thing would apply to workers in the 1930s. The colono and labor movements at big mills like Chaparra and Delicias therefore had a national impact that stretched far beyond Puerto Padre.

In terms of competition, Francisco stood somewhere between Tuinucú and Chaparra. When it looked as if someone might purchase the Elia estate nearby, Rionda called a special meeting of the board of directors. He selected the Chaparra mill to serve as an example of why sugar companies had been so successful in Cuba's East: "The one factor that saved Chaparra and brought it up to what it is today [is] its wonderful command of virgin soil throughout that territory, so that when one portion [gives] out they [create] another cane area at very low prices, and that is the situation, as I understand it, in respect to this particular territory [Elia]." Rionda explained that if other investors purchased Elia, Francisco would have to pay higher wages to workers and a higher percentage of sugar to the colonos. The mill would have to contend with competition in that district, "which Francisco does not have today being Lord of all it surveys in that section." He ended with a simple statement: "Everyone knows what it means to compete for cane."[67]

The tenant colonos of the East were different from the independent colonos in two areas. They were generally not able to play one mill off the other to negotiate better contracts, and they did not own the primary means of production—the land. Based on these facts, Rionda, Ramiro Guerra, and others have implied that the tenant colonos were virtual employees of the mill. Although this may be correct in Marxist economic terms, it is important to consider how the colonos defined themselves. The Association of Colonos of Chaparra and Delicias published a seventy-page almanac in 1926 that allows us to understand just how they saw and positioned themselves in relation to the company, the community, and the nation.[68]

The association's version of colono history must be read critically, as the colonos were writing to forge solidarity within their community and to rouse support from anyone else willing to read their narrative. But precisely because of this bias, we can clearly perceive the message that the vast majority of colonos wanted to project. According to a company memorandum, approximately 90 percent of colonos belonged to the association in 1924 out of a grand total of approximately 1,300 colonos.[69] To company directors and

25   Colonos at Chaparra and Delicias lined up on payday. *Album de vistas del gran central Chaparra,*
      1910, 40.

President Machado, the colonos portrayed themselves as partners of the
company and the natural mediators between the company and workers. But
at the same time they selectively emphasized the fact that they employed
thousands of workers. They could use this fact to threaten the company
with a freeze or slowdown of production or to present themselves to the
state as Cuban employers and a Cuban middle class worthy of recognition
and benefits. When addressing the general public through manifestos and
press interviews, the rich, educated colonos tended to speak of the plight of
their poor, humble counterparts, emphasizing that they were all the same
class—colonos—worthy of support from the nation (see figure 25).

PATRON-COLONO RELATIONS
AT CHAPARRA AND DELICIAS

Reading the early history of the two mills as told in the almanac, whether
the pioneer colonos of Chaparra and Delicias owned their land or rented
it from the mills, they deserved praise for their contribution to the island's
development. The mills provided the money and materials, but the colonos

and their families supplied (or hired) the labor and tended to the clearing, planting, and upkeep of the new cane fields. Since sugar prices were low during the first years of the century, and colonos received only 4 arrobas of cane per 100 arrobas of cane, many were unable to pay off the debts incurred for the initial clearing and planting of lands. The lack of competition for labor in the region and the services offered by the company (including interest-free loans, free use of the railroad, wood for houses, and water tanks) offset the burden of low returns. When the Russo-Japanese war inflated sugar prices from 1904 through 1906, the company contracted out more colonias. Because these new colonias were cleared and planted at higher prices, they were harder hit with debt when prices returned to prewar levels in late 1906.

According to an internal memo written by General Manager R. B. Wood in March 1930, the colonos formed an association in 1906. That year, "the situation at Chaparra became exceedingly tense and very disagreeable." Although the colonos did not openly strike, they carried out a "form of passive resistance" that "interfered seriously with the grinding operations and also with the cultivation and supervision of the fields." Gonzalo Ricardo and Manuel Balan (a prominent local politician) headed the association, but Ricardo left his colonia and moved to Havana amid rumors that orders had been issued for his "definite removal." "Passive resistance was carried out even still further" after his departure, until General Menocal, "either prompted by or with the consent of Mr. Hawley, proposed the establishment of a minimum price [$2.25] to be paid for each hundred arrobas of cane irrespective of the sugar price."[70] Mario García Menocal may have been the one to suggest the minimum. He remained general manager of Chaparra and Delicias until April 1913, when he became the president of Cuba. His brothers and friends from the 1895 war figured among the colonos, and he himself owned a colonia. Or perhaps it was Cubanaco's President Hawley who recognized that it was in the company's best interests to keep the colonos on the company's side. As we saw in chapter 4, many of the colonos held positions in municipal, provincial, and national politics, and these colonos were not averse to using their political clout to push through benefits for the company.

The colonos remembered 1912–13 as a particularly difficult harvest year during which several farmers had to sell their land and its debts to new buyers. Whether the impoverished independent colonos moved away in search of other economic pursuits or became tenant farmers for the mill at that point is unclear. The almanac only states that "nobody wanted a colonia at Chaparra, and yet the colonos, suffering and resigned, continued to fulfill their duties." What saved them from ruin was the increase in sugar prices prompted by the First World War in 1914. Between 1915 and 1919 colonos improved their financial situation considerably, but the postwar depression crushed them again.

The many new sugarmills and colonias created during the First World War boom led to incredibly high wages and prices for plantings, tools, transportation, and food. When the bust came, colonos found that all was worth less than half of what they had paid. According to the almanac, the colonos asked R. B. Hawley to raise the minimum. He increased it to $4, but just for that harvest. The dead season that followed was "a true test of abnegation." The colonos had to ask the company for advances for food, as did the colonos' field workers. Alleging that it did not have enough money to liquidate the colonos immediately, the company kept part of the colonos' money in reserve. The colonos did not protest, and, as the almanac tells it, the Delicias colonos actually made the best of times out of the worst by breaking a worldwide record: "When the mill's siren gleefully announced the one-million-bag record, nobody remembered the colonos, whose limitless perseverance and abnegation made the industrial record possible."

It is interesting to note that the almanac credits Hawley, not Wood or Eugenio Molinet, for the $4 concession in 1920. In 1919, Wood had taken over from Colonel Fonts to become the first American administrator to head Chaparra since its inception. At the same time, Menocal's comrade-in-arms Eugenio Molinet became general manager of the Chaparra and Delicias mills. The 1926 almanac's naming of Hawley perhaps indicates a colono strategy to paint the company's president (who died shortly after the concession) as a "good patron" and the others as intransigent misers, for they remained powerful figures at the time of publication. Hawley's concession is described as one of the last "patient compromises" between workers and company. Colonos felt that the company had been treating them with increasing hostility and insincerity since then. They described the Molinet era as a time when the company began to try to "get as much as possible" out of the colonos by adding "arbitrary interest charges" on their debts and advances, reducing the period of time allowed to deliver burned cane, and adding penalties for badly packed cane carts.

Having painted this picture of an increasingly unfair capitalist "partner," the almanac moves naturally to the colonos' decision to organize and make demands of the company in 1924. On 7 September more than one thousand colonos joined the Colono Association to the triumphant sound of Cuba's national anthem, played by the Municipal Band at Puerto Padre. Men who were, or would become, important figures in local and regional politics led the colonos, and the mayor of Puerto Padre presided over the act of association.[71]

The new association first tried friendly negotiation with the company. It voted to send a committee to New York to tell the company's president, George E. Keiser, about the association and deliver the colonos' request for an increase to 5 arrobas of sugar (per 100 arrobas of cane) at a minimum price of $2.75, among other, lesser demands.[72] As the almanac tells it, the committee was warmly received. Cubanaco's directors pledged a sincere desire to reach a compromise and promised to study the matter. But the directors were not so attentive to two cables that the colono association sent in early October, both of which they ignored.

The colonos opted to take a more aggressive stand. They sent a third cable on 20 October with a veiled threat: "Our situation gets worse every day because our needs are not being adequately attended to by the General Manager Dr. Eugenio Molinet, and the local administrator of Chaparra, R. B. Wood. We have resolved to try to solve everything cordially, and not to use our force for the moment. Please acknowledge receipt by cable." When the directors ignored this third cable, the colonos sent another on 8 November advising Keiser that the colono members had agreed not to cut cane for the next harvest until their grievances were resolved satisfactorily. "We have made this decision," the colonos wrote, "because your commission to discuss the petitions did not arrive and no excuse has been forwarded to explain the delay."

The directors did not respond until 16 December, when they proposed what the association considered "severely insufficient" reforms: to reduce the price of water tanks from $5 to $2.50; to reduce the importation charge for immigrant workers from $7 to $3.50;[73] not to charge interest to colonos who owed less than $24 per acre; to give the colonos slightly more of their advances in cash rather than in credit; and to advance at least $1.60 to each colono for cutting and hauling cane. The directors of the colono association held a meeting on 23 December at which they agreed to maintain their position not to cut cane until the company met their original demands.

On 27 December the colonos reversed their position, agreeing to start the harvest as long as negotiations continued throughout the cutting and harvesting. This reversal reveals the colonos' difficult position in Puerto Padrense society: By going on strike, they withheld jobs from thousands of field workers and, by extension, removed almost all spending for goods and services in the region. The almanac states that they ended the strike to "show their good faith," maintain the "bonds of friendship" between the company and the colonos, and "save the municipality from ruin." "Several commercial operations faced complete bankruptcy," the almanac adds, "and the postponed harvest was doing great damage to the cane into which the workers and colonos had invested so much energy."

The colonos protested again in February 1925, stating that it was impossible to complete the harvest without further reforms. They explained to the directors that the main reason they were insisting on 5 arrobas was to cover their basic needs and to avoid the unpleasant situation whereby individuals were forced to beg the administration for things that should have been covered in the colono contract. Regarding their perennial state of indebtedness, they complained that it was unreasonable for the company to demand repayment of its original investment in the clearing and planting of the colonia when the colono had had to invest equal amounts of capital himself as well as endure the brutal work and isolation.

A Cubanaco memorandum prepared in 1931 reveals the opposite perspective. "The system of colono payments in Cuba is based on the 'Share Crop' principal of tenant farmers," it explained, "a percentage of the product ready for market going to the farmer and the balance to the owner and manufacturer. In 1906," it continued, "an average yield in sugar of 12 percent was high, but using this figure as a standard and paying the colono 4.5 percent, the company received 62.5 percent of the sugar produced from the colono cane and the colonos received 37.5 percent. This was evidently considered an equitable distribution and many planters of Chaparra, who invested no original capital of their own, became wealthy by being paid 4.5 percent."[74] The company's version conflicts with the colono narrative, according to which the colonos did invest on the original colonias and got only 4 percent. The memorandum was correct that some colonos did become rich, but large numbers remained poorer, with less land.

The colonos' protest letter of 1925 complained about the favoritism whereby the administration would sometimes grant requests for money and sometimes not and about the unfair system whereby company field inspectors seemed to decide arbitrarily when to pay one of three prices— 4, 4.25, or 4.5 arrobas. What the colonos may not have realized was that the company could use the tactic of favoritism to get certain colonos on their side. These colonos could then serve as informants and activists against the association. The success of this strategy is revealed time and again in the correspondence in the Cubanaco archives between R. B. Wood and his colono allies. Though never explicitly stated, Cubanaco also likely underpaid colonos deliberately to keep them in debt so that they would remain tied to the company, tied to their land, and morally obliged to the administration for financial loans.

The colono association's 1925 letter concluded by presenting colonos as the deserving and powerful Cuban leaders of the Chaparra and Delicias communities. The association demanded change "not in the name of one man, but in the name of the association, with its ONE THOUSAND, THREE HUNDRED associates, behind which TEN THOUSAND field workers stand and hope to increase their piece of the pie with the extra cents they will receive when our contracts are elevated to FIVE ARROBAS of sugar for every ONE HUNDRED arrobas of cane."[75] The colonos promised to continue to cooperate as they had done "loyally" for twenty-five years but demanded that the company stop keeping them "in a state of ruin." The association reminded the company that the colonos had cooperated with the general manager to solve all conflicts that might affect the smooth production process.

The association then made an observation that clearly shows that the colonos considered themselves not employees but partners of the company and mediators between the company and labor. The letter stated that they had not permitted the field workers to form a labor movement, as had the supervisors who allowed mill workers to organize. The colonos argued that the field workers nevertheless deserved an increase as much as the mill workers, adding that this was another reason to grant the increase to five arrobas. The association gave the company a month to meet its demands, but this time the workers of Chaparra and Delicias pre-empted the colonos with a strike of their own.

WORKERS USE THE POPULIST MOMENT
AT PUERTO PADRE

Railroad workers at Puerto Padre had been the first to organize, creating a branch of the Cuban Railway Brotherhood in early 1924. Near the end of that year, Eduardo Bertot, the second chief of the mill department, and Armando de la Pera, the second chief of the machine workshop, constituted the Union of Workers in the Sugar Industry at Puerto Padre (UTIA). Both leaders appear in the photographs in *Bohemia* magazine as members of the Masonic lodge, which indicates the importance of the autonomous space that such an association created (see figures 26 and 27). On the surface, the union's program was very moderate. It advocated improvement of working-class lives through education and conferences, revealing the influence of Freemasonry and anarcho-syndicalism. On the more assertive side, it also insisted that all workers had the right to stop work or to strike. Moreover, it expressed "solidarity with all the *compañeros* and societies of the Republic" and vowed not to discriminate on the basis of race, sex, politics, or religion.[76] The UTIA's openness to all political groups, ethnicities, and occupations gave it the potential to overcome the racial, ethnic, religious, and occupational divisions that the company worked so hard to maintain. When the union was constituted in 1924, the sugar economy was on the upswing again, but the sugar crash of 1920–21 and the inflationary war years before it were surely fresh in the memories of Puerto Padrense residents. Such experiences and the desire for a more equitable distribution of wealth among workers and merchants functioned to expand the union's influence and support within the community.

The groundwork for a successful opposition movement against the company was thus laid on 20 February 1925, when stevedores at Chaparra's private dock declared a strike to demand that Cubanaco pay the same wages that public dock stevedores had won. The company responded as it always had: by threatening to have the Rural Guard round up the strikers and put them on a train to Sabanazo (outside of company territory). This time, though, the sugar and railroad workers refused to cooperate. Tipped off the

26 Machine-shop workers (including UTIA leaders). Standing, from the left: Emilio Quiñones, Antonio Pérez, José Urrutia, Joaquín Molinet (chief of the machine shop), Eduardo Bertot (second chief of the mills and cofounder of the UTIA), Luis González; sitting, from the left: Alfredo Díaz, Nicolás Arteaga, Armando de la Pera (second chief of the machine shop and cofounder of the UTIA), Miguel A. Hars. *Agricultura y Zootecnia*, special edition, 1924, 16.

27 Masonic lodge at Chaparra. *Bohemia*, 10 June 1923, 14.

night before about the company's plans, the Railroad Brotherhood and the UTIA devised a plan to protect the workers: The train mechanic Evaristo Menéndez opened the water valve so that when the train full of workers and soldiers arrived at Delicias, it had to stop to refill. When the train stopped and the workers heard a prearranged signal (the whistle of the train), workers on the sugar floor at both mills stopped moving the bags. The sugar-floor workers struck to demand fulfillment of a salary increase promised at the end of the previous harvest. The remaining workers at Chaparra and Delicias stopped working shortly thereafter in solidarity, demanding that the dock workers be returned to their jobs, employee housing be provided rent-free, and the union be recognized. Hundreds of workers and their families marched en masse to Puerto Padre. The mayor reported to the provincial governor on February 25 that there were more than 1,500 strikers taking refuge in the city.[77]

Solidarity for the workers (and opposition to the company) stretched across race and class barriers. Farmers and merchants pitched in to support the strikers, offering them free meals at restaurants and private homes in Puerto Padre. The workers created a strike committee that organized a soup kitchen and sent a commission to visit other worker organizations in Las Villas, Camagüey, and Oriente to raise funds and recruit support. The union was able to collect $1,400 during the strike to add to the $1,500 with which it began. It received support from anarcho-syndicalist construction workers and dock workers as far away as Havana, as well as from the moderate Association of Workers in the Sugar Industry (ANIA), also based in Havana. The ANIA had some affiliates in Matanzas and a few delegates scattered across the island, including four at Chaparra. It was an *obrerista*, or self-named socialist, union that advocated cooperation between capital and labor, citing as inspiration Samuel Gompers in the United States and Plutarco Elías Calles in Mexico. It was progressive in that it fought against internal hierarchy—that is, the separation of workers (*obreros*) from more skilled employees (*empleados*). Over the course of 1925, the nationalist ANIA became increasingly irate about sugarmills' tendencies to hire skilled foreign mechanics and engineers over Cubans (Tuinucú offers a prime example) and over the commercial monopolies in the sugar enclaves such as Chaparra and Manatí.[78]

Many field workers in the region threw their support behind the UTIA strike, but field workers as a group did not manage to unionize until the

1930s. They had many obstacles to overcome. Unlike mill workers, who shared a relatively small work and living space on the sugar floor and in the mill town, field workers were spread out among thousands of colonias. The testimony of a former cane cutter named Luis Merconchini reveals that many colonos used a combination of paternalism and force to keep workers from organizing. Some colonos befriended the workers—they lived at the same house, ate at the same dinner table, and helped each other out. These workers, therefore, "did not have the morale to make demands of the colono." Ricardo Torre built housing for workers and provided water service, a general store with reasonable prices, and doctors or medicine as needed. Merconchini considered the colono Vicente Concepción one of the worst employers, yet even he "was smart enough to slaughter a cow and distribute the meat just at the moment workers were ready to rebel." Merconchini ventured that 95.5 percent of colonos were not exploitative "because they realized that well-fed workers would be better workers, but there were bad ones, too; some even killed people—burned them. Monterrey was a good man, a Delegate of the Union. A colono killed him."[79]

Field workers tended to be less literate and less racially and ethnically homogeneous than their counterparts at the mill, making solidarity even more difficult.[80] While exact details on race and ethnicity are hard to come by, photos of skilled office and mill employees indicate that most of them were lighter-skinned than the field workers. Statistics from 1924 show that roughly half of the 9,736 field workers at Chaparra and Delicias were Cuban. The others were from the British, Dutch, and French West Indies, among other places.[81] While new studies have proved incorrect the assumption that "Caribbean" labor was more submissive, one can nevertheless assume that differences in culture and language would create certain barriers, at least during the first years of work together in the fields.

Immigrant field workers had many reasons to join the 1925 strike. José Rodríguez Alejo, a Spanish immigrant who worked as an English translator for Chaparra's immigration department in 1927, described the British West Indians who worked on colonias as "veritable slaves." Company security guards captured the Ingleses if they tried to leave one colonia for another or if they tried to flee to the nearest plantation.[82] The Barbadian immigrant Harold Griffith, who also served as a translator for the department, stated that some Rural Guards actually killed two or three Ingleses, and the administration protected the guards from prosecution. He also mentioned that one colono family earned such a reputation for treating Ingleses badly that the Ingleses refused to work for them.[83]

The fact that the Ingleses were able to take such action demonstrates a certain level of organization on their part. The Barbadians at Chaparra and Delicias created a British West Indian Association that met twice a week "to find out what the Cuban laws were and to make sure these laws were enforced."[84] Rodríguez Alejo's testimony indicates that during the 1921–25 period, many immigrants returned every year; others brought their families; and still others married Cubans or fellow immigrants and put down roots in Puerto Padre. The colonos helped them do so, sending Rodríguez Alejo and the company security guards around to new immigrants' homes to tell them to hide when official inspectors came. After the economic crisis of 1920–21 the company had to sign an agreement promising to return all of the workers to their islands on the harvest's conclusion, paying a 500 peso guarantee for each immigrant. The colonos and Cubanaco got around the agreement by smuggling extra immigrants onto the boats on the way to Cuba and by padding the list of returning immigrants with false names.[85]

Many of the immigrants at Chaparra in 1925 had settled or returned every year since 1921. This helps explain a former cane cutter's observation that the Chaparra and Delicias field workers "joined the [1925] strike out of principle, without knowing what it was about; not a stalk of cane was lifted from the ground after the strike began."[86] Of course, it helped that their employers, the colonos, were also supporting the strike. The colonos did not have much choice, because the workers had widespread support locally and nationally. The question of which came first, the workers' decision not to work or the colonos' decision not to ask them to work, is lost in the historical record. But there is no evidence that anyone broke Chaparra's 1925 strike—colono, field, or factory worker, Cuban, Inglés, or Chinese— before an official state mediator arrived April.[87]

The workers went out of their way to maintain widespread support and respect. To keep the peace at Puerto Padre, they formed a worker police force shortly after arrival. When the Chaparra Light and Power Company threatened to cut off service, the worker committee told the mayor that it would write out receipts and pay for electricity so order could be maintained. Throughout March and early April, the mayor of Puerto Padre sent message after message advising the provincial governor and the secretary of the interior that "the greatest tranquility continues to reign." He told the governor not to send a military intervener because the workers were not causing any trouble in the town. By mid-March, the number of workers still in Puerto Padre had dwindled from roughly one thousand five hundred to two hundred. When Cubanaco administrators officially announced that the harvest would not continue unless colonos and workers returned to their labor without further discussion, dock, mill, and railroad workers left the town in search of employment at other mills. The colonos sent their field workers with more than eight hundred carts full of cane to other sugarmills in the region.[88]

The Cuban government's first inclination seems to have been to support the company, but then came the clearest evidence of the populist moment: Workers started a publicity campaign and wrote a letter directly to the president. According to the union, the military supervisor Emilio Jomarrón tried to help the company by threatening to harm Chinese and Caribbean workers unless they agreed to break the strike at Delicias and Cayo Juan Claro.[89] The UTIA responded by asking the anarcho-syndicalist Worker's Federation of Havana (FOH)—established in 1921 and just beginning to spread its influence to the provinces—to present its protest to government authorities and the Chinese Embassy in Havana. The FOH managed to get an article published on the front page of a national newspaper about the protest.[90] The UTIA's letter, addressed to President Zayas, reported the allegations about Jomarrón. It then stated that the workers were nevertheless staying the course, using the monetary and food aid other collectives were offering them to sustain the six hundred families who remained in the mill towns of Chaparra and Delicias. It should be noted that this was one of the first times that the national press portrayed the Cubanaco mills as something other than fountains of progress and employment.

The press attention and direct appeal from the workers prompted Zayas to send a "special government envoy" (Colonel Eduardo Puyol) to take a more impartial approach to the mediations. On 12 April Colonel Puyol was able to get the company to grant the salary increases to the sugar and dock workers that had been promised at the end of the former harvest; give all of the dismissed workers their jobs back; and recognize the union's delegates. Puyol sent a telegram to the provincial governor, stating: "This morning, the strike was ended at a Mass Assembly of the UTIA of Puerto Padre, and all agreed to resume the harvest tomorrow. The greatest order and enthusiasm reigned at the meeting, and there were repeated cheers for the impartial action of the Government."[91] The UTIA's secretary sent a telegram to the governor the same day that serves to confirm Puyol's statement. It read: "Strike ended with triumph of just cause. Immense jubilation."[92]

Apparently, Puyol achieved the peaceful resolution just in time. A decree signed by President Zayas and the minister of the interior dated 12 April announced that Army Captain Emilio Jomarrón would reassume leadership of the private security force to "enforce public order" at Chaparra and Delicias.[93] Since the decree was published the same day that Puyol sent his telegram, news that the conflict was resolved evidently had not quite made it to Havana. The decree serves as a window into the Liberal Party's strategy of combining mediation with repressive measures, the populist approach that began with Machado in Camagüey in 1924.

The successful strike at Puerto Padre proved inspiring to the whole northern Oriente region, prompting workers from the Railroad Brotherhood and the UTIA to organize a massive May Day celebration in Puerto Padre. Leopoldo Nápoles Díaz remembered it as a "great day of worker solidarity, reuniting [five thousand to six thousand] workers from Santa Lucía, Holguín, Velasco, Manatí, Chaparra, and Delicias."[94] Five days after the celebration, the industrial sugar workers at the Santa Lucía mill constituted their own union, declared themselves a delegation of the UTIA, and presented a list of demands to the directors. They asked for an eight-hour workday; free rent, light, and water; the prohibition of evictions; a 20 percent salary increase; free commerce; and free medical attention. The company studied the demands and then denied them. The workers began a strike on 27 May 1925.

Santa Lucía's strike paralleled the earlier strike movement at Chaparra in some ways: The community rallied to support the strikers; the mayor tried to remain impartial; and the provincial and national government combined mediation with increased repression through the Rural Guard. But there were a few key differences that serve to explain why Santa Lucía's strike failed where that of Chaparra and Delicias succeeded.

First of all, the demands at Chaparra and Delicias were far more moderate and therefore easier to grant. For example, all of the mills on the island used four six-hour shifts—one on, one off—to run the mills continuously at full capacity during the harvest season. No mill workers managed to win the eight-hour work day until the 1933 Revolution. Second, perhaps due to insufficient organizational ground work, worker solidarity did not extend across the sectors at Santa Lucía: Field and railroad workers did not unanimously support the strikes. This made it possible for the company to force workers off the mill, the guards escorting them via the railway. It also allowed the company to recruit Santa Lucía field workers to replace the striking mill workers.[95] Third, as it was later in the harvest season, the company was able to recruit strikebreakers among unemployed populations in Camagüey and Matanzas.

Fourth, and perhaps foremost, the political context was different: The "populist moment" was over.[96] Union Secretary Mariano Aguilera of Santa Lucía related an anecdote that makes this last point blatantly clear:

> Manuel Garrido and I, who were both Freemasons, went to Santiago de Cuba to meet the Provincial Chief of the Rural Guard, Colonel Eduardo Puyol. We went to ask him for help and guarantees for our struggle. He received us courteously, and told us: "I speak to you not as Provincial Chief of the Rural Guard, but as a Masonic brother. I know that your strike is just, as are your demands, and I would gladly offer you guarantees. The problem is, one of the owners of Santa Lucía is an in-law of Machado, and that changes things. Beyond that, *the President gave me strict orders to rapidly liquidate this movement.*"[97]

Machado as president (after the inauguration on 20 May) ruled differently from Machado as president-elect under outgoing President Zayas. Just before his inauguration, Machado made a speech to a group of sugar executives in New York City assuring them that he would promptly introduce anti-strike legislation and that the Cuban Army was "in admirable shape to guarantee the protection of property and the prevalence of peace."[98]

After Machado's inauguration, he began to carry out on a national scale the strategy developed in the Camagüey strike of 1924. Again, he started with the Railroad Brotherhood. He slowly ingratiated himself with the leaders by posing as a fair, impartial mediator while delaying the resolution of a new conflict that stretched, on and off, from March 1925 through May 1926. Appearances took precedence over content. As Machado's new secretary of the interior, Rogerio Zayas-Bazan clearly stated in a letter to the railroad company: "Proceed with your policy, making the workers think that you are really willing to make concessions, even though you don't make them later on."[99]

A preface announcing the darker side of Machado's dictatorship came in September 1925 when a hired assassin gunned down Enrique Varona, one of Cuba's most outstanding leaders of the railroad and sugar workers. Machado followed this brutal assault on the organization of railroad workers with a decree in May 1926 authorizing army troops to occupy the striking railroad centers across the island and imprison the brotherhood's leaders. By killing and jailing the leaders who had organized the railroad workers through 1925 and 1926, Machado cleared the way for more "pliable" leaders to take charge of the Brotherhood.[100]

With the help of Machado's Rural Guard, Cubanaco carried out a similar policy at Puerto Padre. When the 1925 harvest ended at Chaparra and Delicias, the company evicted the UTIA's leaders and families from their homes. According to the Delicias workers' history, they had to wander from one place to the next, using false names to get work. They had to use pseudonyms because mill owners frequently exchanged information about "bad seeds."[101] As the historian of Holguín Jacobo Urbino has noted, the repressive measure had a clear intention: to "decapitate" the sugar workers' movement in a zone where it had become strong and prestigious. To completely destroy the union, the company also gave rank-and-file members an ultimatum: Turn in your union membership card or lose your job. The threat of losing employment in an already depressed economy was effective. One of the island's first powerful sugar unions, the UTIA, was thus destroyed within months of Machado's inauguration.[102]

The company and state backlash against colonos was less extreme. Medium-size and large colonos belonged to the more educated, vocal middle class, and all were potential political supporters. Machado and his soldiers could—and did—exile, remove, and murder workers from the workplace and the island, but they had to be cautious with colonos because they constituted one of Machado's power bases. Race, class, and nationality most likely also played an important role in determining Machado's more favorable treatment of colonos over workers. Field workers especially tended to be darker, poorer, and less literate; moreover, they could be depicted as "foreign," anarchist, or communist agitators. The statistics from Chaparra and Delicias for 1923 support this "national" versus "foreign" breakdown: Approximately 1,390 colonos were Cuban and fewer than 10 were foreign, while only half of Chaparra's and Delicias's 9,736 field workers were Cuban.[103] (See figures 28 and 29.)

28 Colonos sitting on a staircase waiting for their pay at Chaparra. *Album de vistas del gran central Chaparra*, 1910, 41.

29 House of the colono José M. Lasa, Arroyo Seco, Chaparra. The size of Lasa's home suggests that he was one of the wealthier colonos selling cane to the Chaparra sugarmill. *Album de vistas de gran central Chaparra*, 1910, 65.

COLONOS USE THE POPULIST MOMENT

The colonos' reaction to the 1925 strike again demonstrates their perception of themselves as "partners" of the company. They wrote to the manager immediately after the workers declared the strike in February, offering to mediate between the two parties. According to the colono almanac, the manager responded that he was not disposed to enter into any agreement "save the return of workers and employees to their jobs without reservations of any kind." This forced the colonos to "suffer fifty-two days of inactivity." The almanac states that colonos froze production while the Chaparra and Delicias workers struck "because they could not hire replacement workers." (The Chaparra and Delicias workers had the support of worker organizations throughout the republic, and the colonos had no way to protect their property from retaliation.) The almanac praises the "happy arrival" of the government envoy Eduardo Puyol in early April, crediting him for achieving the significant task of forging agreements between the company, workers, and colonos.

The government envoy Puyol's willingness to support workers and colonos—expressed in both the colono narrative and the worker correspondence found at the Santiago de Cuba provincial archives—demonstrates that early 1925 was a propitious political moment for popular negotiations. Gerardo Machado had won the presidential elections on an extremely populist platform in November 1924 and was yet to be inaugurated. The months between the November elections and the May inauguration (which coincided with the sugar harvest) were ideal for worker and colono protests because the incoming president wanted mass support and sugar companies needed workers and colonos to work their mills.

On 4 April 1925 the company signed an agreement reaffirming the promise made in December 1925 to pay 4.5 arrobas and 4.75 arrobas for independent colonos and to divide colonos' profits equally between cash payments and advance-account deposits each pay period. Highly motivated by the company's promises, the colonos, field workers, and mill workers processed a remarkable amount of cane that year, making up for the time lost during the strike. But according to the almanac, the company began to withdraw all benefits as soon as the harvest ended in an effort to sow discontent among colonos against the association. Company correspondence reveals that they did so because paternalism worked best on an individual basis by breeding loyalty and submission. Associations imposed inflexible standards, ruling out the possibility of favoritism. To punish affiliates, the company stopped commercial departments from granting the credits necessary to care for the fields, colonos, and their families. This lack of credit made it difficult for colonos to support not only their own families, but also the field workers who depended on wages from weeding fields during the dead season. The company also ended the harvest before the colonos were ready, leaving more than 30 million arrobas uncut (again hurting both colono and field worker).

When colonos renewed their demand for five arrobas in September 1925 and the directors ignored them again, the colono almanac reports, they "resolved to put their problems in the hands of the Honorable President of the Republic, General Gerardo Machado." The fact that Chaparra and Delicias colonos went to the president reveals Machado's initial success in portraying himself as a "man of the people"—or, at least, as a man of middle-class Cubans who had made it to the status of colono or sugar planter.[104] On 2 November the Chaparra and Delicias Colono Association presented a pamphlet to the president explaining its situation from 1902 to 1925. According to the almanac, the president received the commission "with his usual friendliness and courtesy," congratulating the colonos for their conduct and promising to study the matter seriously. Just over a month later, General Machado called on Mario Miguel García Menocal (General Menocal's nephew), president of the Colono Association, and the vice-presidents J. L. Morris and Agustín Arocena to meet in Havana with E. A. Brooks, the general administrator of Chaparra and Delicias.

The administration at Chaparra proceeded as though no such negotiations were taking place, issuing a circular stating that cane cutting would begin on 15 December. The colono committee members sent a telegram from Havana requesting that the company hold the order, but the acting administrator responded that he was obeying instructions and would wait only until 14 December. The day before the deadline, Brooks, Menocal, Morris, and Arocena met at the Presidential Palace. According to the almanac, the meeting was "extremely cordial," but Brooks asked to consult the directors in New York regarding the request for 5 arrobas "because he lacked the power to resolve the issue." This was no coincidence: Cubanaco used the strategy of sending someone "lacking the power" to make decisions for the company time and again in meetings and legal cases from the company's inception through 1959.

"By request of the colonos, and via the mediation of General Machado," the order to begin grinding was suspended until after Christmas. On 14 December Brooks reported to Machado on his conversations with the directors, and the next day Machado called the colonos to the Capitolio to communicate the results of the conference. According to the almanac, Machado told the colonos that Keiser had agreed to postpone the harvest, and that both he and another witness present at the interview (the president of the Senate) understood Brooks to state that the company was disposed to give 5 arrobas as long as it could abolish the minimum of $2.25 per 100 arrobas. The colonos asked Machado to call another meeting on the following day, which he did. Machado told Brooks that it would be ideal if he could announce the improvements to the colonos before beginning the harvest, and Brooks promised to communicate his request to Keiser.

The colono committee returned to Chaparra highly satisfied with the outcome and thankful for the attention of "the Honorable President of the Republic, who demonstrated at all times his sincere desire to arrive at a definitive solution as cordially as possible." The committee held an "extremely cordial" meeting with Molinet, Wood, and other directors at Chaparra on 19 December, where the administrators all agreed to recommend to the directors in New York that the colonos be granted 5 arrobas of sugar at a minimum price of $2 per 100 arrobas.

Cubanaco ordered the colonos to begin cutting cane "in a most irregular way." Although the almanac does not provide details, the company most likely slighted the colonos who had been most active in the association. Directors also remained silent regarding any formalization of a revised contract. On 8 February 1926 the colonos wrote again to President Machado, but Machado's response must have come after the almanac was published, leaving a blank regarding the events that occurred between that date and the date when R. B. Wood wrote his first memorandum on company–colono relations (6 March 1930). According to Wood's later correspondence, it would appear that the colonos did not win this battle. They continued to receive 4.5 arrobas until 1932.

Colonos at Chaparra and Delicias were not alone in seeking Machado's assistance. Squeezed by high debts and encouraged by the nationalist tone of the elections, colonos across the island organized into "agricultural blocks" or local colono associations. On 5 October 1925 Manuel Rionda forwarded a letter titled "Re: Unjustifiable Moral Support to 'Bloque Agrícola de Camagüey' by Colonos of Tuinucú" to his nephews Leandro, José, Manolo, and Oliver. "I think it is very bad that Tuinucú colonos are supporting other colonos," Manuel wrote, "even out of sympathy, because they have no reason to feel dissatisfied with the treatment they have received at Tuinucú. . . . It is not right that the colonos of Tuinucú join the colonos of other mills to see if they can help those colonos get more." He continued, "If we at Tuinucú treat our colonos as we have, in a very just and beneficial manner for them, why should they help all of the colonos of the province of Camagüey? We have never refused to listen to our colonos, and we remain disposed to continue that way, so they have no reason to join any association."[105]

The Camagüey colonos and many other colono associations called on Machado the populist for mediation in 1925, and Machado received hundreds of letters from individuals, local chambers of congress, solidarity colono associations, and agricultural blocks in support of the colonos of the nation.[106] A common rhetorical strategy in the colonos' letters was to state that they trusted President Machado's judgment and to pledge to do whatever he felt was best. Sometimes this strategy backfired on the colonos—for example, when Machado was close to the men who owned or administered the plantation.[107]

Machado was an expert at maneuvering between colonos and management, whether the management was foreign or Cuban.[108] He had to be, because while Cuban and foreign planters were his most lucrative supporters, many colonos belonged to the well-educated, vocal bourgeoisie that constituted one of his power bases. The colonos seemed to know just what to say to win the sympathy of the press and the nation, putting even more pressure on Machado to come to their rescue.

Machado's populist balancing act became extremely challenging when the Cuban government introduced strict cane quotas to limit the total production of sugar in the hope that a smaller supply would increase the price. On 3 May 1926 the Verdeja Act imposed a decrease of 10 percent from the 1925 sugar crop. Other decrees prohibited the establishment of new cane fields on forest lands and allowed mills to begin harvesting only after 1 January (in contrast to the customary starting dates in November or December).

While many Cuban planters initially supported crop restriction, and the large American producers such as Rionda and Hawley pushed hard for it, most colonos resented it. Having invested all of their lives into making their fields as large and productive as possible, the farmers were hard hit by the decrees to grind only a portion of available cane. Although the Machado regime did not back down from the initiative in response to pressure from the colonos, the quota system did contain a stipulation that the cane supplies of colonos were not to be displaced by administration cane.[109] A study written in 1942 by Ramiro Guerra, the author of *Sugar and Society*, commented in hindsight that "this policy of offering protection to the weak producers" served to "curb the concentration of cane sowings, as well as that of sugar manufacture, in the hands of the strongest producers." He continued, "Theoretical conceptions concerning the best organization of the industry have had nothing to do with the matter. . . . The favorable view toward [control versus laissez faire] won out . . . for considerations of national and political order."[110]

The protectionist legislation, though minimal, demonstrates the success of the nationalist campaign that colonos from the East, including the association at Chaparra and Delicias, had waged. Cuban industrialists also succeeded in getting Machado's administration to introduce protection: The Customs-Tariff Law of 1927 subsidized the expansion of national industry and agriculture with the laudable goal of diversifying the island's economy. The law reduced duties on a wide variety of products that could be processed in Cuba, such as cotton for textile mills and sisal for rope manufacturing. It raised tariffs on manufactured goods to allow Cubans to produce their own cheese, condensed milk, butter, paint, and shoes, among other goods. Livestock and agricultural production diversified under the tariff, as well.[111]

As the next chapter reveals, the Cuban economy's protection and expansion proved to be short-lived. When a more extreme depression hit the nation in the late 1920s and early 1930s, Machado had little chance for popularity even among the island's middle and upper classes. The U.S. government, reeling from its own depression and growing nationalist pressure, lowered Cuba's total sugar quota and passed the Hawley-Smoot Tariff Act, which increased the duty on Cuban raw sugar from the already high "emergency" level of 1.76 cents per pound to 2 cents in 1930. When Cubans began to see the economic crisis prompted by sugar as linked to U.S. policy and

President Machado, a revolutionary opposition took root in the island's cities and countryside. This time, U.S. politicians could not simply send in the Marines. President Herbert Hoover and President Franklin D. Roosevelt had responded to the palpable disgust for U.S. interventionism among Latin Americans with a pledge to be "Good Neighbors."

Revolutionary Rejection of
the Patrons' Compact,
1926–33

7 Cane farmers and workers began to protest and organize in greater and greater numbers from 1926 onward in the countryside and in the cities. The first half of this chapter explores why, in a strike in 1931, colonos at Chaparra suffered a defeat in contrast to their large-scale strike against the company in 1925. The remainder shows that urban and rural workers played a major role in the 1933 insurrection that overthrew Machado. When yet another U.S.-friendly "patron president" replaced Machado, workers contributed to the popular demand for more radical change. A student-military alliance overthrew the interim president, and the regime of the nationalist Ramón Grau San Martín began to legislate what has been dubbed "One Hundred Days of Reform." During the revolution, workers forced managers to leave Chaparra, Delicias, and Tuinucú as their counterparts did at other mills across the island. Different political groups fought for dominance over newly established sugar workers' unions, but workers on the ground at Puerto Padre and Tuinucú maintained the unity necessary to win their demands.

During the nationalist Grau San Martín regime (September 1933–January 1934), cane fires were lit, but the numbers paled in comparison to those in the fight against Spanish rule or the sabotage of the Machado dictatorship. The vast majority of workers wanted not to destroy but to protect the fields and factories and to claim a larger share of the sugar economy. The Depression era had revealed the shallowness of the patrons' compact, so workers and colonos turned to the state for security and welfare (as they did in the United States, Chile, and elsewhere in the Western Hemisphere). The Great Depression and mobilizations of the late 1920s and early 1930s described in this chapter ultimately explain the demise of the patrons' compact and the Cuban state's more lasting embrace of class-based populist rule.

PRELUDE TO REVOLUTION:
THE MACHADO REGIME, 1926–1931

At least in its early years, the Machado regime sought to contain the mobilization of workers and colonos with the populist combination of repression and persuasion. The president might send in the Rural Guard to end a strike on one occasion, but on another he might ask a mediator to convince workers to end the strike in exchange for a few, minimal reforms. Machado certainly hoarded money for himself and his cronies, but he also funneled at least some of the export taxes, payoffs from capitalists seeking contracts, and extremely large loans from Wall Street banks into public-works programs such as a national highway system and the Capitol Building in Havana. Machado's tentative interventions between workers, colonos, and mill owners; his support for the new central highway system (which would finally provide a Cuban alternative to the foreign-owned railroads); and his new Capitolio can be seen as Machado the populist practicing "public theater" on a grander scale.[1] He was essentially asserting that the Cuban state was becoming stronger.

The president's populist position became increasingly untenable as sugar prices dropped from an average 2.96 cents per pound in 1927 to 1.47 in 1930. That year, the United States passed the Hawley-Smoot Tariff Act, which hurt the Cuban economy even more by favoring the producers of beet sugar in the western United States and cane sugar in Louisiana, Hawaii, Puerto Rico, and the Philippines. The regime cut back on public-works projects, and its Tarafa Plan of 1929 lowered cane quotas to limit total production. The crop restriction was momentarily beneficial, but other countries simply increased production, offsetting Cuba's painful efforts to curb the world sugar supply. Prices resumed a downward spiral, and by 1930 the crop restriction was hurting mill owners almost as much as workers and colonos. Since less sugar was being sold at lower prices, workers lost jobs, colonos lost income, and plantation owners lost profits.

Machado had prolonged his political term in 1928 in the name of political and economic stability. The end of public-works projects and the introduction of crop restrictions deprived Cubans of economic opportunities at the same time that Machado's incumbency deprived them of a political avenue for protest. Not just workers and colonos but almost everyone on the island began to resent Cuba's combined state of depression and dictatorship. Politicians from both the Liberal Party and the Conservative Party joined Mario García Menocal's and Carlos Mendieta's Unión Nacionalista in 1931 to try to end the Machado dictatorship through the Río Verde insurrection. Although they landed armed forces in western Pinar del Río and eastern Oriente, they failed to inspire the national uprising (or U.S. intervention) that they had hoped for. Each caudillo led his followers according to his own priorities, thus the Unión Nacionalista was not able to inspire unity among followers.[2] Police reports from Chaparra suggest that both rebels and soldiers used the rebellion as an excuse to steal guns and horses from the company.[3] At the national level, Río Verde had no effect beyond giving Machado an excuse to increase the level of repression. Machado used newly acquired air power for reconnaissance and bombing, naval forces, and army units (dispatched quickly via the new Central Highway) to capture the leaders and crush the rebellion.

Menocal's and Mendieta's rebellion failed in part because Machado had learned from past errors and had finally trained the armed forces to counter the rural insurrectionary strategy that had dominated Cuban revolutionary tradition.[4] As we will see in chapter 8, Fidel Castro, Ernesto Ché Guevara, and other guerrilla leaders returned to precisely this form of rural rebellion during the 1959 Revolution. From the 1930s through the 1950s, though, police and armed forces focused on the new, urban opposition tactics born during the 1933 Revolution. These strategies included the general strike, work stoppages, gun battles, bombings, and political assassinations.

Río Verde was the last major rebellion led by the old caudillos of the 1895 generation. Members of a new generation participated in the opposition movement in much great numbers. For example, Antonio Guiteras, a twenty-five-year-old student activist from Oriente Province, led the La Gallinita rising near Santiago de Cuba. He would become the radical minister of the interior during the nationalist regime of Ramon Grau San Martín in 1933. After Río Verde, Guiteras told a group of Unión Nacionalista leaders: "You have finished the struggle while I am just starting."[5] He spawned the Young Cuba organization, whose members were often dubbed Guiteristas.

Young Cuba was only one among the many organizations students and middle-class professionals could join in opposition to Machado; most of these groups would reemerge as forces of opposition to Batista in the 1950s. Students had to choose among parties such as the University Students' Federation (FEU) that Julio Mella had started in 1925; the University Student Directorate (DEU); the Student Left Wing (AIE); or the secret cells such as the ABC Revolutionary Society or Cellular Organization of Revolutionary Reform (OCRR) that responded to Machado's repression with assassinations and bombings.[6] Meanwhile, workers had to choose leaders from among Guiteristas, ABC cells, communists from the CNOC (who followed directives from Joseph Stalin's Russia), or Trotskyists from the Federation (who combined anarcho-syndicalism with Bolshevik and Leninist principles).[7]

Machado's well-funded police force and army targeted all of these opposition groups. The president lost his populist balance when he abandoned persuasion for extreme repression. Machadista (pro-Machado) military supervisors replaced civilian political administrators, provincial governors, and municipal mayors throughout the island. Machado increasingly relied on the secret police and Rural Guard soldiers to put down the mounting opposition in the cities and countryside. Use of the *ley de fuga* became a common tactic in the cities: Secret service or policemen would round up suspects for interrogation, set them free, and then claim that they had to shoot them because the suspects were trying to run away.

Soldiers in the countryside were equally brutal with any workers or professionals suspected of organizing unions or opposition groups. The Rural Guard would expel them from their homes, put them into prison, and sometimes torture them or hang them from trees. In February 1932 the U.S. Ambassador Harry Frank Guggenheim reported to the U.S. secretary of state that a new military penal code gave the army the power to try all new and pending cases involving explosives, the disruption of transportation and communication facilities, and *the destruction of cane or sugar machinery*.[8] Evidently an increase in the cases of sabotage and destruction prompted the new code.

CUBA LIBRE

30   *The Nation*, 3 May 1933, 136:492. Reprinted with permission.

Other than increasingly relying on military and police force, Machado
looked to the United States. A critical editorial in the U.S. magazine the *Nation* on 3 May 1933 correctly asserted that "Machado has been maintained
in office against the obvious will of the Cuban people by the financial support of our great corporations. More heavily loaded with per capita debt
charges than any other Latin American country, Cuba . . . has been unable
to revolt or default. Machado would doubtless have fallen in 1930 but for
the $50,000,000 lent him by the Chase bank." The interpretation is power-
fully expressed in an adjacent cartoon image (see figure 30). "Wall Street"
holds up a machine-gun-toting Machado puppet that stands over a chained
body—Cuba Libre. Cuban presidents since 1902 had practiced graft and repression to varying degrees, but none before Machado had engaged in corruption under such dire economic conditions and employed such extensive

state violence, including the murder of middle-class journalists, students, and political activists.

PATRONS UNDERMINE THE COMPACT
IN THE COUNTRYSIDE: THE COLONOS

Populist politics could not survive the Great Depression, nor could philanthropic social control at the sugar plantations across the island. Large U.S. corporations such as Cubanaco and the Cuba Company, which had managed to weather the 1920s without deficits, began to lose money in 1930.[9] Manuel Rionda wrote to Oliver Doty in 1929, "Fortunately, the sales last summer show a profit of $194,000 . . . but even this does not permit us to continue paying dividends, so then: (1) out with the idea of paying the colonos but just what they are entitled to; (2) we must cut down expenses; (3) we must cut down our staff. . . . Tuinucú must change its methods, or stop paying dividends, which alternative shall it be?"[10] Rionda posed this as a rhetorical question. To him it was obvious that "benevolent rule" was a luxury. Over the next several years, Doty, the on-site manager, negotiated with Rionda to try not to cut back too much, but Rionda usually won the battles because he held the purse strings.

In January 1930 Doty wrote, "The cost of field work, both of planting fields and ordinary attention, is today, I believe, lower than it has been during any other time, at least during the last twenty years while I have been in Cuba." He explained that despite these low costs, colonos were unable to pay back most of their debts and lacked the funds to hire workers to weed, cut, and haul their cane. Tuinucú only paid an average of $2.32 per 100 arrobas of cane for the whole crop, from which it deducted rent.[11]

The fact that Doty and Rionda exchanged so much correspondence on the colonos' plight, and that they shared the wealth with them during the good years, helps explain why colonos at Tuinucú did not join together and protest until 1934. Their counterparts at Chaparra and Delicias had more reasons to rebel as well as the strength in numbers and experience to do so. In 1931 Cubanaco sparked a new conflict by removing the minimum price for cane. An in-depth memo written by General Manager R. B. Wood on 6 October 1930 had prevented this the previous year with a strong warning that "any change or abrogation of the minimum would precipitate a crisis between the Colonos and Management. Under present conditions, a reasonable forecast would be the adoption by the Colonos of a policy of passive resistance whereby *tareas* [cane supplies] would be seriously reduced and grinding expenses both at the Mill and on Railroad largely increased."

Wood's memorandum provides proof to support the Cubanaco colonos' claim that they were getting a bad deal:

> It should be borne in mind that irrespective of all legal and moral aspects of this matter . . . our actual cost . . . for 100 arrobas of [Administration] cane over a term of years has been higher than [the colono cane minimum of] $2.56. Our Administration cane . . . costs us over $3.00. It should also be considered that Colono cane is, as a general rule, cheaper in our zone than Administration cane and that [even if we reduce this cost as we intend to do with new varieties of cane] I hardly believe this will fall level or below the $2.56.[12]

This quote also demonstrates the fallacy of Guerra's argument in *Sugar and Society* that planters would stop buying cane from colonos and turn to the administration system. Planters might threaten to do so, but no one knew better than them that the colonato was more cost-efficient.

Determined to shift their losses to the colonos, the directors inquired again about removing the minimum in 1931. A larger memorandum was prepared addressing the various sides of the issue. Under "Economic Aspects of the Problem," the memo observed that prior to 1925 the company had suffered a loss due to the difference between the market value of cane and the guaranteed minimum paid to the colonos in only one year (1913). When the minimum was raised in 1925, the company lost small amounts in 1926 and 1928 and very large amounts in 1929, 1930, and 1931. The "Moral Aspect" stated that "there could hardly be any doubt . . . in the minds of any one of the 1400-odd colonos of Chaparra as to the good faith by which the Company has carried out an unwritten agreement to the extent of paying to the colonos approximately $3,000,000 in excess of market value for cane deliveries to the mill." It went on to point out that the colonos had cooperated with the general manager "to the fullest extent" and had "voluntarily agreed" to allow the company to keep more of the cane value as deposit for future cultivation. This, the memorandum concluded, demonstrated that colonos "fully realize the economic impossibility for the Company to have maintained a system of cane payments, on the same basis as when sugar was selling for twice the current value."[13]

The author of the memorandum from 1931 had unrealistic perceptions of colonos' flexibility, to say the least. According to the laws of the land, the final liquidation at the end of one harvest constituted a tacit renewal of the existing contract for the following year. Cubanaco knew this, so it insisted that colonos sign a waiver stating they understood that the minimum would be removed for the next harvest (1932) before they could receive their pay for the previous harvest (1931). For the colonos, this was blackmail, coming just months after they had agreed to leave their hard-earned cash in the company's coffers when the company cried poor. The company's waiver was the last straw for the colonos, prompting a revival of the Colono Association. Manifesto after manifesto was printed for fellow colonos in a propaganda war urging them to stand in solidarity and refuse to sign the circular.

As was the case in 1925, the fact that Puerto Padre was an enclave economy made it easy for the colonos to rally support against the company. Cubans were tired of the stranglehold that the Americans held over their region. U.S. policy—support for Machado's dictatorship and higher tariffs on Cuban sugar—made Cuban nationalism (and anti-imperialism) stronger in 1931 than it had been in 1925. As we have seen, Cubanaco's "greedy twins" had already made enemies of the residents of the area. When the company refused to pay the colonos in 1931 at the end of the harvest (a time when all of the commercial establishments of the region were desperate for consumer purchases), many suppliers had to declare bankruptcy, and outrage spread through the region.

When Cubanaco refused to pay colonos, the thousands of agricultural workers who depended on colonos to pay them did not get paid, either. This cut off all of the merchants' clients except the factory and office workers paid directly by Cubanaco. The Colono Association, the Puerto Padre Chamber of Commerce, several Masonic lodges, the Veterans of Independence Center, the Tobacco Rollers' Guild, and other groups created a Civic Defense Committee to end Cubanaco's monopoly in Puerto Padre. They published appeals in local and national papers, including an impressive document entitled "Manifesto to the Country from the Local Civic Defense Committee of Puerto Padre, Oriente" that raged against Cubanaco's refusal to obey the 1909 Arteaga Law (it continued to pay in tokens rather than cash); the blackmail of the colonos ("Sign or you will not receive your pay"); and the use of foreign labor that left Cubans poor and jobless.[14]

As early as 23 June 1925 an editorial in the national newspaper *La Prensa* had supported the merchants' case:

> Commerce is not free in zones of the large sugar companies. Common law does not reign in these fiefdoms, only the absolute will of the Company directors. There are sugarmills in which a tribute of 10 percent is charged on all commercial goods not coming from the Company. This being the case, it is not at all surprising that a single sugar company, the owner of the "Chaparra," "Delicias," and "San Miguel" sugarmills, realized profits in excess of two million dollars in mercantile operations other than sugar.[15]

A cartoon in *El Colono* magazine from 1931 (figure 31) vividly depicts how the colonos played the "nationalist" card: A fat American man, dressed in a suit and smoking a cigar at his desk, points to a paper that reads "New Contract." A barefoot, desperate-looking colono stands across from him, staring wide-eyed, straw hat in hand. The text reads: "Colono: I need my money. It's been five months since you milled my cane, I cannot tend to my fields, or provide for my most pressing household needs. I want my money / Administrator: Yoo [*Osted*] not friend mine, yoo don't want to sign new contract. If yoo to sign contract, I find money, if no sign, I cannot pay for your cane / Colono: I will not sign this contract, I do not want to be a slave in my nation [*patria*]."[16]

The same issue of *El Colono* contains an interview with the former president Menocal, who supported the movement—at least, rhetorically. "The Chaparra colonos are my old friends; they have my sympathy and affection. I think that they should resolve their problems in a just and fair manner." He ended with a statement that echoed Ramiro Guerra's argument perfectly: "In the sugar industry, colonos represent the only really national interest we have left."[17]

Although the colonos had the outside support of many, they had several enemies within. The correspondence between Wood and his collaborators over the course of 1931 reads like a Greek tragedy, demonstrating the crumbling of colono solidarity in the context of economic crisis. Several colonos worked against the association ideologically and "in the union halls," especially the large colonos who had the most to lose. For example, on 20 May

31   *El Colono*,
     June–July 1931,
     19.

1931 Enrique Tolosa wrote to his brother Mario: "I was shocked to see your name at the bottom of a manifesto to the colonos that included statements that go against your nature; I am positive that you had nothing to do with the writing. . . . I beg you, my dear brother, to resign from the association to protect the honor and prestige of our family. You know that I walk and talk with everyone and in doing so I have been able to determine that the majority of colonos are going to sign the contract with Mr. Wood. Hoping that you will give my advice due attention. . . . Enrique."[18]

The next day J. L. Morris, the owner of a large colonia, forwarded a letter from another colono that stated: "I had a meeting of the colonos from the Pimentel and Torrejon districts, and you can tell Mr. Wood by phone that of those two zones there will be less than five colonos who will not sign, tell him in English that he will triumph." Morris added his own observations to the letter: "I also know that Rafael Cruz is working in his zone. I asked Rafael not to resign from the association as we can use him advantageously in same, without a doubt, the situation is under our control."[19]

Several large colonos quickly succumbed to the company's promises of small reforms and individual rewards, despite the fact that they had been outraged about the waiver at the beginning and actually served as the campaign's first leaders. Every high-profile colono who abandoned the movement undermined the remaining association members' morale. It was the dead season, and as the months wore on, the anxiety prompted more and more colonos to abandon the association and sign the circular. The colono leaders who visited Havana won support from the media, but the company's allies managed to raise some doubts among readers by portraying the leaders as marginal political opportunists with little or no land of their own. There was some truth to these accusations. In the late stages of the campaign, the leaders were indeed small and medium-size colonos. The larger colonos had already abandoned the cause. In contrast to the 1925 struggle, the large colonos became unwilling to stand in solidarity and fight with their smaller "brothers."[20]

The most important factor working against the colonos was where their movement fell in relation to Cuba's agricultural and political cycles. Since it was the dead season, they were not able to threaten to strike effectively or withhold their cane, as they had done in 1925. Wood lightly dismissed their protest in a letter to an official from the Palma sugarmill on 4 May 1931: "We are going pretty well with our Colonos, who have nine long months to shoot off fireworks and their mouths. I believe we will come out o.k. in this matter."[21] He was right. By February 1932, he was able to report that the mills were "grinding at a very high rate and operating under a new form of contract with our colonos, paying 5 arrobas *without any minimum guarantee.*" He added: "Although we had considerable trouble in obtaining signatures to this new contract, since the beginning of the crop everything has been very smooth."[22]

On the political calendar, whereas the colonos' first strike occurred during Machado's flirtation with populism, this second protest came after he had illegally extended his term in 1928 and had begun his most repressive phase. Machado was kind to the Cubanaco colonos once, and he may have been again, had another powerful patron not intervened. In 1931, Eugenio Molinet was Machado's secretary of agriculture. He had been the general manager of Chaparra and Delicias during the 1925 conflict, and his sympathies lay with the company. In a letter on secretary of agriculture letterhead dated 11 June 1931, Molinet advised his friend Wood to "stay firm, be impartial and just, and wait for the storm to pass." He added: "You can count on my loyal cooperation, and I almost dare say the Government's."[23] Although Molinet waxed nostalgic with the colono commission sent to Havana, promising its members that he would work hard to get them a meeting with

Machado, he reported back to Wood sarcastically: "The famous commission wandering around Havana has disappeared, like magic, without being able to meet the President; although I had already briefed the President on the situation, so he would not have been disposed to help them anyhow."[24]

Why did the Chaparra and Delicias colonos lose the battle to maintain the minimum, despite the moral, political, and economic power that they held in the region? By 1931 Machado's regime had become highly centralized. The colonos had set the precedent in 1925 that he was the final arbiter, the "super-patron," so to speak. Thus, when Molinet blocked them from his "good offices" in 1931, they were out of luck. The populist moment had passed, the pressure of a forthcoming harvest was not yet present, and there were no striking workers organizing at Chaparra and Delicias to increase the stakes. The economic situation in the countryside was also considerably worse than it had been in 1925, leading many desperate small and medium colonos to sign the circular in exchange for immediate relief. Finally, whereas in 1925 the larger colonos had participated in creating a unified colono class fighting for a goal through solidarity, in 1931 they quickly aligned themselves with Cubanaco. We might see Eugenio Molinet as the most representative of these cases. Once a middle-class Cuban, head of the sanitation department at Chaparra, and owner of a medium-size colonia, he had become by 1931 a clear ally of American capital embodied in Cubanaco and the dictatorship embodied in General Gerardo Machado. The colonos of Chaparra, Delicias, and other mills across the island would not get their just rewards for all their nationalist propaganda until Machado and Molinet boarded a plane and left the island for good and the 1933 Revolution ushered in a new populist compact.

PATRONS UNDERMINE THE COMPACT
IN THE COUNTRYSIDE: THE WORKERS

At the same time that sugar company administrators strong-armed colonos into agreeing to the removal of price guarantees and other benefits, they cut back on salaries and services that the workers considered essential. As early as 1926, Doty informed Rionda that to reduce expenses Tuinucú would "do no painting whatever in the factory or mill towns; make no repairs to houses whatever except the dwelling house porch; lay off men working on the road to Sancti Spiritus, in the mill towns, gardens, and various other places. Also," he continued, "We will stop wireless broadcasting and cut pensions by 10 percent."[25] Tuinucú cut pensions altogether in 1932 and by that year the most fortunate employees and workers at the mill—those with jobs during the dead-season months—had their monthly salaries cut by 82 percent.[26]

Field workers surely suffered the worst cutbacks. In December 1930 Rionda advised Doty that the extremely difficult jobs of cutting, lifting, and hauling a days' work worth of cane ought not to cost more than 80 cents—50 cents for cutting and lifting and 30 cents for hauling (recall that the average pay in 1906 was $1.80–2.50 per day). "I am sorry to have to reduce the wages of those poor laborers," Rionda wrote, "but I can not see how it can be done otherwise."[27] When Doty did as he was told, Rionda responded with what can only in retrospect be read as extreme naïveté: "You have done well in reducing [the budget] to such an extreme as to make us wonder how much can be done when things are bad. Cuba has great facilities to expand and contract." Referring specifically to the men who hauled cane with their carts, he wrote: "Considering that the oxen earn money and get no pay I should think a man owning *carretas* and hauling at 30 cents makes more money than the cane cutter at 50 cents. Anyhow, these poor devils are the ones that in reality are carrying us! When good times come—if they ever do—we must remember those laborers."[28]

Mills across the island made similar reductions, drastically undermining the patrons' compact. Cubanaco reported in May 1932 that it had "reduced salaries to 33.33 percent of what they were in 1931."[29] A report from Oriente Province's Punta Alegre Sugar Company dated September 1932 observed that "the average daily pay for 1932 was 40 percent less than the averages back in 1910, and some 30 percent less than the seven-year period from 1910 [to] 1917."[30] The British Embassy in Havana asserted one year later that wages across the island had been steadily descending since 1929, adding that it was "probably no exaggeration to say that field workers are worse off in some respects today than in the days of slavery. They are expected to work 10 or 11 hours a day for 25 cents, with seldom more than 100 days' work in the year."[31]

Pay was lower, and there was less work overall. Most mills espoused a strategy of shortening the milling season. From an average of almost five months a year in 1925, the harvest declined to just over two months in 1933. Ursinio Rojas remembers his father and brother getting only 20 cents for each 100 arrobas of cane that they cut and loaded for the Tacajó mill. Because the company was skimping on weeding and planting new cane during the dead season, the cane was rat eaten, old, and full of weeds, making it impossible to cut more than 300 arrobas during the 2:00 A.M. to 11:00 A.M. work hours.[32] The estimated total spent on cane cutters' salaries fell by more than 90 percent during that same period due to lower pay and the shorter harvest.[33] Some mills had to close altogether: There were 163 mills active in 1929, but only 125 in 1933.[34]

The immigrant workers desperate enough to have returned—or remained—in Cuba after the economic downturn found more Cubans competing with them for fieldwork. Harold Griffith told an interviewer that immigration to Chaparra pretty much stopped in 1928 because the Cubans "learned how to pick cane."[35] Certainly, many knew how to cut cane before, but it was a brutally difficult, low-paid job that they would only do in dire straits. Since Cubans were more desperate for employment and nationalism was on the rise, it made sense for sugar companies to replace Jamaicans and Haitians in the fields with Cubans.[36]

Some immigrants managed to secure assistance from their nations of origin. In 1931 and 1932 the U.S. Navy helped repatriate seven hundred Puerto Ricans and large numbers of Virgin Islanders, while Jamaica helped finance the return of some forty thousand workers between 1930 and 1933.[37] This still left many immigrants stranded on the island. In 1931 M. A. Jacobs wrote a petition signed by more than five hundred other British West Indian field workers at Chaparra begging the British Embassy for assistance. "There is no progress," they wrote. "Starvation has taken place and a famine is threatening the island right now. So before many of us should die of starvation and calamities, we are putting our distress to the mother country, asking her for some kind of assistance by which we may be able to leave this island of Cuba." They concluded, "We are just like the children of Israel in the land of Egypt."[38]

Foreign field workers were at the bottom of the economic ladder, but their counterparts at the top also suffered the effects of the Depression. Manuel Rionda advised Oliver Doty in September 1930: "Whenever it can be avoided you should not employ Americans, particularly to fill such places as *puntistas* [those who judge when the cane is the right sweetness at the factory], overseers, and inspectors of cane fields. These can be filled by men in Cuba today who are just as good as Americans or perhaps better—and at one-third the cost!"[39] It is ironic that what the ANIA had sought to do through nationalist pressure in the mid-1920s came about through economic pressure in the 1930s.

Besides cutting jobs, salaries, and the milling season, mills across the island slashed the budgets for schools, medical services, light, and power. The educational expenses at Chaparra and Delicias fell from the 1929–30 level of $41,700 to $9,000 by 1933–34. The company gave fewer discounts for medical services and stopped paying for doctors and teachers in more rural areas. Rural Cubans thus suddenly found themselves unable to remain in their communities. Cubanaco's archives are full of letters and petitions to General Manager R. B. Wood from workers and colonos pleading for the return of schools, teachers, and doctors to their communities in the colonias or mill towns. Workers and small colonos also asked for cash advances or land because they were literally starving. For example, Cándido Fernández wrote in July 1932: "Will you please . . . give me a piece of land on the former 'Campo Sport' [to] cultivate corn, sweet potatoes, beans and etc. I am an old employee of the Analysis Department Central Office, and have six small children to give food."[40]

Other letters in the same file from that period reveal the incredible contrast between the lives of men like Cándido and the administrators. One new administrator at the mill (H. M. Hicks) requested a list of luxury furniture to be shipped from the United States and his dog "couriered" from his former place of employment. R. B. Wood (the "president" of the Chaparra Yacht Club) was called to a meeting in Havana to discuss preparations for the National Sailing Regatta.[41] The same dichotomies existed at Tuinucú. In 1933 Cuban residents were struggling to find food and clothing for their families when Manuel Rionda and his nephew George Atkinson Braga showed up in Manuel's Rolls-Royce.

The patrons' compact fell apart as workers and colonos lost jobs, a place to mill their cane, and their health and education services in one blow. No longer willing to tolerate such harsh conditions and extreme inequality, small colonos and representatives of field and factory workers from 32 sugarmills across the island met in Santa Clara to constitute the National Union of Sugar Industry Workers (SNOIA) in December 1932. They did so despite—and in reaction to—the extreme levels of military repression under Machado. By the second meeting of SNOIA, held the following May at Camagüey, the number of mills represented had grown to 102.

Sugar workers' manifestos from 1932 and 1933 demonstrate how much labor leaders learned from the strike wave of 1925. The proclamations emphasize the need to do solidarity work among workers of the sectors related to sugar, especially railroad and dock workers, but also soldiers, small and medium-size colonos, and farmers of other products in the region. Railroad workers could refuse to run trains that might otherwise bring soldiers to repress a strike. Dock workers could refuse to load sugar made by strike-breakers. Soldiers could refuse to repress workers. Colonos could complete a production blockade against a company by joining striking workers. Finally, merchants, farmers, and other residents near the mills could provide sustenance for striking workers. The manifestos also recognized the important role that women, youth, and immigrants had played in the first strikes. They included a special request to women and youths, urging them to form "Aid Committees" to provide for basic needs and "Anti-Eviction Committees" to protect strikers and their families' homes. Finally, they encouraged foreign and national mill workers and agricultural workers to form strike committees together, coordinating mill and field strikes.[42]

Although a significant number of unions belonged to SNOIA, only a small minority of workers within each mill participated in this early unionization movement. The Railroad Brotherhood at Puerto Padre tried to help Chaparra and its colonias create a new union in 1932, but company coercion largely thwarted these efforts. As the former worker Luis Merconchini tells it, "Nobody wanted to join the union in those years, because joining the union meant losing one's job, and the majority of workers had families with no alternative means of support."[43] With the help of the Rural Guard or private security forces, most companies followed Chaparra's pattern of evicting from their homes (together with their families) anyone accused of organizing a union. This was an effective way to use the apparent worker benefit of housing as a means of control. (Recall that the patrons' compact combined benefits with control in exchange for labor and cooperation.)

When companies barred workers from the legal avenue for protest (unions) after having cut salaries, jobs, and the already minimal social services, workers took to sabotage. Crime reports from Chaparra and Delicias reveal that such acts proliferated during 1932 and 1933. The most common and highest-profile strategy among workers was to set the cane fields on fire. American press sources reported in March 1933 that two million pounds of cane had been torched in the single province of Oriente.[44] Workers stole or destroyed bridges and telephone wires and wood and other materials. They placed obstacles in the way of company trains; left the doors open on cane trains so that cane would fall out as the train moved; and burned, among other things, the barracks of the private security force, a cane-train bridge, and the slaughterhouse. In March 1933, someone even made an attempt on Wood's life.[45] Workers would later adopt similar strategies of sabotage during the equally repressive periods of 1935–38 and 1956–59.

Sabotage may have given workers some moral satisfaction, but it could not relieve their hunger. Many workers had to abandon the countryside to avoid repression and starvation. The Spanish ambassador in Havana described the consequent "caravans of hunger" that came streaming to the cities in search of jobs, food, and a place to settle their families.[46] But companies in the cities were also cutting back on jobs and salaries. Given that sugar was the base of the Cuban economy, the sale of most goods and services depended on Cubans' gaining wages and profits from sugar; the Great Depression thus devastated the entire Cuban economy. Estimated national revenue fell from 708 million pesos in 1925 to only 294 million pesos in 1933.[47] In city and countryside, Cubans responded with strikes and unemployment marches.

REVOLUTION IN THE CITY

On 5 August 1933 workers across the country staged a general strike to demonstrate their sympathy to the Havana bus drivers who refused to pay Machado's transportation taxes. Two days after the strike began, a false rumor spread across Havana that Machado had left the island, and many ecstatic Cubans rushed to the National Palace to celebrate. Policemen surrounded the unarmed civilians and shot at them. Such a large, open confrontation between police and civilians was unprecedented in Cuba, and Cubans renewed the general strike to rid the island of Machado's dictatorship. On 8 August the communist leaders of the CNOC made a deal with President Machado to end the strike in exchange for the economic demands of the workers and the legalization of their party and union (the CNOC and the Communist Party had been declared illegal in August 1925). The strike went on, regardless of the deal. As the Communist Party later recognized in a self-critique to explain the "August mistake," striking workers in the cities and countryside wanted not just improvements in their salaries and benefits but also a conclusive end to Machadista state repression.[48]

"The masses" paralyzed the Cuban economy, and they should be given credit for the fall of Machado. But before the strike could achieve its ultimate goal of ousting Machado and his Congress and army, several officers from that very army escorted him to the airport on 12 August and named an upper-class Cuban, Carlos Manuel de Céspedes, as his successor. (A U.S. mediator, Secretary of State Sumner Welles, had advised the officers to do this under the threat of U.S. invasion.) The appointment of a new president left Machado's Congress intact, along with much of his army. Despite the mass participation in the strike, the events of early August constituted a coup d'état, not revolutionary change.

Workers and middle-class Cubans nevertheless seized the opportunity to flood the streets and celebrate Machado's departure. What they did expressed how they felt, just like the smaller scale workers' "counter-theater" at the mill described in chapter 5.[49] Their actions constituted a clear rejection of the system of patronage and power embodied in President Machado's dictatorship. They targeted and attacked the most notorious elite supporters of the dictatorship, as well as its foot soldiers, the secret police. Thousands of lower- and middle-class Cubans descended on the Presidential Palace and the houses of twenty-eight notorious Machado supporters. The crowd, according to one U.S. observer, "was not chiefly interested in looting. Time and time again, when someone started to carry away a piece of furniture which was intact, he would be met with the cry, 'No, no; it is dirty, dirty,' and the axe would fall upon it."[50] They forced their way into the lower floor of the palace, smashed furniture, and tore up trees and plants in the garden. Someone hung a "For Rent" sign on the main entrance, symbolizing the impression that U.S. and Cuban capitalists could literally buy the patronage of the president.

Besides this rejection of corruption and excess, two other motivations of the crowds became evident—the first shared by most, and the second more prominent among lower-class residents of the city: revenge and hunger. The officers of Machado's army were not targets because they had rejected their unpopular leader, but there were many "mob reprisals" against leaders of Machado's strong-armed killing squad. Someone described as "one of the oldest American residents of Havana" wrote a colorful description of this type of revenge for the *Saturday Evening Post* of Philadelphia: "The relief felt by a long-suffering people expressed itself in blood. . . . Of course the [police] had it coming to them. They had murdered wantonly . . . laughed if they happened to kill the wrong man and jested when they disemboweled boys. . . . It was enough for any man to yell 'There's one!' and point: and then there would be one less!" . . . The crowd tallied a hit at the top of their voices; and after each hit, human eyes turned to look for more bull's eyes."[51]

What the mobs did to the bodies of the policemen once they had been killed reveals elements of revenge, humor, and disdain. Someone placed a cigar between the teeth of former Police Chief Antonio Aincart's corpse as jubilant individuals hung it by the neck from an arc light. The crowds made a bonfire beneath the corpse and danced around it as the rope burned through (according to a perhaps exaggerated account in *Time* magazine). When an ambulance arrived to take away the corpse, the crowds shouted, "Dump Aincart into the sea! He is not fit to be buried in the cemetery with human beings."[52]

One astute observer from the United States noted in the leftist *New Republic* magazine that, while middle-class Cubans waved palm fronds stolen from the presidential garden at the American Embassy, thanking Sumner Welles for helping to rid the island of Machado, another, "more grimly ecstatic" group looted the palace and Machadista houses for food. They lugged off a prize hog, butchered it into small pieces, and distributed them among hungry bystanders. The recipients rushed into the side streets "with bloody joints and hunks of meat" to spark charcoal fires to cook them in.[53] Poor Cubans may in fact have been genuinely interested in taking some of the furniture and goods that middle-class Cubans had the luxury of destroying with the statement, "No, it is dirty." At least in one case, a poor Afro-Cuban woman had the wherewithal to justify taking something in terms that middle-class protesters could accept. She took Machado's linens from the National Palace and waved them to the crowd, declaring that she deserved them "because she was a taxpayer."[54]

President de Céspedes did not bring any immediate relief to the extreme poverty that led to such looting; nor did he significantly reform either the political or military underpinnings of the Machado dictatorship. As the palm-frond wavers mentioned earlier suggest, many Cubans believed that his government had come into office largely as a result of Welles's mediation. According to a popular saying, de Céspedes bore a "Made in the U.S.A." label.[55] Many Cubans continued to use strikes and protests throughout August to demand speedy justice, revenge, and a more equitable distribution of goods.

Riding on this popular wave of protest, Sergeant Fulgencio Batista, other military men, and a group of radical students, professors, and journalists led a bloodless coup against ex-Machadista officers and President de Céspedes on 5 September 1933. This motley group represented the first nationalist-populist coalition in Cuba not recognized by U.S. power. Professor Ramón Grau San Martín became the provisional president, and Sergeant Batista began his meteoric rise to power in the background. (This same Batista would stage a far less popular coup in 1952; his more dictatorial regime from 1952 to 1959 led to the Cuban Revolution of 1959 that brought Fidel Castro to power.)

Grau and his co-conspirators—the University Student Directorate and the sergeants—broadcast an English-language message to Americans in the *New York Times* on 8 October 1933 explaining that they wanted to give Cuba a "New Deal" like the one Roosevelt was implementing in the United States. "We can no longer tolerate puppet governments born of monopolies and concessions," Grau declared, because they make Cuba merely "a sweatshop for the privileged few. . . . Our success will mean a new Cuba, born of new ideals. . . . We are called radicals because we are closely following the tracks of your own National Recovery Act; we are called Communist because we endeavor to return the buying power of the Cuban people." The Student Directorate's speech was far more threatening, proclaiming the revolutionary goal to "conquer economic and political freedom."[56]

Politicians in the United States were concerned, but did not want to jeopardize the new "Good Neighbor" image. The Roosevelt administration therefore assembled the Latin American ambassadors in Washington, told them that there would be no "intervention," and then proceeded to announce that the United States would not recognize the Grau regime until it proved its popularity and ability to maintain order. "Just in case," the United States sent twenty-nine ships to surround Cuba's shores. The overbearing challenge that the United States thus created for Cubans who wanted significant nationalist change is captured in two cartoons in the *Nation* (figures 32 and 33).

The Grau regime introduced a series of reforms that responded directly to the popular demands of the mobilized masses: It repealed the Platt Amendment, gave women the vote, lowered utility and interest rates (nearly all were run by U.S. companies), and gave autonomy to the universities.[57]

32 *"No Sir! We're not
     through yet."*
     The Nation, 30 August
     1933, 137:232. Reprinted
     with permission.

One decree law pledged that government lands and tracts confiscated from Machado's henchmen would be distributed in thirty-three-acre plots to the poor, accompanied by a yoke of oxen, a cow, some seed, and scientific advice.[58] The government also sponsored the inauguration of a National Colono Association and a program of land reform that guaranteed tenant colonos the permanent right to stay on the land they cultivated.[59] This was significant because, as noted earlier, most colonos were Cuban, and many of the sugarmill owners who rented them land were American. The colonos did not gain full ownership of the land, but at least they had more security because landowners could not evict them.

For workers, the regime recognized their right to organize, established a Labor Ministry to arbitrate strikes, workers' compensation, a minimum wage, an eight-hour workday and forty-eight-hour workweek, and a Nationalization of Labor decree requiring Cuban nationality for 50 percent of all employees and 50 percent of total salaries in industry, commerce, and

LIBERTY

The Shadow

33   *The Nation*, 20 September
     1933, 137:315. Reprinted
     with permission.

agriculture. The reforms symbolized a great deal to laborers. For the first
time, the state pledged to intervene in more than an ad hoc or repressive
way between capitalists and labor. The eight-hour workday meant an end
to the exhausting twelve-hour work regime whereby mill workers had to do
one six-hour shift, lose up to an hour walking home to eat and sleep for a few
hours, and then trek back before the bell rang to signal the start of another
six-hour shift.[60] The "third shift" would also mean jobs for some one hundred thousand more workers in the sugar industry alone.[61] The minimum
wage of 50 cents per 100 arrobas for cutting and hauling the sugar crop in
1934 represented a significant improvement, for the rate had gone as low as
20 cents in 1933.

The extremely popular 50 percent law promised to end the practice
whereby foreigners' family members or foreign professionals got positions
that Cubans could fill, leaving only the worst paid and most difficult jobs
for nationals. It required that 50 percent of the jobs in each workplace be

reserved for Cubans. Great numbers of Cubans, many of them Afro-Cubans (who suffered the worst discrimination), staged demonstrations to support the legislation and to demand that it be increased from 50 percent to 80 percent. Companion legislation ruled that only Cubans could lead unions on the island, not foreign citizens. When the communist and the Trotskyist unions published manifestos and newspaper articles condemning the laws as fascist efforts to divide the working classes, mobs stormed the newspapers and targeted their union headquarters. The same laws produced injustices and violence in the countryside. The targets there were the Ingleses and other Caribbean or Asian workers. The Rural Guard practiced raids along with bounty hunters, who tracked down foreigners and deported them—often without their belongings and wages. Working-class Cubans participated enthusiastically in the effort to rid the island of foreigners, whom they perceived as competition for scarce jobs. Communist and Trotskyist union organizers who wanted to forge class solidarity looked on them with distress.[62]

The Grau San Martín regime's most concrete social reforms have been attributed to the left-wing member of the coalition, Minister of the Interior Antonio Guiteras, the leader of Young Cuba. But he and the students who supported him had to compete for workers' loyalty against the communist CNOC (hereafter "Confederation") and the Trotskyist FOH (hereafter "Federation").[63] These two leftist organizations perceived the regime as middle-class, nationalist, and fascist, along the lines of Adolf Hitler's Germany. There were certainly elements of truth to their interpretation. Many members of the original Grau coalition neither enforced nor supported the reforms. By the end of the one-hundred-day administration, Fulgencio Batista, by then chief of the army, was able to consolidate control over the armed forces and get soldiers to take a more repressive approach to workers. While the communist and Trotskyist unions threatened from the left, Batista, his U.S. allies, and the traditional Cuban politicians threatened the Grau regime from the right.[64]

REVOLUTION IN THE COUNTRYSIDE:
MILL OCCUPATIONS AND SOVIETS

Despite all of its division, the 1933 Revolution provided a populist moment with far more potential for worker protest than Machado's short-lived populism. At least for a brief interregnum, the armed forces and state leaders pledged their allegiance to the popular classes and the Cuban nation to a greater extent than any previous regime. Workers certainly rose to the occasion. Sugar workers across the island had already participated in the strikes from June through August that forced Machado to leave; some did so as members of the communist SNOIA. Machado's departure on 12 August elicited outbursts in smaller cities, such as Puerto Padre, similar to those in Havana, combining jubilation, looting, and destruction of pro-Machado newspapers and notorious Machadista homes.[65] But most sugarmills did not erupt into full-scale revolutionary mobilization until Batista led the soldiers' revolt in September. Only then could workers take advantage of a break in the power of the forces of repression. Instead of repressing rebelling workers, soldiers supported them: A U.S. consul observed that mill owners actually preferred not to call in the Rural Guard or the army because the guards fraternized with the mobs and would not "lessen the moral strength of the strikers."[66]

A revolutionary avalanche took place in sugarmill communities across the country after Machado's exile. Workers forced the management to leave many mills. Different political groups then competed to lead the mobilized sugar workers, including the ABC Revolutionary Society of middle-class revolutionaries, the Guiterista students and Labor Ministry officials, the "Bolchevique-Leninista" (Trotskyist) Federation, and the communist Confederation. After a brief overview of sugar workers' activities across the island, the rest of this chapter will zero in on the mobilization of workers at the mills that Rionda and Cubanaco controlled. Chaparra and Delicias played an important symbolic role for the nationalistic Grau regime when Guiteras nationalized them in December 1933 due to Cubanaco's refusal to negotiate with the workers. (They were the only sugarmills that were nationalized during the one-hundred-day reform period.)

Like their poor and working-class counterparts in the cities, some sugar workers reacted violently and with vengeance against the extreme repression they had faced. Most, though, responded to planters' and administrators' control with irony, humor, and dignity. Workers at the Tacajó sugarmill devised a very creative act of vengeance: They installed a loudspeaker that rang a bell on the street corner near an administrator's house so that he could feel what it was like to be deprived of sleep.[67] Inspired by examples from the Russian Revolution of 1917, field and factory workers organized worker soviets to take over, protect, and run the mills from September 1933 through January 1934.[68] In a few isolated cases, as in the occupation of former President José Miguel Gómez's Mabay sugarmill, small colonos joined the workers. A remarkable feature of this revolutionary occupation of sugarmills is that one of the primary goals of strike committees and worker Red Guards (modeled after Russian worker militias) was to protect the mills from any form of destruction or sabotage. It seemed that they wanted to prove that they were not savages but, rather, Cuban citizens worthy of a larger share of sugar profits. They used the fall months from September to December to prepare the fields and mills for the January harvest.

Those not needed for work at the mills marched in flying brigades from mill to mill to support their counterparts to gain demands from other mills. For example, between three thousand and four thousand workers from the Tacajó mill took over a train and rode to the neighboring Baguanos mill, where they confronted the mill management. From there, more than three thousand Tacajó and Baguanos workers and farmers carrying sticks, machetes, and a few small arms marched to the Santa Lucía mill to free the workers from the company–Rural Guard tyranny in that enclave. Some of them were Santa Lucía natives who had been ejected from their jobs and homes after the 1925 strike. On meeting a group of strikers, a Rural Guard sergeant advised them to elect a fifteen-person committee to speak to the mill administrators. The leader said that "he would have to wait for the rest" to see if they would agree. When the sergeant climbed a tree and saw men as far as the eye could see, he stepped aside and allowed them to destroy the sentry post and to break the entry gate's chains that symbolized the company's extreme control over its residents. Workers from all three mills marched through the town and, in a triumphant gesture of counter-theater raised the Cuban flag and the international workers' symbol from Russia—the red flag—on the mill's tall sugar towers. (These towers were a symbol of power and progress like those at Chaparra. Recall the description of them, with their "enormous proportions and reaching boldly upward, as if challenging infinity," in *Bohemia* magazine in 1925.)[69]

Workers raised these homemade flags and sang the national anthem and the communist "Internationale" at sugarmills across the island during the revolution.[70] The rousing lyrics of the "Internationale," versions of which were being sung by workers across the world in the Depression-era 1930s, went something like this: "Arise ye prisoners of starvation, Arise ye wretched of the earth / For justice thunders condemnation, A better world's in birth / No more tradition's chains shall bind us, Arise, ye slaves, no more in thrall / The earth shall rise on new foundations, We who have been nothing shall be all. (Refrain): So comrades, come rally, and the last fight let us face, The Internationale unites the human race."[71]

Back at the Tacajó mill, the strike committee organized marches and demonstrations every afternoon at 3 P.M. to sing the "Internationale," distribute free goods, and hold sporting events, including baseball games. Workers occupied as many as thirty-six mills by the end of September 1933, but workers only made their mills into soviets at Tacajó, Mabay, and Santa Lucía in Oriente; Nazábal, Parque Alto, and Hormiguero in Santa Clara; and Jaronú and Senado in Camagüey. These soviets constituted elaborate experiments in political, juridical, and economic life. Strike committees took over stocks of crude and refined sugar and sold them to pay workers' salaries, to purchase food for families living at the mills, and to stock up on rifles for armed self-defense groups. In the case of Mabay, committees distributed tools, machinery, and more than 66,000 acres of land to peasants and workers. Workers operated the mill without upper-management oversight, opened schools, and established a Justice Tribunal.[72]

Workers at the mills owned by Manuel Rionda did not go quite so far, but their more subtle actions constituted a clear rejection of patronage and control. They wanted to make administrators know how it felt to be a worker. They made them live without servants, eat humble food, and ask permission for just about everything. On 12 September 1933 one of Rionda's nephews reported that workers at Francisco, Elia, Tuinucú, Céspedes, and "all of the other mills of Cuba" had completely frozen all activity in the mill towns and colonias. At Francisco, they "went to the extreme" of cutting off all electricity and refusing to allow anyone to leave without permission from the strike committee. Workers allowed water and electricity to flow at Tuinucú, but only between 6 P.M. and 6 A.M. The strike committees ordered office employees to leave their jobs. These employees and their families complained that their lives were made "almost impossible" when the workers denied them the domestic servants who normally washed their clothes and cooked their meals. Oliver Doty was sick, undergoing treatment in the United States at the time, so workers at Tuinucú imprisoned his replacement, Earl Hine, in his home, letting Hine and his wife leave the mill only after they promised that they would present the workers' demands to the shareholders in Havana and New York.[73]

Workers at Tuinucú not only targeted the loyal office employees and Superintendent Hine; they also categorically rejected their matron Isidora and the system of dependence and charity that she represented. "The strike committee ordered Isidora to leave her Tuinucú," Manuel wrote to his nephew, "and because she did not want to do so, they took away her servants, leaving only her oldest maid Teofila, and her sister Concha. Upon hearing this, we offered to raise daily wages of less than $1.00 by 30 percent and over $1.00 by 20 percent."[74] Another nephew went to the mill to try to get Isidora and Concha to leave because of the family's concern that it was too dangerous for the elderly sisters. But, as her nephew Higinio Fanjul wrote on 14 September, "Isidora would die before abandoning her beloved Tuinucú." He added, "One cannot help but admire her: 87 years old! The saddest part is that some of the people she has protected since their births are among the vanguard of the strike movement. I refused to believe that these movements would make it to mills like Tuinucú and Francisco, but to live is to learn."[75]

Higinio Fanjul complained about the "wave of communism" but stated that the most important thing was to "sprinkle some cash around" because the fundamental cause of the problems was hunger, and "no one deserve[d] the blame more than [U.S. President Herbert] Hoover and Smoot [of the Hawley-Smoot Tariff]." Manuel shared Higinio's opinion that a little money could eliminate the movement. He sent a telegram to the strike committee at Tuinucú that read:

> We are sorry that you have taken this approach. We consider it unnecessary because as soon as the sugar situation improves, and the price of sugar increases, we will be the first to ameliorate the lives of all of those employed at our beloved Tuinucú. In order to avoid misery and sickness, we have authorized Doñas Isidora and Concha to distribute up to $1,000.00 a week during the rest of the month to those faithful, old employees who have found themselves without work for no fault of their own.[76]

In a remarkable gesture given the context of extreme poverty and hunger, the workers rejected this patronizing distribution of funds.[77]

In late September Manuel wrote to his nephew in London that matters "in the interior and in Cuban plantations" were "pretty well muddled." Tuinucú was "in the hands of the working men—very friendly but no work; no one is really in authority. Hine is in Havana and Oliver, here." Manuel preferred to keep American administrators away, since "their presence might precipitate trouble."[78] He was right: As his nephew Higinio Fanjul noted, the mills that were having the least hard time were those where workers had no one to argue with. "In all the mills," Higinio wrote, "including Tuinucú, all of the pigs, chickens, and provisions are running out."[79]

Most mills had strike committees (including lots of women) who set up soup kitchens to distribute such food equitably to all of the residents who remained at the occupied mills. Ursinio Rojas mentioned at least one case—at the Tacajó mill—where strikers made administrators and upper-level employees eat the humble workers' food. One can almost feel his smirk as he wrote: "Sr. Hernández lost quite a bit of weight because he didn't like the 'rancho' that the union made in the soup kitchen."[80] Workers' efforts to "level" elite managers' and employees' access to food and other goods and services reveals their desire to make their superiors perceive the inequalities and the emptiness of the patrons' compact. The redistribution of food and goods, though short-lived, constituted a very revolutionary effort to reverse inequality.

Rionda adopted the attitude that the companies might as well concede whichever demands his nephews considered reasonable to avoid any damage. He wrote to José on 28 September that as far as he was concerned, none of the contracts were worth the paper they were written on "until Cuba has a strong government."[81] Two days later, José reported back on a meeting at the new Labor Ministry office in Havana with the Tuinucú strike representatives Agustín Valdivia, Donato Arcia, and Hernández Díaz. The letter captures the radical change that the 1933 Revolution brought to the island:

> They were much harsher than I thought they would be, and one can say that the "feeling (sentimiento)" of the old Tuinucú has disappeared. This is a changed Cuba. The workers are perfectly organized and united, everywhere, and marked by Communist tendencies. The Government is weak, and can give only minimal guarantees to capital and property. It has placed itself on labor's side to get their support, and that is why the workers feel so strong, ruling the roost, and imposing conditions.

José reported that the hardest condition to swallow was the workers' insistence that worker delegates be recognized to ensure that the company fulfilled those commitments made in the agreement. The Tuinucú managers, he asserted, had always acted in good faith, and he took offense at the implication that they would not honor the commitments. José was incensed when Hernández Díaz referred to the company as *esta gente* (these people) when talking to the government representative Loret de Mola: "And these are the children of those who worked with us in harmony, and who received so many favors from Tuinucú."[82]

Favors no longer sufficed. Workers wanted contracts and government legislation that established fixed social and economic rights, and the 1933 Revolution provided them with the opportunity to win these. According to Agustín Valdivia, Interior Minister Guiteras told him at a meeting in Holguín to "press these people (*apriete a esta gente*)," meaning the Rionda family's interests on the island, which were very large at the time.[83] Precisely to avoid this kind of grouping—workers from all the Rionda mills versus the companies—Manuel advised his nephews to schedule the meetings in Havana with workers from the various mills for different days. Even though they were kept apart, the workers from all of the Rionda mills nevertheless succeeded in winning most of their demands, including higher salaries than the minimum wage that was later established. The minimum wage that President Mendieta established in January 1934 was $1 per day in the cities and sugarmills, but Tuinucú paid $1.20.[84] Tuinucú did not return to "normal" until early March 1934, when it was finally able to begin harvesting the 1933–34 cane crop.[85]

REVOLUTION AT CHAPARRA AND DELICIAS:
WORKERS AND THE STATE VERSUS THE COMPANY

At Chaparra, Delicias, and the private Cubanaco port of Juan Claro, rank-and-file workers managed to forge a new union across ideological and sectoral barriers through meetings, assemblies, and popular demonstrations during the fall of 1933. As in the case of 1925, this can be understood as a form of oppositional politics whereby residents were willing to unite against the company in the context of economic depression, despite their ideological, class, and ethnic differences.

In early September 1933 dock workers declared a strike, and Chaparra and Delicias workers followed suit, demanding an eight-hour workday, a 25 percent salary increase, free rent and utilities, and recognition of their union. About one thousand sugar, dock, and rail workers met at the port and then marched to the Rural Guard's barracks at Delicias, where Wood and his assistant were in hiding. A guard named "Tamayo," already infamous for killing an old man, shot at the workers and killed two. One of the workers entered the barracks, grabbed Tamayo, and hit him with his revolver. More workers arrived and beat Tamayo to death. In a move reminiscent of the action of the mobs against the policeman in Havana, they then tied the guard to a horse's tail, paraded him through the mill town, and burned him. Wood and his assistant H. M. Hicks managed to escape and take refuge on a British merchant ship docked at the port.[86]

The strikers created worker militias to maintain order at the mill and in the surrounding areas. Reports suggested that more than four hundred and fifty workers armed themselves at Delicias. At the Juan Claro port, workers formed thirteen Auxiliary Committees and strategically placed a Red Guard made up of eighty armed sentinels in a fort at the town's entrance. Self-defense committees surrounded the town to keep soldiers or strikebreakers from entering. Many members of the company's armed guard supported the strike.[87] This is not surprising, given that several of the letters of 1932–33 requesting access to credit, land, housing, and electricity came from company guards.

Officers of the U.S. Navy, on inspecting the Puerto Padre district in September 1933, remarked that the workers maintained "unusually good organization," "allow[ed] no depredation or unauthorized visiting," and "continue[d] to be efficient." The same sources remarked that strikers were delivering water by truck and train to areas in need and that they extended "courtesies to citizens like permitting funeral processions to operate on the railroads." The Navy officers also stated that Guiterista university students, a popular support base of the Grau regime, were administering the revolutionary militias, "a well-organized group in each locality having as leaders several men educated in the U.S."[88]

The worker manifestos that remain in the Santiago de Cuba provincial archives indicate that, in fact, many political factions were competing for leadership. The SNOIA led the workers at Delicias and the Juan Claro port, while the Federation's Trotskyist "Partido Bolchevique-Leninista" led workers at Chaparra and in the city of Puerto Padre. The communist Confederation maintained an extremely sectarian stance, attacking the Grau-Guiteras-Batista regime as "bourgeois" and the Trotskyist Federation as divisive opportunists. It accused the Federation of sending only pamphlets while the Confederation sent members to fight and fall with their brothers in arms against Machado, citing the examples of the Haitian comrade Nicolás Simón in Municiones, "the [C]hinese" Wong in Castillo, and comrade Montenegro at the Cayo Juan Claro. One Confederation manifesto asked whether the rival leader González Palacios had on any occasion intervened directly or indirectly to help the workers of Juan Claro achieve more hygienic housing. Then it made a point that underscored the problems born of socialist and anarcho-syndicalist leadership in Cuba's past: "The [Confederation] does not focus on leaders. . . . It is wary of those who erect themselves as leaders because they are to blame for all of the wrongs done to proletarians, up to today." It ended with a quotation from Martí: "With the faith of all, and for all."

The Federation's manifestos spoke more about events in Havana and Europe than Puerto Padre, reflecting the predominance of Spanish anarcho-syndicalist leaders. One manifesto stated that the 50 percent law was turning Cuban workers against their foreign brethren, prompting nationalist mobs in Havana to raid Federation unions to dislodge Spanish leaders and union members. It criticized the Cuban Communist Party and the Confederation for attacking the law only through manifestos, not through strikes. The pamphleteering argument was thus thrown right back at the Confederation—each accusing the other of not putting enough action behind its rhetoric.

According to one Federation manifesto, Confederation leaders in Havana stated that they could not support strikes against the 50 percent law because too many rank-and-file members supported the legislation. The Federation countered that the Confederation was "embracing Estenoz and Ivonnet [the Afro-Cuban leaders of the 1912 PIC rebellion] instead of Marx" and did not attack the 50 percent law and other "manipulative" labor laws because its leaders preferred to stay quiet rather than suffer attacks from the government:

> The Communist Party leaders have all the support of the government that attacks the Federation with blood and fire. This is no coincidence. We Bolshevik–Leninists do not passively contemplate this Stalinist betrayal. But it does not surprise us because it is the repetition of Mexico, China, Germany. . . . We know that the Communist Party . . . will recognize their error and shift directions. Then they will declare war against chauvinism and racism. But it will be too late. . . . That is the same song

they sing in all countries. It is the ill-fated politics of Stalinism. Error after error. Turn after turn. The workers pay, the labor movement derailed and destroyed.

Despite their differences, the manifesto battles between the Confederation and Federation concretely indicate that the two organizations shared the stance of complete rejection of the Grau regime's populist reforms.[89]

Meanwhile, workers on the ground had to decide whether to negotiate with the company and the state during the Grau interregnum. The only worker organization that supported the populist regime and advocated using the space created by it was the Guiterista Young Cuba Party. Officers of the U.S. Navy seemed to think that they led the workers at Chaparra, but if this was the case, it is not clear why the workers did not immediately negotiate with the company via Guiteras's new Labor Ministry in Havana (like the Rionda mill strike committees). As Barry Carr has noted, the Confederation's SNOIA did not emerge as the clear leader at Chaparra and Delicias: "An important issue that is not acknowledged in the contemporary Cuban literature, which tends to link the worker insurgency of 1933 exclusively to the actions and projects of the [communist]-influenced sector of the labour movement."[90] Workers' testimonies and interviews emerging out of Chaparra and Delicias do not explicitly define which party dominated the movement, either.

In contrast, at Tuinucú workers clearly used a template from SNOIA when drawing up their list of demands. Manuel Rionda penciled in numerous notes beside the clauses reading: "What are they talking about?" or "There are none at Tuinucú." For example, beside the sixth demand, "against all discrimination against Jamaicans and Haitians, equal salary for equal work and the right to occupy any job," he wrote: "We have no problem accepting this demand . . . though at Tuinucú, one could count on one's fingers the number of Haitians and Jamaicans who work at the mill towns and colonias."[91] Although Tuinucú's workers looked to SNOIA to help compose their demands, they also opted to use Guiteras and his new Labor Ministry in Havana. (Recall Agustín Valdivia's *esta gente* anecdote and Higinio Fanjul's outrage at the workers' attitude.)

The radical Guiteras worked hard to try to establish more links with Cuban workers to counter Batista's growing power, but beyond accepting his offer of a former Machadista mansion for its headquarters, the

Confederation rejected his requests for support. The Federation toned down its attack on the regime only after its Spanish leaders were replaced with Cubans through the 50 percent law. It is understandable that neither communists nor Trotskyists recognized Guiteras's sincerity: Every pro-worker act he carried out might be reversed by one of Batista's counter-acts. For example, Guiteras would set workers free from jail, but Batista would put them back. In late 1933 while Guiteristas engaged in strike mediation and helped workers form militias to defend themselves and "their" government, Batista and his soldiers toured the country breaking strikes on U.S.-owned plantations and attacking communists to win the support of Ambassador Sumner Welles.[92]

The strike at Puerto Padre continued throughout the fall months. After "considering" the workers' demands presented to them before a delegate of Guiteras's Ministry of the Interior, the company announced that it would grant no reforms and would pay the same wages in 1933–34 as it had in 1932–33, despite national minimum-wage decrees to the contrary. Chaparra's workers were willing to return to work under these conditions, but Delicias's workers refused.[93] (It was a common pattern for Chaparra unions to compromise faster than those of Delicias. Perhaps the patrons' compact was stronger at Chaparra than at Delicias because the general offices for the two mills were located at Cubanaco's "first" mill, or perhaps Delicias had stronger labor leaders.) On 19 December the company stated that it would be unable to mill in the 1933–34 season. It closed the hospital, bakery, butcher shop, and other food shops. Department heads were told to leave their posts, and telegraph, telephone, hospital, and other public services were closed.[94] Workers responded by issuing a manifesto calling for solidarity for the workers who had been locked out (*lokouteado*) of Chaparra and Delicias and a boycott of the Chaparra Light and Power Company, which continued to operate through the strike. The same manifesto explicitly called on the Grau regime to fulfill its rhetoric: "You will be our real defender when you do not allow us workers to be trampled, as we are now."[95]

The interior minister stepped up to the challenge. At least briefly, workers managed to pit the Cuban "state" against one of the most powerful American companies. On 21 December 1933, Guiteras ordered the mayor and the local authorities at Puerto Padre to take possession of the power plant, hospital, and commercial departments at Chaparra and Delicias. This included the general stores, slaughterhouse, ice plant, butcher shops, and bakeries. A U.S. diplomat communicated the Cuban Department of Agriculture's message that they were taken over "on the ground of public need, since they were the only plants existing on the lands of this Company, from which *40,000 to 60,000 people* could secure services and products."[96]

The diplomat's description of the events offers a powerful image of "the state" asserting its new position:

> The acting manager of the company . . . declined to deliver over the company's property unless compelled to do so under force. On December 21, 1933, in the presence of a notary the keys to the commercial departments were delivered to the Mayor, who appeared with troops of the Rural Guard to enforce the order. After similar protest and formalities the entire properties of the [Delicias] Sugar Company, the Chaparra Sugar Company, the Chaparra Light and Power Company and the Chaparra Railroad Company were attached on December 22, 1933, and the acting manager was informed that his administration had terminated.[97]

Two days earlier the Secretary of Agriculture Carlos Hevia had explained the reasoning behind the intervention. He was concerned that if Cubanaco did not grind and the government did not do anything about it, the "one hundred thousand inhabitants of the district" would take matters into their own hands. When Sumner Welles asked the Cuban ambassador to speak to Grau about the intervention in early January 1934, Grau responded that the mills had not been affected, merely the hospital and the stores. This was not the case, and the official admitted that, "in this as in other matters, Dr. Grau is evidently ignorant of what is going on."[98]

Jefferson Caffery wrote a confidential U.S. follow-up report dated 11 January 1934 that placed some of the blame in the hands of Cubanaco: "The recent difficulties at Chaparra and Delicias . . . arise from the fact that the Company can pay average field wages of only about fifteen cents a day." The diplomat received this information from an American newspaper correspondent who had obtained it confidentially from one of the company's accountants.[99] When Cubanaco's directors met with Caffery to request diplomatic support, he asked about these wages. According to a Cubanaco memorandum, "Mr. Wood [stated] that a cutter could make approximately 40 cents per day. Mr. Caffery was rather favorably surprised." Accepting Wood's statement as fact, Caffery then advised Cubanaco to file a formal request for the unconditional return of all properties and to appeal against the constitutionality of the intervention.[100]

British reports provide a broader picture of company–state relations under the Grau regime that help clarify the Cuban state's December "intervention" at Chaparra and Delicias. This unique strategy of government "intervention" to coerce management to accept labor's terms was an important symbol of the state's embrace of populist rule. It would be repeated 101 times between 1934 and 1955.[101] According to a report dated 1 November 1933, many companies had stopped paying taxes, assuming that the regime would soon fall without U.S. recognition. These companies refused to accept Grau's pro-worker decrees and waited in expectation for a counter-revolution. The diplomat's astute conclusion was that "the sugar crop is the supreme test of the administration."[102] A month later, the same observer (Grant Watson) suggested that the administration was looking stronger. Guiteras's action at Chaparra, Watson explained, "has caused other sugarmill owners to modify their attitude toward the Government. . . . Some of them [had been] about to issue an ultimatum to the effect that they would be compelled to close down unless the Workmen's Insurance Law was satisfactorily amended."[103] The intervention at Chaparra sent a strong message to these mill owners: Reform or lose your company.

A report from the American consul at Antilla in early January reveals that he had not figured out what the British Watson had figured out—namely, that social and political struggle in Cuba adapted itself to the agricultural cycle of sugar. "Nominally," the report reads, "the various strikes which have occurred throughout the sugarmills all over the country have resulted in a higher scale of wages, which have not been put into effect as the crop of 1934 has not yet begun. It is believed, at this writing, that the majority of sugarmills will not operate this year not only on account of the wage demands being made by unionized labor but, also, on account of the political and economic chaos at present existing in Cuba."[104]

Cuba was too dependent on sugar to let this prophecy come true. While Batista and his soldiers were willing to stand by and watch, and even to join sugar workers in September and October; as the harvest approached in November and December they opted for repression and the rejection of Grau San Martín. Cuban and U.S. capitalists and politicians played an important role in pushing Batista to take this stance. As early as 4 October Ambassador Welles had told Batista he was the "only individual in Cuba . . . who represented authority."[105] Batista told Welles on 7 October that "delegates of all the important business and financial groups in Cuba" were telling him to create "a government in which the political groups and the commercial interests of the country could have confidence."[106] Finally, Welles and his successor, Jefferson Caffery, made it absolutely clear that the United States would not grant recognition to Grau.

Perhaps to preclude U.S. invasion, or perhaps in response to the capitalists' entreaties for order and peace on the island, but certainly to allow mill owners to begin the sugar harvest, Batista shifted his support from Grau San Martín to Carlos Mendieta's Unión Nacionalista on 15 January 1934. A *New York Times* correspondent's observation at the time underscores the tight relationship between Cuba's agricultural and political cycles: Cubans had set 15 January "as the deadline on which the political situation had to be settled if Cuba was to be able to make a sugar crop this winter."[107]

Politicians in the United States reinforced the new administration almost immediately. They granted recognition to Mendieta—and, by extension, Batista—within five days. They officially recognized the annulment of the Platt Amendment and began to negotiate a new Reciprocity Treaty. Batista must be held accountable for his actions, but the U.S. role in precluding more extensive national reform in 1933 Cuba should not be ignored. One can read with historical irony the *Literary Digest* summary in 1934 of the mainstream U.S. press's take on Batista: "There is nothing in the little brown man's character to justify appellations of 'Little Napoleon' or 'Emperor Batista.' He is smart but has none of the makings of a dictator so far as political ambition is concerned. . . . Long experience in close contact with army leaders taught him . . . the danger of rising too high in a Latin-American republic. He is of the people and his inclination is to support the Government which will do the most for the masses."[108]

In contrast, the interpretation of events by Charles A. Thomson of the *Foreign Policy Review* was far closer to the truth. He had forecast the army's overthrow of de Céspedes before it happened and then foresaw with prophetic accuracy the rise of the "Batista Dictatorship." (In an impressive analytical coup, he came up with this label almost twenty years before it became common shorthand in the political discourse of Cuba.) Thomson's retrospective in January 1936 observed that non-recognition had been a powerful instrument in the hands of the Roosevelt administration. Refusal to recognize the Grau regime, he argued, "helped to doom, as it now appears, the most promising opportunity for a constructive solution of the Cuban problem. . . . The forces of protest have been driven underground, . . . but whether to disappear or to reappear in more aggressive form, the future alone will decide."[109] The forces of protest would indeed reappear, with a vengeance, in the late 1950s, but Thomson was only partly right. Only the hope for a constructive solution can explain the complex populist period from 1933 to 1953, when the forces of protest opted to negotiate with the state rather than try to overthrow it.

On 22 January 1934 Grau sailed into exile in Mexico. Watson's description of the departure shows that the Cuban Revolution and Grau San Martín's brief regime had begun to replace the patrons' compact with this new, more lasting populist form of state rule:

> A crowd of adherents gathered at the wharf and, as the vessel steamed down the harbor, they ran along the sides. They belonged to the poorer classes and were very enthusiastic. They regarded the impractical, consumptive doctor as their champion. He had been in office for only four and a half months, and yet he made reforms, some of which will last. Students of Cuban history will remember his term because a great change came over Cuba. The rule of the sugar magnates was shaken, at any rate, for the present—perhaps forever.[110]

In the end workers and cane farmers managed to use the nationalist, social-reformist movements of the 1930s to create a Cuba that differed greatly from the early republic. The break with tradition is demonstrated at both the national political level and at the local mill-community level. The state, which included the president and his cabinet, the military, judges, prosecutors, and the (new) Ministry of Labor, became mediators who tried to ensure that workers, cane farmers, and sugarmill owners got their fair share of sugar industry profits. At the national level, each group created an association to lobby for spoils, and locally the representatives of these associations—or unions, in the workers' case—went to the state mediators (lawyers, judges, Labor Ministry representatives, and governors). The state thus entered the sugarmills on an unprecedented level, and Batista's soldiers, at least until his 1952 coup, were not merely oppressive forces. They became key players on the local scene, soliciting bribes, marrying into local families, and teaching at schools, among other activities.

At the local level in the countryside, Depression-era patrons chiseled away at the social benefits that held the patrons' compact together. Mill owners and managers overestimated their dependents' tolerance for cutbacks. When these cutbacks revealed the ephemeral nature of patronage and philanthropy, workers and colonos in Cuba demanded more formal, lasting reform and protection from the state, as did their lower- and middleclass counterparts elsewhere in the hemisphere. The transition from company patronage to legislated state welfare under the populist governments of the 1930s, 1940s, and 1950s was rocky, but Cuba was not alone. Populist state legislation and the reaction of capitalists and workers to this legislation paralleled the changes taking place in many countries of the region.[111]

The Populist Compact, 1934–59

8 On 15 January 1935, one year after taking office, the Mendieta-Batista regime issued a decree law that sentenced any perpetrator found guilty of burning or damaging cane fields, mills, or the devices used to transport cane, to life in prison or to the death penalty. The same law summarily tried as common criminals anyone who held "subversive propaganda," participated in solidarity strikes, or presented employers with new demands within six months of a previous strike. Labor activists were defined as outright revolutionaries if they did not follow to the letter extremely rigid new strike procedures. The regime established National Defense Tribunals to try and convict all suspects.[1]

In response, sugar workers invented new ways to commit sabotage clandestinely. In March 1936 an extensive arson campaign affecting roughly 92.5 million pounds of cane prompted a secret-police investigation at Chaparra and Delicias. The perpetrators had apparently used the "burning rag" method whereby a rag was soaked in gasoline, placed at the center of a clearing under a pile of cane leaves, and then set ablaze. It took a while for the fire to reach the rows of cane stalks, allowing the arsonist time to leave the area without a trace.[2] As was the case during the last years of the Machado dictatorship studied in chapter 7, some workers lit the fires because they were desperate for jobs, but others did so as a form of sabotage to counter the repression that left few options open.

The means used to combat repression were the same as in 1928–33—strikes across the island, assassinations and bombings in the cities, and sabotage in the countryside—but the repression itself was of a very different nature. Although the post-1934 period is often labeled a "counter-revolution" in histories of Cuba, the first part of this chapter argues that "authoritarian populism" would be a better label.[3] The new regime did not reverse the revolution; instead, its leaders used violence combined with revolutionary reforms as a means to forcibly incorporate more people into a newly expanded state system of rule. Mendieta blessed with a conservative mantle many of Grau's and Guiteras's reforms in hopes of broadening his support base.[4] Mendieta barely lasted one year, and Batista had little chance to win working-class support until the populist compact deepened during the democratic era surrounding the Second World War, discussed in the latter half of this chapter.

A closer look at Batista's rule in the 1930s and 1940s demonstrates that he was not unlike other authoritarian populists who took power in the Depression-era 1930s such as Getúlio Vargas of Brazil, Anastasio Somoza of Nicaragua, or Rafael Trujillo of the Dominican Republic. These leaders certainly relied strongly on the army as a power base, but they also made concerted efforts to win the support of popular groups such as workers and peasants, and they extended certain benefits to the individuals who joined state-supported unions and associations.[5] The Mendieta–Batista regime can be called "populist" because it constituted a genuine effort to accommodate more peoples' needs into the state via new governmental institutions like the Labor Ministry and the Sugar Stabilization Board (ICAE), on the one hand, and official unions (for workers) and associations (for colonos and mill owners), on the other. Yet the "authoritarian" element must be emphasized, too, because the regime used military force to squeeze out all independent alternatives. Populism is always a combination of force and persuasion, but in 1934 Mendieta and Batista prioritized force to contain the mass-mobilizations of the 1933 Revolution and channel its participants into a new populist state.

The easiest way to understand the Latin American populist model of corporatism (from the Latin *corpus*) is to think in a very schematic way of the state as a body. In "democratic populism," the president and his cabinet

members would be the head that mediated, collected, and redistributed resources among different social groups (symbolically represented as different parts of the body). Workers and peasants organized into local, regional,
and national state-sanctioned unions might make up the legs. Capitalists
organized into regional and national cartels or associations (also state-
sanctioned) might be the arms. The middle-class professionals, small industrialists, service employees, and civil servants might be the stomach and the
armed forces, the neck.

Mexico under Lázaro Cárdenas in the 1930s provides the closest example to this "democratic populist" model, and Cuba achieved more hollow
versions of it during the Batista presidency from 1940 to 1944 and during
the Auténtico Party presidencies under Grau San Martín (1944–48) and
Carlos Prío Socarrás (1948–52).[6] In the case of "authoritarian populism,"
the military either shares the head with the president, as in Cuba's appro-
priately named "Mendieta–Batista" regime (1934–35), or places itself above
the president, as in Brazil's New State regime under Getúlio Vargas from
1937 to 1945.

How these populist corporate experiments ended varied widely. In some
places, such as Brazil and Argentina, they led to brief democratic periods
that were later cut off by military coups; in other places, such as Nicaragua
and Cuba, they transitioned more gradually to military dictatorships and
revolution. The final section of this chapter shows that Cold War anticommunism from 1947 to 1959 emptied Cuba's populist compact of much of its
substance. In Havana and in sugarmill communities, only the leaders and
heads of local branches of corporate bodies such as the Confederation of
Cuban Workers (CTC) and the National Colono Association received benefits from the regime; these benefits did not trickle down enough to keep
members satisfied. Fewer beneficiaries meant less support for the regime,
which helps to explain why the president and sugarmill managers began to
rely more on the army to maintain order. This process, among other problems such as unemployment and economic stagnation (related to Cuba's
monocrop sugar economy) contributed to the triumph of the 1959 Revolution. The chapter begins at the national level because from the 1930s onward, the state actors became more prominent, and we need to be aware of
changes in Havana in order to understand changes in the countryside. This
is the story of cane farmers and workers, but "lobby groups" that supported
or opposed the regimes of the 1930s, 1940s, and 1950s were simultaneously

forming within the military, the education sector, and the professional cadres.[7]

THE DAWNING OF A NEW COMPACT:
AUTHORITARIAN POPULISM, 1934–1936

To understand Cuba's authoritarian populist system of rule, we need to study its leaders Carlos Mendieta and Fulgencio Batista. Mendieta belonged to the Cuban elite, and he was yet another 1898 veteran from Las Villas province (like President Gerardo Machado and President José Miguel Gómez before him).[8] A prominent member of the Liberal Party, Mendieta had hoped for a presidential nomination in 1924 but lost to Machado. He responded to Machado's increasing violence by forming the Unión Nacionalista and attempting the Río Verde rebellion with Menocal in 1931.

On becoming president in January 1934 Mendieta proclaimed new constitutional statutes, granted political amnesty to many, and restrained brutality against all prisoners.[9] He passed legislation in 1934 and 1935 that included getting U.S. politicians to recognize Grau's abolishment of the Platt Amendment, confirming women's suffrage, and expanding social security. For workers, Mendieta reinforced the eight-hour day and legislated collective labor contracts. These contracts applied to all employees and workers of a given company, effectively countering the divide-and-conquer system that companies had relied on before the revolution. He declared it illegal to dismiss workers without cause and made the procedure for dismissal so complicated that it served to protect workers' jobs. He set up a Technical Commission on Minimum Wages that included labor and management representatives and then he set the minimum wage for field workers at an impressive 80 cents (recall that it was 20 cents in 1933). Women were guaranteed "equal pay for equal work," and a Maternity Law established the first general system of worker insurance. Paid vacations followed soon thereafter.

Mendieta may have wanted to steer Cuba on a moderate reformist path out of revolution, but the strike wave that began in 1933 continued to grow exponentially, and the agricultural cycle dictated that his regime would have to take whatever means necessary to begin the 1934 sugar harvest quickly. On January 21 Mendieta ended the government occupation of Chaparra and Delicias, returning them to Cubanaco with the understanding that they would start the harvest. To carry out the transfer to Cubanaco, and to establish order elsewhere on the island for the harvest, Mendieta turned to Batista and his military.[10]

Batista is as complex a man to interpret as other "authoritarian" populists who took power in the 1930s.[11] He was born into a humble mixed-race family in the United Fruit Company's eastern sugarmill enclave—on the other end of the socioeconomic spectrum from Fidel Castro's Spanish family, who subcontracted land to colonos selling cane to United Fruit. Batista worked as a cane cutter, carpenter, tailor, and railroad worker before becoming an army stenographer in 1921 and a sergeant in 1928.[12] On the fateful evening of 3 September 1933 he had been just one of a group of sergeants, corporals, and enlisted men who met at Havana's Camp Columbia barracks to draw up a list of demands regarding basic needs such as housing facilities, food, uniforms, pay, and access to promotion. When the officers on duty refused to submit their petition to the commanding officers, the disaffected military group sent out delegates to get support from other military groups in Havana. By sunrise the next day all of the officers had departed from Camp Columbia and considered the sergeants' and corporals' protest a mutiny.[13]

When civilian opposition groups allied with the sergeants on 4 September, they legitimized the mutiny by making it a political act. The "sergeants" pledged to support the political, economic, and social objectives of the civilians, but as we saw in chapter 7, their allegiance was tentative. On 8 September Batista claimed the position of army chief, thereby gaining the right to commission officers. By the end of 1933 he had removed Machado's loyal officers and commissioned about four hundred new ones (most of them drawn from the ranks of sergeants). This turnover involved a radical social change within the armed forces: A largely non-white, noncommissioned officer corps replaced a white officer corps that was tied to the island's political elite.[14] To use the efficient Spanish-language expression of patronage, *Batistianos* replaced Machadistas at the helm of the armed forces.

It was not immediately clear which segments of society the Batistiano army would buttress. Here, a pattern emerges: The 1933 Revolution, like many other Latin American revolutions, started with middle-class leaders—including students, professionals, and intellectuals—who took power through a dangerous alliance with disaffected members of the military. Machado's soldiers abandoned their commander-in-chief because he was only favoring those officers who were closest to him. The rest of the army had to bear the brunt of the civilians' fury against the dictatorship without getting any of its rewards. This dynamic surrounded the departure of several enduring dictatorships of Central America and the Caribbean, including those of Machado (1925–33), Maximiliano Hernández Martínez in El Salvador (1931–44), and Jorge Ubico in Guatemala (1931–44).[15] What kind of regime followed the dictatorship largely depended on what happened to the military-civilian alliance. In post-1944 El Salvador, the army ruled. In Guatemala, the military backed civilian reformers during the 1944–54 Revolution.[16] In Cuba military and civilian leaders (uncomfortably) shared power from roughly 1933 through 1940, thus the term "authoritarian populism."

Mendieta increased the Cuban state's role with his series of decree laws, Sugar and Coffee Stabilization Boards, and National Defense Tribunals, but the average Cuban was quicker to note the military's infiltration into every realm of society. Just before the 1935 sugar harvest, provincial military authorities asked landowners to prepare lists of agitators and then sent army officials to arrest them. During the harvest, one thousand soldiers moved from Havana to the eastern provinces to protect mills and cane fields. When strikes broke out, the government sent soldiers and members of the newly created "military reserve" to step in as strikebreakers on sugarmills, in utility and telephone companies, and on railroads across the island.[17] Grau and Guiteras followers called a general strike in March 1935 that attracted some two hundred thousand participants. Mendieta declared a state of siege and completely suspended constitutional guarantees for the rest of the harvest. Batista's army and private security forces killed more than one hundred workers and wounded or arrested hundreds more.[18]

It was during this state of siege that Batista's army usurped a vast number of positions formerly held by civilians. The process of military infiltration into civil society had already begun during the final years of Machado's dictatorship, when he sent military officers across the country to replace elected municipal and provincial politicians who had joined the opposition. After Machado's departure, the "mobs" killed some of these officeholders, and the new authorities arrested others. Batista sent army officials to fill the resulting vacuum in local government, supposedly to await political reorganization and elections, but in fact making the army the new powerbroker on the island.[19] A U.S. consul in Santiago de Cuba described the scene in 1935 Oriente Province bluntly:

The Military Commander is, in reality, Governor, Mayor and Police Chief of Santiago. The army's tentacles have grown until they reach out to control insignificant municipal jobs, such as the appointment of street sweepers. . . . These appointments are said to be distributed to close relations and friends of officers and soldiers. . . . Slowly but effectively the Military are replacing the mayors of many municipalities in this Province. Small villages are assigned to the commander of Sergeants and larger places to Lieutenants carrying the title of Supervisor of Police.[20]

These new army powerbrokers mimicked the system of patronage and spoils that had been in place since Cuba's start as a nation in 1902. But the civilian leaders were (at least fraudulently) elected and usually gave a little before they started to take. Their armed replacements behaved more like a Mafia. The U.S. military attaché E. W. Timberlake made this analogy explicit after describing multiple cases of graft. Colonel Rodríguez, for example, persuaded mill owners to "donate" approximately $35,000 to the Provincial Command of Oriente. Colonel José Pedraza managed to deposit $50,000 into his bank account every month from profits made on the numbers rackets. Finally, Rural Guardsmen forced even the most humble members of Cuban society to give them their produce, livestock, and merchandise or suffer beatings with a machete blade and other forms of torture. Timberlake concluded that the chief of staff was like an American gang leader: As long as he guaranteed financial and political gains combined with immunity from punishment, he could count on his lieutenant-colonels' loyalty and obedience as a group.[21]

By ignoring corruption, Batista was able to maintain loyalty within one of the populist authoritarian state's "heads"—the army. In contrast, Mendieta's hold over the state's civilian head—his cabinet—began to fall apart as members resigned in protest against the army's excesses. Mendieta himself resigned in late 1935. Cuba looked more and more like a dictatorship, but "the dictator" saw himself as a revolutionary bringing democracy to the island. In July 1936, Batista advocated "a renovated democracy, under which there should be discipline of the masses and of institutions so that we can establish a progressive State." He added: "We want to teach the masses that capital and labor both are necessary and should cooperate."[22] A year later, he announced: "Many want to forget that I am the chief of a constructive social revolution, and see me as a mere watch-dog of public order. My idea of order is that of an architect rather than that of a police man."[23]

For Batista's populist edifice to stand, "the masses" needed to join its institutions. Before his resignation, President Mendieta had set up the means to incorporate workers through domineering social legislation, and Batista's army stood ready to "discipline" anyone who questioned its terms. A series of presidential decrees disguised as compromises between capital and labor included Decree 3, passed on 7 February 1934, allowing workers to strike but requiring them to give eight days' notice.[24] The law took away the element of spontaneity that made strikes effective. It also gave the companies time to hire strikebreakers and to evict or exile the leaders of the strike before it began. Moreover, since the National Defense Decree prohibited any "unauthorized political meetings," it became increasingly difficult for workers to meet legally at all.

Labor leaders were quick to recognize the controlling nature of these so-called reforms. Communists, Trotskyists, and Guiteras supporters all rejected the populist compact at first. A January 1934 manifesto from the CNOC stated, "We need to resolve conflicts through direct action with the *patrones* (bosses) without intermediaries of any sort. We should not notify the Labor Ministry in any way. Our attitude now must be the same as it was toward Grau and the Labor Ministry: Do not recognize it, ignore it completely, boycott it."[25]

Chaparra, Delicias, and Juan Claro Port workers followed this advice, resolving to reject Decree 3 when they met on Sunday, 11 February 1934. The union addressed its demands exclusively to the patrones, which is not surprising, since Grau's and Guiteras's departure signified the end of the state's Cubanaco "intervention."

In February 1934 the patrons' compact was still all that workers really knew; state intervention—or populism—remained a fleeting promise. By looking at the demands in the collective contract that Cubanaco workers drafted at that time, one gets a sense of what the populist compact would need to win labor's support. Sugarmill and colonia residents wanted to formalize and enhance many benefits that Depression-era patrones considered expendable, including year-round housing, schools, transportation, pensions, health care, and accident compensation. The unions of dock workers, railroad workers, and sugar workers also sought to win more control over hiring and promotions. This began with demands for company recognition of the unions and provision of locales. Another demand called for the re-employment of all laborers who had been dismissed between 1925 and 1934 for labor activism. (Remarkably, this was actually fulfilled when the populist compact deepened in the late 1930s.) Demand 14 insisted that no laborer could be fired until the corresponding mill or colonia union committee had discussed and approved the "record of his case." Demand 34 called for rigorous observance of seniority rights, any exception requiring the approval of a jury that included union representatives. Several other demands sought to achieve the goal of a closed shop—a job ladder whereby only those who belonged to the union could win promotions according to years of service.

All of the above constituted efforts to combat the favoritism and racism (discussed in chapters 4 through 6) that fomented division among the workers. The unions actually attacked racism directly with three "specific demands for Cubans of color": equal salary for equal work, the end of racial segregation in housing and employment, and the right to work in all positions in the mills and their offices. Cuban workers achieved more control over who was hired and fired during the 1934–59 period.[26] Racist barriers were more tenacious.

Three demands hint at what workers considered the proper role for women and families. One called for the establishment of a workroom at the mills where filter cloths could be repaired and sugar bags could be made; the work was to be done "exclusively by women." It is not clear how these tasks were done prior to 1934. Perhaps men no longer wanted to do what they considered "women's work," or perhaps Cubans wanted their wives and daughters to fix products that were previously made or repaired in the United States. In either case, this constitutes evidence that male workers wanted women to be able to supplement their families' income. A few other demands sought to formalize support for midwives.[27] And finally, the most significant demand (never fully achieved) was for the company to grant rent-free parcels of land to all workers and employees of factory, fields, and offices. This went unsaid, but wives and children would be the ones to raise livestock or produce on this land, except during the off-season, when male workers would have free time. As mentioned earlier, the extra food or income that wives and children could generate by washing clothes, raising pigs, or growing banana trees in their yards constituted essential buffers against low wages and unemployment during the prolonged off-season.[28]

The workers were hoping to rebuild the patrons' compact on more solid ground—and with more equal footing. The patrons were intransigent. From 1934 on R. B. Wood and Manuel Rionda continued to receive petitions from individuals, but they consistently rejected them. The harsh tone of their responses to even the smallest requests shows that they felt betrayed by the workers' combative attitudes during the 1933 strikes. For example, when Oliver Doty wrote to Rionda requesting funds to buy a moving-picture projector for Tuinucú's Club House (since "a large percentage of the people who would benefit by this donation are those employees who were faithful to us during the past troubles"), Rionda responded, "There are also a great many of the unfaithful employees that will benefit. . . . Do what you want, but things are not very rosy."[29]

The patrons evidently thought that Mendieta and Batista would be like Machado, spouting populist rhetoric to gain initial support but shifting to repression to guarantee the harvest. The transcript of a 26 January 1934 telephone conversation between Cubanaco's Joseph Harris in Havana and George Keiser in New York describes a meeting in Havana of representatives from all of the big U.S. sugar conglomerates, including the Rionda group, United Fruit, Hershey, and the Royal Bank of Canada. "The consensus of opinion," Harris reported, "was that it was impossible to make the crop at all under present conditions. The only dissenting opinion—Mr. Staples of Hershey[—]reported that they had two mills grinding, but they were paying wages nobody else could afford to pay." A little later in the conversation, Harris stated: "From the point of view of those present today, there is no use being in a hurry until the army takes a firm stand and lets it be known that they intend to run the show." Keiser asked: "Otherwise the labor element will rule?" to which Harris responded, "Absolutely."[30]

Batista did not disappoint them. The words *habrá zafra o habrá sangre* (there will be a harvest or there will be bloodshed) rang out as Batistiano soldiers stormed union headquarters across the island. On 15 February 1934 workers at Chaparra and Delicias found their locale's doors and windows nailed shut. Wood advised his superiors that it would be best not to submit any offers or to even negotiate with the leaders of the 1934 strike because they continued to express defiance against Mendieta's new laws.[31] Wood mentioned that he had heard rumors that workers would commit sabotage in retaliation for the repression, but he did not consider the rumors especially important. He was wrong to dismiss the rumors so quickly. Cubanaco's security records show a spike in the number of sabotage and theft cases during the years 1934–38, when workers had no legitimate union.[32]

Under the guise of enforcing the National Defense Decree, Batista's soldiers crushed the unions of even smaller mills like Tuinucú. The soldiers destroyed papers and furniture, jailed or evicted labor leaders from the mills, and declared their unions illegal. One worker remembered this as the time when an intimidating means of surveillance entered the mill towns: Police cruisers replaced the horses that public and private security guards used to ride on mill-town streets. In the cane fields where cruisers could not pass, Rural Guardsmen wore big hats, carried Springfield rifles and sabers, and rode "seven-foot Texan horses" so they could frighten the mostly thin (undernourished) workers. Batista's soldiers added the Italian fascists' *palmacristi* torture to Cubans' time-honored machete-blade beatings: Anyone who did not say or do what he or she was told to would be forced to drink a liter of oil. The years that immediately preceded the Cuban Revolution from 1955 through 1959 shared many of the characteristics of this era of extreme repression.[33] As mentioned in chapter 6, the Tuinucú workers Eladio Santiago and Arquímedes Valdivia stated that the company could no longer protect them from the Rural Guard's abuses "when Batista arrived." When I pressed them to clarify whether they meant in the 1930s or the 1950s, they responded that it was during both periods. Rita Díaz, a former teacher and political activist from Chaparra who will be discussed later, frequently conflated the 1930s with the 1950s, as well. This is a common pattern, since Batista assumed prominence as an authoritarian military ruler during these periods (versus the era when democratic elections mattered more, between 1940 and 1952).[34]

When Mendieta and Batista shifted from co-optation to coercion in 1934, they reinstituted the patrons' control over their mills, but it was a very contentious "peace." A U.S. Air Force pilot who had to make an emergency landing in 1938 described Puerto Padre as "merely the shipping point for the Cuban-American Sugar Company, which apparently dominates the entire district [and,] according to Mr. Wood, has the native district officials completely under their control." Yet then the pilot added, "Since these two huge mills operate only about 70 days per year, employing around 70,000 natives in the district, there is a great deal of enforced idleness during the 10 months they are not employed. This condition leads to unrest, foments rebellious activities and labor troubles."[35]

Workers from Chaparra, Delicias, Tuinucú, and other mills remember 1935 as a repetition of 1925. Despite all populist promises to the contrary, the state threw its support behind sugarmill owners, not workers. Company correspondence reveals that sugarmill owners used their lawyers and generous bribes to their "friends" to make sure that social measures were diluted and delayed. The most common tactic was to not show up at meetings with Labor Ministry representatives—or to bribe the ministry representatives not to show up—and then to declare the workers' petitions invalid because there was no company or ministry representation. A trick used in 1925 resurfaced numerous times, as well: administrators sent a representative to meetings and then claimed that he was not authorized to make any decisions. In 1939, Cubanaco achieved a real coup when a group of "friendly" workers formed a "legal" union at the Juan Claro Port to replace the former syndicate, thus voiding the impressive collective contract achieved in 1934.

Colonos found themselves in a much stronger position than workers. The same factors discussed in chapter 6 apply here. Because many were middle- and upper-class white Cubans, they found more support in Havana's halls of power. Some literally sat in the Cuban House of Representatives. The governments of the mid-1930s passed a series of decrees to save colonos, reinforcing some measures that Grau had already introduced (such as tenant colonos' right to stay on the land that they worked) and adding others (such as a moratorium on 17 August 1934 to help colonos pay off their debts). A new law sanctioned production quotas for colonos and reinforced state control through the Sugar Stabilization Board (ICAE) that included six colono representatives alongside twelve mill-owner representatives and a presidential delegate.

State legislation protected colonos from being evicted for debt, and quotas guaranteed them a place to sell their cane, but many colonos felt that the quotas were too small to guarantee their livelihood. Chaparra and Delicias colonos won permission to grind more cane when they wrote directly to President Federico Laredo Bru on 18 March 1936. Their letter captures the sense of stagnation and contraction that reigned in Cuba's sugar industry. The era of progress seemed gone forever. "The agricultural zones around Chaparra and Delicias that were once prosperous," they wrote, "now vegetate, listless and pale. We see ourselves, after repeated restrictions, having to leave most of our fields unproductive.... Our cane has contributed to harvests of 1.7 million bags of sugar in the past, but today we are given a quota of only 683,000 bags. This forces us to leave 80 million arrobas of prime cane standing in the fields, increasing our debts and making our workers idle."[36]

Three months later several prominent members of the National Colono Association who had managed to win positions in Cuba's House of Representatives submitted a bill against administration cane that reads like an abstract of Guerra's *Sugar and Society*. They argued that unless measures were taken to avoid the consolidation of the agricultural and industrial sectors in the hands of "a few" (read, U.S. corporations) the "native classes" (read, Cuban colonos) would be displaced from the land. To this nationalist argument the colonos added a class-based one: "The proletariat will have to increase, this being a most serious danger for the stability of the economic system on which the Cuban state and Cuban nationality are based."[37]

The colonos who were making this argument were not Jefferson's small-holding yeoman; most hired large numbers of field workers to administer and work the land that they controlled. There was probably some truth to their argument, though. As outlined in chapters 6 and 7 the field-worker segment of the sugar "proletariat" often supported strikes by mill workers, but on the whole they were slower to organize and make demands themselves for a variety of reasons. One of these is the fact that they were divided up among colonias and often lived in isolated thatch huts within them. (In contrast, mill workers lived in concentrated urban spaces, and many of the homes—even the most humble—had front-porch swings or chairs where workers could share experiences and build a protest movement.)

The fact that the colono congressmen were not "small Cuban farmers" growing cane to sell to "big foreign mills" is revealed in the careful wording of the anti-administration-cane bill of 1936, as well as in subsequent bills that advocated land reform. They proposed that the land be given not to those who worked it, but to those who "enjoyed" or "personally directed" its cultivation. Even Fidel Castro's early revolutionary platforms of the 1950s reflect this inclusiveness. The colonos that headed the National Colono Association had to have the money and education to spend large amounts of time for meetings and lobbying in Havana. Juan Martínez-Alier has written a fascinating national-level study of colono politics from 1934 to 1960 that shows the leaders of the National Colono Association behaving very much like the leaders at Chaparra and Delicias discussed in chapter 6 and 7. When convenient, they included the small colono farmers to play up the image of the downtrodden Cuban peasant. More often they sought to project them-

selves as Cuba's hard-working entrepreneurial middle class. For their summer meetings, they donned a very Cuban business "suit": the white linen
guayabera shirt without jacket or tie.[38]

FALLING THROUGH THE CRACKS:
EDUCATION AND HEALTH CARE IN THE COUNTRYSIDE

Colonos gained far more than workers after 1933, but in certain areas the two
groups shared setbacks in Cuba's transition from patronage to populism.
Access to education at Chaparra and Delicias serves as a case in point. The
problem was that Batista made many promises that he did not fulfill (like his
authoritarian populist counterparts in Brazil and Nicaragua—and in contrast to the more democratic populist Lázaro Cárdenas in Mexico).[39] At the
other end of the spectrum, patrons such as R. B. Wood and Manuel Rionda
felt so betrayed by their subordinates that they obliged only the smallest
requests. Batista the populist made overly ambitious promises, and patrons
stepped aside to let "the state" shoulder social responsibilities too quickly.
Residents on sugarmills across the island fell through the cracks.

Education was a contentious issue to start with. The tension between the
two "heads" of the authoritarian populist compact came to blows over the
planned construction of roughly two thousand three hundred rural schools
in 1936. After winning the presidency that year (largely because Batista preferred him to the conservative General Mario García Menocal), Miguel
Mariano Gómez tried to regain some of the civilian ground that his predecessors had lost to Batista's military.[40] Within weeks of being inaugurated, he
reorganized the armed forces' command and dismissed some three thousand
civil servants. Most of them were military reservists. He distributed the positions to Liberal Party and Unión Nacionalista functionaries and named two
close relatives to head the army and navy. Batista vigorously disapproved.
But what pushed Batista to make Congress impeach the new president was
Gómez's veto of Batista's proposal to impose a new tax on sugarmills to
extend education to the rural population using armed-forces personnel.[41]

In an effort to win popular support, Batista the populist had dedicated
part of the 1936 military budget to send out about seven hundred and fifty
army teachers to rural areas that had no schools. They introduced new agricultural techniques and taught disease control, reading, and writing to some
thirty-five thousand children and twenty thousand adults. The program

was expensive but popular, so Batista proposed a 9 cent tax on every bag of sugar to increase the military's budget. Gomez called Batista a "fascist" and argued that the Department of War had no right to run the schools in the first place. Owners of large sugarmills objected to the tax. Batista responded effectively with a time-honored threat: If sugar companies did not pay, he could not guarantee that troops would protect mills and cane fields.[42]

Gómez was impeached in December 1936, and the mill owners accepted the sugar tax as a sort of insurance against labor trouble.[43] Cubanaco used the tax as an excuse to rapidly withdraw funding from schools in the mill towns and colonias. On 28 August 1939, R. B. Wood wrote to the company's president George Keiser: "I agree with you completely that in view of our large tax payment for 'Cívico Militar' schools . . . we should not continue to make any excess payment . . . but unfortunately the operation of the schools has become . . . our principal talking point . . . with the Government for any favors or attentions we ask from them, and with the laborers for the maintenance of the present wage scale." Showing a hint of obligation toward the old patrons' compact, Wood added: "The two subsidiary schools at Chaparra have only two teachers but attract 221 children from the lowest laboring strata with no other opportunity to acquire a knowledge of reading and writing."

The directors in New York were not sympathetic. Keiser's letter of 6 September 1939 reads:

> What we want to make very plain is that if we and other sugar mills are to pay for the whole social program in Cuba, which we seem to be doing . . . we cannot continue to run social and philanthropic enterprises at our own expense as well. As you know, for years we were willing to run the schools and the hospital for the benefit of the people in our community. Now, however, the Government wishes to take over such activities by the school tax and also by the maternity and various other taxes, and give us no credit for them, and we can see no other course but eventually, if not perhaps immediately, . . . to close all activities that do not contribute to the manufacture of sugar.

Keiser still gave Wood the option of keeping the schools open but insisted that reductions be made and suggested a start date of 1 November instead of 1 October.

Keiser's final words demonstrate the difference between the social-democratic ideal and the Cuban reality: "As in all these matters we feel eventually that the only way relief can be given is by the people themselves demanding it from the Government, and as long as we continue to suppose these philanthropies, such will not be the case."[44] Wood passed on Keiser's response to colono and worker protesters and advised them to write to Batista. They may have done so, but they continued to write to Wood and the directors in New York, as well, in hopes that the patrons' compact would endure.[45]

Sometime between 26 September and 21 October Cubanaco made the decision to completely close all of its schools. Colonos, workers, and public functionaries flooded the directors' offices with petitions, but Keiser stood firm. "Outlook for coming crop so demoralized," he cabled the United Front of Associations and Lodges, "that obliged to suspend disbursement activities other than manufacture sugar. . . . Chaparra and Delicias this year have already paid Cuban government over $60,000 school tax. Some or all of this money should be available for schools in our district. Our only suggestion you secure portion of these funds from government for company to operate Chaparra and Delicias schools. Company has tried to secure government assistance but regret without success."[46]

The historical record of what happened next is unclear, but as late as February 1942 Wood received a letter from the Puerto Padre Rotary Club saying that President Batista still had not responded to their pleas. "Since the economy has improved," they wrote, "could you not reopen the schools?"[47] A youth club sent a much more aggressive letter the same month: "We know that this company closed the schools in retaliation against the demands that workers have been making to make the company fulfill the new laws. We simply cannot understand how the company can justify such aggression against our country's culture."[48] Finally, on 15 April 1943, after almost five years of silence, an Education Ministry secretary wrote to Wood asking about the number of classrooms, students, and teachers that needed to be replaced.[49] That the state finally turned its attention to education at Chaparra in 1943 is no coincidence: Cubans went into national shock when that year's census revealed a drastic fall in the literacy rate.[50] For too many years, Cuban presidents had used the Education Ministry merely for patronage appointments. When sugarmill companies cut back on social spending, these two factors combined to take a serious national toll on literacy.

Education and health benefits were never great under the patrons' rule, but populism made them even less accessible, at least at the sugarmills. Cuba's social-democratic constitution of 1940 (discussed later) officially placed the onus back on companies to provide education and health care for their workers. But the golden years of the patrons' compact were long gone, and the populist state never delivered in the realms of rural health care and education. The child of a large colono, Fidel Castro was struck by the poverty that surrounded him in rural Oriente of the 1940s and 1950s: "In those immensely extensive fields, where there were huts, thatched-roof shacks, impoverished villages and sugarmills, it was hard to find a single very poor classroom for the 200 or 300 children who lived in the area; there were no books, very few school materials and sometimes not even a teacher. It was only in the hamlets that sprang up around the big sugarmills that there were one or two physicians who basically cared for the families of the foreign sugar companies' local managers and senior operatives."[51]

Census statistics from 1953 confirm these impressions: There was one teacher per one hundred and fifty-nine children in rural areas versus one teacher per eighteen children in the cities, and fully 44 percent of the rural population had not gone to school.[52] Only 7.5 percent of Havana residents were illiterate, in contrast to 43 percent of rural Cubans. Roughly 60 percent of doctors and dentists serviced the 21 percent of Cubans who lived in Havana. This left very few resources for the Cubans who lived outside the capital.[53] These urban-rural disparities help to explain the rural population's support for Fidel Castro's revolution in 1959.[54]

THE COMPACT DEEPENS: SUGAR COORDINATION AND THE POPULAR FRONT, 1937–1944

Whereas populism hurt sugarmill communities in the realms of education and health care, it allowed them to win impressive gains against mill owners in other areas. The Sugar Coordination Act of 1937 permanently established a new system of profit sharing between workers, colonos, and mill owners according to a sliding scale that moved with the price of sugar. Described by one analyst as "the crowning piece of legislation—and—consequently, the cornerstone of the Cuban political system until 1959," it was fundamentally populist in that it guaranteed redistribution among society's classes.[55] It also offered so much nationalist protection for Cuban colonos and mill owners that they were able to "Cubanize" much of sugar production before the 1959 Revolution. By the late 1950s administration cane had practically disappeared, and colonos officially provided 94 percent of cane to Cuba's sugarmills.[56] Cubans also held almost 70 percent of the sugar industry by then, up from under 30 percent in 1925.[57]

Politicians in the United States turned a deaf ear to the inevitable protests of the Rionda group, Cubanaco, and other U.S. corporations against the Coordination Act. President Roosevelt's New Dealers prioritized Cubans' political and economic stability—and thus their ability to consume more U.S. products—above the profits of a few U.S. sugar magnates.[58] The populist compact hurt individual U.S. sugarmill owners, but ultimately U.S. politicians still held the reins of the Cuban economy. In 1934 Cuba had signed a new Reciprocity Treaty that gave the United States reduced tariffs on fully 406 categories of merchandise, versus the 251 categories guaranteed preference in 1902. These U.S. products won higher tariff reductions (25–60 percent versus 20–40 percent in 1902). In exchange Cuba got a smaller share of the U.S. market for sugar, rum, and tobacco than it had won in 1902. The new treaty reversed the diversification process that Machado's 1927 tariffs had allowed Cubans to begin. This contrasted sharply with populist Mexico, where Cárdenas introduced protectionist tariffs to let domestic producers make what was previously imported—a widely used populist policy called import-substituting industrialization.[59]

The main reason Cuban elites agreed to the 1934 Reciprocity Treaty and the Jones-Costigan Sugar Act (passed that same year) was that they still believed sugar was their best alternative, and they desperately wanted a secure market for it. The new agreements set quotas for Cuban sugar in the U.S. market at rates that were more stable, though not always higher, than those of the world market. The 1937 Sugar Coordination Act divided Cuba's total sugar quota among mills,[60] and specified that the mill had to grind at least 30,000 arrobas of cane per year from each of its colonos (grinding administration cane only if extra quota remained). The act made mill owners pay at least 5.5 arrobas of sugar for 100 arrobas of cane to landowning colonos and 5 arrobas to tenants. It also gave the "right of permanent occupancy" to tenant colonos and fixed their rent at a very low rate. Last but not least, the act specified that wages for sugar workers should go up or down according to the average price of sugar. Companies and colonos followed this rule until 1947, when post–Second World War sugar prices spiked so high that the employers refused to give workers their corresponding pay. The move sparked another massive strike wave, but the Cold War climate made it harder for workers to claim their due.

International factors help to explain why the social climate was much more favorable to workers in 1937. The populist compact grew deeper as Batista shifted further to the left and labor leaders shifted more to the center. The 1937 Sugar Coordination Law was followed by a general amnesty for political prisoners, a very progressive Labor Code in 1938, and a Supreme Court decision that same year ruling that "labor relations were not a private matter." The ruling obliged proprietors to furnish salary and production details to the state so that it could serve as mediator between bosses and workers, in true populist form.

Three main factors contributed to Batista's shift to the left. Communists, anarcho-syndicalists, and Auténticos (supporters of Grau San Martín) forged a popular front that staged massive demonstrations and an international campaign to win amnesty for all political prisoners and to raise funds for the struggle against the fascist regime of Francisco Franco in Spain. Batista visited the Cárdenas regime in Mexico and saw a democratic populist model that he wanted to emulate—a model that workers, too, wanted to emulate. Finally, the U.S. alliance with Russia against fascism in Europe during the Second World War put pressure on the "Good Neighbors" to soften their approach to communists and to distance themselves from any fascist tendencies at home.[61] The confluence of pressure for democracy and unity against fascism finally created a long enough "populist moment" for Cuban workers to achieve deeper reforms between 1937 and 1947. The economic climate in the early to mid-1940s was also good for the Cuban economy because the Second World War curbed European beet-sugar production and increased demand on the world market for sugar. This literally gave populist leaders more to distribute.

Domestic factors also contributed to the shift. Grau San Martín, living in exile in Miami, constituted a very popular alternative to Batista. Ousted before he had the chance to turn against workers or engage in corruption, Grau was remembered for the popular decrees of 1933. Batista the populist tried to ally with Grau, as did the communists, but he refused both of their advances, pushing them toward each other. Cuba's first presidents had sought a power base in mill owners. Machado and Grau added industrialists and colonos to the mix. In 1938 Batista moved further from his army power base and invited workers into the state. He legalized the Communist Party and allowed it to start a newspaper and radio station in the hope that communists could organize "the masses" around their new democratic "savior." He officially stepped down as chief of the army and began campaigning for the 1940 presidential elections.

Communist leaders started plans for a new national union (to replace the CNOC that Batista himself had dissolved after the March 1935 strike) at the first Congress of Latin American Workers celebrated in Mexico in 1938. The location of the meeting shows that Cuban labor leaders' decision to ally with the new "democratic" Batista did not take place in a vacuum. The Soviet Comintern influenced these leaders—advocating a popular front of socialists, communists, and middle-class parties against fascism—but so did the profound populist transitions taking place next door in Mexico.[62]

Memories of the sectarianism that had divided the labor movement during the 1933 Revolution must also have figured heavily in communist leaders' decision to ally with other political factions in 1939. Members of the FOH and the CNOC, once so viciously pitted against each other, joined together under the able leadership of an Afro-Cuban tobacco worker named Lázaro Peña. He was a communist who possessed a great deal of political tact and ability to negotiate with leaders of other persuasions.[63] This openness served the organization well: By the end of 1939, the new Confederation of Cuban Workers (CTC) boasted more than two hundred thousand members. Two years later there were almost three hundred and fifty thousand.[64] Approximately three-quarters of unionized workers belonged to the CTC. The rest belonged to independent unions or to Grau's National Worker's Commission headed by Eusebio Mujal. Mujal tried to force a split in the CTC in 1942, but he backed down when he realized that workers believed in the need for labor unity against fascism.[65]

Workers perceived the great rewards that a united, self-defined "working class" could reap from populist presidents and a booming wartime sugar economy. Colonos had already organized as a class to make demands from Machado, Grau, and Mendieta; they continued to do so (successfully) under Batista and the Auténticos. By allowing the CTC to thrive, and by offering large concessions to workers in exchange for political support, Batista was the first president to truly give workers a stake in Cuban politics.

Company administrators believed that this was just a passing populist moment, like 1924 or 1933. In January 1940 R. B. Wood explicitly stated this

when he chose to appeal a case found in favor of Cubanaco's dock workers. He explained to his superiors that the general labor unrest and the
forthcoming elections made it the worst time for them to talk about wages.
"There is bound to be a reaction against the continued demands of labor,"
he reasoned, and then he proposed that an appeal to the Supreme Court
would function as a perfect delaying tactic.[66]

Wood was wrong. This populist moment lasted through two administrations, and the reaction did not really come until the end of Grau's second
regime, in 1947. His delaying tactic did work in terms of agricultural timing. As Wood predicted, a rehearing was not held until April, at which time
the crop was practically complete and Cubanaco took "measures to insure
efficient operation during the dead season"—in other words, it fired the
troublemakers and got rid of extra workers. The dragged-out negotiations
effectively made the increase applicable only to the next harvest.[67]

The CTC leaders quickly figured out how to use the space created by
domestic and international politics to preclude this kind of legal trickster-
ism. Back in March 1935 the workers had had no choice but to modify their
stance after the repression that followed the failure of the general strike
(and the assassination of Guiteras three months later). Communist leaders
slowly began to advocate working from within the system to avoid more
violence. From late 1935 onward, the Havana-based unions issued circulars
to workers on sugarmills across the island explaining how to make unions
legal and trained unions to combat more successfully the tactics that companies such as Cubanaco were using to get around legislation. Ursinio Rojas,
jailed in 1935 for his organizing activity at the Tacajó mill, learned many of
these tactics in prison, where he came into contact with communist organizers and workers from across Cuba. He described the prisons as "universities
for revolutionaries," where the *Communist Manifesto* was read aloud and
prisoners learned the benefits of unity by forming cooperatives to share
donations. The prisoners' family members collected items such as medicine,
soap, toothpaste, and books through new popular-front "anti-fascist, pro-
political amnesty" organizations like the Democratic Federation of Cuban
Women (FDMC).[68]

Like union leaders in Mexico under Cárdenas or Nicaragua under Somoza, Cuban leaders decided to try to push the state's superficially pro-
labor legislation further, making it real by engaging it from within. They
opted to join state-sanctioned unions to make them powerful, slowly taking

over leadership of formerly "yellow" unions. If we picture Batista as the architect that he himself claimed to be, then we can say that he and Mendieta built some very thin walls that the CTC filled with concrete. The workers' decision to engage the new legislation was what made Cuba "populist" in this era, for leaders as far back as Menocal had tried to set up false labor congresses, but not enough participants attended to make them legitimate.[69]

Sugar workers in particular made impressive advances in salaries and benefits between 1939 and 1947 under the new National Federation of Sugar Workers (FNOA)—renamed the National Federation of Workers in the Sugar Industry (FNTA) in 1945 to include workers from the very bottom of the industry (field workers in the colonias) to employees at the very top (formerly separated into the National Association of Sugar Office Employees and the National Association of Sugar Technicians).[70] The August 1945 congress included two hundred unions representing an estimated four hundred and eighty thousand workers.[71] The unified "sugar worker class" was able to lobby the populist presidents alongside its "colono class" counterparts. A report in 1947 from Cubanaco's R. B. Wood noted that, "during the last five or six years, because of presidential decrees, sugar companies have had to increase salaries of workers and employees by over 200 percent from the base salaries of 1940."[72] Batista's Decree 100 had increased salaries by 50 percent in 1942, and in 1943 he extended the "right of permanent employment" to sugar workers. This deterred mill owners from firing workers to cut back on labor costs.

Grau San Martín was eager to court the workers' support when he won the presidency in 1944, especially since the communist leaders of the CTC threatened to call a general strike if he replaced them with Auténticos. The communists led up to one-third of all unionized workers and even more of the sugar workers, so alienating them would risk the kind of strike that would give Batista an excuse to stage a military coup against him. The new president's Auténticos and the communists reached a compromise: Lázaro Peña remained secretary general, and the remaining executive committee positions were divided evenly.[73] To shore up support, Grau proceeded to give sugar workers a wage hike of 32 percent for the 1945 harvest.[74] The average salary for sugarmill workers more than doubled between 1940 and 1945, reaching almost $2 per day.[75] During the 1940s, the executive continued to decree wage increases, and labor courts decided in favor of workers in three out of five dismissal cases.[76]

Back in 1939 popular domestic mobilizations, diplomatic pressure, and a desire to win the presidency democratically had pushed Batista to organize a Constitutional Convention. The resulting 1940 Constitution was perhaps the most progressive in Latin America, at least on paper. Communists played a major role in the convention, drafting the twenty-seven articles that affected labor. Among other benefits, the constitution granted "tenure" to employees after six months on the job, promoted wage increases in urban trades, granted social-security benefits to parts of the working class, and recognized the right to organize. In sum, it established the Cuban welfare state.[77]

Hugh Thomas and Robert Hoernel, among others, have emphasized that the triumphs of the labor movement reflected in the 1940 Constitution, and subsequent laws were extremely uneven. Specifically, they argue that agricultural laborers did not share many of the advances.[78] This is certainly the case for field workers in coffee, and it was sometimes the case for field workers in the sugar industry. However, field workers in sugar did gain many benefits when men such as Jesús Menéndez and Melanio Hernández helped them to organize and make demands (see figure 34). These men, like Enrique Varona before them, saw the importance of crossing the occupational (and often racial) divide between factory and field. It is significant that Jesús Menéndez and Melanio Hernández were both cane cutters—and then mill workers—at the mills before they began to organize and win impressive demands for sugar workers. It is also significant that they were both Afro-Cuban (recall that mill workers tended to be lighter-skinned than field workers and that union demands included instituting the right of mulattos and blacks to move up the job ladder free from discrimination). Because so many Afro-Cubans joined Menéndez and Hernández in the ranks of organized labor, they were able to combat more—though by no means all—of the employment and wage inequities between blacks and whites that applied elsewhere in the hemisphere.[79]

Born in a tobacco zone in Santa Clara in 1911, the great-grandson of a female slave and son of Liberation Army veterans, Jesús Menéndez took a job as a tobacco worker when he was thirteen years old. He had only four years of primary education. He started cutting cane at fourteen, got a job in the purging house at the Constancia sugarmill, joined the Communist Party at twenty, and founded the mill's first union. He was jailed in 1932 for organizing a hunger march of more than three thousand people in Las

34 Jesús Menéndez, "the General of
the Cane." Museo Jesús Menéndez,
Havana.

Villas and was released in 1933. He narrowly escaped an assassination attempt after the March 1935 strike and resurfaced in 1936 to lead a new sugar
union at Constancia. Soldiers sacked the union locale and put Menéndez in
jail. When he was released, he began to organize a provincial labor federation that would include sugar and tobacco workers. He left his position as
secretary general of the new Provincial Workers Federation of Santa Clara
(founded in 1938) upon being elected to the CTC's executive committee
in 1939. He participated in the 1939 Constitutional Congress and helped
organize the first National Sugar Workers' Federation that same year. He
served concurrently as leader of the FNOA (later FNTA) and as a communist congressman in the House of Representatives from 1940 until his death
at thirty-six in 1948.[80]

Menéndez visited Tuinucú and Chaparra frequently, and such visits to
sugarmills across the island informed many of the demands that he ended
up making at the national level through the sugar federations.[81] Chaparra
workers remember him fondly for his jovial, down-to-earth character and
talk of him walking through cane alleys and the dusty streets of Pueblo
Viejo to meet with leaders, workers, and their families. On 9 August 1943

Menéndez's FNOA demanded the *higienización* (urbanization and sanitation) of mill towns and colonias across the island. This was precisely to improve on the humble conditions that he knew so well from such visits—isolated huts in the cane fields and makeshift shantytowns on the outskirts of mills. The FNOA's goal was to mandate proper homes with cement floors for all workers in small colonia hamlets and in neighborhoods adjacent to mills, such as Chaparra's Pueblo Viejo, giving all workers access to collective stores, electricity, and light. He toured the island advocating these measures and won the support of workers from all sectors, as well as from medical professionals and intellectuals. Higienización became law, but like so many other pieces of social legislation in Cuba, it was never properly enforced.

One very impressive FNOA goal was achieved, at least briefly, during the immediate postwar years of 1945–47. This was when workers won the *diferencial azucarero*. The Sugar Coordination Act stipulated that at the end of each year, colonos would receive the difference between the average price of sugar during the harvest and the average price for the whole year. Under Menéndez's leadership, the workers demanded that that diferencial be extended to workers. The famous call for sugar workers that rang out from the 1940s through 1959 was "demand the diferencial with the point of your machetes!"[82]

Menéndez also demanded another diferencial from the United States— the difference between the rising costs of imports from the United States (due to postwar inflation) and the cost of Cuban sugar being sold to them (fixed by the Reciprocity Agreement). In October 1945 Menéndez traveled to Washington, D.C., with the FNTA's beloved accountant Jacinto Torres to force their way into trade negotiations over Cuba's sugar quota. Delegations of colonos, mill owners, and Cuban and U.S. diplomats were present at the meeting, along with the U.S. Commodity Credit Corporation that would buy the sugar. Menéndez faced racial discrimination in Miami, on the train, and in Washington, but he and Torres managed to overcome all of these obstacles to convey the economic facts to the Americans. The Cubans went home without a new agreement, as would two more delegations before July 1946, when Cuba suspended sugar shipments.

The U.S. secretary of agriculture traveled to Cuba and ended up signing an agreement accepting Menéndez's *garantía* (guarantee clause) linking the price of Cuban sugar to an index based on the price of a group of basic products that Cuba bought from the United States. To the Association of Mill Owners, who seemed ready to sign any agreement under the motto/excuse, "Without sugar, there is no country," Menéndez countered, "Put sugar to work for Cuba."[83] This was an unprecedented victory: It marked the first time that a "Third World" country established a compensatory commercial agreement with a developed capitalist state.[84] Sugar workers received $29 million of the $36 million garantía distributed on 10 December 1946. Thanks to the garantía that they won the next year—after another widespread struggle that united workers and colonos—workers ended up with total salaries 40.6 percent higher than those in 1946, the highest wage in the history of the sugar industry.[85]

Unity gave the working class as a whole more strength to win demands under the populist presidencies of the 1940s, and the same rule applied to sugar workers. When the FNOA became the FNTA in 1945, this announced the "unity" goal at the national level. Numerous testimonies highlight the fact that Menéndez had long been working toward this goal at the local level. At Chaparra and Delicias, he helped to organize unions in the colonias as well as at the factories. The single union allowed Cubanaco workers to win impressive benefits for both sectors. Chaparra mill and field workers remember the mid-1940s as the era when they had "some of the best collective contracts in the nation": Field workers won the right to land on which they could supplement their incomes and feed their families, and mill workers won an impressive array of benefits highlighted in the appendix (the Cubanaco collective contract of 1946).[86]

The self-described Chaparra housewife Minina Blanco provided one example of how Menéndez forged such unity. She remembers him grabbing a couple of sticks and breaking them easily into two and then three pieces. He then grabbed a handful of sticks and showed his audience that, when held together, they were impossible to break. "This is how all of us workers must be, united to be stronger."[87] He was also skilled at negotiating with elites. A series of books on the national hero reveal story after story of standoffs between diplomats, mill owners, colonos, and workers being broken by the lanky, handsome Menéndez's sly dimpled grin and brilliant compromise solutions.

Tuinucú workers benefited enormously from Menéndez's skills. In the early 1940s, a group of field workers asked the leader—by then, nationally

35   Tuinucú union headquarters, completed in 1941. Photograph by the author.

known as "the General of the Cane"—to help them organize a union (see figure 35). Jesús had once worked as a cane cutter at one of Tuinucú's colonias,
and he was a close friend of the Tuinucú mill workers' union leader Melanio
Hernández. Jesús instructed his friend Hernández to gather field workers,
mill workers, and the workers' families together for a general assembly in
the wee hours of the morning. In effect, his strategy was to assemble the
entire sugar community, with the notable exception of colonos and mill
managers.

When Menéndez arrived on the scene, he found an assembly hall full of
Tuinucú workers, machetes in hand and families by their sides. The "general" could not have been happier. He told Melanio to bring him a type-
writer and advised his audience that this was an ideal moment to demand
not just recognition of a field workers' union, but also the most pressing
needs of field and factory workers and employees. The workers, represented
by the master negotiator Jesús, told Tuinucú colonos and managers that if
their demands were not met, no field worker would cut the cane, or pile it,
or move it, and no mill worker would process it at the factory. The colonos
had to recognize the field workers' union, and colonos and management
granted field and factory workers most of their demands.[88]

COLD WAR UNDERMINES THE COMPACT, 1947–1955

It took sugar workers a long time to achieve this unity. Combined with the favorable economic and political climate for workers in the late 1930s and early 1940s, unity allowed workers to challenge company and colono power. At the best of times, solidarity was difficult to sustain in the face of populist co-optation from above and occupational (and other social) divisions from within. The onslaught of Cold War politics and anticommunist populism from 1947 onward rendered unity even less achievable. Field and factory workers at Chaparra, Delicias, Tuinucú, and other mills on the island united, then separated, on numerous occasions over the course of the 1940s and 1950s.

On 22 January 1948 an army captain shot Jesús Menéndez on the platform of a train station in Oriente. His body was placed on a train to Havana, and as the train passed, crowds of people stood by every station holding up their fists and shouting: "Unity, CTC!" Thousands were waiting in Havana, too, and organizations from all over the Americas sent cables condemning the crime. One hundred thousand people marched from the Capitolio to the Colón cemetery on 25 January 1948, after a two-day wake. This was the largest, most disciplined concentration of people that Havana had ever witnessed.[89] (See figure 36.)

Menéndez had spoken passionately about the importance of standing united, and for many years the FNTA and the CTC had been able to maintain such unity. Yet even before his murder, Cold War politics had begun to foment division. On 12 March 1947 U.S. President Harry S Truman proclaimed the "Truman Doctrine" to "support free peoples who are resisting attempted subjugation by armed minorities or by outside pressure." The way that U.S. politicians applied the doctrine in practice was to help opposition groups remove communists from leadership or government positions, to declare communist parties illegal, and to channel funding toward conservative armed forces.[90]

With the support of U.S. anticommunism behind them, the Auténticos began a direct attack on communist leadership of the unions. It started at the top, with the CTC congress scheduled to take place in April 1947 (one month after Truman's declaration). What exactly happened is difficult to ascertain, and it must be stated that Cuba's Cold War period from 1947 through 1959 is extremely difficult to evaluate as a historian. There is a real challenge

36   Jesús Menéndez's funeral, Havana,
     1948. Museo Jesús Menéndez,
     Havana.

in filtering out partisanship from the sources on the labor movement, and the presidential archives are largely inaccessible. Oral histories also pose a challenge because descriptors such as *el movimiento* or *los unitarios* seem to be used interchangeably to refer to the Communist Party and Fidel Castro's Twenty-Sixth of July Movement, despite the fact that the Communist Party did not throw its support behind the movement until shortly before the fall of Batista. Pro-communist memoirs will generally condemn Auténticos but sometimes have to acknowledge the fact that Auténtico leaders continued to stage strikes and win demands throughout the period.

What can be safely asserted is that from 1947 onward, the government's approach to the labor movement began to shift away from persuasion and more toward force. Workers remember—and Cubanaco records confirm—that they were arrested more frequently than they had been during the 1940–46 period. They were jailed for things like demanding the diferencial or for trying to hold Unitario CTC meetings versus the new Auténtico-dominated CTC (Unitarios labeled this new CTC the CTK, for "Strike-breakers' Union").[91]

In 1947 Grau's anticommunist Labor Minister Carlos Prío Socarrás legalized the Auténtico CTC under Eusebio Mujal over Lázaro Peña's Unitario CTC. When the Unitario CTC staged a general strike, Prío had 115 labor leaders arrested and encouraged employers to fire all strike participants.[92] Prío won the presidency in 1948, and the repression intensified. Histories of Tuinucú and Chaparra both describe the army sacking their union locales and placing Auténticos in charge. Again, we need to be cautious when considering sources from this era. And yet it can safely be asserted that when leaders were physically expelled from unions—something that occurred to a certain extent in 1947 but to an even greater extent after Batista's military coup in 1952—unions lost much of their legitimacy. By extension, the populist leaders under the Auténtico regime of 1948–52 and the Batistiano regime of 1952–59 evidently had less broad popular support, given that they rested on such shallow and repressive organizations.

Cold War politics and mounting corruption and violence under Auténtico leadership began to undermine the state's legitimacy achieved through the 1937–47 populist compact. The 1940s witnessed a proliferation of violent revolutionary parties fighting for patronage positions, members, and "turf" in the Congress, on the University of Havana campus, and in union locales across the country. Many of the organizations had their roots in the 1933 Revolution, including the ABC Revolutionary Society, the University Student Federation (FEU), and the Student Left Wing (AIE in the 1930s; renamed Revolutionary Student Directorate [DRE] under José Antonio Echeverría in the 1950s). This was the resurfacing that Charles Thomson of *Foreign Policy* had predicted back in 1936.

Fidel Castro took part in these violent clashes as a law student at the University of Havana before he joined what many reformists hoped would be a viable political alternative to the hopelessly corrupt Auténticos— Eduardo Chibás's Ortodoxo Party.[93] Chibás, who had been a prominent student leader in 1933, broke with the Auténtico Party in 1947 to create the "Orthodox" Cuban Revolutionary Party. The party's name, like its leader, discredited the "Authentic" Cuban Revolutionary Party by exposing case after case of high-level government corruption. When Chibás shot himself during a radio broadcast in 1951 in a dramatic act that ended in death, he left many Cubans demoralized.[94] The Auténticos seemed hopelessly greedy, but the Ortodoxo Party no longer provided a viable alternative without Chibás's charismatic leadership. Batista hovered in the background, desperate to return to the presidency to "fix" the order that the Auténticos had broken. He was running a distant third to the Ortodoxo and Auténtico candidates in the 1952 presidential elections, so he staged a coup to pre-empt them.[95]

Batista's coup on 10 March 1952 shares some striking parallels with Machado's prolongation of power in 1928. In both cases, the revolution did not materialize immediately. There were scattered strikes in reaction to the event (including a short-lived protest strike at Tuinucú), but general strikes would not take place until several years later. Students, politicians, and military men began to plot how to depose the dictator immediately. These plots—and the absence thereof during the populist era from 1940 through 1952—demonstrate the important stabilizing role that electoral politics played, even when it was extremely corrupt.[96]

The fact that the United States supported both Machado and Batista militarily and diplomatically after their illegal assumption of power undermined the dictators' legitimacy for Cubans from all strata. The two leaders were frequently portrayed as puppets for U.S. power (recall figure 30, the 1933 *Nation* cartoon in chapter 7). Both negotiated large loans from U.S. banks and then engaged in obvious graft. In Batista's case, the loans were from the U.S. government's export-import bank rather than private, "Wall Street" banks, but this made little difference to Cuban nationalists. Batista granted tax breaks to U.S. capitalists and tried to break down some of organized labor's gains, ostensibly to attract more investors to the island and to improve the economy. His regime claimed such enormous kickbacks on these new investments that they did little for Cubans as a whole. Finally, Batista looked more like Machado because the Cold War policy of the United States precluded the possibility of a renewed alliance with the communists. (The popularity of their working-class CTC was long gone, in any case, undermined by years of divisive Auténtico rule.) Without the communists providing a way to incorporate workers, Batista was left with only two real support bases: the army and U.S. politicians.

For a few years Batista tried hard not to alienate the official populist groups. Within five days of his coup, big organizations like the Association of Mill Owners, the Association of Colonos, and the CTC all agreed to accept Batista as Cuba's new ruler. The author Aureliano Sánchez Arango offers a logical explanation for this in regard to the CTC: "The unions had become cells of an economic animal; whatever happened beyond the margins of the economy did not matter to them."[97] This certainly applied to the official unions, and their compromising leaders reaped great rewards from their ties to Batista. He gave them $1.347 million between 1952 and 1958, plus $3.67 million for their social-security fund.[98] He also tried to buy workers' support by improving on the wage increases, vacations, and summer hours that his Auténtico predecessors had established. As for colonos, Batista raised their share of the value of the cane from 48 percent to 49–50 percent. He also increased all colonos' grinding factor from 30,000 arrobas to 40,000 arrobas during the 1953 harvest, when demand and prices for sugar were higher because of the Korean War.[99]

DICTATORSHIP EMPTIES THE COMPACT

Batista's fundamental problem in the 1950s was that the head of a populist state could not "balance society's parts" if the parts themselves did not have enough "society" in them. Batista practiced favoritism and nepotism to such an extent that he undermined what little integrity remained for populist institutions like the Colono Association and the CTC. In some ways, Batista represented a return to individualistic patronage politics. He and his wife doled out "discretionary funds" and positions to individuals that they wanted as friends (such as journalists and lawyers) to try to rally more support.[100] These favored few alienated the vast majority of the populist institutions' associates, stealing away their access to the state and its benefits.

The journalist Raul Cepero Bonilla made this point clearly in his critical articles for *Prensa Libre* during the 1950s, which have been republished as *Política Azucarera, 1952–1958*. "We need to free sugar questions from Associations, Law Firms, and Ministers," he argued, "to make them accessible to the man on the street." Cepero described the sugar industry as an immense state-run cartel. He attacked the "vicious" system that made sugar and molasses speculation official policy. The Sugar Stabilization Board (ICAE) that allocated quotas to sugarmills and cane farmers and sold Cuba's sugar to international buyers was made up of lawyers and representatives from export companies who engaged in inside trading to the detriment of Cuba's sugar industry as a whole. Batista had "politicized" the leadership of the Mill Owner Association and the National Colono Association to such an extreme that Cepero suggested they should be re-baptized the "Association of Lawyers of Mill Owners and Colonos." Finally, Cepero relayed a story told to him by a mill owner about how the three leaders of the institute imposed their mandate. They would keep members waiting for hours to force as many as possible to lose patience and leave before they waltzed in. When they arrived, they would announce the motions that they wanted approved as though they had already been approved, exerting pressure at gunpoint by announcing, "Batista would like this to pass." As a result, the regime forced the association's members to sanction the ICAE officials' outrageous salaries and official speculation.[101]

A similar lack of democracy reigned in the unions. They supposedly represented large numbers of workers. In 1951 at least half of the workforce, more than a million people, paid union dues to more than two thousand one hundred trade unions. But the numbers were deceiving. For example, the vast majority of sugar workers no longer opted to pay dues for "their" unions. Rather, mill owners and colonos automatically deducted the dues from wages to distribute among leaders of local unions, the FNTA, and the CTC.[102] Union dues had been plummeting since 1948, and Prío responded by imposing an obligatory union fee on all sugar workers (Decree 1300 in April 1951). The FNTA's new "cooperative" leaders returned Prío's favor by shelving a list of demands prepared for the 1952 harvest that included one for a 40 percent wage increase.[103] In exchange for the CTC's support in 1952, Batista extended the obligatory union fee to all labor sectors. Eusebio Mujal, boss of the CTC (and a Batistiano senator), reportedly made more than $280,000 a year during the dictatorship years.[104]

Not enough people were being incorporated into the state, so as the 1950s wore on, Batista had to rely increasingly on violence instead of persuasion. The police cruisers and guardsmen on imposing Texan horses returned to intimidate mill residents, as they had in 1935. Soldiers expelled a great number of workers from the unions and regularly entered workers' homes and assemblies to search for communists. Eladio Santiago, Arquímedes Valdivia, and Rita Díaz all spoke of the need to hide communist and Unitario leaders in safe houses or cane fields when the Rural Guard came around to look for them. Tuinucú's Arquímedes Valdivia remembers Auténtico CTC leaders (followers of Eusebio Mujal) stuffing ballots, threatening to have workers fired, falsifying voter lists, and splitting field workers from factory workers. One department head would not let communist CTC members (Unitarios) leave the workplace during voting hours for union elections. Valdivia added a refreshingly nuanced qualifier to this anecdote that contrasts with the written sources' partisanship: "Some Unitarios sold out, and some Auténticos were honest."[105] By the mid-1950s, though, the official union movement was compromised to company and state leaders to the extreme. Batista's mandatory union dues took away any choice from the workers as to whether or not they wanted to be in the unions, and this gave the union leaders less motivation to make themselves accountable. The stories of corruption of the ICAE and union leaders are only a few examples among many of the decay of 1950s populism.

Sugar workers remember the late 1940s and the 1950s as a time when the army "mafia" returned to their mills. The Second World War and the Korean War (1950–53) brought a burst of prosperity, and with it came gambling, prostitution, and racketeering. As in the Havana of the 1950s so famously depicted in Francis Ford Coppola's *The Godfather II*, Batista's politicians and military men reaped handsome profits from the vice at the mills. In an interesting parallel to the celebrations in 1933 over the departure of Machado, after the departure of Batista, Cubans attacked symbols of elite power such as the mansions of Menocal and the Riondas, but they also destroyed symbols of U.S. power and military racketeering—Havana's grand casinos.[106]

Vice, corruption, and violence encouraged sugarmill companies to ignore or defy many of the labor gains of 1937–47. Workers responded with strikes, production slowdowns, shadow leadership, and sabotage. The worker José Adan Romero Rojas narrates a strike in 1950 at Chaparra when factory workers demanded bonus pay for the days they would have worked if not for the faster production brought on by technological changes at the mill. This was not unlike the protests surrounding "Taylorism," when workers were asked to do more precise jobs, faster, elsewhere in the Americas.[107] The union leadership presented the demands to the Ministry of Labor, but "the haughty *Mister* Wood" was intransigent.

The union needed unanimous worker support to win, but it was not allowed to hold meetings during the harvest. The union "consulted the masses" via small groups in numerous sessions in the mill towns. Its representatives explained the plan that the shadow Unitario CTC leadership was advocating from Havana—the *paso de jicotea* (literally, "turtle step," or what social historians call foot dragging). This action demonstrated the strength of the union and the depth of workers' hostility toward the foreign company. The pay for faster production was not achieved via foot dragging, so workers started to abandon the factory, leaving only what Adan calls the "enemies of the working class, the submissive and cowardly strike-breakers."[108] The strikebreakers were in fact field workers brought in by the Rural Guard. Since the technology to which mill workers were reacting did not affect field workers, the union left them out of the discussions. This was evidently a mistake. The administration tried bribes to get the union leaders to stay away from the Labor Ministry, and when that did not work, they tried death threats. All of this was to no avail: On 29 March 1950 after more than six hours of discussion between the union leaders and the "*yanqui* administration," President Prío signed Decree 1931 granting six days of bonus pay to all of the sugar workers in the country.[109]

The demand for bonus pay closely relates to a series of other demands that workers made to try to counter the largest problem in Cuba—unemployment. Violence and corruption go a long way toward explaining why there was a revolution in 1950s Cuba, but the fundamental structural problem in 1959 was the same as it had been in 1933: dependence on one product that required large numbers of workers only a few months of the year. The Reciprocity Treaty of 1934 had only exacerbated the problem, reducing the employment possibilities for the working class and middle class alike. A former worker at the Violeta sugarmill, Angel Santana Suárez, vividly described the unemployment of the 1950s: "It became more common to see hundreds of companions walking the roads at the beginning of each harvest season, carrying their possessions in straw bags and asking the unions to help them find work. How many times they asked us to let them cut a bundle of cane so they could continue on their way or to let them work half a day in order to earn 'water and charcoal'! Hundreds, thousands of times!"[110]

Workers would fight against being fired for what the employers insisted were "just causes," all the way to the Supreme Court. Mill owners tried—and sometimes managed—to "buy" workers' positions from them, offering them money not to return the following harvest. Workers fought tooth and nail against any form of mechanization, resisting tractors in the cane fields and containers (instead of bags) on the docks. The populist laws and 1940 Constitution protected workers' jobs reasonably well until Batista's coup. But according to the U.S. economist Philip C. Newman in *Cuba before Castro*, "Since 1953, the interpretation of the 1933 laws has been considerably more lenient." He noted that strikes were allowed only after ten days' notice to the Labor Ministry and assured investors that the "intervention" tactic used frequently during the Auténtico years to force companies to concede to labor demands had not been applied since 1953. He added: "The rigidity of past attitudes by unions and governments has been considerably relaxed." His word choice reflects the perspective that mill owners and colonos would share. From the workers' perspective, the unions were not "relaxed," but useless (15).

In October 1954 just when reparations were scheduled to begin for the 1955 harvest at Chaparra and Delicias, Cubanaco announced that it would cut a considerable number of jobs for reasons of economy. The workers refused to accept these layoffs and demanded that their union declare a strike. The Auténtico union leaders fled, ostensibly to escape Rural Guard repression so they could lead the workers. This left them free to maneuver with the company and sell out the movement, which was what they had done in the past. A group of Unitario workers occupied Puerto Padre's City Hall to raise the strike's profile. Two days later, the Rural Guard stormed the building and put them in jail.

The women of Chaparra and Delicias, who had already mobilized support for the Unitarios, created two commissions. One small group went to the police chief to demand freedom for the jailed workers. The other group burst into the mayor's home to protest the abuses and demand his intervention. The mayor fainted from the shock of the noise and confusion.[111] The Afro-Cuban Ester Villa Nápoles led Chaparra's women, and Rita Díaz led the women from Delicias; Villa was married to the Unitario activist Tomás González, and Díaz had gone to Havana to study before returning to the mill as a teacher and organizer for the Democratic Federation of Cuban Women (FDMC). When asked about the event fifty years later, Villa still remembered removing French braids to let her thick black hair hang free in an intimidating mane, and she laughed at the memory of the fainting mayor.[112]

As a leader of the FDMC, which had been formed during the 1937–47 democratic opening, Díaz had already begun to build a strong female auxiliary force that could buttress the strike movement at Chaparra and Delicias. Batista had declared the FDMC illegal after Fidel Castro and a group of young middle-class revolutionaries, including several women, tried to take over the Moncada barracks in Santiago de Cuba on 26 July 1953. Yet women immediately resumed organizing patriotic and cultural associations, local clubs, and sewing clubs to rally support for the revolution. During the 1954–55 strike, Women's Committees formed at Chaparra and Delicias and at the Juan Claro Port, where dock workers held a solidarity strike for their "industrial brothers."

The women got the Rural Guard to give them the key to the union locale, and they kept it open throughout the strike. They held nightly meetings and thus prevented Batista's fake military union leaders from using the Auténtico CTC leaders' absence as an excuse to take over the union. (Rita Díaz concurred with Valdivia that there were at least a few decent Auténtico leaders, and she added that they felt a certain obligation to the workers because they were elected, even though the elections were "marred by political maneuvers.") Many workers and the Auténtico union officials reinforced the strike by fundraising among other mill workers in northern Oriente, perhaps out of fear that they would lose their positions if they did not show honor in the struggle. As in 1925 and 1933, civil, social, cultural, and religious institutions in Puerto Padre supported the workers with financial aid. During 104 days, the strike committee distributed rice, beans, lard, vegetables, and the meat acquired from a few confiscated cows, among families at Chaparra and Delicias. They also provided food for the children in public schools. The dock workers refused to carry sugar bags even though Christmas was approaching, thus forfeiting the salaries that could have bought presents for their children.

Rita Díaz recalled with pride that the strike took place when the Batista dictatorship was in full swing, at a time when the Rural Guard regularly appeared at union assemblies on horseback with sabers in hand. The agents of Batista's new Bureau for the Repression of Communist Activities interrupted many of the meetings, detaining women and union members more than once to take them to Holguín for National Defense Tribunals. Batista revived the tribunals as yet another means of repression from the Mendieta–Batista era of 1934–36.

As in the battles of 1925 and 1933, Chaparra and Delicias workers won national public support against the foreign Cubanaco. Popular pressure led the Labor Ministry to rule that Cubanaco could not lay off any workers. The women stood fast until they saw proof that the ruling was enforced. Jeffrey Gould found communities using similar tactics during the harshest years of the Somoza dictatorship in Nicaragua. Male leaders would be forced to hide, so women would organize strikes or land occupations. When the soldiers asked them, "Who is your leader?" they would declare, "We lead as equals."[113] In both the Cuban and Nicaraguan cases, women shielded combative male labor leaders from Rural Guard repression and at the same time defended their communities from company abuses.

Díaz recalled the women of Chaparra and Delicias demonstrating a level of class-consciousness whose roots were in the revolutionary tradition of that region, the frequent scene of powerful worker and colono battles for rights, later converted into national gains that would achieve their climax in the 1959 Revolution."[114] Díaz was correct: The powerful nationalist, oppositional movements that developed at the Cubanaco enclave in 1925 and 1933 and during the complex populist decades of the 1940s and 1950s often had broader effects on national policy toward colonos and workers. Among other examples, this was the case for the triumph in gaining bonus pay, as described earlier, and for Machado's protective colono legislation discussed in chapter 5. Chaparra and Delicias were the first and only mills to be "intervened" in 1933, and Chaparra was among the first mills that the Cuban revolutionary government nationalized and made the property of the state after the breakdown of Cuban-U.S. relations in July 1960.[115] The workers renamed the mill "Jesús Menéndez," and the nationalized Delicias would soon after be renamed "Antonio Guiteras."

From the mid-1950s onward, as the dictatorship hardened, workers adopted the 1933 strategies of the general strike and sabotage. In December 1955 two workers named Conrado Rodríguez and Conrado Bécquer organized what became known as the "strike of the Conrados" with the help of the shadow Unitario CTC and middle-class students from the Directorio Revolucionario organization. The strike was one of the largest in Cuban sugar workers' history, attracting some five hundred thousand workers despite the Auténtico CTC's and the FNTA's warnings against it.

Workers demanded an end to restrictions on the sugar harvest, pay based on a fixed price of 5 cents per pound, and a diferencial equal to 8 percent of workers' salaries. (Colonos and mill owners, with the help of the ICAE, were trying to withhold the diferencial by hiding profits in their accounting practices.) The workers managed to paralyze more than fourteen mills, including Tuinucú, but Batista's soldiers savagely repressed workers at Chaparra, Delicias, and elsewhere on the island in the so-called Bloody Christmas. Batista ended up giving workers a diferencial, but it was only 1 percent instead of 8 percent. Batista, Mujal, and FNTA leaders were bought off by mill owners and colonos in 1955 just as Grau had been bought off by the U.S. Credit Corporation in 1948 when he agreed to annul Menéndez's garantía clause.[116]

The CTC and the FNTA, populist institutions that were once such strong tools for the new self-defined "working class" and "sugar-worker class," had become vehicles for the personal enrichment of a few. The 1955 strike that workers organized despite CTC and FNTA orders to the contrary helped to demonstrate how thin dictatorship and favoritism had rendered one of the thickest walls of Cuba's populist edifice.

EPILOGUE: CANE FIRES AND
REVOLUTIONARY PARALLELS

After landing a revolutionary force of eighty-two men on Cuban shores, Fidel Castro and about a dozen other revolutionaries who survived capture by Batista's soldiers took refuge in the eastern mountains of the Sierra Maestra to build a guerrilla army. The evidence is uneven as to what relationship sugar workers, colonos, and even mill owners had to this Twenty-Sixth of July Movement (M-26–7) from the time the guerrillas landed in December 1956 through the overthrow of Batista in December 1958.[117] What is clear is that cane fires resumed an important place in the symbolic battle between revolutionaries and the status quo.

One of Castro's comrades-in-arms wrote: "Revolution in Cuba means burning sugarcane—it did in 1868, 1895, and 1930–33, and it did for us."[118] In February 2000 I asked two former field workers at Tuinucú if they had ever burned cane fields. The ninety-two-year-old Rafael Gutiérrez Rodríguez and Armando Cruz García, roughly twenty years his junior, began to shake their heads, but then their friend and local historian Eladio Santiago pushed them: "You *never* burned cane?" At that point Cruz took me aside and told me that they did burn cane at Tuinucú. He said that cutters occasionally did so to get more work if the quota was too small, and during the 1950s revolution, workers did so extensively as a form of sabotage.[119] Cruz left Tuinucú to join Ché Guevara in the Escambray mountains near Santa Clara in the late 1950s. Other revolutionary workers, including Eladio Santiago and Arquímedes Valdivia, remained at the mill, where they collected funds and supplies for the guerrilla army and organized clandestinely to burn cane, make Molotov cocktails, and commit other forms of sabotage.

Evidence from Chaparra, Tuinucú, and other mills on the island proves Ramón Eduardo Ruiz's oft-cited study on the Cuban Revolution wrong in its assertion that "labor remained aloof from the Revolution; only the upheaval of 1933 had drawn the worker into its vortex. . . . Not once did organized labor heed Castro's call for a general strike."[120] Batista's favoritism and repression had rendered "organized labor" a shell of its former (1939–47) self. The corrupt leadership of the Auténtico CTC did not join the revolution, but many workers who were supposedly "organized"—like Gutiérrez, Rodríguez, Santiago, and Valdivia of Tuinucú—did join, or they at least did what they could to support the insurrection from within the heavily repressed sugarmills. Guerrilla leaders in the mountains and radical students and professionals in the cities certainly deserve much of the credit for making the 1959 Revolution happen.[121] After seeing how much workers participated in shaping the Cuban state over the course of the twentieth century, and how much the populist compact had failed them by the mid-1950s, it cannot be true that they remained aloof from the revolutionary struggle.

Several impressive similarities exist between the 1959 Revolution that ends this book and the nineteenth-century struggles that began it. The timing of the revolutionary triumph is noteworthy: U.S. policymakers and Batista's longstanding individual supporters from the Cuban military and from the middle and upper classes abandoned the dictator as the 1959 harvest approached. The kind of violence and repression practiced by Batista, like that of Weyler in the 1890s, served to alienate rural peasants, workers, and even middle- and upper-class Cubans to the point of pushing them into the ranks of a revolutionary cross-class movement. The Associations of Colonos and Sugarmill Owners not only sent officers and cabinet members to demand Batista's resignation, but sugarmill owners, colonos, cattlemen, bankers, and industrialists contributed several million pesos to finance the rebellion.[122]

This support made sense, and it was not so different from when nineteenth-century mill owners decided to abandon the colonial compact. Batista's corrupt and violent regime was stealing more than capitalists and colonos were willing to accept. The regime was no longer able to guarantee "peace and prosperity" in the face of the mounting insurrection. And most important, the middle-class revolutionaries who led the insurrection carefully recruited middle-class and elite support with moderate political programs.

In the famous "History Will Absolve Me" speech that Castro made before being jailed for the attack on the Moncada barracks in 1953, the charismatic young leader demonstrated a keen knowledge of the problems of Cuba's countryside (learned from his childhood in the colonia in Oriente) and the problems of its cities (learned from his student years in Havana). He managed to gain support from many who were suffering under the broken populist compact:

> Seven hundred thousand Cubans without work . . . five hundred thousand farm laborers inhabiting miserable shacks, who work four months of the year and starve for the rest of the year . . . four hundred thousand industrial laborers and stevedores whose retirement funds have been embezzled, whose benefits are being taken away, whose homes are wretched quarters, whose salaries pass from the hands of the boss to those of the usurer, whose future is a pay reduction and dismissal . . . one hundred thousand small farmers who live and die working on land that is not theirs . . . who, like feudal serfs, have to pay for the use of their parcel of land by giving up a portion of their products; who cannot love it, improve it, beautify it or plant a lemon or an orange tree on it, because they never know when a sheriff will come with the rural guard to evict them from it.

Castro listed some of the M-26–7's strongest supporters last: teachers, professors, and small-business men "weighted down by debts" and "harangued by a plague of filibusters and venal officials," as well as "ten thousand young professionals . . . who come forth from school with their degrees . . . only to find themselves at a dead end with all doors closed, and where no ear hears their clamor or supplication."[123]

"History Will Absolve Me" promised land reform, but with generous compensation for landowners. Large colonos saw this as a chance finally to buy the land that they had only been able to "control." Small colonos were promised a larger quota, but this did not threaten the larger colonos. It was assumed that the quota would come from what little remained of administration cane's quota or from an end to the highly unpopular national sugar restrictions. "History" stressed the goals that lower-, middle-, and upper-class Cubans shared of increasing employment and national income by stimulating industrialization and agricultural diversification. It assured capitalists that new taxes would not be needed; the revolutionary government ould pay for these programs by eliminating corruption and excessive military spending. Castro's "Manifesto to the People of Cuba" of 1955 was even more moderate than "History Will Absolve Me," and the same applies to the other M-26–7 manifestos issued before the fall of Batista.[124]

The battles over cane fires that raged in the 1890s reappeared in the 1950s and for the same reason: Civilian leaders in exile tended to be more moderate and more focused on U.S. public opinion than rebel leaders on the island. In the summer of 1958 the rebel army passed an order requiring sugarmill owners to pay a "levy" of 15 cents on each 250 pound bag of sugar "or suffer the consequences."[125] Civilian leaders in exile pleaded with the guerrillas to cease this "blackmail" of North American firms, complaining that it was contributing to bad press in the United States, but the rebels did not listen.[126] Former President Carlos Prío Socarrás joined the fray when he outfitted a plane from his home in exile in Miami to have it drop live phosphorus on cane fields and buildings in Cuba.[127]

Like their nineteenth-century predecessors, revolutionaries realized that the modern "burning-torch" policy to destroy the harvest was the best way to get sugar workers to join the insurrection. Early in November 1957 the rebel army torched ten sugarmills around the Sierra Maestra, and by the middle of the month they had burned some forty-four thousand tons from twenty thousand acres. Celia Sánchez, one of the most important leaders in the movement, noted on 9 November 1957, "The environment is ripe to attack the rice. . . . This action, together with the cane burning, can accelerate the strike."[128] Castro himself announced in November 1957 that insurgents would burn cane fields "no matter who owned them." In other words U.S. property would not be spared. Cubanaco took matters into its own hands by ordering rifles and tear-gas bombs and obtaining assurance from the U.S. State Department that it would help evacuate some fifty Americans at Chaparra and Delicias, if needed.[129]

The rebel army called for the destruction of the 1958 sugar harvest under the motto: "Either Batista without the harvest or the harvest without Batista. . . . After the tyrant is in the tomb . . . we shall have a harvest of liberty." Sugar workers received a one-page pamphlet with instructions on how to set the fires, including the suggestion to tie a gasoline-soaked sponge to a rat's tail.[130] In response Batista tried to "save face" and prove that he could still protect the fields, much like the Spanish colonial administrators who forced Francisco Rionda to mill in 1895. Shored up by a seemingly endless supply of military aid from the Cold Warriors of the United States, the dictator sent military equipment and armies into the fields to combat the fires. He gave permission to start grinding in December 1957 (earlier than usual) and permitted soldiers to fire on "all suspicious people." Mujal of the Auténtico CTC asked workers to "stand guard against the torch." There must have been more hype than reality to Castro's threats, because mill owners still managed to make $680 million dollars on the 1957 harvest, $200 million more than in 1956 and more than in any other year since 1952.[131]

Some of the parallels between the 1930s and the 1950s have already been highlighted, but a few more merit attention here to explain why Castro managed to triumph over Batista, on the one hand, and over other opposition leaders, on the other. Batista practiced a modern version of Machado's *ley de fuga* whereby prisoners would be released, then the dictator's henchmen would kill them. Desperate for political legitimacy and under strong diplomatic pressure from the United States to achieve it, Batista allowed several general amnesties over the course of the 1950s. He usually waited a few days or weeks and then announced another "state of siege." Castro issued the 1955 "Manifesto" that helped to make his movement so popular when Batista freed him in an amnesty. Castro escaped the fate of many other opposition leaders by hiding first in Mexico, where he organized the M-26–7 guerrilla army, and then in the eastern mountains of the Sierra Maestra, from whence he ran the insurrection from 1956 to 1959. Batista's "amnesties," combined with his powerful urban forces of repression, served to destroy even the most moderate middle- and upper-class opposition leaders in the cities.[132]

Batista's repression and Castro's moderate platforms based on a broad understanding of Cuba's urban and rural problems helped the M-26–7 win the 1959 Revolution. So did Castro's return to the rural expeditionary tactic, first used in the nineteenth-century revolutions. Batista's forces were so focused on targeting revolutionaries in the cities that they were unable to capture the guerillas in the eastern mountains.[133]

A few final historical parallels deserve attention. The first is that revolutionaries in the 1950s faced the same regional challenge as the anticolonial guerrillas of the nineteenth century. Urban revolutionaries attacked the Batista regime to the best of their ability using the terrorist and secret-cell tactics first developed in 1933, and guerrilla leaders gathered support in the countryside surrounding their bases in the eastern Sierra Maestra mountains. But the 1950s revolution was won when, and only when, the guerrilla columns of Ché Guevara and Camilo Cienfuegos defeated a heavily armed military detachment in central Cuba and marched into Santa Clara to occupy it on 31 December 1958.[134]

Batista's General Eulogio Cantillo, military chief of Oriente Province, took over from the dictator when he boarded a plane to the Dominican Republic in the early hours of 1 January 1959. He left for three main reasons. Isolated and demoralized, the dictator's soldiers and generals had abandoned him just as Machado's soldiers and officers had abandoned him in 1933.[135] U.S. public opinion against the dictator and Batista's refusal to soften his repressive rule finally swayed the White House policymakers away from the Cold Warriors of the Pentagon: They cut off the military aid and diplomatic support that Batista desperately needed. (True to Good Neighborly form, the CIA, State Department, and U.S. ambassadors cast around for a moderate alternative to Castro or Batista. They tried to forge alliances between civilian leaders of the opposition and dissenting military leaders—to no avail.) Last but certainly not least, Batista left because M-26–7 columns were moving toward Havana from central Cuba.

Events surrounding Batista's departure were similar to those that surrounded Machado's, but there was a crucial difference in order. Soldiers became demoralized; the United States abandoned the dictator; and there was a general strike. In 1933 the general strike gave Machado the final push off the island, leaving his officers in charge (at least briefly, until the sergeants took over). In 1959 Fidel Castro was outraged when he heard of General Cantillo's appointment. The revolutionaries did not want another fragile civilian-military alliance like that of 1933. The M-26–7 therefore used the same popular tactic that revolutionaries had used in 1933, calling a general strike on 1 January 1959. It was so successful that it allowed the rebels to dissolve the army altogether.[136] This would be one among many crucial differences to explain the longevity of the Cuban Revolution of 1959 versus the Cuban Revolution of 1933 and Guatemalan Revolution of 1944–54 before it or the Chilean Revolution of 1970–73 after it.[137]

The final historical parallel is that, while many sugar workers had been too repressed to act during the insurrections of 1933 and 1959, they asserted and won their demands after. Upon Batista's departure, the vast majority of workers joined the general strike and forced Batista's generals to abdicate to Fidel Castro and the rebel army. Upon assuming power, the new revolutionary regime's challenge was to get the economy ready for the 1959 harvest after having completely paralyzed it during the insurrection and general strike. When the charismatic, romantic revolutionary leader Fidel Castro asked workers to stop the strikes, they did. But they flooded the new Agrarian Reform Institute with letters. Most of the M-26–7 program centered on land under the slogan "Land to the Tiller," so workers would couch their demands by asking for "land or work."[138]

Colonos also lobbied the regime, and they got their demands before the workers. The first Agrarian Reform Law passed in 1959 gave colonos the right to buy land. As Martínez-Alier explains, "It would seem that the revolutionaries in May 1959 were thinking that a land reform which got rid of the American companies' landed properties and gave ownership of the land to farmers and small tenants was good enough."[139] The reform did not mention work or land for agricultural laborers, instead favoring the gradual division of large landholdings and the creation of cooperatives on confiscated Batistiano land.

Colonos demanded the state's "intervention" in mills because the mills did not pay off colono sugar quotas at the end of the harvest. And then workers demanded state "intervention" in colonias because they did not pay workers their wages during the harvest or offer to pay them for weeding when the 1959 off-season started. In their defense, colonos and mill owners emphasized that they faced serious credit issues in the post-revolutionary economic climate of uncertainty. Banks did not want to lend them money, and from the colonos' perspective, weeding could wait for better times.

Workers prompted a radicalization of revolutionary policy both through their letters and through their actions. In 1959 and 1960, a small number of workers got jobs in cooperatives; tenants of various types stopped paying rent and won ownership titles for the land they occupied. Practically all of the colonos and squatters seemed to be getting land, but many workers were falling through the cracks. The national agrarian archives include some five hundred letters from individual workers asking for land. The same archives note at least forty instances of illegal land occupations by workers in 1959–60. Great numbers of letters from unions and individuals explained that cooperatives were not enough and that companies were keeping the best land and were not creating enough jobs. The letters asked for, and sometimes won, the state's "intervention" in mills and eventually colonias, as well.[140]

The sources are not yet accessible to carefully elaborate what workers and colonos gained—or lost—from the revolution. What is undeniable is that their initial actions rapidly pushed the revolutionary state further to the left. This included the nationalization of industries and sugarmills and much more thorough land reforms.[141] The later land reforms actually pushed many large and medium-size colonos to leave the country. Historians have documented a similar process whereby the masses radicalized the triumphant revolutionary regimes in Mexico of the 1930s and Chile of the 1970s.[142] And we saw variations of this pattern in Cuba's nineteenth- and twentieth-century revolutions.

The reforms and nationalization in Cuba prompted a resurgence of cane fires, this time by individuals who rejected Castro's revolution. "Counter-revolutionaries" from the Escambray Mountains of Las Villas province started fires at Tuinucú by entering the fields at night. Exiles dropped lit torches onto the cane fields of Chaparra, Delicias, and other mills on the island from airplanes launched from Miami. Manuel Rionda's nephew, Manolo Rionda, was among the band of Cuban exiles who staged a much more aggressive attack on the revolution. He landed at the Bay of Pigs in 1961 to try to overthrow Castro's regime.

Conclusion

In the end, the stories of workers, colonos, and mill owners traced in this book prove that we can only understand how systems of rule are created and adjusted by paying attention to the action of the popular groups that the system seeks to "incorporate."[1] Revolutionaries used cane fires to try to raze the old order and make way for a new one. Each revolution had its successes. The Ten Years' War and the Little War that followed it freed the slaves and prompted the division of sugar production into industrial and agricultural sectors. Three distinct social classes emerged from this division to play important roles in state formation in twentieth-century Cuba—the mill owner, the colono cane farmer, and the sugar worker.

The 1895 Revolution broke the colonial compact, freeing Cuba from its colonial rulers. New electoral politics carved out some (albeit limited) space for popular participation in Cuban politics. Foreign mill owners spread sugar production eastward with the help of Cuban patron middlemen such as Mario García Menocal, and workers and colonos tried to negotiate the best deal that they could within the new patrons' compact. At the national level, caudillo veterans of the wars for independence tried to balance U.S. capital and political demands with the needs of their popular and elite Cuban clientele.

The economic crash of 1921 underscored the economic and political frailty of the caudillo–clientele system of rule, and the organizations of veterans, colonos, and workers prompted the Cuban government to become more inclusive through popular nationalism in the mid-1920s (at least at the rhetorical level). The Great Depression hit harder, bringing a shift back to exclusion and dictatorship, but the masses made the state more inclusive again through the 1933 Revolution, with its more profound, class-based popular nationalist reform. What came next was a two-year period of right-of-center populism to "contain" the popular energies of the revolution. Only then could a more democratic populist system of rule emerge. President Batista and President Grau San Martín, organized workers, and colonos significantly altered the political, social, and economic structures of Cuba from the late 1930s through the late 1940s. During the popular-front and Democratic Spring periods, the Cuban state looked much like some of its more widely recognized Latin American populist counterparts.

The new social legislation and more nationalist politics on the island prompted U.S. capitalists to make a gradual retreat from sugar from the mid-1930s through Batista's 1952 coup d'état.[2] Those remaining on the island and their Cuban capitalist counterparts sought to sidestep social legislation while workers joined together—mill and field, white and black, Cuban and British West Indian, communist, anarcho-syndicalist, and Auténtico—to make the social legislation and constitution of the 1930s and 1940s more autonomous, democratic, and real.

That colonos succeeded in improving their lot is demonstrated in the pro-colono government legislation and press coverage from the late 1920s through the 1950s. Colonos' demands even made their way into Fidel Castro's revolutionary program. As to workers, their success is demonstrated in the positive social legislation passed in the late 1930s and early 1940s. It is also reflected in the fact that the most influential labor confederation changed from advocating rejection of Cuban state institutions to promoting engagement and negotiation from within. This very change reveals the transformation that mass popular mobilization provoked in the Cuban state: from openly repressive dictatorship in 1932 to "populist" regimes from 1933 to 1956.

"Populist" is surrounded by quotation marks because, as we saw, the inclusion of popular groups varied immensely during the period. The early years included top-down labor legislation combined with extreme repression. The far more significant inclusion of popular groups came during the 1937–47 period, and then the second Auténtico administration introduced a highly insidious form of populism that divided labor unions from within and undermined much of the power workers had accumulated. First Auténticos and then Batistianos intervened in unions, pushing the communists across the island into "shadow unions" at the local and national levels. A more extensive discussion of Cuba's populist and dictatorship periods still lies ahead, but I hope that this study has proved that by paying attention to how popular, middle-class, and elite groups at the local level affect the national, and vice versa, we can arrive at a more nuanced vision of Cuban history.

Through tracing the construction of day-to-day relations and systems of rule in Cuba's sugarmills and national halls of power, this study raises several broader theoretical reflections. Social and political relations in many early-twentieth-century American nations can be seen as variations on the theme of patronage at the local level and caudillismo at the national level. Within the many variations on the patrons' compact and the capitalist management of communities, the experience of the Chaparra Sugar Company underscores an important lesson. While the enclave initially facilitated rapid profits and enforced inequality through a combination of co-optation and coercion, it simultaneously created the potential for workers and colonos to absolutely freeze production—when they got around their differences. In this respect Ramiro Guerra's thesis can be flipped on its head: Because there were more foreign-owned enclaves in the East, colonos and workers there ended up having more power than those in the West. They organized strong oppositional movements against the "imperialist" companies, won support from the region and the nation, and pushed through local and national reforms.

Across the Americas, the patrons' philanthropy and progressivism faltered with the agricultural depression of the early 1920s and then froze with the larger social and economic shock of the Great Depression starting in 1929. That was when workers and cane farmers in Cuba (and different popular groups elsewhere) began to see themselves as distinct classes and organized as such to demand social-democratic "rights" and "protection" from the state. As Lizabeth Cohen wrote about the transition from paternalism to social democracy taking place simultaneously in the United States, "With this notion of rights . . . workers were moving beyond the hierarchical authority relationships implicit in paternalism, which made them dependents. As contributing members of society, they made no apologies for taking relief, social security ... insurance ... mortgages, and ... jobs from the state."[3] Cuba's transition from the company welfare programs described in chapters 4 and 5 to state legislated welfare under the populist governments of the 1930s and 1940s described in chapter 8 was nowhere near as thorough as it was in countries like the United States, Chile, or Mexico, but it was similar to the changes in Brazil and Nicaragua.

Cuba fits into the larger Latin American pattern better than most studies recognize. To understand the 1959 Revolution, we need to look more closely at the Cold War years that preceded it. As this study proves, veterans, mill owners, planters, and colonos, among other groups in the Cuban state, pushed and pulled politics in many different directions between 1868 and 1959, and the stories of these groups are important ones to tell. The Cold War backlash beginning in 1947 began to sap the populist institutions of their social-democratic value by again prioritizing individual clients instead of class groups. Jeffrey Gould has traced a similar pattern in Nicaragua, where peasants helped the Sandinistas win their revolution by proving that populist Somocista rhetoric was completely empty.[4] Cuban and Nicaraguan histories confirm the argument that the Cold War squeezed out much of the space that popular groups had carved out for themselves within mid-twentieth-century populism.[5]

The populist compacts forged by workers, middle-class groups, and the state during the eras of the popular front and the Democratic Spring set up the architecture of reform, nationalism, and social rights. Popular participants made these reforms more real, and they made them deeper, by lobbying the state through mass organizations such as unions, federations, associations, and political parties. Today, political scientists and diplomats speak of the need to create a "civil society" in Latin America to create "deeper," more participatory democracies. The mid-twentieth-century populisms were built on "mass" or "class" groupings instead, but it seems to me that the idea is the same: to get more people to have a stake in the state.

A final reflection relating to Latin America as a whole is that, to better understand state formation and rebellions in the twentieth century, historians must pay more attention to the role of middle sectors such as mid-level management groups in companies and midsize farmers in the countryside. Such sectors include citizens with a broad range of educational and

economic positions in society, and this gives them equally broad potential
for participation in the dependent economic states in which they live. We
have seen that the colonos were able to depict themselves as the small, help-
less farmers of the nation at one moment, the wronged educated middle
class at another, and the powerbrokers between capital and labor in a third.
In this vein, I must second Juan Martínez-Alier against other historians:
Cuba was not merely a society divided between dependent U.S. puppets
and dispossessed impoverished masses.[6] It had a well-organized and demanding nationalist middle-class group—the colonos. What needs further
research is the relationship between Cuba's colonos and its industrialists
and professionals. One thing is certain: Ruiz, who was wrong about the level
of working-class participation in the 1959 Revolution itself, was also wrong
about Cuba's middle class when he wrote, "The nebulous stratum between
the upper and the lower echelons of Cuban society was made up not of
one but of several sectors, none of which, either separately or as a whole,
had a consciousness of class."[7]

My goal in writing this book has been to tell the story of Cuban history
in a way that newcomers to the field can grasp. The way that I organized a
vast array of historical "facts" and debates was to argue that Cuba moved
through three broad systems of rule from the 1760s to the 1960s: the colonial
compact, the patrons' compact, and the populist compact. I would hate for
anyone closing this book to leave with the impression that history is "neat,"
though. Nothing and nobody ever fit perfectly within any model, and the
compacts that I present throughout this book are meant to be understood
as always shifting and never all-encompassing systems of rule. In fact, what
seems to have killed the compacts on all three occasions was lack of fulfillment combined with mass-mobilization by the groups who were squeezed
out of the compact. I invite everyone to delve deeper into Cuban history,
because through it we can learn a lot about popular participation and the
many forms of "democracy" that it can forge.

In 2002 the Cuban government finally ended more than two hundred
years of dependence on sugar. Supply had been surpassing demand on the
world market quite consistently for decades, and substitutes like aspar-
tame were drawing greater numbers of consumers and contributing to the
downward spiral in sugar prices. The Soviet Union had prolonged Cuba's re-
liance on sugar from the 1960s to the 1980s by guaranteeing oil in exchange
for sugar, but after the fall of the Berlin Wall in 1989, the Cuban govern-

ment turned toward tourism as the primary engine of the island's economy. The Sugar Ministry closed about half of its sugarmills and has continued to phase out production in many more since then.

Tuinucú, now called Melanio Hernández, forges on because of its rum distillery. (The government's strategy includes diversifying away from sugar but also building on sugar byproducts such as rum and paper.) Chaparra, now Jesús Menéndez, ground its last harvest just before my most recent visit in 2005. David González, a journalist with the *New York Times*, captured the ambiance at the closing mills perfectly in an article he wrote in 2002:

> Noel Ibáñez, a lanky man with stubbly gray bristles, insisted that even at 58 he was not worried. . . . "The important thing to know is why we have to do this. . . . I am not without hope. I have the guarantee of working or studying. I have the right not to be unemployed. In other parts of the world, that does not happen." [After gazing at the] gigantic mill with its arched windows, broken panes and faded revolutionary slogans . . . he allowed himself a moment of nostalgia. "The smell of molasses is what I'll miss," he said. "Remember, we are talking about something historic in our country."[8]

The communities that planted cane and made it into sugar, some of them hundreds of years old, have adapted (and contributed to) other transitions—from colonial rule to the patrons' compact, from patronage to populism, dictatorship, revolution, and socialism. The thousands of people who depended on these agro-industrial complexes for so many years now face the difficult challenge of learning new skills or growing new crops. They will adapt, but they should be allowed a moment of nostalgia to remember the sounds, smells, and life surrounding the mills and the cane fields before their communities pass into pages of history books.

Selections from the 1946 Chaparra and
Delicias Collective Contract

Between: The Union of Workers and Employees of the Chaparra and Delicias Sugar-mills and their Colonias, including Office, Retail Stores, Bakery and Railroad Branches, represented by Mr. José Jomarrón Velazquez, Secretary General, Luis Merconchini Gonzalez, Official Delegate, and Carlos Cué Lopez, Secretary of Finances, hereafter referred to as "the Union."

And: The Cuban American Sugar Mills Company, proprietor and operator of the Chaparra and Delicias Sugarmills, located in the Municipality of Puerto Padre, Province of Oriente, with offices at Chaparra, represented by Mr. Ralph B. Wood, General Administrator of these sugarmills, hereafter referred to as "the Company."

They have agreed to the following Collective Contract, formed according to Decree-Law Number 446 of 1934, and Decree Number 798 of 1938:

ARTICLE I

A The stipulations of this contract will apply to the work done in all of the Union sections and branches at Chaparra and Delicias.

B The Company will be represented by the respective heads, foremen, or overseers of each section or department.

C The Union will identify the delegates of each section or department that this contract covers for the General Administrator of Chaparra and Delicias.

D The Union delegates should inform the General Administrator of any infraction against this collective contract committed in the workplace at the end of the workday; this does not exempt delegates from fulfilling their own work obligations efficiently.

E If the delegate within the section or department is unable to resolve a claim, it should be brought to the attention of the Union Executive members, who will try to resolve the matter with the General Administrator.

F Both parties express their firm determination to maintain cordial relations between the legal representatives of the respective organizations.

ARTICLE II The recognition of the Union makes implicit the recognition of representatives of this organization in all work places.

A The Company will continue to maintain the Delicias and Chaparra Union headquarters in the premises that they [currently] occupy, providing water, electricity, telephone and ice free of charge, as is now the case.

B The Company agrees to grant a plot of land beside the highway to the Union for a new building to be used for social occasions.

C The company will only deduct fees from workers' wages that the Laws authorize; any other advances or deductions must be agreed upon directly by individual workers or employees and the Company, and must be authorized directly by the workers or employees with their signature.

ARTICLE III The Company will continue to charge Chaparra and Delicias workers, their parents, their children, and their cohabitants 60 percent less for Chaparra Railroad Company tickets. The company will also continue to give 6 pesos per month to each one of the union sections covered by this contract for use on the public railroad. . . .

ARTICLE IV The Company will offer jobs to all of the workers and employees who were working during the 1944–45 harvest for the 1946 harvest.

ARTICLE V The Company will make a promotion list for all positions in each department or section for the harvest period, as follows:

A The promotions within each department or section will be decided as per workers' capacity, efficiency and seniority, according to the job ladder. If the Company or the Union is concerned that the worker entitled to promotion does not possess the capacity and efficiency required for the new position, the worker will do a test before a Commission that includes the head of the department or section that he belongs to, a worker from the Chaparra or Delicias sugarmill (of the same job category or of a higher category) designated freely by the Union, and the General Administrator of the sugarmill.

B The Company must notify the Union, at least twenty-four hours in advance, if it intends to call someone to work, according to the job ladder derived from payroll lists. The Union will confirm if the worker in question is next on the job ladder, and, if not, the Company must make pertinent adjustments to call the right person. Seniority will be determined within each section within each department, as long as the rights of workers are not affected. The personnel called "laborers (*peones*)" remain outside of the section job ladders; these workers should be placed on a separate job ladder in the department in which they work, taking note of their efficiency and seniority within this department. Each harvest year worked will be calculated as one year of seniority. In exceptional cases, where there is a high demand for work or service in another section or department, personnel can be moved from one section or department to another; once the demand returns to normal, the personnel will return to their original positions. New personnel may be hired, as long as they possess the requisite capacity and efficiency to fulfill their work duties.

C Missing work, in any department, for a full year will annul seniority rights (if the worker is to blame for the absence). If the worker returns, seniority rights will start from zero, beginning with the year of his return. Workers can request permission to miss work for one year from the Administration and the Union; the latter two will agree upon how to proceed with each case separately, and will communicate their decision to the worker.

D As is custom, the Company will prepare the list of personnel whom it will need for the dead time and will send it to the Union twenty-four hours in advance as well as posting it in a public place.

E No workers or employees can carry out jobs that they do not customarily do. All workers or employees who are asked to do jobs of higher caliber will gain the pay or wage that corresponds to this position.

ARTICLE VI Workers and employees who are away from their usual place of employment at breakfast or lunch time, on Company orders, are entitled to $0.80 for lunch and $0.25 for breakfast. Office employees will continue to receive the food stipends currently established.

A The Company will continue to provide waterproof shelters to those who have them at the moment, and it will also provide additional shelters for the auxiliary workers and workers at Vázquez. . . . The workers are responsible for taking care of these shelters.

ARTICLE VII   Apprenticeships will adjust to effective legislation, and the Company will place the requisite apprentices in each department.

ARTICLE VIII   The work day will be regulated according to the effective legislation.

A   Shifts will continue in the same form in both sugarmills.

ARTICLE IX   All time worked in excess of the legal eight-hour day will be considered overtime and will be remunerated at 1.5 times the regular pay. If a worker has completed his eight-hour shift, and is called back for extra work, he is guaranteed a half days' pay at 1.5 times his salary, even if he works less than four hours, and a full days' pay at 1.5 times his salary if he works any more than four hours (even if it is less than eight hours).

A   If personnel from the sugarmill workshop departments must travel outside the mills to fulfill their jobs, the hours of travel from the moment at which they leave until the moment of return will count towards their eight-hour shift.
B   During the harvest period, all of the workshop personnel must work on Sundays; they will be paid for eight hours of work but will only work six hours and twenty minutes.
C   Overtime pay will be added to the weekly paycheck the same week that the hours are worked.

ARTICLE X   The Company will give workers vacation pay as per the terms and conditions established in Article 67 of the Constitution of the Republic of Cuba and in accordance with the effective Decrees, Regulations, and other legal dispositions on the matter.

A   Occasional workers will receive vacation pay two times a year; one, at the end of the harvest period, and the other on December 22.

ARTICLE XI   No worker or employee can work more than eight hours per day when unemployed people are available to do the work. . . .

A   A worker or employee must be paid (and allocated seniority rights) for any period in which he is inactive for causes other than his own will.

ARTICLE XII   Each worker will be allocated twenty minutes for eating during his shift, and these breaks will be staggered so as to ensure that the work of the sugarmills is not interrupted in any way.

ARTICLE XIII   Wages will be paid in legal currency with only the deductions authorized or specifically ordered by government legislation. Worker and employee pay stubs will reflect the reasons for each deduction. The Company will continue to make the same deductions that are currently in place.

A   The Company will pay the wages established by the Constitution, and as per that same Constitution, day laborers must be paid on a weekly basis, with only the deductions authorized by the Law.

ARTICLE XIV   Deductions for medical and hospital benefits will be according to the following scale:

Weekly pay up to $18.75: 1.20 percent
Weekly pay up to $75.00: 1.80 percent
Monthly pay up to $75.00: 1.20 percent
Monthly pay over $75.00: 1.80 percent
Maximum: $2.70

A   The Company will provide an identification card to each worker entitled to these benefits that also lists his family members who have a right to these services (see Article XXVI.)

ARTICLE XV   No worker can be dismissed without justified cause, as per the government legislation in place. . . .

. . .

B   The Company will facilitate lands to the workers of both sugarmills as is established in Article 47 of the 1937 Sugar Coordination Law, and will maintain those already so allocated, facilitating the requisite oxen and farming equipment; the workers are obliged to take care of these in due form and to give them back upon finishing the harvest.
C   Salaries and wages will be paid in accordance to the Law of Sugar Coordination, Agreement 50 of the National Commission on Minimum Wages, and other obligatory legal dispositions.

ARTICLE XVI   The laborers (*peones*) of each department will only be responsible for cleaning the area where they work.

A   When the Company summons a worker, he will be paid for at least one half-shift or for a full-shift, according to the schedule.
B   Occasional and substitute employees and workers will be considered first for new permanent positions during the harvest period or the dead time, according to their seniority.

ARTICLE XVII The Company will maintain the houses and laborers' quarters in which the workers and employees protected by this contract live; beginning repairs street by street according to the most pressing needs, and it will not grant houses to any private individuals while there are workers and employees lacking them.

A The Company will fulfill the currently vigilant legal requirements on *higienización* (urbanization and sanitation).

ARTICLE XVIII The Company will maintain free housing, water, and electricity for the workers who currently enjoy these benefits; in the future, the Company will cover the expenses for houses that become vacant according to the working applicant's situation. The Company also agrees to provide 20 kilowatts of free electricity per month for domestic use to all workers, whether they live in the free housing provided by the Company on its premises, in their own houses, or in houses rented within the radius of the central Delicias and Chaparra sugarmills and Puerto Padre, as long as they are within the company's distribution network. If consumption exceeds 20 kilowatts, the worker must pay for it.

A If possible, the Company will extend the distribution network to the houses located in "La Loma," the neighborhood adjacent to Chaparra, and to "La Represa,"
adjacent to Delicias.
B If possible, the Company will extend electricity service to those workers covered
by first paragraph of this article who currently lack such service.

ARTICLE XIX The Company will pay seasonal monthly employees who work in the industrial branches of either sugarmill during the harvest an extra fortnight of pay on completion of the harvest, whatever day of month it is, as long as they are still working when the milling concludes.

A Workers and employees will be paid harvest-time wages and salaries for work that
they begin up to fifteen days before the beginning of the harvest through to fifteen
days after the completion of the harvest, as long as they are doing the same work
that they usually do during the harvest; in any case, these wages and salaries cor-
respond to the work that they are actually doing.

ARTICLE XX No worker or employee can do tasks other than those specifically listed for that position in the job description that the Company must give to each worker at the beginning of every work period. The worker cannot be given a position and then asked to fulfill tasks that are in fact from a superior job category.

ARTICLE XXI   When a worker has suffered a small accident that does not impede him from fulfilling his usual tasks, he is nevertheless entitled to one day's pay and free transportation to go to Court.

ARTICLE XXII   The Company will maintain the car that currently provides transportation services between San Manuel and Delicias. During the dead time, if at least eight workers who reside in Vazquez need to get to Delicias for work, this car will transport them to and from Vazquez.

A   The Administration will study the possibility of changing the present itinerary of the cane trains that pass through San Manuel with the goal of solving the transportation problem for workers who live there.
B   If a worker is not notified twenty-four hours in advance that he is not required, and he arrives at the workplace, he has the right to a half-day's pay. Field workers (*los trabajadores de la zafra*) are excluded from this benefit, since they do not work in shifts.

ARTICLE XXIII   The Company and the Union agree to fulfill all of the dispositions related to work, hygiene, and social needs.

A   The company will introduce adequate sanitary services within both of the sugarmills and in their workers' quarters.

ARTICLE XXIV   The members of the Union, Union delegates, and the heads and overseers of the Company and its administrators hereby pledge to maintain mutual respect.

ARTICLE XXV   The workers who occupy the positions of General Secretary, Organization Secretary, Correspondence Secretary, Treasurer, Official Delegate, Propaganda Secretary, and Culture Secretary of the Union have the right to one leave without pay per work period, be it during the harvest, dead time, or repair time, in order to fulfill their union duties, contingent on previous request in writing to the General Administrator and provided that their leave never surpasses a five-month period.

A   It is agreed that these leaves of absences will be terminated immediately upon the worker's or employee's return to the work.

ARTICLE XXVI   The company will provide hospital and medical services to the workers and employees protected by this contract, as well as to their parents, mothers, children and partners, and younger siblings who are the worker's or employee's dependents. It will also maintain the system of house calls during the day as well as at night.

A   When a nocturnal emergency forces the doctor to use one of the sugarmills' vehicles to attend to the patient, the company will cover the costs associated with this travel.

B   The company guarantees that ambulance services will be provided effectively, and is responsible for this service.

C   Workers and employees are entitled to free medical tests if requested by a doctor and to 50 percent of X-ray expenses, as are their parents and mothers, children and partners, and younger siblings who live with them.

D   The company will study the possibility of re-opening the room in the Chaparra Hospital to serve workers' and employees' sisters and wives.

E   The Company will continue to cover the costs of burial for all workers who pass away within the mill towns of these sugarmills, whether or not they were previously hospitalized, providing a simple wood coffin, painted black, and a hearse, if the family of the deceased worker does not have the means to cover the expenses themselves. . . .

ARTICLE LIV   Both parties agree to register this collective contract in the Registry of Pacts and Agreements at the Ministry of Labor, according to Decree 446 of 1934 and Decree Law 798 of 1938.

ARTICLE LV   The present collective contract will be vigilant until the 30 September 1947.

Havana, March 21, 1946
The Cuban American Sugar Mills Company; Signed, Ralph B. Wood; Dr. Ernesto Freyre; [two illegible signatures].
The Union of Workers and Employees of the Chaparra and Delicias Sugar Mills and Their Colonias; Signed, José Jomarrón Velazquez; Luis Merconchini Gonzalez; Carlos Cué Lopez; Roberto Vilar; Dr. José E. Ramos.

Notes

PREFACE AND ACKNOWLEDGMENTS

1 "Sugarmill" is written as a single word throughout this book, following the translation of *ingenio* in Moreno Fraginals's foundational study titled *The Sugarmill*.
2 Zanetti, "Historia y azúcar," 17.
3 I capitalize "East," "West," and "Center" when referring to regions of Cuba.

INTRODUCTION

1 Cristóbal Díaz Ayala, "Caña Quemá" (*quema* is slang for *quemada*, or burned), on Duo Los Compadres (Lorenzo Hierrezuelo and Francisco Repilado), *Cantando en el Llano*, Tumbao Cuban Classics, TCD-061.
2 The term *colono* means "farmer" in Brazilian historiography, as well, but for most other Latin American nations, such as Argentina, it is more closely linked to "immigrant settler." It will be used interchangeably with "cane farmer" in this study. A small body of work touches on Cuban colonos in the nineteenth century, including González Sánchez, "Del esclavo al colono"; Iglesias García, *Del ingenio al central*; and Scott, *Slave Emancipation in Cuba*, and *Degrees of Freedom*. On the twentieth century, see Zanetti, "El colonato azucarero cubano en 1959," as well as selected references in Martínez-Alier and Martínez-Alier, *Cuba*; Guerra y Sánchez, *Sugar and Society in the Caribbean*; Dye, *Cuban Sugar in the Age of Mass Production*; Pollitt, "The Cuban Sugar Economy and the Great Depression"; Ayala, *American Sugar Kingdom*; and McAvoy, *Sugar Baron*.

3 A Galician farmer who first came to Cuba to fight in the war of 1895–98, Castro managed to purchase 800 hectares of land and lease an additional 10,000 hectares. He grew cane and ran a store and workshop himself and leased out much of the land to other cane farmers (called "*subcolonos*"). Castro, *Fidel*, 34–36.

4 The change in policy is mentioned in Secret Police Agent Francisco Micó Urrutia's "Informe" about cane burning at Chaparra and Delicias, forwarded by Rafael Balart Perera, chief of the Secret Police, Santiago, to the governor of Santiago, 22 March 1936, Santiago, Gobierno Provincial (STGO, GP), legajo 312, expediente 16 (hereafter "leg." is used for *legajo* ("bundle"), and "exp." for *expediente* ("file").

5 Letter, 23 January 1928, Braga Brothers Collection (hereafter BBC), Record Group (RG) 2, series 10, Tuinucú: Doty, Oliver K., Letters File. Much of the correspondence in the Braga Brothers Collection is in Spanish. Unless otherwise noted, all translations are my own.

6 Men owned most cane farms, but there were a few cases of women purchasing or inheriting cane farms as daughters or widows.

7 Braga, "A Bundle of Relations," 47.

8 Guillermoprieto, *Dancing with Cuba*, 88.

9 Captain J. A. Ryan, Santa Clara, to Chief of Staff, Havana, 28 December 1906, National Archives of the United States, Record Group 395 (hereafter USNA, RG 395), Division of the Army of Cuban Pacification, entries 1007–8, item 40, file 44, 3–4. Most worker testimonials describe field labor as something that was done "from dusk 'til dawn." An earlier source suggests that cane cutters worked from 4 A.M. to 11 A.M., took a one-hour break, and then resumed cutting and hauling until 6 P.M. Enrique Cresi in *El Productor* (Havana), 24 January 1890, cited in Cabrera, "Enrique Cresi," 131–32.

10 Aisnara Perera, e-mail to the author, 6 April 2006.

11 Many expert cane-cutter families moved to the city for better education and jobs, so urban volunteers had to be recruited, and they had a hard time mastering leaf removal. The negative economic and environmental impact outweighed its advantage. Burned shoots grew again but did not last as long, and far more weeds grew on burned fields than on those that were harvested "green," making the harvesting more expensive. Oscar Zanetti, e-mail to the author, 8 April 2006.

12 See Okihiro, *Cane Fires*; Richardson, *Igniting the Caribbean's Past*.

13 Thompson, *The Making of the English Working Class*, 10.

14 The first Industrial Revolution (related to the mechanization of the textile industry, the advent of metal machine tools, and expanded trade via canals and roads) transitioned into its second phase around 1850, with the arrival of steam-powered ships and railways. See Hobsbawm, *The Age of Revolution*; Wells, "Did 1898 Mark a Fundamental Transformation for the Cuban Sugar Industry?"

15 For more on elite mentalities, see Bradford Burns, *The Poverty of Progress*.

16 For more on social compacts, see Arrom and Ortoll, *Riots in the Cities*, 5; Milton, *The Many Meanings of Poverty*.

17 The post-1959 socialist compact that ended the populist period is, as yet, too recent to analyze.

18 John Lynch uses the term "primitive caudillos" for the leaders who achieved Spanish American independence in the early 1820s and battled for the presidency thereafter. For much of South America and Mexico, *caudillismo* declined with the rise of liberal dictatorships that used armies, railroads, and taxes to consolidate national power from the 1850s onward. Lynch, *Caudillos in Spanish America*, passim. Mexico seems to have witnessed a rebirth of caudillismo during and after the 1910 Revolution, when national power broke down, and Cuba experienced caudillo rule shortly after gaining independence, from roughly 1906 through 1921. U.S. powerholders imposed the civilian leader Tomás Estrada Palma from 1902 to 1906, but from 1906 onward, liberals and conservatives maintained small groups of armed followers in the countryside that they used to claim power in Havana.

19 I use the term "capitalist welfare" to indicate capitalists' or corporations' support for social welfare to avoid conflation with the current U.S. usage of "corporate welfare" to describe government subsidies for corporations.

20 Kazin, *The Populist Persuasion*, introduction.

21 This interpretation reigned until the early 1970s. See, e.g., Di Tella, "Populism and Reform in Latin America," in a book whose title tells it all—*Obstacles to Change in Latin America*; Germani, "El rol de los obreros y de los migrantes internos en los orígenes del peronismo," 435–88. The negative portrayal of populist leaders is enjoying a resurgence in Latin American media coverage of early-twenty-first-century leaders like Hugo Chavez in Venezuela, Evo Morales in Bolivia, and Manuel López Obrador in Mexico. On contemporary Latin American populism, see also de la Torre, *Populist Seduction in Latin America*; Laclau, *On Populist Reason*.

22 The literature on populism in Latin America is voluminous. Some of the most innovative studies include Brennan, *Peronism and Argentina*; Conniff, *Latin American Populism in Comparative Perspective*; French, *The Brazilian Workers' ABC*; Gould, *To Lead as Equals*; James, *Resistance and Integration*; Knight, "Populism and Neo-populism in Latin America, especially Mexico"; Turits, *Foundations of Despotism*. Bethell and Roxborough, *Latin America between the Second World War and the Cold War*; Adelman, "Andean Impasses"; and Grandin, *The Last Colonial Massacre*, also underscore the positive aspects of mid-twentieth-century populist rule.

23 Grandin, *The Last Colonial Massacre*, 4.

24 This interpretation is put forth most clearly in Ruiz, *Cuba*. Although the source is dated (it was published in 1968), it remains a staple that Cubanists and Latin Americanists frequently cite. Robin Blackburn put forth in "Prologue to the Cuban Revolution," 52–91, the argument that Cuba lacked a nationalist middle class in 1963, and it was taken up by a number of other writers, including Hugh Thomas in his encyclopedic *Cuba, the Pursuit of Freedom* and *The Cuban Revolution*.

25 García-Pérez's *Insurrection and Revolution* includes oral interviews, newspaper articles, and legal documents from the province of Matanzas that suggest that

workers became at least as important as—if not more important than—students and members of the middle classes to the triumph of the Cuban Revolution when it shifted to its insurrectionary phase from 1956 to 1959. In a larger sense, Cuba fits the argument Charles Bergquist made based on his research in Chile, Argentina, Venezuela, and Colombia. He wrote, "workers, especially those engaged in production for export, have played a determining role in the modern history of Latin American societies. Their struggle for material well-being and control over their own lives has fundamentally altered the direction of national political evolution and the pattern of economic development in the countries of the region." *Labor in Latin America*, vii.

26 See Martínez-Alier, "The Peasantry and the Cuban Revolution from the Spring of 1959 to the End of 1960," chap. 5 of *Haciendas, Plantations and Collective Farms*.

ONE The Colonial Compact

1 Pérez, *Cuba*, 103. This migration continued in the 1860s, after the Dominican Republic won its independence. Between 1868 and 1894, more than four hundred thousand civilians emigrated to Cuba from Spain, and more than two hundred thousand soldiers were stationed there. Most settled in the West, where earlier waves of Spaniards had settled. Tone, *War and Genocide in Cuba*, 93.

2 Brazil was also very slow to end slavery. The Brazilian monarchy emancipated slaves only two years after Cuba, in 1888.

3 They are therefore discussed at greater length in chaps. 5–7.

4 Carl Ortwin Sauer argues that by overworking Indians in tasks other than food production and barring them from fishing in boats out of fear that they might run away, the Spanish literally starved the Indian population. Sauer, *The Early Spanish Main*. Alfred Crosby emphasizes other important biological and ecological factors in *The Columbian Exchange*.

5 Rodríguez García and Morales Fuentes, "Apuntes para la historia del antiguo central Tuinucú hasta 1959," 10.

6 McNeill, *Atlantic Empires of France and Spain*, cites evidence to support the estimate of four thousand slaves, in contrast to the more commonly cited estimate of ten thousand slaves that likely originated in a misreading of 1,700 as 10,700 at the Archivo General de las Indias. The source in question is Francisco López de Gmarra a Arriaga, 27 April 1763, SD 2210, cited ibid., 167. Many slaves were bought unofficially, but not likely as many as eight thousand. This first section of chapter 1 draws on Knight, *Slave Society in Cuba during the Nineteenth Century*, chap. 1.

7 Zanetti and García, *Sugar and Railroads*, 1.

8 Moreno Fraginals, *El ingenio*, 2:96.

9 Knight, *Slave Society in Cuba during the Nineteenth Century*, 17. For more on the environmental impact of sugar, including the destruction of Cuban forests, see Funes Monzote, *From Rainforest to Cane Field in Cuba*, passim.

10 For a concise discussion of sugar and its pairing with slavery, see Mintz, *Sweetness and Power*; Curtin, *The Rise and Fall of the Plantation Complex*.

11 Scott, *Slave Emancipation in Cuba*, 24–25.

12 Zanetti and García, *Sugar and Railroads*, 7. Cuban sugar's percentage of the world market increased from 13.64 in 1820 to a high of 31.15 in 1855. See Moreno Fraginals, *El ingenio*, 3:35–36.

13 Corvea Alvarez, *Los ingenios de la villa de Sancti Spiritus*, 10.

14 The colonies included Brazil, Barbados, Jamaica, and Saint-Domingue (Haiti). Haiti was abandoned because of the revolution, not soil exhaustion. Planters did not necessarily move from one colony to the next; many remained in Brazil and on the British sugar isles. It was merely that the new colony became the new top world producer because virgin lands were more productive and therefore more profitable.

15 Barrera Figueroa, *Estudios de Historia Espirituana*, 101.

16 Corvea Alvarez, *Los ingenios de la villa de Sancti Spiritus*, 22.

17 From Trinidad's *Registro de la Propiedad*, cited in National Archives of Cuba, Fondo 154. Valle-Iznaga (hereafter ANC, Valle-Iznaga), 2/22, T. VI-A.

18 Schwartz, *Lawless Liberators*, 29–30; Pérez, *Cuba*, 85; Klein, *The Atlantic Slave Trade*, 211.

19 For details, see Scott, *Slave Emancipation in Cuba*; Knight, *Slave Society in Cuba during the Nineteenth Century*; and Paquette, *Sugar Is Made with Blood*.

20 Historians have debated whether the "conspiracy" was real or a figment of Spaniards' imagination to justify the repression of mulattos. For a thorough investigation of the revolt, see Paquette, *Sugar Is Made with Blood*. See also Childs, *The 1812 Aponte Rebellion in Cuba and the Struggle against Atlantic Slavery*.

21 There is great debate among historians regarding how much outside events influenced slaves. The two extremes are best exemplified by Genovese, *From Rebellion to Revolution*, on the outside-influence factor, and Craton, *Testing the Chains*, on autonomous organization. Viotti da Costa, *Crowns of Glory, Tears of Blood*, offers a nuanced and convincing combination of the two factors. For details on the abolition of slavery in Haiti, see Fick, *The Making of Haiti*. For details on the rest of Spanish America, see Reid Andrews, *Afro-Latin America*.

22 Slaves from the same "Zaza" plantation would later join the war of independence in 1869. Barrera Figueroa, *Sancti Spíritus*, 65–68.

23 Corvea Alvarez, *Los ingenios de la villa de Sancti Spiritus*, 24.

24 Fick, *The Making of Haiti*, passim.

25 Corvea Alvarez, *Los ingenios de la villa de Sancti Spiritus*, 24.

26 Jorge Ibarra cites a *Harper's Magazine* article from March 1865 commenting on the harsh regime in Cuba. "In Alabama, slaves are treated like gentlemen compared to the treatment they get here." Ibarra Cuesta, *Ideología mambisa*, 31.

27 It is not specified whether the "blacks" were slaves or wage laborers. Sancti Spiritus Property Registry, cited in Rodríguez García and Morales Fuentes, "Apuntes para la historia del antiguo central Tuinucú hasta 1959," 23.

28 Barrera Figueroa, *Sancti Spíritus*, 75.

29 Pérez de la Riva, *El barracón y otros ensayos*, 471, cited in Scott, *Slave Emancipation in Cuba*, 29.

30 Barrera Figueroa, *Sancti Spíritus*, 74; Scott, *Slave Emancipation in Cuba*, 29–30.

31 Scott, *Slave Emancipation in Cuba*, 110.

32 Ibarra Cuesta, *Ideología mambisa*, 17.

33 Scott, *Slave Emancipation in Cuba*, 110.

34 Ibid., 39.

35 Knight, *Slave Society in Cuba during the Nineteenth Century*, 57. This was not Spain's only reaction to the U.S. Civil War. In December 1866 Cuba's captain-general cautioned local officials to be wary of how the abolition of slavery in the neighboring republic would affect "the links of obedience and respect which the colored race should entertain for the white and on which the tranquility of this territory largely depends." The same communication instructed these officials to "fulfill . . . without excuse nor pretext of any kind . . . whichever regulations have been passed regarding the respect and obedience the colored race owes the white." An exceptional study on race, class, and gender in nineteenth-century Cuba by the historian Veronica Martínez-Alier (now Stolcke) documents how this segregationist message was followed to the letter: Not a single license for an interracial marriage was granted for the next ten years. Eleven years before the captain-general's order, the civil governor of Oriente had explicitly stated the racist logic: "By authorizing marriages between one and the other [race] the links of subordination of the colored people to the white will tend to be subverted and weakened. . . . The day would come when those encouraged by the example of unequal marriages which favor them will aspire impetuously to achieve a rank which society denies them and as a consequence public order would be upset; it is therefore the Government's duty to prevent such a situation at all cost." Martínez-Alier, *Marriage, Class and Color in Nineteenth-Century Cuba*, 31–32, 46.

36 Benedict Anderson describes the processes of national identity formation in South East Asia and elsewhere in *Imagined Communities*.

37 Political mobilization took place during conspiracies such as the 1844 Escalera rebellion, but the mobilization was covert rather than open.

38 de Céspedes, *Escritos*, 1:104–5, as translated in Ferrer, *Insurgent Cuba*, 18–21.

39 Louis Pérez states in *Cuba*, 113–14, that it was 95 percent.

40 Rodríguez García and Morales Fuentes, "Apuntes para la historia del antiguo central Tuinucú hasta 1959," 23.

41 Knight, *Slave Society in Cuba during the Nineteenth Century*, 159.

42 Pérez, *Cuba*, 119–20.

43 The tax ranged from 6 percent to 12 percent. Knight, *Slave Society in Cuba during the Nineteenth Century*, 159.

44 Cepero Bonilla, *Azúcar y abolición*, 182.

45 In 1862, sugar plantations in the East averaged only 53 slaves, while those in the West averaged 143 slaves. The calculations are based on Scott, *Slave Emancipation in Cuba*, 22, table 5.

46 In 1862 sugarmills in the two eastern provinces averaged 5,500 pesos in annual profits per mill versus the other provinces' 17,500 pesos. There were 356 sugarmills in the East and 1,175 in the West. The calculations are based on ibid.

47 Knight, *Slave Society in Cuba during the Nineteenth Century*, 156.

48 A few other pockets in the East shared the profile of that of the majority of the West. Pockets of Pinar del Rio and Santa Clara (particularly the mountainous regions) also looked more like the East than the West. Ferrer, *Insurgent Cuba*, 18–21.

49 Captain General Lersundi, 24 October 1868, in Archivo Histórico Nacional, Sección Ultramar, 4933/1, book 1, doc. 55, as translated in Ferrer, *Insurgent Cuba*, 24.

50 "Ordén del día," Bayamo, 29 October 1868 in de Céspedes, *Escritos*, 1:117, cited in Ferrer, *Insurgent Cuba*, 24.

51 Scott, *Slave Emancipation in Cuba*, 58.

52 The Assembly of Guáimaro had declared all inhabitants of the republic "entirely free" in April 1869, but the Reglamento de Libertos, passed shortly thereafter, required freed slaves (called *libertos*) to work for a nominal wage for their former masters or for new masters dictated by a government office. Scott, *Slave Emancipation in Cuba*, 47. Both Rebecca Scott and Ada Ferrer emphasize the deeply ingrained racial attitudes born of a mature slave society that most insurgent Creole leaders shared toward blacks and mulattos.

53 Cepero Bonilla, *Azúcar y abolición*, 190.

54 Ferrer, *Insurgent Cuba*, chap. 2. Other historians, including Rebecca Scott and Franklin Knight have done similar demographic research to determine the profiles of East versus West.

55 The Spanish left some of these prisoners in Cuba and exiled others to Spain or Africa. Barrera Figueroa, *Sancti Spíritus*, 91.

56 The Sancti Spiritus historians Orlando Barrera Figueroa, Domingo Corvea Alvarez, Judith Rodríguez García, and Madelyn Morales Fuentes all agree on this point. The introduction to *Héroes humildes*, by the insurgent leader Serafín Sánchez of Sancti Spiritus, mentions one battle in which twenty of the eighty soldiers accompanying Sánchez were Chinese. Sánchez, *Héroes humildes*, 15. Sánchez also mentions patriotic tailors, doctors, teachers, foremen, cattle ranchers, and the slaves that they brought with them.

57 The land tax was 3.5 percent. Cepero Bonilla, *Azúcar y abolición*, 182.

58 Tuinucú's weapons included 19 Remington rifles, 9 Lanenier carbines, 2 hunting rifles, and 3,750 rounds of ammunition. 31 March 1874 document from the Sancti Spiritus archives, cited in Corvea Alvarez, *Los ingenios de la villa de Sancti Spiritus*, 26.

59 Máximo Gómez fought with Spanish forces against Haiti in 1861 and continued to serve with Spanish forces against his Dominican countrymen when they

began fighting for independence in 1863. When the Dominican Republic gained independence in 1865, he had to abandon his family's property and emigrate to Cuba. The Spanish army did not reward him for his service and forced him to take early retirement in 1867. Outraged, he joined the Cubans in their war agaist Spain in 1868. Because he knew Spanish tactics and was an excellent commander, the Cubans gave him the rank of colonel and quickly promoted him to general. Tone, *War and Genocide in Cuba*, 61.

Serafín Sánchez was a land surveyor who led many into battle during the 1868, 1879, and 1895 wars for independence. Like Fidel Castro, he was educated by Jesuits and was the son of a large landowner (although his father was a cattle rancher rather than a cane farmer). The Sancti Spiritus Provincial Archive is named after this hero of all three struggles for independence.

60 The report, cited in Corvea Alvarez, *Los ingenios de la villa de Sancti Spiritus*, 28 and note 31, is dated 11 August 1876.

61 Ibid., n. 32. "La Propaganda" Periódico Liberal, 20 November 1881, Sancti Spiritus, in Santiago Serrano R., "La incidencia de un central azucarero en la comunidad 'Tuinucú Ayer y Hoy,' " 9.

62 Barrera Figueroa, *Sancti Spíritus*, 91.

63 Informe del Insurección en Santi Espíritu, June 1870, 5/64, Fernández Duro Collection, Real Academia de la Historia (Madrid) as translated in Schwartz, *Lawless Liberators*, 43.

64 Ferrer cites a revealing poem popular in Camagüey at the time: "The two cocks of the earth / are having an atrocious war / and the one who conquers in war / will be eaten with rice / by the blacks." Ferrer, *Insurgent Cuba*, 48–49.

65 Ibid., 59–60.

66 Cepero Bonilla, *Azúcar y abolición*, 257.

67 Santa Clara is just west of Sancti Spiritus, still within the colonial province of Las Villas.

68 Ferrer, *Insurgent Cuba*, chap. 2; Pérez, *Cuba*, 124.

69 Tone, *War and Genocide in Cuba*, 3; Pérez, *Cuba*, 124. At least one Cuban historian has presented a different case that emphasizes the distance between the reformist leadership and the revolutionaries in the fields. Citing a number of rebel victories in Las Villas and farther east before, during, and after the Martínez Campos columns moved across the island, Jorge Ibarra argues that the rebels could have fought on. He posits that the revolution ended because the rebel government was both unaware of ongoing guerrilla victories and far too eager to accept Spain's offer of reform. Ibarra Cuesta, *Ideología mambisa*.

70 M. Gómez to Manuel Sanguily, 1 October 1877, cited in Ibarra Cuesta, *Ideología mambisa*, 111.

71 Barrera Figueroa, *Sancti Spíritus*, 98–99; Ferrer, *Insurgent Cuba*, 72.

72 Scott, *Slave Emancipation in Cuba*, 116.

73 Ferrer, *Insurgent Cuba*, 73–74; Scott, *Slave Emancipation in Cuba*, 118.

74 Ferrer, *Insurgent Cuba*, chap. 3. Cuban analyses of the event share this same conclusion; see, e.g., Barrera Figueroa, *Sancti Spíritus*; Ibarra Cuesta, *Ideología mambisa*.

75 Moreno Fraginals, *El ingenio*, 3:60.

76 Cuba produced 553,364 tons in 1878 and 775,368 tons in 1879. In 1880 and thereafter, Cuban sugar's percentage of the world market declined, again for reasons that will be discussed later. Moreno Fraginals, *El ingenio*, 3:37; Rodríguez García and Morales Fuentes, "Apuntes para la historia del antiguo central Tuinucú hasta 1959," 25.

77 Whereas sugar had traded at 10–12 Spanish *reales* in 1868, by 1878 the price had fallen to 5–7 *reales*. Rodríguez García and Morales Fuentes, "Apuntes para la historia del antiguo central Tuinucú hasta 1959," 27.

78 Cuban Economic Research Project, *A Study on Cuba*, 95.

79 Scott, *Slave Emancipation in Cuba*, 206. For a detailed analysis of the forming of the trust and the ensuing lobby-group wars over U.S. sugar tariffs, see Ayala, "The Horizontal Consolidation of the U.S. Sugar Refining Industry," and "The Sugar Tariff and Vertical Integration," chaps. 2–3 of *American Sugar Kingdom*.

80 I discuss in chap. 6 how risk and profits shifted between sugarmill and colono according to the different payment systems and changing sugar and labor prices.

81 Iglesias García, *Del ingenio al central*; Scott, *Slave Emancipation in Cuba*, 211.

82 Rebecca Scott drew this conclusion from nineteenth-century census data, and photographs and interviews suggest the same conclusion for the twentieth century. Scott, *Slave Emancipation in Cuba*, 241.

83 Iglesias García, *Del ingenio al central*, 69.

84 For more on whitening policies in Cuba, see Scott, *Slave Emancipation in Cuba*, 213–218. On Latin America, see Reid Andrews, *Afro-Latin America*, chap. 4. For more on nineteenth-century racial theory, see Hannaford, *Race*; Stocking, *Race, Culture, and Evolution*.

85 Over the course of his time in Cuba, Ferrer was a Spanish military officer, a colono, and a grocery-store owner in Sancti Spiritus. Deposition of Ramon Ferrer, Sancti Spiritus, 1 October 1903, 2–3, National Archives of the United States, Record Group 76, Spanish Claims 1901, case no. 240, *Central Tuinucú Sugarcane Manufacturing Company v. United States of America* (hereafter USNA, RG 76, 240), pt. 1, folder 2.

86 Cuban Economic Research Project, *A Study on Cuba*, 92.

87 "There was a dynamic to the process of emancipation," Rebecca Scott explains, "that transcended the will of the individual participants, a dynamic whereby loss of authority led to further loss of authority, *patrocinado* initiatives created their own momentum, the approaching end of the *patronato* [tutelage] made self-purchase cheaper, and the decreasing importance of slavery made government enforcement of *patrocinado* rights less difficult." Scott, *Slave Emancipation in Cuba*, 193. For example, with the help of a small group of abolitionists and free black

supporters, slaves would argue that they were not registered or that they were older than their masters' records said. Both situations entitled them to freedom.

88 Iglesias García, *Del ingenio al central*, 4.

89 Rodríguez García and Morales Fuentes, "Apuntes para la historia del antiguo central Tuinucú hasta 1959," 30–31.

90 The merchant initiating the proceedings was Antonio Iznaga del Valle (from Trinidad). Tuinucú bill of sale (1892), ANC, Valle-Iznaga, 2/22, T. VI-A.

91 Gonzalo Iturrioz, "Sobre el Ingenio Tuinucú," *Diario de Cienfuegos*, 14 January 1886. I thank David Sartorius for pointing this article out to me at the library of the Instituto de Literatura y Lingüística in Havana.

92 "Rionda Exhibit 15: Translation of Certificate Relating to Title and Liens on Tuinucú Estate," from *Registro de la Propiedad*, "Tuinucú" Inscription 14 (October 9, 1888), 17:192, USNA, RG 76, case no. 240, pt. 2, folder 2.

93 Deposition of Manuel Rionda, Washington, D.C., 15 September 1903, 20, in USNA, RG 76, case no. 240, pt. 1, folder 7.

94 His death by drowning is confirmed in the *Registro de la Propiedad* entries, but the details are not recorded. Braga, "A Bundle of Relations," 39.

95 Moreno Fraginals, *El ingenio*, 3:38.

96 Ibid., 76–77. The percentage was 58.47 in 1860.

97 Pérez, *Cuba between Empires*, 32–33.

98 Approximately 47,100 stayed of the 104,600 who had entered between 1891 and 1894. Iglesias García, *Del ingenio al central*, 71.

99 Tone, *War and Genocide in Cuba*, 28.

TWO Revolutionary Destruction

1 Deposition of Máximo Cisneros, Sancti Spiritus, 6 February 1903, 11, USNA, RG 76, case no. 240, pt. 1, folder 2.

2 As James Scott has written, "A revolution is . . . an interregnum. . . . State-centric descriptions of this period typically emphasize its anarchy, chaos, and insecurity[; however,] the term 'local sovereignty' might serve better." James C. Scott, "Foreword," in Joseph and Nugent, eds., *Everyday Forms of State Formation*, ix.

3 I researched the Sancti Spiritus networks by cross-referencing the listings of mayors and governors in Riera Hernández, *Cuba política*, with Cuban and U.S. archival data on local war heroes from 1895 to 1898 and the 1906 Liberal Rebellion, following Orlando García's, Rebecca Scott's, and Michael Zeuske's methodology to trace Liberal Party networks in Cienfuegos, Santa Clara. See, e.g., Zeuske, "Los negros hicimos la independencia," 201–17.

4 Pérez Guzmán et al., *Guerra de Independencia 1895–1898*, 47–60, mentions that even after Weyler was replaced by a more moderate leader who sought again to protect rather than destroy cane and tobacco, Spanish soldiers continued to embrace Weyler's destruction strategy. See the section "Azúcar, tabaco y la guerra bajo el régimen autonómico," 47–60.

5 For more detail, see Schwartz, *Lawless Liberators*, 98–159.

6 Corvea Alvarez, "Sistema defensivo de fortificaciones españolas en la ciudad de Sancti Spíritus," 12.

7 Guerra, *The Myth of José Martí*, 77, mentions forty-nine out of approximately two hundred P R C clubs in 1898, citing Estrade, "Los clubes femeninos en el Partido Revolucionario Cubano," 178–79. See Guerra, *The Myth of José Martí*, chap. 2, for a pathbreaking discussion of women and gender in the 1895 Revolution, as well as for analysis of the divisions between civilian leaders in exile and military leaders in Cuba. Helg, *Our Rightful Share*, and Stoner, *From the House to the Street*, also offer important insights into women and gender in the 1895 Revolution.

8 For details, see Balboa Navarro, *La protesta rural en Cuba*; Schwartz, *Lawless Liberators*. Pérez, *Lords of the Mountain*, analyzes the same topic using newspaper sources and building on Eric Hobsbawm's bandit theory. Rosalie Schwartz and Imilcy Balboa Navarro build original theories based on stronger archival bases, as do Manuel de Paz Sánchez, José Fernández Fernández, and Nelson López Novegil.

9 Schwartz, *Lawless Liberators*, 122.

10 Ibid., 19.

11 de Paz Sánchez et al., *El bandolerismo en Cuba*, 276–77, quotes a 31 December 1890 letter in which the infamous bandit Tuerto Rodríguez asked "don Francisco Rasco" (probably a misreading of the handwritten "don Francisco Rionda") to send money by way of a Tuinucú security guard. Eladio Santiago, a former office employee at Tuinucú, recalls seeing evidence from the accounting department that Tuinucú paid off bandits in the early twentieth century so they would leave the estate alone. Eladio Santiago Serrano, interview by the author, Tuinucú, 1 February 2000.

12 Called the "Directorio Central de las Sociedades de la Raza de Color." de la Fuente, *A Nation for All*, 37; Helg, *Our Rightful Share*, 53–54.

13 Ferrer, *Insurgent Cuba*, 7; Ibarra Cuesta, *Ideología mambisa*, 52. Ada Ferrer's book offers an impressive analysis of how raceless nationalism played out in the three independence wars.

14 Ferrer, *Insurgent Cuba*, 4.

15 Early in the century, mainland Spanish Americans had generated the concept of "Americanos" with much the same goal of fortifying cross-class, cross-racial armies against the Spanish colonial regime. Over the course of the nineteenth century, lighter-skinned elites began to introduce literacy and landholding requirements, chipping away at universal manhood suffrage to monopolize political power. See Chasteen, *Born in Blood and Fire*, for a concise overview of this process. For more on the concept of raceless nationality in nineteenth-century and twentieth-century Cuba, see Bronfman, *Measures of Equality*; de la Fuente, *A Nation for All*; Fernández Robaina, *El negro en Cuba*; Helg, *Our Rightful Share*; Ibarra Cuesta, *Ideología mambisa*; Scott, *Slave Emancipation in Cuba* and *Degrees of Freedom*.

16 Helg, *Our Rightful Share*, 56–57; Schwartz, *Lawless Liberators*, 159.

17 Helg, *Our Rightful Share*, 57.

18 Ibid., 58.

19 Tone, *War and Genocide in Cuba*, 94–95.

20 Evidence regarding the revolutionary forces in Las Villas is in the USNA and BBC sources listed in this chapter, as well as in Helg, *Our Rightful Share*, 58.

21 These caudilloesque forces made the Las Villas Brigade of the Liberation Army extremely top-heavy and difficult to coordinate. Zeuske, "Los negros hicimos la independencia," 201–17.

22 García Galló, *Esbozo biográfico de Jesús Menéndez*, 31–32.

23 Rosalie Schwartz remarks that the brigand auxiliaries "did not lash out against local authorities or landowners. The outposts of the despised civil guard remained intact, and the planted fields remained untouched. . . . The absence of a mass uprising," she argues, "reflected the characteristic self-interest of the *habanero* [resident of Havana]. He assessed the consequences and did not like the odds. Familiarity with the government's harsh policies of retribution weighed heavily in the balance. Reluctant to take risks in the absence of reasonable assurances of success, and with the separatist leadership captured or killed, he waited." Schwartz, *Lawless Liberators*, 232–37.

24 Customs agents tipped off by Spanish informants had repeatedly foiled their earlier attempts to reach the island by confiscating boats and war materiel.

25 Pérez, *Cuba between Empires*, 44–45.

26 Francisco Rionda to Don Francisco Albert y Paula, 10 March 1896, as translated by "A.Y.C." for the Spanish Treaty Claims Commission, Olazar exhibit 1, USNA, RG 76, case no. 240, pt. 1, folder 5.

27 According to the Spanish secret archives consulted by the prosecution. Vol. 8, Spanish Treaty Claims Commission, Brief for the Claimant, "XI. The Military Situation in Sancti Spiritus," 18, USNA, RG 76, case no. 121: *Mapos Estate v. United States*.

28 Deposition of Raimundo Sánchez (Serafín's brother), Sancti Spiritus, 17 September 1903, USNA, RG 76, case no. 121, pt. 2, folder 1; deposition of José Miguel Gómez, Havana, 17 February 1903, USNA, RG 76, case no. 121, pt. 1, folder 3.

29 Deposition of Manuel Rionda, Washington D.C., 15 September 1903, 8, 60–64, USNA, RG 76, case no. 240, part 1, folder 7.

30 Sancti Spiritus, 23 November 1895, cited in Churchill, *Winston S. Churchill*, 9.

31 Captain Eugenio Pérez de Lema, Madrid, Spain, 11 February 1905, 7, USNA, RG 76, case no. 240, pt. 3, folder 3.

32 Manuel Rionda y Polledo, incoming correspondence, 1896–1917, BBC, RG 2, series 1, file: Rionda family.

33 Officer Antonio Chies Gómez, León, Spain, 13 February 1905, 30, USNA, RG 76, case no. 240, pt. 3, folder 3.

34 Pérez, *Cuba between Empires*, 53–56, 119–24.

35 Hidalgo de Paz, *Cuba 1895–1898*, 26–32.

36 José Martí and Máximo Gómez, "Circular: la política de la Guerra," as translated in Pérez, *Cuba between Empires*, 126.

37 They may have worried more about the Cuban sugar industry's recovery after the war than did the Dominican-born Máximo Gómez. Antonio Maceo, Camagüey, to Tomás Estrada Palma, New York, 21 November 1895, in Maceo, *Antonio Maceo*, 131; Tone, *War and Genocide in Cuba*, 60–65.

38 Documents from the Official Archives of the Kingdom of Spain, 30 November 1895, USNA, RG 76, case no. 240, pt. 3, folder 2.

39 Chies Gómez, León, 13 February 1905, 24, USNA, RG 76, case no. 240, pt. 3, folder 3.

40 Pérez de Lema, Madrid, Spain, 11 February 1905, 7, USNA, RG 76, case no. 240, pt. 3, folder 3.

41 Ibid.

42 Deposition of Máximo Cisneros, Sancti Spiritus, 6 February 1903, 8, USNA, RG 76, case no. 240, pt. 1, folder 2.

43 Francisco Rionda to Juan M. Ceballos, BBC, RG 2, series 1, file: Francisco Rionda y Polledo (April–December 1897).

44 Máximo Gómez to Tomás Estrada Palma, July 1897, *Boletín del Archivo Nacional* 30 (January–December, 1931): 71–72, as translated in Pérez, *Cuba between Empires*, 133.

45 Enrique Cresi in *El Productor* (Havana), 24 January 1890, cited in Cabrera, "Enrique Cresi," 131–32.

46 Pérez, *Cuba between Empires*, 136.

47 Headquarters of the Army Liberation, "Proclamation," 4 July 1986, as translated ibid., 136.

48 Ibid., 128.

49 Documents from the Official Archives of the Kingdom of Spain, USNA, RG 76, case no. 240, pt. 3, folder 2.

50 Máximo Gómez, "Circular," 6 November 1895, as translated in Pérez, *Cuba between Empires*, 136.

51 For a good discussion of the same question in Mexico, see Wells and Joseph, *Summer of Discontent, Seasons of Upheaval*.

52 Deposition of Máximo Cisneros, Sancti Spiritus, 6 February 1903, p. 29, USNA, RG 76, case no. 240, pt. 1, folder 2.

53 Ibid., 33.

54 Tone, *War and Genocide in Cuba*, 48.

55 The number of months varied from year to year. Many supplemented their incomes with day labor during the tobacco and coffee harvests.

56 José B. Rionda, Sancti Spiritus, 7 February 1903, p. 25, USNA, RG 76, case no. 240, pt. 1, folder 1.

57 Juan Soria, the overseer on the colonia Esperanza, testified that he and fifty or sixty workers were staying in a large barracks "right in the very center of the work, where the work was being done," when the cane fields nearby were set on fire in

April 1896. Juan Soria, Sancti Spiritus, 2 October 1903, USNA, RG 76, case no. 240, pt. 1, folder 4.

58 "News from Havana," *Willett and Gray Statistical Sugar Trade Journal*, 30 January 1896, 4. At least at one estate, the Los Caños mill in Guantánamo, "virtually all of the estate's workers" went to the insurrection, according to a Spaniard testifying to the Claims Commission. Deposition of Marcos Margadas, 5, USNA, RG 76, 120 (Sheldon), pt. 2, cited in Scott, *Slave Emancipation in Cuba*, 290.

59 "Cuba," *Willett and Gray Statistical Sugar Trade Journal*, 9 January 1896, 3.

60 "News from Havana," *Willett and Gray Statistical Sugar Trade Journal*, 16 January 1896, 3.

61 Cuba produced only 300,000 tons in 1896. Moreno Fraginals, *El ingenio*, 3:39.

62 Deposition of the carpenter Juan Echevarne, who watched the estate during Francisco Rionda's absence between 1896 and 1899. Sancti Spiritus, 6 February 1903, p. 53, USNA, RG 76, case no. 240, pt. 1, folder 1.

63 Pérez, *Cuba between Empires*, 55.

64 Ibid., 54; *Willett and Gray Statistical Sugar Trade Journal*, volumes for January–February 1896.

65 The first decree was passed on 15 February 1896; it was for Sancti Spiritus, Camagüey (Puerto Principe), and Oriente. Pérez, *Cuba between Empires*, 55.

66 Tone, *War and Genocide in Cuba*, 66–67, 93, 197. As mentioned earlier, for more on female revolutionaries, see Guerra, *The Myth of José Martí*, and works by Lynn Stoner cited in the bibliography.

67 For more on re-concentration, see Pérez Guzmán, *Herida Profunda*; Tone, *War and Genocide in Cuba*, 193–224.

68 Ironically, the British would use the same strategy in the Boer War only a few years later, as would the United States in the Philippines (which it occupied in 1898, along with Cuba and Puerto Rico). This may explain why the U.S. Congress officially absolved Weyler in 1902, despite the fact that re-concentration caused a massive public outcry among U.S. citizens—an outcry that the U.S. administration used to justify intervention. Mexico's Federal Army used re-concentration in 1910, and the French established "*agrovilles*" in Indochina in the 1940s (which became U.S. "strategic hamlets" in Vietnam in the 1960s). Tone, *War and Genocide in Cuba*, 222. Fulgencio Batista used re-concentration against revolutionaries in the 1950s, and Fidel Castro used it against counter-revolutionaries in Escambray (Las Villas) in the 1960s. Other twentieth-century cases abound. To mention a final example, the Guatemalan military's "scorched earth" policy uprooted entire indigenous communities using the same logic: Remove the ocean (peasant support) and the fish (guerrillas) will die.

69 "Document No. 4," in Documents from the Official Archives of the Kingdom of Spain, USNA, RG 76, case no. 240, pt. 3, folder 2.

70 The note is extremely subtle in Spanish. "Sirvase acompañar al Portador de esta, pues de su pronta presentación depende el que se eviten graves males de los que traigo a Ud. responsable." Exhibit A, in Francisco Rionda, 26 August 1896, protest

to the State Department, presented to Consular Agent P. D. Buzzi at the United States of America at Tunas de Zaza, USNA, RG 76, case no. 240, pt. 3, folder 3.

71 Deposition of Máximo Cisneros, Sancti Spiritus, 6 February 1903, pp. 29, 42–44, USNA, RG 76, case no. 240, pt. 1, folder 2.

72 Exhibit B, in Francisco Rionda, 26 August 1896, protest to the State Department presented to Consular Agent P. D. Buzzi at the United States of America at Tunas de Zaza, USNA, RG 76, case no. 240, pt. 3, folder 3.

73 Some Spaniards, when asked by the commissioner of Spanish Treaty Claims in 1903, stated that it was the other way around—that is, Francisco asked Pin for protection because he wanted to grind. Chies testified that he had never sent a note, but Buzzi did certify Chies's signature on Exhibit B to be the "true and genuine signature of said officer" in the documentation accompanying Francisco Rionda's protest to the State Department of 26 August 1896 . USNA, RG 76, case no. 240, pt. 3, folder 3.

74 José B. Rionda, Sancti Spiritus, 7 February 1903, p. 10, USNA, RG 76, case no. 240, pt. 1, folder 1.

75 Francisco Rionda, 26 August 1896, protest to the State Department, USNA, RG 76, case no. 240, pt. 3, folder 3.

76 Deposition of Máximo Cisneros, Sancti Spiritus, 6 February 1903, 11, USNA, RG 76, case no. 240, pt. 1, folder 2.

77 José B. Rionda, Sancti Spiritus, 7 February 1903, pp. 13–14, USNA, RG 76, case no. 240, pt. 1, folder 1.

78 Juan Echevarne, Sancti Spiritus, 6 February 1903, pp. 3, 5, 25–28, USNA, RG 76, case no. 240, pt. 1, folder 1.

79 "Brief for the Claimant," pp. 21–24, USNA, RG 76, case no. 240, pt. 1, folder 1.

80 The soldier, Thomas Ashburn, had helped U.S. forces to protect sugar plantations during the Philippine War for Independence, which began shortly after U.S. occupation in 1898. Thomas Ashburn, Cienfuegos, 7 October 1903, question 34, USNA, RG 76, case no. 240, pt. 1, folder 4.

81 Máximo Cisneros, who was a soldier under Ferrer's command during the Ten Years' War, corroborated Ferrer's story. Deposition of Máximo Cisneros, Sancti Spiritus, 6 February 1903, p. 2; deposition of Ramon Ferrer, Sancti Spiritus, 12 February 1903, p. 3, both in USNA, RG 76, case no. 240, pt. 1, folder 2. (There are two depositions from Ferrer—one for the defendant, cited earlier, and this one for the claimant.)

82 Pedro Velazco Jiménez burned the cane as a member of the Honorato Regiment, under orders from José Miguel Gómez. Pedro Velazco Jiménez, Sancti Spiritus, 29 September 1903, p. 7, USNA, RG 76, case no. 240, pt. 1, folder 4.

83 Mapos Sugar Company, case no. 121, in U.S. Department of Justice, *Special Report of William E. Fuller*, 47.

84 José Antonio Jiménez y Cañizares, Sancti Spiritus, 22 September 1903, p. 4, USNA, RG 76, case no. 240, pt. 1, folder 3.

85 Ramon Sobrino, Sancti Spiritus, 25 September 1903, p. 4, USNA, RG 76, case no. 240, pt. 1, folder 3.

86 José B. Rionda, Sancti Spiritus, 7 February 1903, pp. 16–17, USNA, RG 76, case no. 240, pt. 1, folder 1.

87 Braga, "A Bundle of Relations," 47–49.

88 Depositions of Manuel Ferrer, Sancti Spiritus, 11 February 1903, pt. 1, folder 2; Juan Echevarne, Sancti Spiritus, 6 February 1903, pt. 1, folder 1; and Máximo Cisneros, Sancti Spiritus, 6 February 1903, pt. 1, folder 2, all in USNA, RG 76, case no. 240.

89 Ferrer had to travel at night because neither insurgents nor Spanish forces wanted neutral residents to move between countryside and town for fear they might be spies. Depositions of Manuel Ferrer, Sancti Spiritus, 11 February 1903, pt. 1, folder 2.

90 Francisco Rionda, Sancti Spiritus, to Manuel Rionda, New York, 15 February 1987, BBC, RG 2, series 1, file: Rionda y Polledo, Francisco (Pancho), April–December 1897. Note that Francisco's letters are all in Spanish; direct quotations in English are my translations.

91 Francisco Rionda, Matanzas, to Manuel Rionda, New York, 29 March 1898, BBC, RG 2, series 1, file: Rionda y Polledo, Francisco (Pancho), March 18–July 1898.

92 Francisco Rionda, Sancti Spiritus, to Manuel Rionda, New York, 15 February 1987, BBC, RG 2, series 1, file: Rionda y Polledo, Francisco (Pancho), April–December 1897.

93 Letters from Rionda family (Francisco, Isidora, Concha, Elena, Elenita) to Manuel Rionda, BBC, RG 2, series 1.

94 Corvea Alvarez, "Sistema defensivo de fortificaciones españolas en la ciudad de Sancti Spíritus," 17.

95 Tone, *War and Genocide in Cuba*, 215.

96 Francisco Rionda, Matanzas, to Manuel Rionda, New York, 29 March 1898, BBC, RG 2, series 1, file: Rionda y Polledo, Francisco (Pancho), March 18–July 1898.

97 Captain Nicolas Yero, 28 September 1903, Sancti Spiritus, p. 8, USNA, RG 76, case no. 240, pt. 1, folder 3. Yero switched sides near the end of the war, joining the insurgents in 1898.

98 Francisco Rionda, Sancti Spiritus, to Manuel Rionda, New York, 12 March 1897, BBC, RG 2, series 1, file: Rionda y Polledo, Francisco (Pancho), April–December 1897.

99 Manuel Ferrer, Sancti Spiritus, 11 February 1903, pp. 3–7, USNA, RG 76, case no. 240, pt. 1, folder 2.

100 See, e.g., Pérez, *Cuba between Empires*, 141–63.

101 Paquette, *Sugar Is Made with Blood*, 251.

102 Arbelo, *Recuerdos de la última Guerra por la independencia de Cuba*, 56, cited in Helg, *Our Rightful Share*, 59.

103 My thanks to Thomas Klubock for pointing this out to me. Guerra, *The Myth of José Martí*, discusses the vision of female and civilian versus military revolutionar-

ies, as does Stoner in *From the House to the Street* and "Militant Heroines and the Consecration of the Patriarchal State."

104 "To the President of the Republic of the United States of America," enclosure in Fitzhugh Lee to Richard Olney, 24 June 1896, Richard Olney Papers, cited in Pérez, *Cuba between Empires*, 157.

105 The reasons behind U.S. intervention are outlined in chapter 3. For more on the war's contested title change and its historiography, see Pérez, *The War of 1898*.

106 Whereas Havana (10.3 percent) and Matanzas (30.6 percent) together produced 40.9 percent of the total crop in 1902, versus Oriente (16 percent) and Camagüey (2.6 percent), which together produced 18.6 percent, by 1922 the figures were 20.2 percent (7.7 percent, Havana; 12.5 percent, Matanzas) versus 55.9 percent (32.3 percent, Oriente; 23.6 percent, Camagüey). Moreno Fraginals, *El ingenio*, 3:61.

107 That year, Santa Clara produced 20.9 percent, versus Camagüey's 23.6 percent and Oriente's 32.3 percent. Moreno Fraginals, *El ingenio*, 3:61.

108 This argument is put forth convincingly in Scott, " 'The Lower Class of Whites' and 'The Negro Element,' " 179–191, and Zeuske, "Clientelas regionales, alianzas interraciales y poder nacional en torno a la 'guerrita de agosto' 1906," 127–56.

THREE U.S. Power and Cuban Middlemen

1 Garnett to British Legation, Havana, 18 September 1906, Public Records Office, Foreign Office Papers (hereafter PRO, FO), 371/56, doc. 126.

As mentioned in the introduction, the Liberal and Conservative parties in Cuba did not have clear ideological differences, as they did elsewhere in Latin America over the boundaries between church and state, federal versus state power, and so on. They merely represented separate clientele networks with a different leader at the top. In fact, the parties divided, changed names, and re-constituted themselves several times during the first two-thirds of the twentieth century, and leaders and members frequently changed allegiances. For details on early-twentieth-century political parties, see Ibarra Cuesta, *Cuba 1898–1921*; Riera Hernández, *Cuba política*.

2 Van Horne was born in the United States and knighted by Britain for building the Canadian Pacific Railway from the Atlantic to the Pacific coast. The company's authorized capital was $8 million, divided into 160 shares priced at an incredibly high $50,000 each. Zanetti and García, *Sugar and Railroads*, 217.

3 Pérez, *Cuba*, 187.

4 British Legation, Havana, to Sir E. Grey, London, 10 September 1906, PRO, FO, 371/56, doc. 271.

5 W. H. Taft to Helen Taft, 20 September 1906, Taft Papers, cited in Pérez, *Cuba under the Platt Amendment*, 104.

6 Zanetti, "Historia y azúcar," 17. For more on elite mentalities and the embrace of "modernity," see, e.g., Pérez, *On Becoming Cuban*; Bradford Burns, *The Poverty of Progress*; and Meade, *Civilizing Rio*.

7 Miguel de Carrión, "El desenvolvimiento social de Cuba en los últimos veinte años," *Cuba Contemporánea* 9 (September 1921). 19–20, cited in Pérez, *Cuba under the Platt Amendment*, 141.

8 Garnett's letter shows Estrada Palma's reputation for venality. A popular saying demonstrates that the second Cuban president, José Miguel Gómez (1909–12), had a similar reputation: "The shark bathes in it but splashes it around." The third president, Manuel García Menocal (1913–21), surpassed his two predecessors by far, allegedly entering the presidency with one million pesos and leaving it with forty million pesos. López Segrera, "La economía y la política en la república neo-colonial," 153.

9 My understanding of how U.S.-Cuban relations developed from 1898 through 1902 draws most strongly from studies by Jorge Ibarra, Philip Foner, Louis Pérez Jr., Julio Le Riverand, and Michael Zeuske. Le Riverand and other post-1959 Cuban historians tend to emphasize U.S. manipulation; Zeuske and Pérez add more attention to the Cuban actors who participated and engaged with U.S. power.

10 Wartime damage during the first year of the 1895–98 War for Independence slashed total Cuban production by more than 70 percent, the number of tons produced going from 983,265 in 1895 to 286,229 in 1896. In contrast, in 1906, 1912, and 1917, Cuban sugar production actually increased in relation to the previous year's crop. See table 2 on p. 87 above for production details for 1902–19.

11 My argument draws on Aline Helg's insightful *Our Rightful Share*, combining elements of her attention to race and ideology with the more race- and region-based arguments of Scott, "Fault Lines, Color Lines, and Party Lines," 61–106, and Zeuske, "Clientelas regionales, alianzas interraciales y poder nacional en torno a la 'guerrita de agosto' 1906." Much of the primary political data in Zeuske's regional study and my own comes from Ibarra Cuesta, *Cuba 1898–1921*, and Riera Hernández, *Cuba política*. This study follows Zeuske's and Scott's lead, building on the nuanced vision of U.S. hegemony and political power in Cuba as clearly expressed in Pérez, "Dependency," while trying to trace a clearer picture of domestic Cuban state formation through local history found in Cuban provincial sources and U.S. diplomatic records from the occupations of 1898–1902 and 1906–1909.

12 "Doctors" is the term used for the middle-class intellectuals who led revolutionary movements across the Americas. Lester Langley points out that triumphant generals and middle-class intellectuals took power across the American continent in *America in the Age of Revolution*. In *Cuba 1898–1921*, Jorge Ibarra cites the novel *Generales y Doctores* as one of many works of fiction that emphasize the role of war heroes in early-twentieth-century Cuban society and politics.

13 This pattern of intervention is most evident in Panama, Mexico, Haiti, the Dominican Republic, and Nicaragua, but it has been replicated in other parts of the

world, such as the Middle East. Foner, *The Spanish-Cuban-American War and the Birth of American Imperialism*, 2:671–72; Pérez, *Cuba between Empires*, 378. See Grandin, *The Last Colonial Massacre*, for a comparative discussion of U.S. policy during the Cold War era, when Good Neighbor diplomats were replaced by secret Central Intelligence Agency strategists.

14 See LaFeber, *Inevitable Revolutions*; Wood, *The Making of the Good Neighbor Policy*.

15 Haiti symbolized the "worst case scenario" for elites across the Americas during the nineteenth century and twentieth. See Geggus, *The Impact of the Haitian Revolution in the Atlantic World*.

16 As early as 1823 the future U.S. President John Quincy Adams declared: "If an apple severed by the tempest from its native tree cannot choose but fall to the ground, Cuba, forcibly disjoined from its own unnatural connection with Spain, and incapable of self support, can gravitate only toward the North American Union, which by the same law of nature cannot cast her off from its bosom." He offered to purchase Cuba from Spain in 1825, but the Spanish government refused to negotiate. After paying $7 million to Russia for Alaska, the administration of U.S. President James Polk offered $100 million for Cuba in 1847, but the Spanish government declined again (Cuba was one of Spain's first colonies, and it remained strategically and monetarily important). Tone, *War and Genocide in Cuba*, 246. For an excellent discussion of the competing interests within American foreign policy and the myths and realities of intervention, see Ayala, *American Sugar Kingdom*, 23–74; Pérez, *The War of 1898*.

17 The literature on Martí is vast. For an innovative new contribution, see *The Myth of José Martí*, in which Lillian Guerra analyzes the different national aspirations of civilians, military leaders, and imperialists.

18 Louis Pérez makes this argument powerfully in *Cuba between Empires*, as does Michael Zeuske in "1898."

19 Foner, *The Spanish-Cuban-American War and the Birth of American Imperialism*, 2:354.

20 General William Shafter refused to allow García and his troops to enter the city under the pretext that the Cubans might attack Spanish soldiers and property. This came after a series of slights against Cuban forces including the general tendency to assign them to auxiliary duties such as building roads and encampments for American soldiers.

21 Acta Capitular no. 30, 1898, Archivo Histórico Provincial de Sancti Spiritus, Fondo: Ayuntamiento, República Mediatzada, 1899–1958 (hereafter APSS, RM), as cited in Barrera Figueroa, *Estudios de Historia Espirituana*, 138. Máximo Gómez and José Miguel Gómez were very close collaborators, exchanging over one hundred letters between the end of 1897 and 1898. As mentioned earlier, they were not related. José Miguel Gómez took over the leadership of Santa Clara forces after the death of Serafín Sánchez. Zeuske, "Los negros hicimos la independencia," 218.

22 Foner, *The Spanish-Cuban-American War and the Birth of American Imperialism,* 2:400; Pérez, *Cuba between Empires,* 245.

23 Pérez, *Cuba between Empires,* 245–47.

24 This argument is drawn from studies by Michael Zeuske, Louis Pérez Jr., and Lillian Guerra. All three historians offer important insights into the process of Cuban engagement with U.S. imperialism.

25 Foner, *The Spanish-Cuban-American War and the Birth of American Imperialism,* 2:401.

26 Le Riverand, *La República,* 10.

27 Foner, *The Spanish-Cuban-American War and the Birth of American Imperialism,* 2:440.

28 Incidentally, the $3 million "gift" was actually left over from the amount allocated by Congress for the Spanish-American War. Foner, *The Spanish-Cuban-American War and the Birth of American Imperialism,* 2:441.

29 Ibid., 2:443.

30 Of this total, $35 million was a loan from U.S. banks; the rest was from the Cuban Treasury.

31 Martínez Ortiz, *Cuba,* 2:54 and following pages, cited in Zeuske, "Los negros hicimos la independencia," 214; see also Ibarra Cuesta, *Cuba 1898–1921,* 194–95.

32 The agency's name, Guzmán and Company, was designed to attract the caudillos' followers. It suggested more equal power sharing between him and the investors than there actually was. Zeuske, "Los negros hicimos la independencia," 216.

33 *Congressional Record,* vol. 31, 15 April 1898, pt. 4, 3882, as cited in Pérez, *Cuba between Empires,* 186.

34 For a discussion of "idealists" and "imperialists," see Williams, *The Tragedy of American Diplomacy,* 18–90.

35 For example, Wood reversed most of the revolutionary improvements in education that Alexis E. Frye, Brooke's superintendent of schools, had introduced. Frye's commitment to incorporating Cuba's historical experience and the principles of the revolution into a vastly expanded educational system contrasted with Wood's desire to Americanize the Cuban population and promote U.S. annexation. After dismissing Frye, Wood imported U.S. textbooks about George Washington, Thomas Jefferson, and Abraham Lincoln in place of José Martí, Antonio Maceo, and other Cuban martyrs. Le Riverand, *La República;* Portell Vilá, *Nueva historia de la República de Cuba.*

36 "Forty white prostitutes have appeared," the police chief of Sancti Spiritus reported in 1900, as well as "eight of color, and six foreign, all clandestine." The colonial Spanish regime registered prostitutes and had them pay taxes, and U.S. occupying forces maintained the same procedures. This particular request, however, was not for taxes but for the population census of 1900. APSS, RM, leg. 351, exp. 1012.

U.S. agents sought to impose the North American vision of "modern" women's roles. In May 1900 the mayor of Sancti Spiritus received a request that several women be selected for study in a school where they could learn to teach kindergarten and home economics in Havana. The goal of the school was to "popularize and spread domestic science or the teaching of proper administration of the household as broadly as possible across the island." Chapter 5 discusses how Elena Doty introduced the same kind of "training" through her women's club at Tuinucú. APSS, RM, leg. 163, exp. 369. Santos, "The Peaceful Invasion of 1900," mentions many clashes over appropriate gender roles. Americans considered Cuban ideas on protecting a woman's honor rather extreme. For more on U.S. versus Spanish Caribbean ideas on gender, see Pérez, *On Becoming Cuban*; Suarez Findlay, *Imposing Decency*.

37 Barrera Figueroa, *Estudios de Historia Espirituana*, 139. We need to read critically the descriptions of Americans in local histories such as that by Orlando Barrera, written after the 1959 revolution. However, in this case the evidence cited earlier supports Barrera's claim regarding prostitution. The way the occupation is remembered is also important in and of itself. The Afro-Cuban veteran Esteban Montejo remembered a clear case of gender conflict in Cienfuegos in 1899. Some American soldiers said, "Fuky, Fuky, Margarita," to Cuban women, provoking Cuban men to attack the American soldiers in retaliation. Barnet, *Biography of a Runaway Slave*, 197.

38 The myth of racial equality forged during the war nevertheless remained a part of Cuban national discourse. Aline Helg argues that the myth limited Afro-Cuban mobility because when Afro-Cubans organized as a group to claim their rights, as they did in 1912, the state called them "racist" and repressed them. Alejandro de la Fuente agrees with Helg in part, but he emphasizes that electoral politics and the myth of racial democracy provided Afro-Cubans with some avenues for mobility. For excellent discussions of race in later colonial and early republican Cuba, see de la Fuente, *A Nation for All*; Helg, *Our Rightful Share*; Duke, "The Idea of Race"; Ferrer, *Insurgent Cuba*; and Rebecca Scott's work.

39 Mayor García Cañizares, Sancti Spíritus, to General Wilson (military governor of Las Villas Province), 1 September 1899, APSS, RM, leg. 163, exp. 362.

40 He was replaced by a relative nonentity named Tomás Pina. According to Mario Riera Hernández, the Sancti Spíritus native José Miguel Gómez, who was the governor of Las Villas at the time, helped push Cañizares out. Perhaps Cañizares was not a cooperative enough sub-caudillo. Riera Hernández, *Cuba política*, 11.

41 Pérez, *Cuba under the Platt Amendment*, 38.

42 Americans accumulated windfall profits during the French Revolution and Napoleonic Wars (1789–1815) because the United States could sell wartime staples such as wheat and cotton to all of the belligerents, including Britain, France, and Spain. In 1808, Britain and France declared that the United States had to choose a side, which led President Thomas Jefferson to decide that the United States should turn inward, developing its own agriculture and industries. Over the course of the nineteenth century, American industrialists pushed for higher protection through tariffs on imported industrial goods and subsidies

for domestic industries, and American agriculturalists demanded the opposite: lower tariffs to encourage agricultural export profits and lower-priced imported goods for the domestic market. Most of Latin America did not benefit from a similar inward period of protected industrial development because Britain insisted on "free," "open" markets in exchange for recognition of independence in the 1820s. The United States did essentially the same thing to Cuba in 1902, forcing a very uneven "reciprocity" agreement on Cubans in exchange for recognition.

Only a few countries with large populations (and thus, large domestic markets) such as Argentina and Brazil could have achieved the type of balanced economic growth that the United States, Canada, and western European nations achieved by building industrial and agricultural bases, but even the smaller Latin American nations could have made a few essential products instead of importing them, thus diversifying their economies beyond just exports of agricultural products with very unstable prices on the world market.

43 Ayala, *American Sugar Kingdom*; Foner, *The Spanish-Cuban-American War and the Birth of American Imperialism*; Ibarra Cuesta, *Cuba, 1898–1958*.

44 McAvoy, *Sugar Baron*, 31.

45 Most communal estates in the West had already been divided and sold during periods of sugar expansion in the eighteenth century and nineteenth.

46 Pérez, "Insurrection, Intervention, and the Transformation of Land Tenure Systems in Cuba," 247.

47 Most of these investors were U.S., British, or European shareholders of companies incorporated in the United States. Pérez, "Insurrection, Intervention, and Transformation of Land Tenure Systems in Cuba," 252. Pérez cites two sources for the statistics: Carpenter, "Cuba in 1905," 11, and Jenks, *Our Cuban Colony*, 143–44.

48 The next chapter will explore the establishment and growth of Chaparra. Manuel Rionda wrote on 22 August 1901, "Este ingenio . . . tiene ya armada la casa pero les falta instalar tres veces más maquinarias que nosotros." Archivo Provincial de Las Tunas (hereafter APLT), Fondo: The Francisco Sugar Company, leg. 1, exp. 24, cited in Pichs Brito, "Una compañía azucarera," 6.

49 "Mammoth Sugar Plant to be Established in Cuba," *Courier-Journal* (Louisville, Ky.), 24 March 1901, cited in Foner, *The Spanish-Cuban-American War and the Birth of American Imperialism*, 2:477; Pérez, *Cuba between Empires*, 360.

50 Pérez, *Cuba between Empires*, 360.

51 I chose not to make the UFCO sugarmills a case study for this book because they were run quite differently from other mills on the island, hiring workers almost exclusively instead of using the Cuban colono system for growing cane (this is discussed further in chapter 6). Moreover, Cuban students supervised by Oscar Zanetti and Alejandro García wrote a solid analysis of the mills in 1976—one of the very few scholarly Cuban sugarmill case studies ever produced. García and Zanetti, *United Fruit Company*. The study's subtitle, "A Case of Imperialist

Domination in Cuba," reveals its only weakness: the 1970s Marxist intellectual slant.

52 Pérez, "Insurrection, Intervention, and Transformation of Land Tenure Systems in Cuba," 252. (His figures are from Carpenter, "Cuba in 1905," and Jenks, *Our Cuban Colony*.)

53 The land was purchased earlier that year "from its native owners." "Rionda Exhibit No. 20: Annual Report of the Central Tuinucú Sugarcane Manufacturing Company to the Stockholders. Crop 1901–1902," p. 5, USNA, RG 76, case no. 240, pt. 2, folder 1.

Farther west, still within the province of Las Villas, Edwin Atkins purchased two estates beside his Soledad mill near Cienfuegos.

54 Pérez, *Cuba between Empires*, 360. For a wider discussion of the expansion of U.S. interests in Cuba and across the Caribbean, see McAvoy, *Sugar Baron*, and Ayala, *American Sugar Kingdom*.

55 *Congressional Record*, vol. 32, 281, as cited in Foner, *The Spanish-Cuban-American War and the Birth of American Imperialism*, 2:470.

56 And the capitalists who produced and imported sugar duty-free from Hawaii.

57 Pérez, *On Becoming Cuban*, 221.

58 Zanetti and García, *Sugar and Railroads*, 221.

59 Civil Order 34, passed in February 1901, also allowed foreigners to purchase land to establish or expand railroad construction. "Vast tracts of land were thus subject to expropriation in the pursuit of an enterprise owned almost entirely by foreign capital. Railroad companies . . . routinely attached [extra] property." Pérez, "Insurrection, Intervention, and Transformation of Land Tenure Systems in Cuba," 245.

60 Tuinucú Sugar Company, "Annual Report 1924," 9–10, Harvard Business School, Baker Library, Historical Collections Department (hereafter HB, HCR).

61 I borrow the concept of "everyday forms of resistance" from Scott, *Domination and the Arts of Resistance*.

62 J. A. Ryan, Ranchuelo, Santa Clara, to chief of staff, Army of Cuban Pacification, Havana, 28 December 1906, USNA, RG 395, item 40, file 44, 3–4.

63 Ibid., 8.

64 G. W. E. Griffith, Havana, to Sir Edward Grey, London, 6 October 1906, PRO, FO, 371/56, doc. 340.

65 The current provinces of Cienfuegos and Santa Clara were part of the colonial province of Las Villas, as was Sancti Spiritus. The Liberal Party was an alliance of the Las Villas group and the Havana-based "Zayista" followers of Alfredo Zayas (a nationalist lawyer, and brother of Juan Bruno Zayas, a Liberation Army leader who helped invade the West). The case for Las Villas as a springboard to national power is from Zeuske, "Los negros hicimos la independencia," 202, 221.

66 Ibid., 225. The geography of the rebellion is described in "Cuban Secretary of State Report, Havana, 28 August 1906," cited in PRO, FO, 371/56, doc. 154.

67 Captain Wirt McCreary to military secretary, Army of Cuban Pacification, 16 December 1906, USNA, RG 395, item 25, file 25.

68 Second Lieutenant C. S. McReynolds to military secretary, Army of Cuban Pacification, 27 September 1908, USNA, RG 395, item 25, file 25.

69 Helg, *Our Rightful Share*, 147.

70 de la Fuente, *A Nation for All*, 72–73.

71 The author of the report does not say what these subsequent events were. PRO, FO, 371/1359, doc. 371.

72 Stephen Leech, Havana, to Sir Edward Grey, 5 June 1912, PRO, FO, 371/1359, doc. 42; Leech to Grey, 1 May 1912, PRO, FO, 371/1359, doc. 39.

73 For an excellent discussion of the PIC movement, see Helg, *Our Rightful Share*.

74 Beaupré to the secretary of state, Havana, June 14, 1912, USNA, RG 59, 837.000/793, as cited in de la Fuente, *A Nation for All*, 74.

75 27 March 1917, PRO, FO, 371/2923.

76 Giovannetti-Torres, "Black British Subjects in Cuba," 73–79.

77 3 May 1917, PRO, FO, 371/2923.

78 Letter from residents of Paso Estancia, Oriente, to U.S. consul, Santiago, cited in 17 May 1917 British Legation Report, PRO, FO, 371/2923.

FOUR The Patrons' Compact

1 Sugar production may have increased even more than it did in 1906, 1912, and 1917, had the rebellions not taken place, but the contrast with the 1895–1896 statistics cited above demonstrates that the movements came nowhere near the impact a "revolution" could have on sugar production on the island.

2 The role of gendered rhetoric in twentieth-century Cuba offers a promising avenue for future research. K. Lynn Stoner has contributed extensively on women in Cuba, but the island's historiography lacks studies like the ones Eileen Findlay has written for Puerto Rico (cited above) or Susan Besse has written for Brazil. I have not seen any sources documenting Fulgencio Batista using the kind of state-as-family language that Besse found his contemporary Getúlio Vargas using in Brazil and Sandra McGee-Deutsch and others found the Peróns using in Argentina. The challenge is to find more sources on Batista: as of yet there is no "Batista" archive analogous to the Getulio Vargas Foundation and similar archives in Argentina. See Besse, *Restructuring Patriarchy*; Deutsch, "Gender and Sociopolitical Change in Twentieth-Century Latin America," 259–306.

3 Eladio Santiago Serrano, interview by the author, Tuinucú, 1 February 2000.

4 J. A. Ryan, Ranchuelo, Santa Clara, to chief of staff, Army of Cuban Pacification, Havana, 28 December 1906, USNA, RG 395, item 40, file 44, 3.

5 Summary of Report by Lieutenant Wilson, 30 July 1907, USNA, RG 395, item 207, file 53.

6 United States War Department, *Report on the Census of Cuba, 1899*.

7 Beaupré to secretary of state, Havana, June 14, 1912, USNA, RG 59, 837.000/793, as cited in de la Fuente, *A Nation for All*, 74.

8 One of the best studies that documents the transition for the United States is Cohen, *Making a New Deal*. Klubock, *Contested Communities*, builds a convincing case that the Chilean state actually copied welfare ideas from the capitalists.

9 The land for Manuel Rionda's "Francisco Sugar Company" in Camagüey was purchased earlier than Chaparra's, but Rionda always credited Hawley with pioneering the concept of a work that would open up and set production records in eastern Cuba. McAvoy, "Lion's Tail, Mouse's Head," 16.

10 As mentioned earlier, Chaparra was quickly followed by the establishment of the United Fruit Company's "Boston" and "Preston" in Nipe Bay, Oriente, and thereafter by many others of the same model (large, privately owned land, ports, railroads, and towns).

11 *Louisiana Planter and Sugar Manufacturer*, 8 December 1900, 363. I thank Muriel McAvoy for sending me a copy of this article.

12 The García Menocal men chose to go by Menocal rather than García because their maternal line played a prominent role in Cuba's nineteenth-century wars for independence. Monsignor Carlos Manuel de Céspedes García Menocal, interview by the author, Havana, 25 April 2000.

13 J. M. Clark, Cuba, to Manuel Rionda, United States, 12 May 1899, BBC, RG 2, series 1, file: Clark, J. M.

14 Ibid.

15 "Mammoth Sugar Plant to be Established in Cuba," *Courier-Journal* (Louisville, Ky.), 24 March 1901, cited in Foner, *The Spanish-Cuban-American War and the Birth of American Imperialism*, 2:477.

16 A U.S. military report dated May 1907 stated that Plá owned private railroad lines from the port to San Manuel, as well as "the ground and many of the buildings" in Puerto Padre itself. "The other buildings are owned by the occupants," it added, "but they pay 5 per cent of the valuation of the property, for annual rent to Francisco Plá." USNA, RG 395, item 45, file 51, 5.

17 Santa Cruz y Mallén, *Historia de Familias Cubanas*, 1:264; *Cuba Contemporánea: Las Seis Provincias en Tres Tomos: Oriente* (1943).

18 Libro Diario, 1905, Archivo Provincial Histórico de Las Tunas, Fondo: Cuban American Sugar Company (hereafter APLT, CASC), leg. 2, exp. 14, 24.

19 Marrero Zaldívar, "Dulce amargo de una historia obrera." A similar argument is made in Urbino Ochoa et al., "Las primeras luchas obreras en los centrales Chaparra y Delicias."

20 Beyond the fact that Cuban authorities are naturally quite cautious about letting foreign researchers look at twentieth-century land registries (U.S. sugarmill companies have lawsuits pending against the Cuban government for property nationalized after the 1959 Revolution), there is the problem of shifting municipal and provincial boundaries in the region. Chaparra overlapped four municipalities, Holguín, Las Tunas, Puerto Padre, and Gibara. Some documents were filed

in Holguín or Las Tunas; others were funneled to Santiago de Cuba (the provincial capital of Oriente). After a re-division of Cuban provinces in the 1970s,
they were supposedly shifted back and divided among the provincial archives of
Holguín, Las Tunas, and Santiago. The end result is that it is extremely difficult
to follow land transfers using any single archive.

Cuban researchers list some of the tactics for early-twentieth-century land
takeovers that United Fruit company representatives and their Cuban allies used
a few years later to acquire land in nearby Banes, Oriente. In García and Zanetti,
United Fruit Company, 57–58. Strategies included hiring lawyers to falsify land
titles within communal estates, or to prove legitimate Cuban land titles false by
identifying and exaggerating small discrepencies over transfers that took place
during the colonial era.

21 "Memorandum about *pesos* of *posesión* in Las Salinas." George Henson, New
York, 18 December 1928, APLT, CASC, leg. 24, exp. 310.
22 R. B. Wood, Chaparra, to Mr. Keiser, New York, 21 February 1929, APLT, CASC,
leg. 24, exp. 310.
23 Puerto Padre, 11 February 1911, STGO, GP, leg. 130, exp. 10.
24 Manuel Machado and M. de Oca to R. B. Wood, Puerto Padre, 5 December 1932,
APLT, CASC, leg. 50, exp. 558.
25 Pérez, "The Pursuit of Pacification," 327.
26 "Tacit pact" is my translation of *entente cordiale*, the French term used by Eva
Canel in *Lo que ví en Cuba a través de la isla*, 290.
27 Omar Villafruela, interview by the author, Chaparra, 19 February 2000; McAvoy,
Sugar Baron, 40.
28 M. Carlos Manuel de Céspedes García Menocal, interview by the author, Havana,
25 April 2000.
29 de la Riva, "Los recursos humanos de Cuba al comenzar el siglo," 1:31.
30 Unfortunately, the source does not provide information about salaries during the
dead season or specify the portion of the total that went for salaries versus wages
for day labor. *Impresiones de la República de Cuba en el siglo XX*, 249, 255.
31 *Album de vistas del gran central Chaparra*. The text is in English on one side and
Spanish on the other. There is one copy of the book at the National Library of
Cuba in Havana.
32 "Los Grandes Centrales," 13, 15, 17, 24. I found this source thanks to Louis Pérez's
excellent discussion of Cuban and American culture in "The Meaning of the
Mill," in Pérez, *On Becoming Cuban*, 220–38.
33 "Los Grandes Centrales," 13, 15, 17, 24.
34 General Manager R. B. Wood to mill worker Julio Batista, 14 October 1929, and
other letters, in APLT, CASC, leg. 46, exp. 528.
35 Canel, *Lo que ví en Cuba a través de la isla*, 286; Martí, *Films cubanos*, 106–8, cited
in Pérez, *On Becoming Cuban*, 222.
36 Martí, *Films cubanos*, 106–8, cited in Pérez, *On Becoming Cuban*, 222.
37 *Agricultura y Zootecnia*, July 1924, 34.

38 Vega Suñol, *Presencia norteamericana en el area nororiental de Cuba*, 112–30.

39 For more on baseball and cricket in Cuba, see Pérez, *On Becoming Cuban* and the many sources on which he builds his argument.

40 *Album de vistas del gran central Chaparra*, 6.

41 *Agricultura y Zootecnia*, July 1924, 86; "Los Grandes Centrales," 19.

42 APLT, CASC, leg. 48, exp. 545.

43 It was Rionda's understanding that these unions were "local to their respective plantations" and "had no connections with any outside group." Manuel Rionda to Gerard Smith, 29 October 1919, BBC, RG 2, series 10, as cited in Lauriault, "Virgin Soil," 337.

44 The worker history described the guardsman, whose name was Arias, as a "servile and illiterate man." Personal archive of Omar Villafruela, director of Museo de los Hermanos Almejeiras, Chaparra.

45 The archivist Marina Pichs Brito of Las Tunas and Omar Villafruela both mentioned the nickname "Las Gemelas Golosas" to me during informal conversations in February and May 2000 at Las Tunas and Chaparra.

46 USNA, RG 395, items 48, 62, file 51.

47 Harold Griffith (former Chaparra employee), interviewed by Víctor Marrero, Chaparra, 15 July 1991, tape recording, Oficina del Historiador de la Ciudad de Las Tunas (hereafter OHLT).

48 He remained on the board of directors of the Cuban-American Sugar Company after he became president in 1913.

49 Canel, *Lo que ví en Cuba a través de la isla*, 293–94.

50 *Agricultura y Zootecnia*, July 1924, 69. They reasoned that a bargaining merchant "may have paid double what the product was worth to spare a fight" with the seller, or "because he did not know exactly what he was buying," and he would pass that expense on to the consumer. The "misunderstood" product was likely to be some luxury good, exported from the United States and consumed in Cuba thanks to the copious U.S. advertising and the allure of "superior" U.S. products. See Pérez, *On Becoming Cuba*, passim, for a discussion of the complex cultural and commercial relations between Cuba and the United States.

51 I have not been able to locate prices to test the validity of this argument.

52 *La Prensa*, 23 June 1925, 2, cited in Pérez, *On Becoming Cuban*, 229.

53 After Cuba's 1899 census documented that about one-third of the population was Afro-Cuban, racist Cubans and U.S policymakers passed legislation prohibiting black immigration and allowing only whites in hopes of "whitening" the overall population. See de la Fuente, *A Nation for All*, 44, and see chap. 1 for the colonial counterpart to this policy—the 1880s promotion of the colono cane-farming system as a way of bringing white families to Cuba.

54 Urbino Ochoa et al., "Las primeras luchas obreras en los centrales Chaparra y Delicias," 29. Note that this source details the permanent population of Chaparra as just over four thousand, based on the Cuban census. The U.S. military source cited in n. 46 above estimates the population level at roughly five thousand. The

difference can be explained by the fact that the military surveyor visited Chaparra during the harvest period (in July 1907), so there were more domestic and foreign migrant workers present in the area at the time.

55 Canel, *Lo que ví en Cuba a través de la isla*, 286–87.

56 Fernández, *De memorias y anhelos*, 24. I thank Jorge Giovannetti-Torres, José Abreu, and Elia Sintes for pointing me to this source.

57 Canel, *Lo que vi en Cuba a través de la isla*, 293; Urbino Ochoa et al., "Las primeras luchas obreras en los centrales Chaparra y Delicias," 1.

58 Luis Merconchini, interview by Víctor Marrero, Delicias, 21 August 1990, tape recording, OHLT.

59 Canel, *Lo que ví en Cuba a través de la isla*, 288–89.

60 Marrero Zaldívar, "Dulce amargo de una historia obrera," 1.

61 R. B. Wood to Captain Eduardo Hidalgo, chief of the Guardia Jurada (Private Guard), Delicias, APLT, CASC, leg. 46, exp. 531.

62 Elmer V. Thompson, director, West Indies Mission for the Training of a Native Gospel Ministry ("Fields: Cuba and Haiti, Headquarters: P.O. Box 131"), Placetas, Cuba, to R. B. Wood, Chaparra, 9 February 1939, APLT, CASC, leg. 198, exp. 3864.

63 Tomás González Romero and Ester Villa Nápoles, interview by the author, Chaparra, 5 September 2005; Tomás González Romero and Ester Villa Nápoles, interview by Víctor Marrero, 17 April 2007, Chaparra.

64 For details on the most extreme case (at the Francisco sugarmill), see Lauriault, "Virgin Soil."

65 Manuel Rionda to Albert Strauss, New York, 16 March 1917, BBC, RG 2, series 10, file: Liberal Rebellion (1917).

66 *Gráfico*, Havana, 17 May 1913, ANC, Fondo Donativos y Remisiones, box 456, no. 7.

67 Ibarra Cuesta, *Cuba 1898–1921*, 284.

68 Riera Hernández, *Cuba política*, 218–20.

69 Stephen Leech, Havana, to Sir Edward Grey, 5 June 1912, PRO, FO, 371/1359, doc. 42.

70 Leech to Grey, 1 May 1912, PRO, FO, 371/1359, doc. 39.

71 They did not want a doctor (Zayas) to win, and were more confident that General Menocal could beat him than the Liberal General Asbert. Ibarra Cuesta, *Cuba 1898–1921*, 337.

72 García Galló, *Esbozo biográfico de Jesús Menéndez*, 25.

73 On 16 June 1916, Menocal approved a law on compensation for work accidents, but the coverage was extremely minimal. Ibarra Cuesta, *Cuba 1898–1921*.

74 This paragraph is derived from Stoner, "Militant Heroines and the Consecration of the Patriarchal State," 21–22.

75 The Spanish name for the saint is "Virgen de la Caridad del Cobre." Ibid., 21.

76 Domínguez, *Cuba*, 71.

77 Stubbs, *Tobacco on the Periphery*.

78 Carr, "Mill Occupations and Soviets," 135; Dumoulin, *Azúcar y lucha de clases*, 182.

79 Stephen Leech, Her Majesty's Legation, Havana, to A. J. Balfour, 7 January 1917, PRO, FO, 371/2923.

80 Santiago Serrano R., "Historia del movimiento obrero en el central Melanio Hernández (antes Tuinucú)"; Urbino Ochoa et al., "Las primeras luchas obreras en los centrales Chaparra y Delicias."

81 Primelles, *Crónica cubana*, 499.

82 "Orden Público 288," signed by Mario García Menocal, 23 October 1917, STGO, GP, leg. 1705, exp. 2; Ambassador William Gonzales, Havana, to secretary of state, Washington, D.C., 29 September 1917, USNA, RG 59, 836.504/13.

83 Vicente Martínez to Samuel Gompers, 21 October 1917, cited in Ibarra Cuesta, *Cuba 1898–1921*, 352.

84 *Gaceta oficial: Edición extraordinaria* 47, STGO, GP, leg. 1705, exp. 5.

85 Manuel Rionda, "To the Cuba Cane Sugar Corporation," BBC, RG 2, series 10, file: Cuba Cane, Papers Related to, Goethals Report, 23. The Cuba Company was Manuel Rionda's "brainchild." See McAvoy, *Sugar Baron*.

86 Unfortunately, the records regarding salaries and wages at Tuinucú and Chaparra are sporadic, so I have not been able to systematize when and how much they changed from year to year.

87 The literature on early-twentieth-century immigration to Cuba is increasingly rich. Among other works, see Giovannetti-Torres, "Black British Subjects in Cuba"; Hoernel, "A Comparison of Sugar and Social Change in Puerto Rico and Oriente," 123; Alvarez Estévez, *Azúcar e inmigración*, 68, 87; Carr, "Identity, Class, and Nation," 83–116; Knight, "Jamaican Migrants in the Cuban Sugar Industry"; Chomsky, "Barbados or Canada?," 415–462, and McLeod, "Undesirable Aliens," 599–623.

88 Giovannetti-Torres, "Black British Subjects in Cuba," 42.

89 *Agricultura y Zootecnia*, July 1924, 77.

90 Letter from Chinese worker and lists of immigrants, jobs, and pay, APLT, CASC, leg. 39, exp. 456.

91 For more on the difference between the treatment of Haitians and Ingleses, see Carr, "Identity, Class, and Nation"; McLeod, "Undesirable Aliens."

92 Giovannetti-Torres, "Black British Subjects in Cuba."

93 Various documents in STGO, GP, legs. 786–89.

94 de la Fuente, *A Nation for All*, 124.

95 Ibarra Cuesta, *Cuba 1898–1921*, 346.

96 Ibid., 357–58.

97 Martí, *Films cubanos*, 100.

98 Emphasis mine. Stephen Leech to Foreign Office, 27 April 1917, PRO, FO, 371/2923.

99 Stephen Leech to Foreign Office, 27 April 1917, PRO, FO, 371/2923.

100 "Tumba la caña, anda lijero; corre, que viene Menocal, sonando el cuero," as cited in Canel, *Lo que ví en Cuba a través de la isla*. Riera Hernández, *Cuba política*,

229, cites a slight variation: "Anda lijero, corta la caña, que ahí viene el mayoral, sonando el cuero."

FIVE Patrons, Matrons, and Resistance

1   Captain Earl Brown, Corps of Engineers, to adjutant, 2nd Battalion of Engineers, Camp Columbia, Havana, 1 April 1907, USNA, RG 395, item 77, file 70. This population estimate must have included the colonias surrounding Tuinucú, because the mill town itself had only one workers' barracks that housed approximately one hundred Spanish workers, at the time. The population figure for Chaparra is from Urbino Ochoa et al., "Las primeras luchas obreras en los centrales Chaparra y Delicias," 29.

2   Rionda's system of rule paralleled Fordism more in social terms. He tried to make workers feel like they were part of the "family" and practiced social control through the subtle means described in this chapter such as housing policies. He did not mimic Henry Ford's assembly-line system used for cars or try to create a bigger domestic market of consumers by offering high wages to workers. For more on Fordism, see Montgomery, *Worker's Control in America*, 113–38; Cohen, *Making a New Deal*, 100.

3   The words of the British historian E. P. Thompson are appropriate here: "We need to be careful not to idealize [patronage], but it can be a profoundly important component of ideology and of actual institutional mediation of social relations." He uses the term "paternalism," but for the sake of simplicity I am using "patronage" to include both "boss–worker" local relations and "patron–client" state relations. Thompson, *Customs in Common*, 24.

4   Until the sugar boom during the First World War, when more veterans turned to sugarcane farming.

5   Tello was Major-General Serafín Sánchez's brother. The fact that he was a colonel rather than a major-general like Menocal may explain why he could not mobilize as many workers. José Rionda, Tuinucú, to Manuel Rionda, New York, 25 January 1905, BBC, RG 2, series 1, file: Rionda, José.

6   Pedro Alonso, Noreña, Spain, to Manuel Rionda, New York, 14 January 1913, BBC, RG 2, series 1, file: Alonso, Pedro.

7   Manuel Rionda to Frederick Strauss, 28 May 1908, BBC, RG 2, series 3, vol. 1.

8   Manuel Rionda to Messrs. Czarnikow, McDougall and Company, New York, 30 January 1905; Manuel Rionda to C. Czarnikow, London, 14 December 1906, BBC, RG 2, series 5, box 1, as cited in Giovannetti-Torres, "Black British Subjects in Cuba," 19.

9   Santiago Serrano R., "La incidencia de un central azucarero en la comunidad 'Tuinucú Ayer y Hoy,'" 30.

10 Manuel Rionda to Pedro Alonso, 25 July 1916, BBC, RG 2, series 1, file: Alonso, Pedro.

11 Eladio Santiago Serrano, interview by the author, Tuinucú, 1 February 2000.

12 de la Fuente, *A Nation for All*, 99.

13 Eladio Santiago Serrano, interview by the author, Tuinucú, 1 February 2000. For more on racial practices in public spaces, see de la Fuente, *A Nation for All*; Guridy, "Racial Knowledge in Cuba."

14 Italicized words are underlined in the original. Manuel Rionda to José "Pepe" Rionda, 3 February 1906, BBC, RG 2, series 3, vol. 1.

15 Eladio Santiago Serrano, interview by the author, Tuinucú, 1 February 2000.

16 Manuel Rionda to Leandro Rionda, 18 October, 1916, BBC, RG 2, series 2; Lauriault, "Virgin Soil," 308.

17 They took a ferry from Miami to Havana. Braga, "A Bundle of Relations," 178.

18 José Rionda, Tuinucú, to Manuel Rionda, 19 January 1905, BBC, RG 2, series 1, file: Rionda, José B. Tuinucú.

19 Isidora Rionda, Tuinucú, to Manuel Rionda, New York, 6 March 1902, BBC, RG 2, series 1, file: Rionda y Polledo, Isidora.

20 Manuel Rionda, New York, to Elena Doty, Tuinucú, 16 October 1918, BBC, RG 2, series 10, file: Tuinucú Sugar Company—Correspondence 1917 [1919] (hereafter Tuinucú, Correspondence 1917 [1919]).

21 Manuel Rionda to Isidora "Madrina" Rionda, 16 June 1906, BBC, RG 2, series 3, Manuel Rionda y Polledo Travelling Letterbooks, 1905–26, vol. 1.

22 Manuel Rionda to Isidora "Madrina" Rionda, 10 February 1906, BBC, RG 2, series 3, vol. 1.

23 Manuel Rionda to Isidora "Madrina" Rionda, 10 February 1906, 13 April 1906, 16 June 1906, BBC, RG 2, series 3, vol. 1.

24 Concepción Rionda, Tuinucú, to Manuel Rionda, New York, 19 July 1915, BBC, RG 2, series 1, file: Rionda, "China" [Concepción], Sancti Spiritus.

25 Thompson, *Customs in Common*, 45–46.

26 "Los Grandes Centrales," 19.

27 Tomás González Romero and Esther Villa Nápoles, interview by Víctor Marrero, Chaparra, 17 April 2007.

28 Tomás González Romero and Ester Villa Nápoles, interview by the author, Chaparra, 5 September 2005.

29 The literature on gender and social reform in early-twentieth-century U.S. cities is vast. For the United States, see Frankel and Dye, *Gender, Class, Race, and Reform in the Progressive Era*. For Argentina, see Guy, *Sex and Danger in Buenos Aires*.

30 Thompson, *Customs in Common*, 66. For more on how to interpret worker anecdotes and jokes, see James, *Doña María's Story*.

31 Santiago Serrano R., "La incidencia de un central azucarero en la comunidad 'Tuinucú Ayer y Hoy,'" 33.

32 Isidora Rionda, Tuinucú, to Manuel Rionda, New York, 5 May 1914, BBC, RG 2, series 1, file: Rionda y Polledo, Isidora, Sancti Spiritus.

33 Isidora Rionda, Tuinucú, to Manuel Rionda, 9 May 1918, BBC, RG 2, series 1, file: Rionda y Polledo, Isidora, Sancti Spiritus.

34 Santiago Serrano R., "La incidencia de un central azucarero en la comunidad 'Tuinucú Ayer y Hoy," 23.

35 Valdivia Hernández, interview by the author, Tuinucú, 12 May 2000.

36 The labor movement at Tuinucú and beyond (especially the importance of contact between sectors) will be discussed in much greater detail in the next two chapters.

37 Santiago Serrano R., "La incidencia de un central azucarero en la comunidad 'Tuinucú Ayer y Hoy.'"

38 Arquímedes Valdivia Hernández, interview by the author, Tuinucú, 1 February 2000.

39 Ibid.

40 Ibid. Company documents suggest that at the peak of the 1933 strike, Doty was not actually present at the mill, but this negotiation may have occurred before he left.

41 Eladio Santiago Serrano and Arquímedes Valdivia Hernández, interview by the author, Tuinucú, 12 May 2000.

42 When I pressed them to clarify whether they meant in the 1930s or the 1950s, they responded that it was during both periods. Chapters 7 and 8 will discuss the transition from company to state power further.

43 Manuel Rionda, untitled seven-page description of Tuinucú for an American audience, typed ms., BBC, RG 2, series 10, Tuinucú, Correspondence 1917 [1919], 6.

44 Ibid. In a similar vein, administrator Eugenio Molinet contemplated "prizes" to reward the colonos who dedicated themselves to food crops on the largest scale. Chaparra owner Robert Hawley forwarded Manuel Rionda a letter from Eugenio Molinet stating, "we have in Chaparra 400 rozas prepared and destined for [food], and there is great enthusiasm shown among a great many colonos . . . This will be a trial, and if it gives the results expected, I will propose to you for next year a plan to reward the colonos who cultivate their fields best, and who prove themselves to be the best farmers." He did, in fact, establish three such colono prizes in 1917. Eugenio Molinet, Chaparra, to Manuel Rionda, Havana, 31 March 1916, BBC, RG 2, series 1, file: Hawley, R. B.; Eugenio Molinet, Chaparra, to R. B. Hawley, New York, 10 September 1917, BBC, RG 2, series 1, file: Hawley, R. B. (Cuban-American Sugar Company).

45 Elena Doty to Manuel Rionda, 18 July 1915, BBC, RG 2, series 10, Tuinucú, Correspondence 1917 [1919]. The Chinese presence in Cuba is a fruitful avenue for future research. See Choy et al., *Our History Is Still Being Written*; Jiménez Pastrana, *Los chinos en las luchas por la liberación cubana*; and López, "One Brings Another."

46 Manuel Rionda to Elena Doty, 14 August 1917, BBC, RG 2, series 10, Tuinucú, Correspondence 1917 [1919].

47 Manuel Rionda to Elena Doty, 16 October 1918, BBC, RG 2, series 10, Tuinucú, Correspondence 1917 [1919].

48 The amount is left blank in the file copy. "Memorandum," 17 June 1919, BBC, RG 2, series 10, Tuinucú, Correspondence 1917 [1919].

49 Frank Jones to Manuel E. Rionda [Manuel Rionda's nephew], 12 February 1925, BBC, RG 2, series 10, file: Tuinucú: Radio Station at the Plantation.

50 Manuel Rionda to Frank Jones, 6 April 1925, BBC, RG 2, series 10, file: Tuinucú: Radio Station at the Plantation.

51 *Heraldo de Cuba*, 14 February 1925, BBC, RG 2, series 10, file: Tuinucú: Reports on This Sugar Estate.

52 The author of the letter wrote "*administración extranjera*," which likely reflects the workers' perspective that the mill was run by foreigners. Oliver and Elena Doty, the on-site administrators, were American, and Manuel and Isidora were Spanish. Milliken, "Arreglando el mundo: un caso práctico," *El Mundo*, 13 December 1924, in BBC, RG 2, series 10, file: Tuinucú: Reports on This Sugar Estate.

53 Manuel Rionda to Ricardo Bianchi, 29 April 1927, BBC, RG 2, series 10, file: Tuinucú: Ricardo Bianchi [member of Municipal Council of Sancti Spiritus].

54 Ricardo Bianchi to the president and councillors of the town of Sancti Spiritus, 20 April 1927, BBC, RG 2, series 10, file: Tuinucú: Ricardo Bianchi.

55 "Rionda Exhibit No. 20: Annual Report of the Central Tuinucú Sugarcane Manufacturing Company to the Stockholders. Crop 1901–1902," 14–15, USNA, RG 76, case no. 240, pt. 2, folder 1.

56 "Although you have not told me whether you wish to resume paying bonuses this year," he wrote, "as we had done prior to the collapse of the sugar market, I enclose a list of bonuses for this year which I would suggest, provided you wish to do so." Oliver Doty to Manuel Rionda, 10 April 1923, BBC, RG 2, series 10, file: Tuinucú: Bonuses (1921).

57 Manuel Rionda, New Jersey, to Oliver Doty, Tuinucú, 19 April 1923, BBC, RG 2, series 10, file: Tuinucú: Bonuses (1921).

58 Oliver Doty to Manuel Rionda, 18 October 1922, BBC, RG 2, series 10, file: Tuinucú: Salaries and Wages.

59 Acta, Secretaría de Gobernación, 28 September 1933, BBC, RG 2, S. 10, file: Tuinucú, Labor Troubles.

60 Klubock, *Contested Communities*, 58.

61 Leonor may have been a servant or chef who worked at the Rionda family home or a clerk at the store. These were the only two places women officially worked at the sugarmill. Manuel Rionda to Oliver Doty [the letter from Isidora to Manuel is mentioned in his letter to Doty], 6 April 1925, BBC, RG 2, series 10, file: Tuinucú: Radio Station at the Plantation, Jones, Frank H.

62 Thompson speaks about this difference of perspectives (charity versus rights) in rural Britain, in Thompson, *Customs in Common*, 72. Scott, *Domination and the Arts of Resistance*, applies it more broadly, as I am doing here.

63 Even the promise of a house was not always solid. When sugar prices fell in the late 1920s, Manuel advised Oliver Doty to cut the $3,000 allocated to building a

two-family house "even at the risk of the inconvenience to the two employees." He only authorized the $1,500 Doty allocated for repairs on "family homes" because "they would probably deteriorate more otherwise . . . like you, I think that $1,500 spent on 94 houses in the mill town is not exorbitant." Manuel Rionda to Oliver Doty, 23 May 1927, BBC, RG 2, series 10, file: Tuinucú: Cane Left Uncut at End of Crop.

64 Studies on workers by E. P. Thompson and Catherine LeGrand proved inspirational for trying to find the workers' perspective in sources written by "the bosses." Many ideas come from LeGrand, "Informal Resistance on a Dominican Sugar Plantation during the Trujillo Dictatorship," 555–96.

65 José Rionda's words that I translate as "dismiss" and "annoying" are *botar* and *quisquillosos*, respectively. José Rionda, Tuinucú, to Manuel Rionda, 13 February 1911, BBC, RG 2, series 1, file: Rionda, José B., Tuinucú.

66 One arroba equals roughly twenty-five pounds of cane.

67 A longer discussion of colono pay and negotiations with the mills follows in chapters 6–8. Pedro Alonso, Tuinucú, to Manuel Rionda, 6 April 1905, BBC, RG 2, series 1, file: Alonso, Pedro (1902–8), Tuinucú.

68 Pedro Alonso, Tuinucú, to Manuel Rionda, 26 April 1905, BBC, RG 2, series 1, file: Alonso, Pedro, Tuinucú.

69 José Rionda, Tuinucú, to Manuel Rionda, 9 February 1911, BBC, RG 2, series 1, file: Rionda, José B., Tuinucú.

70 "News Letter from Our Havana Office," *Louisiana Planter*, vol. 60, 16 February 1918, 103.

71 Colectivo de autores, *Memorias de un viejo mundo azucarero*, 8.

72 Cozzens, *Cock Pit*.

73 Rojas, *Las luchas obreras en el central Tacajó*, 33.

74 Silvestre Rionda, Tuinucú, to Manuel Rionda, New York, 21 April 1902, BBC, RG 2, series 1, file: Rionda, Silvestre.

75 Manuel Rionda to Isidora "Madrina" Rionda, 9 April 1907, BBC, RG 2, series 3, vol. 1.

76 Manuel Rionda to "José, Leandro, Rafael, Manolo, y Bernardo," 24 November 1907, BBC, RG 2, series 3, vol. 1.

77 R. B. Wood to E. Hidalgo, chief of private police force, Chaparra, 13 March 1937, APLT, CASC, leg. 48, exp. 543. To this day, it is extremely difficult to get permission to visit the sugar factory floors. Unfortunately, I was unable to go inside Chaparra or Tuinucú; I regret that I cannot offer a more detailed description of the place of work of the principal subjects of this book.

78 Doty's letter does not mention what kind of infection it was.

79 Oliver Doty to Manuel Rionda, 6 February 1929, BBC, RG 2, series 10a–c, file: Tuinucú: Doty, Oliver K., Letters (1929), Tuinucú.

80 Pedro Alonso, Tuinucú, to Manuel Rionda, 6 April 1903, BBC, RG 2, series 1, file: Alonso, Pedro, Tuinucú.

81 Thomas Klubock discusses "San Lunes" in *Contested Communities*, 45. E. P. Thompson discusses "Saint Monday" in "Time and Work Discipline," in *Customs in Common*, 374.

82 Rojas, *Las luchas obreras en el central Tacajó*, 35.

83 This data is based on a survey of all of the legal files: e.g., APLT, CASC, leg. 49. For example, in exp. 546, the chief of the Telephone Department reported the data about the telephone wire theft and its uses directly to R. B. Wood on 11 February 1938: APLT, CASC, leg. 46, exp. 525.

84 Manuel Fernández Pupo to R. B. Wood, Chaparra, 2 December 1932, APLT, CASC, leg. 50, exp. 558.

85 For an excellent study of how this played out among workers in Mexico, see French, *A Peaceful and Working People*.

86 E. Hidalgo to R. B. Wood, 7 August 1939, APLT, CASC, leg. 49, exp. 546. Although this report is from a later era, Chaparra administrators' concern for sanitation reigned from the early decades of the twentieth century onward.

87 Rojas, *Las luchas obreras en el central Tacajó*, 35.

88 Eladio Santiago Serrano, interview by the author, Tuinucú, 1 February 2000.

89 Letter from *los vecinos* [the neighbors] to Emilio Abreu, Subteniente Escd. no. 42, Chief of Rural Guard Post, forwarded to H. M. Hicks, general administrator, on 15 July 1937. The authors state that they complained to Mr. Wood about this "shameful situation" and asked him to cut the bushes around the chalet and to keep it lit, but neither he nor the private guard would do anything about the problem.

SIX   Patronage to Populism

1 The increase appears in both business correspondence and in the national and international media.

2 Benjamin, *The United States and Cuba*, 203, n. 14, cited in Pollitt, "The Cuban Sugar Economy and the Great Depression," 10.

3 This was chiefly due to vertical integration and economies of scale. Many American companies (like the Cuban-American Sugar Company) also owned refineries in the United States, so when prices for raw sugar decreased, they could produce sugar more cheaply in their refineries. Because the American mills tended to be larger than the Cuban mills, they secured higher profits during stable years, softening the blow during depression years. For details, see Dye, *Cuban Sugar in the Age of Mass Production*.

4 Benjamin, *The United States and Cuba*, 203, cited in Pollitt, "The Cuban Sugar Economy and the Great Depression," 10.

5 Alexander, *A History of Organized Labor in Cuba*, 35. For more on the foundation of the PCC, including the important influence of foreigners like Mexico's Enrique Flores Magón as well as Cubans such as student Julio Antonio Mella, see Córdova, *Clase trabajadora y movimiento sindical en Cuba*, 126–34; Instituto

de Historia, *Historia del movimiento obrero cubano*, 1:230; and Rojas, *Las luchas obreras en el central Tacajó*, 54.

6   Although "fall" and "winter" are not perfect translations for the Cuban seasons, I will use the terms for ease of reference; the harvest took place between approximately December and July until the mid-1920s and between January and February or March thereafter.

7   Burned cane had to be processed rapidly or it would lose all of its value, as mentioned earlier. The company planned which fields would be cut and milled each year. By burning cane, colonos might get to "jump the line," thus throwing off the milling schedule and privileging their cane before other colonia or company cane.

8   Oliver Doty to Manuel Rionda, 23 March 1921, BBC, RG 2, series 10, file: Tuinucú: Colonos—Accounts and Liquidations (hereafter Tuinucú: Colonos—C-AL).

9   Oliver Doty to Manuel Rionda, 3 August 1921, BBC, RG 2, series 10, Tuinucú: C-AL.

10   Oliver Doty to Manuel Rionda, 16 February 1922, BBC, RG 2, series 10, Tuinucú: C-AL.

11   Oliver Doty, Tuinucú, to Leandro Rionda, Havana, 11 April 1922, BBC, RG 2, series 10, Tuinucú: C-AL.

12   Pollitt, "The Cuban Sugar Economy and the Great Depression," 7. See also Buell et al., *Problems of the New Cuba*, 220; Moreno Fraginals, *El ingenio*, 3:38–39, for statistics on millions of tons.

13   Ibarra Cuesta, *Cuba 1898–1921*, 358.

14   As mentioned earlier, although the Arteaga Law of 1909 declared the token system illegal, sugar companies continued to use it to a greater or lesser extent until 1959. The companies would defend the system by arguing that they were short of cash until the sugar from the harvest was sold. The tokens were particularly bad for immigrant workers, who frequently had to leave Cuba without collecting all of the pay due to them.

15   Parallel developments occurred in other new communities forged by capitalism in Guatemala, Venezuela, Costa Rica, and Nicaragua. See Smith, "Culture and Community," 2:197–217; Roseberry, "Images of the Peasant in the Consciousness of the Venezuelan Proletariat"; Gudmonson, *Costa Rica before Coffee*; and Gould, *To Lead as Equals*.

16   See McAvoy, *Sugar Baron*, chaps. 6–7.

17   Pollitt, "The Cuban Sugar Economy and the Great Depression," 7.

18   Pérez, *Cuba*, 225; Thomas, *Cuba, the Pursuit of Freedom*, 544, cited in Lauriault, "Virgin Soil," 351. See Speck, "Prosperity, Progress, and Wealth," 50–86, for details on the few mills that actually went to Cuban banks.

19   Buell et al., *Problems of the New Cuba*, 342.

20   An excellent discussion of U.S.-based sugar producers versus U.S. corporations that produced sugar in Cuba can be found in DeWilde, "Sugar," 162–72.

21   In "By Way of Prologue," in Ortiz, *Cuban Counterpoint*, xix.

22 The Liberal Party, upon its inception, was an alliance of José Miguel Gómez's "Miguelista" Las Villas group and the Havana-based "Zayista" followers of Alfredo Zayas (a nationalist lawyer and brother of Juan Bruno Zayas, a leader of the Liberation Army that invaded the West). Their leadership rivalry lasted through the early twentieth century; the two leaders and their clienteles moving frequently from pragmatic alliances to frustrated splits.

23 Primelles, *Crónica cubana*, 239–47.

24 Pérez, *Cuba under the Platt Amendment*, 248–49.

25 As discussed in chaps. 3 and 4, the so-called Reciprocity Treaty undermined diversification and led to an excessive concentration on sugar and tobacco by granting low tariffs to a great range of American consumer exports in exchange for a 20 percent reduction on only two, highly fluctuating Cuban export products, sugar and tobacco. Meanwhile, the Platt Amendment (and the 1906–9 U.S. intervention justified by the amendment) created a political environment whereby many Cubans opted to stage rebellions to force a U.S. intervention through which they hoped to win control of the presidency from the opposition party.

26 "Otros sectores se solidizaron con los azucareros . . . y la población expresó su simpatía con el movimiento." Instituto de Historia, *Historia del movimiento obrero cubano*, 217.

27 Pérez, *Cuba Under the Platt Amendment*, 175–256.

28 "Con el pueblo y a pie." Aguilar, *Cuba 1933*, 53.

29 This thesis is most clearly stated in French, "Workers and the Rise of Adhemarista Populism in Sao Paulo, Brazil," 1–43.

30 H. C. Lakin [president of the Cuba Railroad] to A. Gruber [vice-president in charge of operations], 30 December 1923, in Archivos de los Ferrocarriles de Cuba, Division Camagüey, Fondo Permanente, exp. 100–17, cited in Zanetti and García, *Sugar and Railroads*, 309.

31 Adán, an important figure in the Camagüeyan Railroad Workers' Brotherhood, was of reformist leanings. Arévalo, an important dock workers' leader in the 1910s, had switched from dock to rail workers when accused of mismanaging the dock union's fund. Zanetti and García, *Sugar and Railroads*, 457, n. 40.

32 Ibid., 310.

33 Ibid., 457, n. 44.

34 Barry Carr explores some of the challenges to organization and the forms of worker autonomy in " 'Omnipotent and Omnipresent'?" 260–91, and "Mill Occupations and Soviets," 129–58.

35 Zanetti and García, *Sugar and Railroads*, 314.

36 Ibid., 315.

37 The authors describe it as a "resounding victory" for the workers, but unfortunately they do not provide details on the demands won. Ibid., 316.

38 Instituto de Historia, *Historia del movimiento obrero cubano*, 218.

39 "The Cuban-American Sugar Company to the National City Company, New York, March 7, 1921" and "The Cuban-American Sugar Company, Annual

Report Section: Revised 3 January 1931," HB, HCR, folder: Cuban-American Sugar Company.

40 Horace J. Dickinson, 6 May 1922, USNA, RG 59, no. 488, roll 88, no. 369, as cited in Hoernel, "A Comparison of Sugar and Social Change in Puerto Rico and Oriente," 134. In reference to a statement of crops made by the Cuban-American Sugar Company from 1920–1932, Manuel Rionda observed that Chaparra and Delicias were "among the lowest cost producers—and have their own shipping port." Manuel Rionda to B. Forster, Bank of Manhattan Trust Company, 17 August 1933, BBC, RG 2, series 10, file: Cuban American.

41 Martínez-Alier and Martínez-Alier, *Cuba*; Pollitt, "The Cuban Sugar Economy and the Great Depression"; Dye, *Cuban Sugar in the Age of Mass Production*; and Ayala, *American Sugar Kingdom*.

42 Higinio Fanjul to Aurelio Portuondo, Havana, 14 September 1933, BBC, RG 2, series 11, file: Correspondence with Higinio Fanjul, Manuel Rasco, and Cuban Trading Company, Havana, Cuba (21 April 1933–19 December 1933).

43 As mentioned in chap. 2, Europe raised tariff barriers against foreign sugar imports, allowing European planters to develop highly capitalized, efficient sugar production that led to a large supply of cheap sugar flooding the world market in the late nineteenth century. For a more complete discussion of the birth of the *colonato*, see Iglesias García, *Del ingenio al central*.

44 See Scott, *Slave Emancipation in Cuba*, conclusion, 279–93.

45 Deposition of Manuel Rionda, Washington D.C., 15 September 1903, p. 20, USNA, RG 76, case no. 240, pt. 1, folder 7.

46 Italicized words are underlined in the original source: Manolo Rionda to Manuel Rionda, 18 February 1905, series 12, as cited in Lauriault, "Virgin Soil," 282.

47 "*Trancarlo*" is translated as "locking the colono in" and "*amarrar*" as "tying up." Plácido Alonso to Manuel Rionda, 12 May 1908 and May 1910, BBC, series 14, vol. 2, as cited in Moyano Fraga, "*Central*-Colono Relations within the Cuban Sugar Industry," 60.

48 BBC, RG 2, series 1, file: Joseph I. C. Clarke.

49 Copy of letter from D. A. Galdós, vice-president, Cuba Railroad Company, Camagüey, to Manuel Rionda, Manatí Sugar Company, New York, BBC, RG 2, series 10, file: Tuinucú: Miscellaneous Papers (1912–15).

50 Oliver Doty, Tuinucú, to Manuel Rionda, New York, 9 December 1924, BBC, RG 2, series 10, Tuinucú: C-AL.

51 See García and Zanetti, *United Fruit Company*, 124–28.

52 Whereas Guerra, the nationalist, argued that colono autonomy was a good thing because it meant that the island's wealth remained in Cuban hands, Alan Dye, the economic historian, argued that colonos created bottlenecks in supply and detracted from western sugar plantations' profits, thereby widening the gap in technology already extant between the older western mills (that tended to be Cuban) and the larger new eastern mills (that tended to be American).

53 This study looks at Chaparra, but a similar story can be told for the Francisco mill just slightly west of Chaparra. See Lauriault, "Virgin Soil."

54 Speck, "Prosperity, Progress, and Wealth," 66.

55 Ibarra Cuesta, *Cuba 1898–1921*, 70–80.

56 Ibid., 418–425; Riera Hernández, *Cuba política*.

57 "Large" was defined as capable of producing over 500,000 arrobas of cane (1 arroba equals 25 pounds).

58 The one hundred names were predominantly cane farmers, but a few were chief administrators or owners of sugarmills; some were all three, at different stages of their careers. In compiling the list, Jorge Ibarra erred on the side of caution. When the names were particularly common or where Roloff listed an official as from the eastern part of the island and the same name turned up as a colono in the West, the names were not included unless a third source confirmed that it was the same individual. Ibarra's sources include the *Times of Cuba*, December 1918, February 1921, and February 1926. Ibarra Cuesta, Cuba, 1898–1921, Apendice F, Relación de oficiales del Ejército Libertador que se convirtieron en grandes colonos, 418–25.

59 The Afro-Cuban Colonel Gabino Gálvez became a large colono at Tuinucú during the First World War and governor of Santa Clara in the 1930s. He fits the pattern in that he was one of the three colonos demanding more for their cane at Tuinucú in 1919, while others agreed to lesser terms. Oliver Doty to Manuel Rionda, 24 November 1919, BBC, RG 2, series 10, file: Tuinucú Correspondence 1917 [1919].

60 The estimate of Chaparra's production for 1902–1903 mentions that "the *colonias* are on company land except for a few that are owned by the colono." STGO, GP, leg. 2867, exp. 6.

61 Secretaría de Agricultura, *Industria azucarera de Cuba 1913–1914*, 409.

62 The pre-1930 annual sugar reports and statistics at Cuba's national archives and at the Institute of History in Havana grouped cane ground by tenant colonos together with administration cane. *Memoria de la Zafra realizada en el año 1926 a 1927*, ANC, AIC, leg. 4, exp. 33.

63 *Memoria de la Zafra realizada en el año 1926 a 1927*, ANC, AIC, leg. 4, exp. 35.

64 The year 1937 was the first in which administration cane versus colono cane was clearly documented in the statistics—a fact that in itself reflects the growing political clout of colonos. The total cane ground was 166,912,866 arrobas at Chaparra and Delicias and 144,464,085 arrobas at Boston and Preston. The statistics from the same year reveal the sizes of the Cuban American colonias: The majority were medium-size. Chaparra and Delicias combined had 368 colonos with less than 20,000 arrobas; 462 colonos with less than 30,000; and a grand total of 1,169 colonos. The source does not differentiate between independent and company colonos. STGO, GP, leg. 313, exp. 19.

65 Several books, theses, and dissertations based on Manuel Rionda's records at the Braga Brothers collection in Gainesville, Florida, have made similar arguments,

including Ayala, *American Sugar Kingdom*; Dye, *Cuban Sugar in the Age of Mass Production*; Lauriault, "Virgin Soil"; Marconi Braga, "No Other Law but Supply and Demand"; and Moyano Fraga, "*Central*-Colono Relations within the Cuban Sugar Industry."

66 "Study Made January 22, 1913, Relative to Colonos at FRANCISCO," BBC, RG 2, series 10, file: Miscellaneous.

67 Special meeting of the board of directors, May 13, 1919, BBC, series 90, minute book 3, as cited in Lauriault, "Virgin Soil," 346–47.

68 *Memoria de la Asociación de Colonos de los Centrales "Chaparra" y "Delicias" Correspondiente a los años 1924 a 1925 y 1925 a 1926.*

69 R. B. Wood, 6 October 1930, APLT, CASC, leg. 41, exp. 473.

70 Ibid. Although neither the colonos nor company officials mention any colono associations between 1906 and 1924, a cictation by Jorge Ibarra provides evidence of an association during the years 1915/1916. Ibarra's appendix mentions the *Memoria de la Asociación de Colonos de Chaparra y Delicias de 1915/1916* published in 1917 by La Moderna Poesía in Havana. The source was not at the National Library or in the archives or library of Las Tunas, and Jorge Ibarra, whom I thank for trying to assist me in this matter, has not been able to locate his notes regarding its contents or whereabouts.

71 The *Cuba Review*'s Havana correspondent, George Reno offered an interesting observation regarding such political ties in his September 1925 editorial: "The [cooperative spirit between colono and company] as a rule, has prevailed, and would probably continue were it not for a disturbing element in the person of some local politician who, in order to gain fame and the good will of his constituents, poses as a protector and advocate of the rights or interests of the colonos. This advocate, who usually is a provincial office holder or a Representative in Congress, informs the colonos that if they will all work together, and follow his leadership, he will compel the companies . . . to give the colonos a larger share of the returns . . . The politician has everything to gain and nothing to lose." *Cuba Review*, vol. 23, September 1925, 10–11. Reno's observation reflects the changing politics within Cuba whereby nationalist rhetoric gave the electorate more power in the 1920s than they had had in the earlier republican years—politicians felt compelled to appeal to colonos, and colonos appealed to or became politicians themselves.

72 The colonos included a promise to give the company 40 cents out of the $2.75 for their cultivation accounts kept by the company—an increase from the previous 25 cents allocated for that purpose. They agreed to pay interest, but only on debts above $36 per acre (versus the previous amount of $18). They also demanded that burned cane be received without penalty, unless the cane was in bad condition, in which case the colono would be notified one day in advance by the field inspector. A final demand was for the cane to be appraised by *two* technicians, one hired by the colono and the other by the company (to prevent company abuse).

73 As mentioned earlier, Chaparra and Delicias had secured permission from the government to import large numbers of temporary workers for the harvest, pri-

marily from the British and Dutch West Indies. The company brought the workers by boat, and then distributed them among the colonos to work as field hands. At Chaparra and Delicias, the colonos had to pay for part of the transportation costs.

74 "Notes prepared in anticipation of conference between R. B. Wood, E. A. Horné, and Rosales y Lavedán (Arturo Mañas), regarding *Colono Situation—Chaparra and Delicias*," Havana, 4 February 1931, APLT, CASC, leg. 41, exp. 473.

75 The capitalized text is in the original.

76 Urbino Ochoa et al., "Las primeras luchas obreras en los centrales Chaparra y Delicias," 4.

77 Mayor of Puerto Padre to provincial governor, Santiago, 25 February 1925, STGO, GP, leg. 1706, exp. 18; Fernández, "Historia del movimiento obrero del Central Antonio Guiteras (antes Delicias)," 10–13; and Urbino Ochoa et al., *Datos para la historia*, 3–6.

78 Fernández, "Historia del movimiento obrero del Central Antonio Guiteras (antes Delicias)," 11; Asociación Nacional de la Industria Azucarera, *Memoria de la labor realizada durante el Segundo año de su fundación de 1924 a 1925*.

79 Luis Merconchini, interview by Víctor Marrero, Delicias, 21 August 1990, Delicias, tape recording, OHLT.

80 As will be discussed later, the colonos probably did manage to keep field workers from organizing in some cases. One Chaparra field worker told historian Víctor Marrero that some colonos used paternalism effectively to keep workers from organizing, and some used force. Barry Carr has also theorized that factory workers faced fewer barriers to organization than field because they tended to be more racially and ethnically homogeneous, more literate, and they worked and lived in larger, concentrated groups. Luis Merconchini [labor organizer], interview by Víctor Marrero, Delicias, 21 August 1990, Delicias, tape recording, OHLT; Carr, "Mill Occupations and Soviets," 129–58.

81 Of the workers, 5,046 were Cuban; 2,726 were from the British West Indies; 1,008 were from Haiti; and 956 were from the Dutch Islands. *Agricultura y Zootecnia*, July 1924, 39.

82 José Rodríguez Alejo, interview by Víctor Marrero and Olga Cabrera, Chaparra/Delicias, 15 September 1992.

83 The colono's name was Vitalianos Peña. Harold Griffith Guana, interview by Víctor Marrero, Chaparra/Delicias, 15 July 1991.

84 Ibid.

85 José Rodríguez Alejo, interview by Víctor Marrero and Olga Cabrera, Chaparra/Delicias, 15 September 1992, tape recording, OHLT. There are several repeats and remarkably similar names among the roughly five hundred names contained in the post-harvest "repatriation" lists of 1924 from Chaparra. See "Relación de Inmigrantes del Caribe Oriental Repatriados . . . por cuenta de la Chaparra Sugar Company," lists dated August–October 1924, ANC, AIC, leg. 4, exp. 45. Unfortunately, these lists have gone missing from the ANC. I thank

Jorge Giovannetti-Torres and César Ayala for sending their notes on the lists to me.

86 "Nos sumamos temáticamente a esta huelga, sin saber en que consistía la huelga . . . La caña que estaba en el suelo no subo." Luis Merconchini, interview by Víctor Marrero, Delicias, 21 August 1990, tape recording, OHLT.

87 A letter from a Manatí administrator to Manuel Rionda suggested as early as 18 October 1924 that efforts were being made among field workers to unionize. "The labor situation at Chaparra has recently taken a turn for the worse. Through Mr. Perez Puelles, Mayor of Puerto Padre, who was here yesterday, I learned that not only the colonos have formed a union but also the factory and railroad laborers of Chaparra, and now it appears that efforts are being made in the direction of also unionizing the cane cutters." Letter no. 5 from Morell to Manuel Rionda, BBC, RG 2, series 10, file: Labor Trouble, Manatí Sugar Company.

88 Although the sources do not mention it, this cane was likely previously con-tracted to Chaparra and Delicias. Provincial governor, Santiago, to minister of the interior, Havana, 17 March 1925, STGO, GP, leg. 1706, exp. 18.

89 In an interesting parallel that may indicate wider use of the ethnic-strikebreaker strategy, the administrators at Rionda's Manatí mill just west of Chaparra brought from 150 to 200 Chinese men "as a precautionary measure" in October 1924, when dock workers at that mill began to organize. The UTIA and colono association at Puerto Padre raised Rionda's concern that unionization would spread to Manatí. Morrell, auxiliary administrator at Manatí, Oriente, to Manuel Rionda, president, New York, 9 October 1924, BBC, RG 2, series 10, file: Labor Trouble, Manatí Sugar Company.

90 There was no date, and I have been unable to determine which paper it was, but it was definitely published during the strike (21 February–12 April 1925). The article is on display in the Neo-Colonial Republic Room at the Museum of the Revolu-tion in Havana.

91 Puyol to provincial governor, Santiago, STGO, GP, leg. 1706, exp. 18.

92 Ariz, Bertot, and La Pera to provincial governor, Santiago, STGO, GP, leg. 1706, exp. 18.

93 Decree, 12 April 1925, STGO, GP, leg. 308, exp. 15.

94 Leopoldo Nápoles Diaz "Mirin," interview by Maritza Labrada Verdecia, 18 No-vember 1987, Puerto Padre, cited in Urbino Ochoa et al., "Las primeras luchas obreras en los centrales Chaparra y Delicias," 7.

95 Mayor of Gibara to provincial governor, Santiago, 1 June 1925, STGO, GP, leg. 1706, exp. 19 (Santa Lucía).

96 Urbino Ochoa, "El movimiento obrero y comunista en el territorio de la actual Provincia de Holguín," 1.

97 Emphasis mine. The story is secondhand—the Union Secretary, Mariano Agu-ilera, told it to José Aviles. Interview with José Aviles by Jacobo Urbino Ochoa, Archivo Histórico Provincial de Holguín, Interview Collection, 3.

98 *Willett and Gray Statistical Sugar Trade Journal*, 30 May 1925, 226.

99   Zanetti and García, *Sugar and Railroads*, 319.

100 Oscar Zanetti and Alejandro García make this argument, ibid., 319–20.

101 Fernández, "Historia del movimiento obrero del Central Antonio Guiteras (antes Delicias)," 11. The correspondence in the Braga Brothers Collection at the University of Florida, Gainesville, has many such communications, as does the Cuban-American Sugar Collection in Las Tunas.

102 Charles Ingram (former worker at Delicias), interview by Maritza Labrada, 30 October 1987, cited in Urbino et al., "Las primeras luchas obreras en los centrales Chaparra y Delicias," 8.

103 *Agricultura y Zootecnia*, July 1924, 39–40.

104 The colonos also lobbied senators and representatives from Oriente to support or vote down legislation that affected them, the almanac publishing several cases whereby the officers voted as the colonos had requested. This, again, demonstrates the strength of nationalist politics whereby colonos had more power during the populist era of the mid-1920s.

105 Manuel Rionda to Francisco Alonso, copied to Rionda nephews, 5 October 1925, BBC, RG 2, series 10, file: Tuinucú: Asociación de Colonos.

106 The lengthy correspondence is contained in ANC, Fondo Secretaría de la Presidencia, leg. 97, exp. 1.

107 This was the case with the Cuban Cane mills, whose agents Aurelio Portuondo and Higinio Fanjul visited Machado in December 1925 to ask him to order their colonos back to work. Two days after their visit, on December 5, Machado issued a decree that the harvest must begin in five days, but the same decree acknowledged that the colonos had "certain problems for which solutions must be found," and these were submitted to an arbitration committee made up of eighteen colono representatives, ten mill owners, and four government representatives on 7 December. F. Gerard Smith to Charles Hayden, Havana, 8 December 1925, BBC, RG 2, series 10c, Sugar Industry in Camagüey Province, Cuba, 1899–1926, cited in McAvoy, "Lion's Tail, Mouse's Head," chap. 10, 10.

108 Thomas, *Cuba, the Pursuit of Freedom*, 568, n. 19.

109 Borges, *Compilación ordenada y completa de la legislación cubana*, 1:584, cited in Aguilar, *Cuba 1933*, 56.

110 Guerra y Sánchez, *La industria azucarera de Cuba*, as translated in Pollitt, "The Cuban Sugar Economy and the Great Depression," 13–15. See also Santamaría-García, *Sin azúcar, no hay país*.

111 Pérez, *Cuba*, 250–51.

SEVEN Revolutionary Rejection

1   By "public theater," I mean physical or symbolic demonstrations of power designed to assert control and impress the general public. Chapter 5 discusses how this "public theater" played out at the local level with patron mansions on one side and "counter-theater" worker resistance on the other.

2 Whitney, *State and Revolution in Cuba,* 72.

3 E. Hidalgo, chief of Policia Jurada (Company Guard), to R. B. Wood, general manager, 2 September 1931, APLT, CASC, leg. 47, exp. 535.

4 Pérez, *Army Politics in Cuba,* 58–59.

5 Tabares del Real, *Guiteras,* 154.

6 So named because each cell, made up of about ten members, would operate independently of the others so that if Machado's police caught one, those remaining would not be detected. The leading cell was "A."

7 Whitney, *State and Revolution in Cuba,* offers the most detailed English-language study of these organizations.

8 Emphasis is mine. Harry F. Guggenheim to secretary of state, 18 February 1932, USNA, RG 59, 837.00/3230, cited in Pérez, *Army Politics in Cuba,* 64.

9 Cubanaco suffered a loss of $5,547,159 in 1921 but made cumulative earnings of 32,271,934 from 1922 through 1929. Not until 1930 did it suffer another net loss (of $1,362,437). "The Cuban-American Sugar Company: First Mortgage Collateral Sinking Fund Gold Bonds 8% Series due 1936," 15 March 1931, HB, HCR, folder: Cuban-American Sugar Company. Compañia Cubana, a subsidy of the American-owned Cuba Company, continued to report profits in 1928 and 1929—$235,035.64 and $47,298.34, respectively—but recorded net losses from 1930 through 1933. It did not return to a net profit on its sugarmill operations until the year ending 30 June 1934 (the profit was $50,396.80). "Compañia Cubana Annual Reports for Fiscal Years 1928 to 1934," series 7, box 156 in Cuba Company Archives, Special Collection, College Park Libraries, University of Maryland.

10 Manuel Rionda to Oliver Doty, 31 January 1929, BBC, RG 2, series 10, file: Tuinucú: C-AL.

11 Oliver Doty to Manuel Rionda, Tuinucú, 14 January 1930, BBC, RG 2, series 10, file: Tuinucú: C-AL.

12 R. B. Wood to directors, New York, 6 October 1930, APLT, CASC, leg. 41, exp. 473.

13 R. B. Wood, E. A. Horné, and Rosales y Lavedán (Arturo Mañas) regarding *Colono Situation—Chaparra and Delicias,* Havana, 4 February 1931, APLT, CASC, leg. 41, exp. 473.

14 July 25, 1931, APLT, CASC, leg. 41, exp. 474.

15 Cited in Asociación Nacional de la Industria Azucarera, *Memoria de la labor realizada durante el Segundo año de su fundación de 1924 a 1925,* 194.

16 The colonos had an easy time playing the "nationalist" card because approximately 1,390 of them were Cuban (5 more were North American, and 2 or 3 were Spanish). *Agricultura y Zootecnia,* July 1924, 39; *El Colono,* June–July 1931, 19; and APLT, CASC, Fuera de Caja no. 224, leg. 41, exp. 474.

17 *El Colono,* June–July 1931. It was Director Vicente Grau who interviewed Menocal, describing him as "Ex-Presidente de la República, Mayor General del Ejército Libertador," and "Fundador de los Centrales Chaparra, Delicias, Palma y Sta. Maria." In the interview, Menocal takes credit for establishing the minimum of $2.25 for

4 arrobas of sugar (for 100 arrobas of cane), and states that at his Palma and Santa Marta mills, he established the same minimum but guaranteed even more— 5 arrobas of sugar per 100 arrobas of cane. "I believe that we should protect the colonos, as best we can, guaranteeing them a price that allows them to work."

18 APLT, CASC, leg. 40, exp. 474.

19 Ibid.

20 I use "brothers" to emphasize how opportunistic the larger colonos were about claiming that they were "all one class" of farmers when making demands to the president or talking to the press when, in fact, large disparities remained between the huge landowner who subcontracted colonias and the small farmer who tended the colonia with his family. Most colonos were male, but there were a few cases of widows or daughters who inherited colonias and used their sons or hired help to run them.

21 APLT, CASC, leg. 7, exp. 77.

22 Emphasis is mine. R. B. Wood to General Maxwell, South Porto Rico Sugar Company, APLT, CASC, leg. 7, exp. 77.

23 The Spanish reads, "Casi me atrevo a afirmar que también cuente con la del Gobierno." APLT, CASC, leg. 41, exp. 474.

24 Eugenio Molinet to R. B. Wood, 24 June 1931, APLT, CASC, leg. 7, exp. 77.

25 Oliver Doty to Manuel Rionda, 22 July 1926, BBC, RG 2, series 10, file: Tuinucú: Improvements (Capital) and Extraordinary Repairs.

26 Monthly salaries totaled $137,426.00 during the dead season of 1927 versus only $25,242.00 during the dead season of 1932.

27 Manuel Rionda, New York, to Oliver Doty, Tuinucú, 27 December 1930, BBC, RG 2, series 10, file: Tuinucú: Doty, Oliver K., Correspondence (1931).

28 Manuel Rionda, New York, to Oliver Doty, Tuinucú, 14 January 1931, BBC, RG 2, series 10, file: Tuinucú: Doty, Oliver K., Correspondence (1931). Testimony from Arquímedes Valdivia suggests that the cart-drivers in fact deserved more money, for they had one of the most demanding jobs at the sugarmills. "My grandfather [a colono] felt terrible waking his cart-driver up in the morning because he barely had time to sleep. When the others finished their work, the driver had to spend another two hours feeding the oxen, and then he had to wake up before the others to prepare the oxen again. Life was very hard. There were four, or sometimes six bulls for each cart, and he had to prepare them all." Arquímedes Valdivia Hernández, interview by the author, Tuinucú, 12 May 2000.

29 R. B. Wood to Maxwell, South Porto Rico Sugar Company, 26 May 1932, APLT, CASC, leg. 7, exp. 77.

30 Punta Alegre Sugar Company to R. B. Wood, 15 September 1932, APLT, CASC, leg. 7, exp. 77.

31 PRO, FO, 371/16575, doc. 304.

32 Rojas, Las luchas obreras en el central Tacajó, 57.

33 Les années trente à Cuba, 34.

34 Carr, "Mill Occupations and Soviets," 132.

35 Harold Griffith Guana, interview by Víctor Marrero, Chaparra, 15 July 1991, tape recording, OHLT.

36 E. A. Wakefield, "Political Situation in Nuevitas Consular District," 6 February 1931, USNA, RG 84, Havana Post Records, pt. 10, 1931, 800 Cuba, as cited in Carr, "Identity, Class, and Nation," 105.

37 Ibid., 104.

38 PRO, FO 369, K7511/7084/214, cited in Carr, "Identity, Class, and Nation," 105. Robert Whitney, Barry Carr, Marc McLeod, and Jorge Giovannetti-Torres, among others, have emphasized that British West Indian subjects wrote frequently to the British Embassy in Cuba, leading Cuban authorities and many mill owners to favor the importation of less literate and "connected" Haitians. As shown in chapter 5, Cubanaco opted for approximately 50 percent *Ingleses* during the greatest period of dependence on immigrant field labor, from 1917 through 1928, but tended to avoid Jamaicans, who were the best able to defend themselves through their literacy, mobility, and access to Jamaican consuls.

39 Manuel Rionda to Oliver Doty, 22 September 1930, BBC, RG 2, series 10, file: Tuinucú: Doty, Oliver K., Letters.

40 The original letter is in broken English. Chaparra, Cándido Fernández to H. M. Hicks, Auxiliary General Manager, 20 July 1932, Chaparra, APLT, CASC, leg. 50, exp. 558.

41 Yacht Club, Havana to president of Nautical Club, Chaparra, 26 July 1932, APLT, CASC, leg. 50, exp. 558.

42 "SNOIA: Proyecto de Resolución para la II Conferencia Nacional," 16 June 1933, Instituto de Historica, Fondo: 1er Partido Marxista Leninista y otros, leg.: Organización de los Trabajadores Sindicales Nacionales, exp.: SNOIA (hereafter IH, SNOIA), doc. 1/8:87/3.1/1–6.

43 Cited in Marrero Zaldívar, "Dulce amargo de una historia obrera."

44 Charles W. Hackett, "Mexican Constitutional Changes," *Current History* (May 1933): 214.

45 Club Atlético Chaparra to R. B. Wood, Chaparra, 30 March 1933, APLT, CASC, leg. 50, exp. 558.

46 Carr, "Mill Occupations and Soviets," 133.

47 *Les années trente à Cuba*, 34.

48 "IV Conferencia Nacional de la Unidad Sindical, CNOC, "La Situación actual, analisis de las luchas y tareas del movimiento sindical revolucionario," 6, Instituto de Historica: Conferencia Nacional de Obreros Cubanos (hereafter IH, CNOC), 1/8:7/2.1/56–64.

49 For more on how to "read" the actions of the popular classes, see Scott, *Domination and the Arts of Resistance*; Thompson, "The Moral Economy of the English Crowd in the Eighteenth Century," 76–136.

50 Herring, "The Downfall of Machado," 17–18.

51 Lefevre, "Soldier and Student Control in Cuba," 36.

52 *Time*, 28 August 1933.

53 Strode, "Behind the Cuban Revolt," 204–7.

54 Ibid.

55 Thomson, "The Cuban Revolution: The Fall of Machado," 259.

56 Cited in McAvoy, *Sugar Baron*, 256.

57 For more on the impressively strong student and women's movements, see Whitney, *State and Revolution in Cuba*; Stoner, *From the House to the Street*.

58 McAvoy, *Sugar Baron*, 258.

59 Pérez, *Cuba*, 268.

60 The former worker Ursinio Rojas explains that this exhausting work schedule, combined with the noise and heat at the mills, had a terrible effect on workers' nerves and bodies. Sickness was very common. Rojas, *Las luchas obreras en el central Tacajó*, 59–70.

61 Córdova, *Clase trabajadora y movimiento sindical en Cuba*, 204.

62 Carr, "Identity, Class, and Nation," 103–9.

63 The latter was the same Federación de Obreros de la Habana that had helped Chaparra and Delicias publish their protest to Zayas in 1925.

64 Whitney, *State and Revolution in Cuba*, 105–7.

65 Rita Díaz, interview by the author, Havana, 10 September 2006.

66 "Strikes by the Sugar Workers in Province of Santa Clara," Alexander Knox, American consul, Cienfuegos, 28 August 1933, USNA, RG 59, 837.5045/44.

67 Portuondo Moret, *El soviet de Tacajó*, 69, cited in Carr, "Mill Occupations and Soviets," 135.

68 *Soviets* were grassroots workplace and community councils named after the 1905 and 1917 Russian revolutions.

69 "Los Grandes Centrales," 13.

70 Carr, "Mill Occupations and Soviets," 139–58; Urbino Ochoa et al., *Datos para la historia*, 120–37.

71 Adapted from the Spanish and English versions of the song as found on www .angelfire.com/pq/svechka/#CASTELLANO.

72 Carr, "Mill Occupations and Soviets," 155.

73 Hine was the "neat freak" administrator whom workers ridiculed in the anecdote cited in chapter 5.

74 Manuel Rionda to Bernardo Braga, London, 15 September 1933, BBC, RG 2, series 4, vol. 3.

75 Higinio Fanjul to Aurelio Portuondo, 14 September 1933, BBC, RG 2, series 11, file: Correspondencia con Higinio Fanjul, Manuel Rasco, and Cuban Trading Company, Havana.

76 Manuel Rionda, president, Tuinucú Sugar Company, to Tuinucú [Comité Central], 11 September 1933, BBC, RG 2, series 4, vol. 3.

77 Transcript of telephone conversation, Manuel Rionda, New York, to Bernardo Braga, London, 18 September 1933, BBC, RG 2, series 4, vol. 3.

78 Manuel Rionda to Bernardo Braga, London, 26 September 1933, BBC, RG 2, series 4, vol. 3.

79 Higinio Fanjul to Aurelio Portuondo, 25 September 1933, BBC, RG 2, series 11.

80 Rojas, *Las luchas obreras en el central Tacajó*, 83. Also Grant Watson to Foreign Office, London, enclosing letter from A. Hopton Jones, 16 September 1933, PRO, FO, 371, A 7120/255/14, cited in Carr, "Mill Occupations and Soviets," 153.

81 Manuel Rionda, New York, to José Rionda, Havana, 18 September 1933, BBC, RG 2, series 2, vol. 78.

82 The word he used that I have translated as "feeling" is *sentimiento*. José Rionda to Manuel Rionda, 30 September 1933, BBC, RG 2, series 10, file: Tuinucú, Labor Troubles.

83 Arquímedes Valdivia told me this anecdote about his father, Agustín, in an interview, 1 February 2000, Tuinucú.

84 Oliver Doty to Sindicato de Obreros y Empleados de la Industria Azucarera, Sección del Central Tuinucú, Tuinucú, 11 January 1935, BBC, RG 2, series 10, file: Tuinucú, Labor Troubles.

85 Manuel Rionda, New York, to Dr. Santiago Urías, Gijón, Spain, 12 March 1934, BBC, RG 2, series 2, vol. 78.

86 Luis Merconchini, interview by Víctor Marrero, Delicias, 21 August 1990, tape recording, OHLT; Fernández, "Historia del movimiento obrero del central Antonio Guiteras (antes Delicias)." U.S. records confirm the workers' story. On September 6 the U.S. Ambassador Welles wrote to the Secretary of State, "General rioting throughout the Chaparra and Delicias sugar estates belonging to the Cuban-American Sugar Company broke out yesterday and in view of their belief that the situation was completely out of control the Manager Mr. R. B. Wood and the Assistant Manager Mr. Hicks took refuge on a British steamer." Welles, Havana, to secretary of state, Washington, D.C., 6 September 1933, USNA, RG 59, 837.00/3765.

87 "SNOIA Report on the Provincial Conference of Oriente, 17–18 September 1933," 19 September 1933, IH, SNOIA, doc. 1/8:87/15.1/1–10.

88 Cuba Embassy Post Records, pt. 12 800, Cuba 1933—Reports from Ships, commanding officer *U.S.S. Dupont*, 8 October 1933, to commander, Special Service Squadron, Station File at Puerto Padre, Cuba, 27 September–7 October 1933, entry dated 30 September 1933, USNA, RG 84, as cited in Carr, "Mill Occupations and Soviets," 156.

89 The myriad manifestos can be found in STGO, Tribunales de Defensa Nacional, "Juicios establecidos por propaganda subversiva" files; APL, CASC, esp. leg. 197, exp. 2961, leg. 197, exp. 3870; ANC, Fondo Especial; and IH, SNOIA. For more on the communist stance, see Carr, "From Caribbean Backwater to Revolutionary Opportunity"; Whitney, *State and Revolution in Cuba*. For more on Trotskyists, see Fernández, *Cuban Anarchism*; Shaffer, *Anarchism and Countercultural Politics in Early Twentieth-Century Cuba*; and Soler, "El Trotskismo en Cuba."

90 Carr, "Mill Occupations and Soviets," 156.

91 Tuinucú Sugar Company to Comité Conjunto, Sección de Tuinucú, 26 September 1933, BBC, RG 2, series 10, file: Tuinucú, Labor Troubles.

92 Tabares del Real, *Guiteras*, 197, 282–83.

93 "Memorandum sobre las huelgas en los centrales Chaparra y Delicias y la ocu-
pación de los mismos por el gobierno," Joseph B. Harris, manager, Cuban-
American Sugar Company, Havana, to Jefferson Caffery, special representative
of the President of the United States, American Embassy, Havana, 23 December
1933, USNA, RG 59, stack 250, row 26, decimal file 1900–1939, box 1339, 337.115
SM/665–337.1153 CU.

94 Grant Watson to Sir John Simon, 19 December 1933, PRO, FO, 277/226.

95 "Tribunal de Defensa Nacional. Juicios establecidos por propaganda subversiva,"
Chaparra Chapter of SNOIA manifesto, n.d., STGO, "Tribunal de Defensa Nacional. Juicios establecidos por propaganda subversiva."

96 Emphasis mine. U.S. Chargé d'Affaires Samuel S. Dickson to secretary of state, 30
December 1933, USNA, RG 59, stack 250, row 26, decimal file 1900–1939, box 1339,
337.115 SM/665–337.1153 CU.

97 Samuel S. Dickson, chargé d'affaires ad interim to secretary of state, 28 December
1933, USNA, RG 59, stack 250, row 26, decimal file 1900–1939, box 1339, 337.115
SM/665–337.1153 CU.

98 Sumner Welles to assistant secretary, Department of State, 9 January 1934,
USNA, RG 59, stack 250, row 26, decimal file 1900–1939, box 1339, 337.115 SM/665–
337.1153 CU.

99 Jefferson Caffery to secretary of state, 11 January 1934, USNA, RG 59, stack 250,
row 26, decimal file 1900–1939, box 1339, 337.115 SM/665–337.1153 CU.

100 Joseph B. Harris, Havana, to George E. Keiser, president, Cuban-American Sugar
Company, 11 January 1934, USNA, RG 59, stack 250, row 26, decimal file 1900–1939,
box 1339, 337.115 SM/665–337.1153 CU.

101 Domínguez, *Cuba*, 62.

102 Grant Watson to Sir John Simon, PRO, FO, 371/16575, and surrounding documents.

103 "Memorandum for the Minister re: the Situation at Chaparra," Grant Watson to
Sir John Simon, 30 December 1933, PRO, FO, 277/226.

104 "Current Wages in the Antilla Consular District," 8 January 1934, USNA, RG 59,
837.5041/63.

105 Sumner Welles to secretary of state, 5 October 1933, 837.00/4131, USNA, RG 59,
cited in Pérez, *Army Politics in Cuba*, 97.

106 Sumner Welles to secretary of state, 7 October 1933, 837.00/4146, cited in Pérez,
Army Politics in Cuba, 97.

107 Cited in McAvoy, *Sugar Baron*, 259.

108 "Cuba's Procession of Presidents," *Literary Digest*, 27 January 1934, 14.

109 Thomson, "The Cuban Revolution: Reform and Reaction," 276.

110 Grant Watson to Sir John Simon, Havana, 29 January 1934, PRO, FO, A/1127/
29/14, no. 13 (confidential), cited in Whitney, *State and Revolution in Cuba*, 121.

111 For the case of Nicaragua, see Gould, *To Lead as Equals*. For the Dominican Republic, see Turits, *Foundations of Despotism*. For Brazil, see French, *The Brazilian*

Workers' ABC; Wolfe, *Working Women, Working Men*; and Weinstein, *For Social Peace in Brazil*. For Chile, see Klubock, *Contested Communities*. For Argentina, see Brennan, *Peronism and Argentina*; James, *Resistance and Integration*. For Mexico, see Hamilton, *The Limits of State Autonomy*; these are only a few of the many studies that describe the growth of populism and state intervention in post-1930s Latin America.

EIGHT The Populist Compact

1 Decreto-Ley no. 813, signed by President Carlos Mendieta and Secretary of Justice Raúl de Cárdenas, *Gaceta Oficial* 3 *(extraordinaria)*, 15 January 1935, STGO, GP, leg. 312, exp. 10. The "National Defense Tribunals" decree law passed on 6 March 1934. Buell et al., *Problems of the New Cuba*, 15–16, 202–203. Joanna Beth Swanger describes these tribunals in relation to coffee workers in "Lands of Rebellion."

2 Secret Police Agent Francisco Micó Urrutia's "Informe" about cane burnings at Chaparra and Delicias, forwarded by Rafael Balart Perera, chief of Secret Police, Santiago, to governor of Santiago, 22 March 1936, STGO, GP, leg. 312, exp. 16.

3 I discuss the historiography of populism in the introduction. Robert H. Dix, "Populism," 29–52, coined the terms "authoritarian populism" and "democratic populism" but did not include Cuba in his discussion. I define them more carefully through the corparatist metaphor of the body.

4 Domínguez, *Cuba*, 78–79. The first section of this chapter draws ideas from Whitney's detailed study of the 1930s and 1940s in chaps. 6 and 7 of *State and Revolution in Cuba*, and Pérez's *Army Politics in Cuba*.

5 For the case of Getúlio Vargas and other populists in Brazil, see French, *The Brazilian Workers' ABC*; Weinstein, *For Social Peace in Brazil*. For the case of Anastasio Somoza in Nicaragua, see Gould, *To Lead as Equals*; Walter, *The Regime of Anastasio Somoza*. For Rafael Trujillo in the Dominican Republic, see Derby, *The Dictator's Seduction*; Turits, *Foundations of Despotism*.

6 For the case of Cárdenas in Mexico, see Córdova, *La política de masas del cardenismo*; Hamilton, *The Limits of State Autonomy*. These books focus on the "big picture"; many other excellent, more recent studies look at the complex effects of Cárdenas's populist rule in the provinces.

7 For more on these other groups, see Domínguez, *Cuba*; Paterson, *Contesting Castro*; Suchlicki, *University Students and Revolution in Cuba*; Whitney, *State and Revolution in Cuba*; and Pérez, *Army and Politics in Cuba*, which offers a strong analysis of the middle classes, as do many other studies by this author.

8 True to the elite pattern discussed in chapter 2, he joined late in the war for independence after the United States intervened and it was safe to assume that Cubans would triumph over Spaniards.

9   Domínguez, *Cuba*, 78.

10 Mendieta ended the government intervention at Chaparra and Delicias, yet he also solidified the legal procedures for future interventions of private companies when public needs clashed with company intransigence. Zanetti, "The Workers' Movement and Labor Regulation in the Cuban Sugar Industry," 189–191; Sims, "Cuba's Organized Labor," 46.

11 On Getúlio Vargas of Brazil, see Levine, *Father of the Poor?* On Anastasio Somoza of Nicaragua, see Gould, *To Lead as Equals*; Walter, *The Regime of Anastasio Somoza*. On Rafael Trujillo of the Dominican Republic, see Derby, *The Dictator's Seduction*; Turits, *Foundations of Despotism*.

12 By "mixed-race," observers usually suggest that he had Chinese, indigenous, or Afro-Cuban heritage. See Argote-Freyre, *Fulgencio Batista*; Whitney, *State and Revolution in Cuba*, 122.

13 These are the events as told in Pérez, *Army Politics in Cuba*, 79–93. There is a certain level of disagreement among historians as to who approached whom first—the students, or the sergeants.

14 The newly commissioned officers included 363 sergeants, 26 corporals, 32 privates, 28 warrant officers, and 63 civilians. Pérez, *Army Politics in Cuba*, 79–93.

15 Although "the military" is sometimes portrayed monolithically in Latin American history, several excellent studies have delved into the battles between the conservative "right" and the (usually junior) "left" within the armed forces. The studies that informed my research are Loveman, *For La Patria*; for Argentina, James, *Resistance and Integration*, and Deutsch, *The Argentine Right*; for El Salvador, Stanley, *The Protection Racket State*; for Guatemala, Gleijeses, *Shattered Hope*, 16–22; and for Cuba, Pérez, *Army Politics in Cuba*.

16 Jacobo Arbenz, who was president from 1950 to 1954, was initially part of the army, but he resigned from his post as defense minister before running for the presidency and he worked with civilian political parties during his term in office. Gleijeses, *Shattered Hope*, 74.

17 Pérez, *Army Politics in Cuba*, 102–3.

18 Ibid., 103–7; Domínguez, *Cuba*, 78; Sims, "Cuba's Organized Labor," 46.

19 Pérez, *Army Politics in Cuba*, 104.

20 William P. Blocker to American Embassy, 29 November 1935, file (1935) 800, American Consulate, Santiago de Cuba, Miscellaneous Correspondence, USNA, RG 84, cited ibid., 105.

21 Major E. W. Timberlake, military attaché, G-2 reports dated 1 December 1937, 16 February 1938, and 5 May 1938, file 2012–133 (84, 86, 88), USNA, RG 165, cited in Pérez, *Army Politics in Cuba*, 106.

22 Russell B. Porter, "Dual Regime Denied by Batista," *New York Times*, 5 July 1936, 1–2, as cited in Whitney, *State and Revolution in Cuba*, 133–34.

23 *Havana Post*, 23 June 1937, as cited ibid., 149.

24 Whitney, *State and Revolution in Cuba*, 125.

25 "Circular sobre la lucha contra Decreto Ley de prohibición de huelgas," n.d., IH, SNOIA, 1/8:87/6.1/13–18.

26 I say "Cuban workers" rather than "workers," because many foreign workers ended up losing their jobs when the government began to apply the 50 percent law more strictly in the late 1930s. These conclusions are based on a reading of the series entitled "Sindicatos" from the 1930s through the 1950s in APLT, CASC. As mentioned earlier, workers managed to force Cubanaco to rehire all of the labor activists dismissed between 1925 and 1934, and they established a job ladder and dismissal procedures that the company had to follow. The company ended up having to bribe people to leave their jobs to get rid of specific positions because government legislation made it nearly impossible to cut jobs from the mills.

27 The two demands regarding midwives read, "Chaparra, Delicias, Vazquez and Cayo Juan Claro [shall have] midwives paid for by the company and the colonos" and "Midwives will be furnished with the necessary equipment and materials required in their profession."

28 National Syndicate of Laborers of the Sugar Industry, Syndical Section of Chaparra—Oriente, "Bases Which Will Be Presented to the Cuban-American Sugar Company, Owner of Centrals Chaparra and Delicias, by the Various Syndicates of this Region," enc. no. 4, dispatch 512, 13 February 1934, Embassy at Havana, USNA, RG 59, stack 250, row 26, decimal file 1900–1939, box 1339, 337.115 SM/665–337.1153-CU.

29 Oliver Doty, Tuinucú, to Manuel Rionda, New York, 29 May 1935, and Manuel Rionda, New York, to Oliver Doty, Tuinucú, 4 June 1935, BBC, RG 2, series 20, file: Tuinucú: Doty, Oliver K., Correspondence (1935).

30 Memorandum on 26 January 1934 telephone conversation between Mr. Harris in Havana and Mr. Keiser in New York, USNA, RG 59, stack 250, row 26, decimal file 1900–1939, box 1339, 337.1153-CU.

31 Memorandum on 15 February phone conversation between R. B. Wood and Joseph B. Harris, Havana representative, Cubanaco, submitted by H. Freeman Matthews, chargé d'affaires ad interim to secretary of state, USNA, RG 59, stack 250, row 26, decimal file 1900–1939, box 1339, 337.115 SM/665–337.1153-CU.

32 This conclusion is based on a comparison of the Jurado files in APLT, CASC.

33 Testimony by Manuel Suarez Gómez in Colectivo de autores, *Memorias de un viejo mundo azucarero*, 40. The detail about the Texan horse is from Fidel Castro's memories of growing up in Oriente province. "Key address by Dr. Fidel Castro Ruz, President of the Republic of Cuba, Major General Calixto García Square, Holguin," 1 June 2002, http://www.cuba.cu/gobierno/discursos/2002/ing/f010602i.html.

34 Eladio Santiago Serrano and Arquímedes Valdivia Hernández, interview by the author, Tuinucú, 12 May 2000; Rita Díaz, interview by the author, Havana, 10 September 2006.

35 W. J. Slattery, USNA, RG 38, Records of the Office of the Chief of Naval Operations, box 1007, H-11-a (7114A-22885), NM-63, entry 98.

36 Chaparra and Delicias Association of Colonos to the president of the Republic, 18 March 1936, STGO, GP, leg. 312, exp. 16. Cubanaco may have lost some of its quota to the smaller Cuban mills that nationalist legislation was favoring. This legislation will be further discussed below.

37 One of the congressmen who proposed the 1936 bill was Eduardo Puyol Canal; perhaps the same "Colonel Eduardo Puyol" who mediated between workers and companies under Zayas then Machado in 1925 had made it to the status of colono. Martínez-Alier and Martínez-Alier, *Cuba*, 78; Martínez-Alier, *Haciendas, Plantations, and Collective Farms*, 97.

38 The Spanish words that I translate as "enjoy" and "personally direct" are *disfrutar* and *dirigir personalmente*. Martínez-Alier, *Haciendas, Plantations, and Collective Farms*, 97, 112; Martínez-Alier and Martínez-Alier, *Cuba*, 78.

39 The historiography on Cárdenas is vast, and there is a great deal of debate about how many promises he was actually able to fulfill. Compared with the performances of Batista, Somoza, and Vargas, his accomplishments are impressive. In the 1930s, little evidence exists that Batista inspired the kind of individualistic bare-minimum populism that prompted hundreds of letters from humble citizens of Brazil to the "Father of the Poor." See Levine, *Father of the Poor?* Appendixes.

40 Miguel Mariano was José Miguel Gómez's nephew.

41 Pérez, *Army Politics in Cuba*, 108.

42 Whitney, *State and Revolution in Cuba*, 132.

43 Ibid., 133.

44 His n.b. reads, "While on this subject we asked you in our letter of August third if you could not arrange to reduce the expenses of the Hospital either by reduction in the number of people . . . or again if we could not secure some assistance from the appropriate governmental department." APLT, CASC, leg. 49, exp. 548.

45 As mentioned earlier, such letters would be difficult to find because the Batista presidential archives are not accessible, in contrast to those of populists such as Getúlio Vargas, Lázaro Cárdenas, and even Cuba's Gerardo Machado (recall the letters mentioned in chapter 6).

46 George E. Keiser to "Todas Asociaciones Instituciones Logias Centrales Chaparra Delicias Unidas Agrupaciones Padres Familias," 23 October 1939, APLT, CASC, leg. 49, exp. 548.

47 16 February 1942, APLT, CASC, leg. 49, exp. 548.

48 27 February 1942, APLT, CASC, leg. 49, exp. 548.

49 Ministro de Educación, Junta de Educación, Secretario Jorge Martínez Carmona to General Administrator, Chaparra, Delicias, and San Manuel, 15 April 1943, APLT, CASC, leg. 49, exp. 548.

50 Domínguez, *Cuba*, 71.

51 "Key Address by Dr. Fidel Castro Ruz, President of the Republic of Cuba, in Holguín Province," 1 June 2002, http://www.cuba.cu/gobierno/discursos/2002/ing/f010602i.html.

52 Portuondo, *Historia de Cuba*, 627.

53 Farber, *The Origins of the Cuban Revolution Reconsidered*, 20–21.

54 Ibid.

55 Ibid.; Domínguez, *Cuba*, 85.

56 The "officially" is there because sometimes companies disguised administration cane by inventing colonias for the paper trail; a few such cases existed at Tuinucú and Chaparra. Martínez-Alier and Martínez-Alier, *Cuba*, 81.

57 Ibid., 63.

58 Hoernel, "A Comparison of Sugar and Social Change in Puerto Rico and Oriente," 168.

59 Farber, *The Origins of the Cuban Revolution Reconsidered*, 11.

60 The U.S. quota added to an estimate of the amount of sugar to be sold domestically and in markets outside the United States.

61 Such "fascist" tendencies included the forceful suppression of opposition, belligerent nationalism, racism, and militarism. The international and domestic factors listed earlier and later are drawn from several sources, including Whitney, *State and Revolution in Cuba*; Zanetti, "The Workers' Movement and Labor Regulation in the Cuban Sugar Industry," 193.

62 The Comintern was an international communist organization founded in Moscow that advised Communist Party members abroad from 1919 to 1935. For more on communism in Cuba, see Carr, "From Caribbean Backwater to Revolutionary Opportunity."

63 Córdova, *Clase trabajadora y movimiento sindical en Cuba*, 234.

64 Spalding, *Organized Labor in Latin America*, 228.

65 Ibid., 230.

66 R. B. Wood to George E. Keiser, 18 January 1940, APLT, CASC, leg. 198, exp. 3868.

67 Ibid.

68 Rojas, *Las luchas obreras en el central Tacajó*, 96.

69 As mentioned in the introduction, in many of the early studies on populism elsewhere in Latin America, Marxist scholars condemned workers for not having enough "class-consciousness" to reject populist leadership. They argued that populist leaders such as Juan Perón and Getúlio Vargas "duped" workers into supporting them by presenting themselves as fathers to the poor, saviors for the workers, etc. Daniel James's trailblazing study on Perón presents the far less judgmental (and more convincing) argument that workers chose to engage with the populists because they offered the best alternative to violent repression under the more conservative regimes that preceded them. See James, *Resistance and Integration*, introduction.

70 Villafruela, *El General de las Cañas*, 14.

71 Sims, "The Cuban Sugar Workers' Progress under the Leadership of a Black Communist," 11.

72 R. B. Wood to Compañía General de Seguros y Fianzas de Sagua la Grande, S.A., 12 February 1947, APLT, CASC, leg. 71, exp. 811.

73 Spalding, *Organized Labor in Latin America*, 230.

74 Sims, "Cuba's Organized Labor," 48.

75 The rate for mill workers increased from 96.4 cents in 1940 to 198.5 cents in 1945; for field workers, it went from 70.7 cents in 1940 to 180.4 cents in 1945. IH, Fondo: Museo Obrero, leg. Organizaciones de Trabajadores Azucareros, 1924–75, Fichero no. 8, 8/E15/G4/C1/12; Colectivo de autores, *Memorias de un viejo mundo azucarero*; Zanetti, "The Workers' Movement and Labor Regulation in the Cuban Sugar Industry," 183–205.

76 Pérez Stable, *The Cuban Revolution*, 44.

77 Sims, "Cuba's Organized Labor," 47.

78 Hoernel, "A Comparison of Sugar and Social Change in Puerto Rico and Oriente," 203–8; Thomas, *Cuba: The Pursuit of Freedom*, 1122.

79 For details on race and the labor market, see de la Fuente, *A Nation for All*, 99–137; Pérez, *Cuba*, 306–7.

80 Sims, "The Cuban Sugar Workers' Progress under the Leadership of a Black Communist," 10; Villafruela, *El General de las cañas*, 7–21.

81 He also helped workers make specific local demands. For example, during a visit to Chaparra in 1942, Menéndez saw the inhumane condition of the Caribbean workers' barracks across the way from the union locale. He spoke to the union leaders about it, and together they presented a protest to the British Embassy. The vice-consul visited the mills and demanded that Cubanaco make improvements. Villafruela, *El General de las cañas*, 13.

82 "*El diferencial en la punta de la mocha.*" This is the definition of the *diferencial* in Colectivo de autores, *Memorias de un viejo mundo azucarero*, 216.

83 The motto of the Association of Mill Owners was *Sin azúcar, no hay país*, and that of the FNTA was *El azúcar al servicio de Cuba*. Other workers remember it being *Sin trabajadores, no hay azúcar* (Without workers, there is no sugar).

84 Sims, "The Cuban Sugar Workers' Progress under the Leadership of a Black Communist," 12.

85 Zanetti, "The Workers' Movement and Labor Regulation in the Cuban Sugar Industry," 197.

86 Luis Merconchini, interview by Víctor Marrero, Delicias, 21 August 1990; José Rodríguez Alejo, interview by Víctor Marrero and Olga Cabrera, Chaparra/Delicias, 15 September 1992, tape recording, OHLT.

87 Villafruela, *El General de las cañas*, 25.

88 Santiago Serrano R., "Historia del movimiento obrero en el central Melanio Hernández (antes Tuinucú)."

89 García Galló, *Esbozo biográfico de Jesús Menéndez*, 150–76.

90 Grandin, *The Last Colonial Massacre*.

91 Alexander, *A History of Organized Labor in Cuba*, 117.

92 Spalding, *Organized Labor in Latin America*, 231.

93 Thomas, *The Cuban Revolution*, 24.

94 A friend of Chibás's doctor told a colleague that Chibás had ascertained exactly where he could place the gun to carry out the dramatic gesture without actually risking his life, but unexpected excessive bleeding led to his death. Conversation with Marial Iglesias, Toronto, 24 November 2006. For more on Cuba's political culture of martyrdom, see Pérez, *To Die in Cuba*; Stoner, "Militant Heroines and the Consecration of the Patriarchal State," 71–96.

95 Pérez, *Cuba*, 287–88.

96 Domínguez, *Cuba*, 136.

97 A. Sánchez Arango, "Breve historia del movimiento sindical cubano," *Jornada* (Caracas), 1 May 1963, 109, cited in Córdova, *Clase trabajadora y movimiento sindical en Cuba*, 319.

98 Domínguez, *Cuba*, 94.

99 Ibid., 427.

100 Ibid., 94.

101 Cepero describes the three ICAE leaders as *jinetes*, which can be translated as "horsemen" or "whores" in Cuban slang. Cepero Bonilla, *Obras históricas*.

102 Sims, "Cuba's Organized Labor," 53.

103 Zanetti, "The Workers' Movement and Labor Regulation in the Cuban Sugar Industry," 199.

104 Spalding, *Organized Labor in Latin America*, 233.

105 Eladio Santiago Serrano and Arquímedes Valdivia Hernández, interview by the author, Tuinucú, 12 May 2000. Rita Díaz, interview by the author, Havana, 10 September 2006.

106 Paterson, *Contesting Castro*, 226.

107 See Farnsworth-Alvear, *Dulcinea in the Factory*; Klubock, *Contested Communities*; Montgomery, *Workers' Control in America*; and Winn, *Weavers of Revolution*.

108 Adan Romero Rojas, *A través de mis recuerdos*, 10–11.

109 Ibid., 10–13.

110 Ewell, "Angel Santana Suárez," 87.

111 The Spanish text reads, "Ante la irrupción brusca y la algarabía [hullabaloo] de tantas mujeres, el alcalde se desmayó." Colectivo de autores, *Memorias de un viejo mundo azucarero*, 162.

112 Tomás González Romero and Ester Villa Nápoles, interview by the author, Chaparra, 5 September 2005.

113 *To Lead as Equals* is the title of Jeffrey Gould's book.

114 Díaz, "La huelga que decidieron las mujeres," in Colectivo de autores, *Memorias de un viejo mundo azucarero*, 160–67.

115 Why these relations broke down is the subject of great debate, but most attribute it to a combination of U.S. assumptions of hegemony and the revolutionaries' deep-rooted desire for independence. The nationalization of sugarmills came in a roundabout way. The Soviet Union sold oil to Cuba for less than U.S. prices,

but the U.S. refineries in Cuba refused to process it. Cuba nationalized the oil refineries, and the United States responded by drastically cutting Cuba's sugar quota. At the same time, Cuban workers and peasants were also pressuring the Cuban government to radicalize agrarian and nationalist reforms. See Paterson, "A Complete Break: How Did the United States Let This One Get Away?," in Paterson, *Contesting Castro*, 241–63; Martínez-Alier , "The Peasantry and the Cuban Revolution from the Spring of 1959 to the End of 1960," in Martínez-Alier, *Haciendas, Plantations, and Collective Farms*, 127–47.

116 The 1955 sugar strike is a fruitful avenue for future research when more government sources become available on the 1950s. See Bonachea and San Martín, *The Cuban Insurrection 1952–1959*; Cardona Bory, "La huelga azucarera de diciembre de 1955 y la alianza obrero-estudiantil." Gladys Marel García-Pérez emphasizes the importance of sugar (and other) workers' strikes and sabotage actions in Matanzas and elsewhere on the island in *Insurrection and Revolution*, her provincial case study of 1950s Matanzas that analyzes why Fidel Castro's movement triumphed in 1959.

117 The Twenty-Sixth of July name came from the date in 1953 that Fidel Castro and his small band of rebels attacked the Moncada army barracks in Santiago de Cuba.

118 Franqui, *Family Portrait with Fidel*, 163. I thank Marc McLeod for sending me this citation.

119 His initial reticence to talk about such sabotage was likely due to the fact that U.S. sugar companies, including the former owners of Chaparra and Delicias, have legal cases that are still pending in U.S. courts for compensation from the Cuban government for the nationalized properties.

120 Ruiz, *Cuba*, 14. García-Pérez's *Insurrection and Revolution* provides reams of evidence from the province of Matanzas proving workers' activism in the struggle against Batista.

121 On students, see Sweig, *Inside the Cuban Revolution*, and Suchliki, *University Students and Revolution in Cuba, 1920–1968*; on the guerrillas, see Thomas, *The Cuban Revolution*, and studies by Louis Pérez, Marifeli Pérez Stable, Thomas Paterson, Cole Blasier, and Ramón Bonachea and Marta San Martín.

122 Domínguez, *Cuba*, 129.

123 Castro, "History Will Absolve Me," 306.

124 Domínguez, *Cuba*, 130–31.

125 Thomas, *The Cuban Revolution*, 225.

126 Paterson, *Contesting Castro*, 179.

127 Ibid., 83.

128 Sweig, *Inside the Cuban Revolution*, 78.

129 Paterson, *Contesting Castro*, 99–101, 113–17. Upper-level employees wrote to the administration throughout 1959 asking permission to take "leaves of absences" in the United States until the "troubles" blew over. Many of them are probably still resident in the United States today. APLT, CASC, leg. 209, exp. 3154.

130 Thomas, *The Cuban Revolution*, 190.

131 Ibid., 190.

132 Paterson, *Contesting Castro*; Pérez, *Cuba*.

133 Pérez, *Army Politics in Cuba*, 58–59.

134 Blasier, "Social Revolution," 38.

135 For powerful interpretations of the Batista army and the regime's decay, see Pérez, *Army Politics in Cuba*; Paterson, *Contesting Castro*.

136 Pérez, *Cuba*, 311–13.

137 Cuban guerrillas could draw the lesson about the dangers of civilian–military alliances from 1933, and the prominent leader Ché Guevara could draw it directly from Guatemala, where he had witnessed the army–CIA overthrow of the Arbenz regime.

138 Martínez-Alier, "The Peasantry and the Cuban Revolution from the Spring of 1959 to the end of 1960," chap. 5 of *Haciendas, Plantations, and Collective Farms*, 127–47.

139 Ibid., 132.

140 Ibid., 136.

141 McAvoy, *Sugar Baron*, conclusion.

142 For the Mexican and Chilean cases of land occupations by workers and nationalization, see Hamilton, *The Limits of State Autonomy*; Winn, *Weavers of Revolution*.

CONCLUSION

1 As the international and domestic political and economic climate changed from the 1850s through the 1950s, it affected how much leaders did or did not seek to incorporate these popular groups.

2 As mentioned earlier, Cubans held almost 70 percent of the sugar industry by 1959, in contrast to the roughly 70 percent that was "North American" in 1925. Martínez-Alier and Martínez-Alier, *Cuba*, 63.

3 Cohen, *Making a New Deal*, 285.

4 Gould, *To Lead as Equals*.

5 See Grandin, *The Last Colonial Massacre*; Gould, *To Lead as Equals*.

6 See n. 24 of the introduction.

7 Ruiz, *Cuba*, 13.

8 David González, "Cuba's Bittersweet Move to Trim Its Sugar Crop," *New York Times* 9 October 2002.

ABC Revolutionary Society: Each cell, made up of about ten members, would operate independently of the others so that if the police caught one, those remaining would not be detected. The leading cell was "A."

Administration System: Companies would purchase large tracts of land and hire workers to grow and cut cane on it instead of purchasing cane from landowning cane farmers (independent colonos) or tenant colonos (also called sugarmill colonos or controlled colonos). Used mostly by the United Fruit Company in eastern Cuba.

Anarcho-Syndicalism: Socialism and anarcho-syndicalism were opposed to a state run by capitalists. Socialists wanted to reform the state by letting workers run it, whereas anarcho-syndicalists wanted to get rid of the state altogether to allow grassroots workplace and community councils—called soviets after the Russian Revolutions of 1905 and 1917—to run their own affairs.

Auténtico Party: Created by Ramón Grau San Martín as an "institutionalized" version of the 1933 Revolution. Its full name was the Authentic Cuban Revolutionary Party.

Batistianos: Supporters of Fulgencio Batista, who was head of the army starting in 1933. Batista was elected president from 1940 to 44 and then returned to power from 1952 to 1959 through a military coup.

Caudillos: Usually war heroes from the provinces who became heads of political parties. A wide network of personal and business relationships extended from the caudillo and his war companions to individuals throughout the nation

to make up the ruling or opposition party. When in power, the caudillo, acting
as patron, would dole out jobs, contracts, and favors to party members and
supporters (clients) in exchange for their political support.

CNOC (also referred to as "the Confederation" in this book): National
Confederation of Cuban Workers, formed in 1925 and declared illegal in 1935
by Fulgencio Batista. Communist labor union that followed directives from the
Comintern international revolutionary directorate in Moscow (in Josef Stalin's
Russia).

Colonato: The system of production whereby farmers (*colonos*) grew cane to sell to
a nearby sugarmill in exchange for cash, sugar, or credit at sugarmill company
stores. A *colono* might be a small farmer growing and tending cane with his
family to sell to the nearest sugarmill, or a comfortable middle-class owner or
renter of medium-sized plots of land. A few were large landowners who rented
out their land to *subcolonos*. The cane farms were called *colonias*.

Compact: Unstated agreement on how to keep the peace on a day-to-day basis.
Patterns in relationships that established the boundaries of acceptable behavior
that all parties recognized. System of rule.

CTC (Confederation of Cuban Workers): Members of the FOH and CNOC of the
1920s and 1930s joined together in 1939 during the popular-front era of the Second World War. The CTC was led by communists until 1947, when the Communist Party was declared illegal and the Auténticos took over.

Diferencial Azucarero: The 1937 Sugar Coordination Act stipulated that at the end
of each year, colonos would receive the difference between the average price of
sugar during the harvest and the average price for the whole year. Under Jesús
Menéndez's leadership, the workers achieved the demand that that diferencial be
extended to them.

FEU (University Students' Federation): Started by Julio Mella in 1925; students also
mobilized in the Student Left Wing, called the AIE in the 1930s and renamed
the DRE (for Left-Wing Student Directory) under José Antonio Echeverría in
the 1950s.

FNOA/FNTA (National Federation of Sugar Workers). The FNOA was formed
in 1939. Jesús Menédez renamed it the National Federation of Workers in the
Sugar Industry (FNTA) in 1945 to include field workers as well as employees
who formerly had been separated into the National Association of Sugar Office
Employees and the National Association of Sugar Technicians.

FOH (also referred to as "the Federation" in this book): Worker's Federation
of Havana, founded in 1924. Trotskyist labor union that combined anarcho-
syndicalism with Bolshevik and Leninist principles; also called the Partido
Bolchevique-Leninista.

Garantía: Jesús Menéndez's guarantee clause linking the price of Cuban sugar to an
index based on the price of a group of basic products that Cuba bought from the
United States. It represented the difference between the rising costs of imports

from the United States (due to postwar inflation) and the cost of Cuban sugar being sold to them (fixed by the 1934 Reciprocity Treaty).

Guiteristas: Followers of Antonio Guiteras, who was minister of the interior under Grau San Martín during the 1933 Revolution's "One Hundred Days of Reform" and leader of the Young Cuba opposition movement against Carlos Mendieta and Fulgencio Batista in 1934 and 1935.

Higienización: The sugar union's demand for proper homes with cement floors, access to collective stores, electricity, and light for all workers in small colonia hamlets and in neighborhoods adjacent to the mills, such as Chaparra's Pueblo Viejo.

ICAE (Sugar Stabilization Board): The Cuban state controlled the production and sale of sugar by distributing specific cane quotas to sugarmills and the colonos selling to these mills. The ICAE initially included six representatives of the colonos alongside twelve representatives of the mill owners and a presidential delegate.

Ley de fuga: Secret service or policemen would round up suspects for interrogation, set them free, and then claim that they had to shoot them because the suspects were trying to run away.

M-26-7 (Twenty-Sixth of July Movement): Fidel Castro's revolutionaries named after the 1953 date on which he and a small group of rebels tried to take over the Moncada barracks in Santiago de Cuba.

Machadistas: Supporters of President Gerardo Machado (1924–33).

Pacíficos: Civilians; free or enslaved people who remained outside the insurgent or Spanish forces during the wars for independence, rebellions, and revolutions of the nineteenth century and twentieth.

Palmacristi: Italian fascists' torture that Cuba's secret police and Rural Guardsmen used in the 1930s and 1950s. Anyone who did not say or do what he or she was told would be forced to drink a liter of oil.

Paso de jicotea: Literally, "turtle step"; a form of protest in which workers slow down production to protest against the company.

PCC (Communist Party of Cuba): Formed in 1925 but declared illegal later that year, the PCC would provide many of the most active and disciplined leaders of the incipient sugar workers' movement and would resurface legally as the Popular Socialist Party (PSP) in the late 1930s before being declared illegal again in 1947.

PIC (Independent Party of Color): Afro-Cuban political party founded by Evaristo Estenoz in 1908 and brutally repressed by José Miguel Gómez's Liberal Party in 1912.

Plan de machete: Used by Cuba's Rural Guardsmen, who beat victims using the thick side of their machetes.

PRC (Revolutionary Party of Cuba): José Martí established the party in New York City in 1892 to organize and raise funds for a new independence struggle. Estrada Palma dissolved it in 1898.

Pueblo Viejo: Chaparra's "Old Town"; the neighborhood where workers, servants, prostitutes, and other, less fortunate residents constructed their homes and huts. It was adjacent to the mill town where the employees and administrators lived in more luxurious homes.

SNOIA **(National Union of Sugar Industry Workers):** Established in December 1932, SNOIA was replaced by the FNTA and the FNOA in the 1940s.

Sobrinismo: Nepotism (literally, "nephewism"); an island-wide problem in the late nineteenth century and early twentieth whereby Spanish bosses gave the best positions to their relatives, leaving Cubans with the lowest-paying jobs or no jobs at all.

Soviets: Grassroots workplace and community councils named after the Russian Revolutions of 1905 and 1917.

Unión Nacionalista: A party that Mario García Menocal and Carlos Mendieta formed to try to end the Machado dictatorship (1928–33). It staged the Río Verde insurrection in 1931.

Unitarios: This term is used interchangeably with "*el movimiento*" to refer to followers of the illegal Communist Party (Popular Socialist Party) and Fidel Castro's Twenty-Sixth of July Movement (M-26–7), despite the fact that the Communist Party did not throw its support behind the movement until shortly before Batista's fall in 1958. The CTC Unitario was the communist "shadow" union after the Auténticos took over the CTC in 1947.

Select Bibliography

MANUSCRIPT COLLECTIONS

Archivo Histórico Provincial de Holguín
    Gobierno Municipal, Ayuntamiento Neocolonial
Archivo Histórico Provincial de Las Tunas (APLT)
    Fondo Cuban-American Sugar Company (CASC) referred to as Cubanaco in text
    Fondo Francisco Sugar Company
    Protocoles Notariales
Archivo Histórico Provincial de Sancti Spíritus M. G. Serafín Sánchez (APSS)
    Fondo Ayuntamiento, República Mediatizada (RM)
    Protocoles Notariales
Archivo Histórico Provincial de Santiago de Cuba (STGO)
    Gobierno Provincial (GP)
    Tribunales de Urgencia/Tribunales de Defensa Nacional
Archivo Nacional de Cuba, Havana (ANC)
    Fondo Valle-Iznaga (Valle-Iznaga)
    Fondo Secretaría de Agricultura, Industria y Comercio (AIC)
    Fondo Secretaría de la Presidencia
    Fondo Donativos y Remisiones
    Fondo Especial
Braga Brothers Collection, Special Collections, Smathers Library, University of
    Florida, Gainesville (BBC)

Cuba Company Archives, Special Collections, College Park Libraries, University of
    Maryland
Harvard Business School Historical Collections Department, Baker Library, Harvard
    University, Boston (HB, HCR)
Instituto de Historia, Havana (IH)
    Fondo Museo Obrero
    Fondo Organizaciones de Trabajadores Sindicales Nacionales
    Sindicato Nacional de Obreros en la Industria Azucarera (SNOIA)
    Confederación Nacional de Obreros de Cuba (CNOC)
    Federación Nacional de Trabajadores Azucareras (FNTA)
Public Records Office (PRO)
    Foreign Office Papers, Kew Gardens, London (FO)
United States National Archives (USNA)
    Microform 1900–29, Reading Room boxes 1930–35, College Park, Md.
    Record Group 59: State Department Records, Internal Affairs of Cuba, College
        Park, Md.
    Record Group 76: Spanish Treaty Claims Commission, College Park, Md.
    Record Group 395: Records of the Military Intelligence Division, Washington,
        D.C.

INTERVIEWS

By the author
de Céspedes García Menocal, Monsignor Carlos. Havana, 25 April 2000.
Díaz, Rita. Havana, 10 September 2006.
González Romero, Tomás, and Ester Villa Nápoles. Chaparra, 5 September 2005.
Santiago Serrano, Eladio. Tuinucú, 1 February 2000, 12 May 2000.
Valdivia Hernández, Arquímedes. Tuinucú, 1 February 2000.
Valdivia Hernández, Arquímedes, and Eladio Santiago Serrano. Tuinucú, 12 May
    2000.
Villafruela, Omar. Chaparra, 19 February 2000.

By Víctor Marrero, audiotape recordings at the Oficina del Historiador
de la Ciudad, Las Tunas (OHLT)
González Romero, Tomás, and Ester Villa Nápoles. Chaparra. 25 March 2007.
Griffith Guana, Harold. Chaparra, 15 July 1991.
Merconchini, Luis. Chaparra/Delicias, 21 August 1990.

By Víctor Marrero and Olga Cabrera, audiotape recordings at the
Oficina del Historiador de la Ciudad, Las Tunas (OHLT)
Rodríguez Alejo, José. Chaparra/Delicias, 15 September 1992.

PERIODICALS

Agricultura y Zootecnia
Bohemia
Cuba Contemporánea
Cuba Review
Current History
El Colono
Foreign Policy Reports
Havana Post
Literary Digest
Louisiana Planter and Sugar Manufacturer
Memoria de la Zafra
The Nation
New York Times
Time
Willett and Gray Weekly Statistical Sugar Trade Journal

BOOKS, DISSERTATIONS, JOURNAL ARTICLES, AND OTHER PRINTED MATERIAL

Adan Romero Rojas, José. *A través de mis recuerdos*. Municipio Jesús Menéndez: Casa de Cultura José de la Luz y Caballero, 1985.

Adelman, Jeremy. "Andean Impasses." *New Left Review* 18 (November–December 2002): 41–72.

Aguilar, Luis E. *Cuba 1933: Prologue to Revolution*. Ithaca: Cornell University Press, 1972.

Album de vistas del gran central Chaparra. N.p., 1910.

Alexander, Robert J. *A History of Organized Labor in Cuba*. Westport, Conn.: Praeger, 2002.

Alvarez Estévez, Rolando. *Azúcar e inmigración, 1900–1940*. Havana: Editorial de Ciencias Sociales, 1988.

Anderson, Benedict. *Imagined Communities: Reflections on the Origin and Spread of Nationalism*. London: Verso Press, 1983.

Arbelo, Manuel. *Recuerdos de la última guerra por la independencia de Cuba, 1896 a 1898*. Havana: Imprenta Tipografía Moderna, 1918.

Argote-Freyre, Frank. *Fulgencio Batista: From Revolutionary to Strongman*. New Brunswick, N.J.: Rutgers University Press, 2006.

Arrom, Silvia M., and Servando Ortoll, eds. *Riots in the Cities: Popular Politics and the Urban Poor in Latin America, 1765–1910*. Wilmington, Del.: Scholarly Resources, 1996.

Asociación Nacional de la Industria Azucarera. *Memoria de la labor realizada durante el segundo año de su fundación de 1924 a 1925, que la Junta Directiva presenta a los*

Señores Asociados. Havana: Imprenta y Papeleria de Rambla, Bouza y Cía, 1925.

Ayala, César. *American Sugar Kingdom: The Plantation Economy of the Spanish Caribbean, 1898–1934.* Chapel Hill: University of North Carolina Press, 1999.

Balboa Navarro, Imilcy. *La protesta rural en Cuba. Resistencia cotidiana, bandolerismo y revolución (1878–1902).* Madrid: Consejo Superior de Investigaciones Científicas, 2003.

Barnet, Miguel, ed. *Biography of a Runaway Slave.* Willimantic, Conn.: Curbstone Press, 1994.

Barrera Figueroa, Orlando. *Estudios de historia espirituana.* Sancti Spiritus: Ediciones Luminaria, 1994.

———. *Sancti Spíritus: Sinopsis histórica.* Santiago de Cuba: Editorial Oriente, 1986.

Benjamin, Jules R. *The United States and Cuba: Hegemony and Dependent Development, 1880–1934.* Pittsburgh: University of Pittsburgh Press, 1977.

Bergquist, Charles. *Labor in Latin America: Comparative Essays on Chile, Argentina, Venezuela, and Colombia.* Stanford, Calif.: Stanford University Press, 1986.

Besse, Susan. *Restructuring Patriarchy: The Modernization of Gender Inequality in Brazil, 1914–1940.* Chapel Hill: University of North Carolina Press, 1996.

Bethell, Leslie, and Ian Roxborough, eds. *Latin America between the Second World War and the Cold War, 1944–1948.* Cambridge: Cambridge University Press, 1992.

Blackburn, Robin. "Prologue to the Cuban Revolution." *New Left Review* 21 (October 1963): 52–91.

Blasier, Cole. "Social Revolution: Origins in Mexico, Bolivia, and Cuba." In *Cuba in Revolution,* edited by Rolando E. Bonachea and Nelson P. Valdés, 18–51. Garden City, N.Y.: Doubleday Anchor Books, 1972.

Bonachea, Ramón L., and Marta San Martín. *The Cuban Insurrection 1952–1959.* New Brunswick, N.J.: Transaction Books, 1974.

Borges, Milo A. *Compilación ordenada y completa de la legislación cubana.* Havana: Editorial Lex, 1952.

Bradford Burns, E. *Poverty of Progress.* Berkeley: University of California Press, 1983.

Braga, George Atkinson. "A Bundle of Relations." Typed ms., n.d., Braga Brothers Collection, University of Florida, Gainesville.

Brennan, James, ed. *Peronism and Argentina.* Wilmington, Del.: Scholarly Resources, 1998.

Bronfman, Alejandra. *Measures of Equality: Social Science, Citizenship, and Race in Cuba, 1902–1940.* Chapel Hill: University of North Carolina Press, 2004.

Buell, Raymond Leslie, et al. *Problems of the New Cuba: Report of the Commission on Cuban Affairs.* New York: Foreign Policy Association, 1935.

Cabrera, Olga. "Enrique Cresi: Un patriota obrero." *Revista Santiago* 36 (December 1979): 131–32.

Canel, Eva. *Lo que ví en Cuba a través de la isla* (1916), reprint ed. Santiago de Cuba: Editorial Oriente, 2006.

Cardona Bory, Pedro. "La huelga azucarera de diciembre de 1955 y la alianza obrero-estudiantil," Havana: n.p., n.d.

Carpenter, Frank G. "Cuba in 1905." *Cuba Review* 3 (November 1905): 11.

Carr, Barry. "From Caribbean Backwater to Revolutionary Opportunity: Cuba's Evolving Relationship with the Comintern, 1925–34." In *International Communism and the Communist International, 1919–1943*, eds. Tim Rees and Andrew Thorpe, 234–53. Manchester: Manchester University Press, 1998.

―――. "Identity, Class, and Nation: Black Immigrant Workers, Cuban Communism, and the Sugar Insurgency 1925–1934." *Hispanic American Historical Review* 78, no. 1 (1998): 83–116.

―――. "Mill Occupations and Soviets: The Mobilisation of Sugar Workers in Cuba, 1917–1933." *Journal of Latin American Studies* 28 (1996): 129–58.

―――. "'Omnipotent and Omnipresent'? Labor Shortages, Worker Mobility, and Employer Control in the Cuban Sugar Industry, 1910–1934." In *Identity and Struggle at the Margins of the Nation-State: The Laboring Peoples of Central America and the Hispanic Caribbean*, edited by Aviva Chomsky and Aldo Lauria-Santiago, 260–91. Durham: Duke University Press, 1998.

Castro, Fidel. *Fidel: My Early Years*. Melbourne: Ocean Press, 2005.

―――. "History Will Absolve Me." In *The Cuba Reader: History, Culture, Politics*. Durham: Duke University Press, 2000.

Cepero Bonilla, Raúl. *Azúcar y abolición* (1948), reprint ed. Havana: Instituto Cubano del Libro, 1976.

―――. *Obras históricas*. Havana: Instituto de Historia, 1963.

Chasteen, John Charles. *Born in Blood and Fire: A Concise History of Latin America*. 2d ed. New York: W. W. Norton, 2006.

Childs, Matt D. *The 1812 Aponte Rebellion in Cuba and the Struggle against Atlantic Slavery*. Chapel Hill: University of North Carolina Press, 2006.

Chomsky, Aviva. "'Barbados or Canada?' Race, Immigration, and Nation in Early Twentieth-Century Cuba." *Hispanic American Historical Review* 80, no. 3 (August 2000): 415–62.

Choy, Armando, Gustavo Chui, Moisés Sío Wong, and Mary-Alice Waters. *Our History Is Still Being Written: The Story of Three Chinese Generals in the Cuban Revolution*. Atlanta: Pathfinder, 2005.

Churchill, Winston S. *Winston S. Churchill: War Correspondent, 1895–1900*, edited by Frederick Woods. London: Brassey's, 1992.

Cohen, Lizabeth. *Making a New Deal: Industrial Workers in Chicago, 1919–1939*. Cambridge: Cambridge University Press, 1990.

Colectivo de autores. *Memorias de un viejo mundo azucarero*. Havana: Editorial de Ciencias Sociales, 1990.

Collier, Ruth Berins, *Shaping the Political Arena: Critical Junctures, the Labor Movement, and Regime Dynamics in Latin America*. Princeton: Princeton University Press, 1991.

Conniff, Michael, ed. *Latin American Populism in Comparative Perspective*. Albuquerque: University of New Mexico Press, 1982.

———. *Populism in Latin America*. Tuscaloosa: University of Alabama Press, 1999.

Córdova, Arnaldo. *La politica de masas del cardenismo*. Mexico City: Ediciones Era, 1986.

Córdova, Efrén. *Clase trabajadora y movimiento sindical en Cuba, Volumen 1: 1819–1959*. Miami: Ediciones Universal, 1995.

Corvea Alvarez, Domingo. *Los ingenios de la villa de Sancti Spiritus (hasta 1879)*. Sancti Spiritus: Ediciones Jarao, 1999.

———. "Sistema defensivo de fortificaciones españolas en la ciudad de Sancti Spíritus." Typed ms. borrowed from the author, Sancti Spiritus, n.d.

Cozzens, James Gould. *Cock Pit*. New York: William Morrow, 1928.

Craton, Michael. *Testing the Chains: Resistance to Slavery in the British West Indies*. Ithaca: Cornell University Press, 1982.

Crosby, Alfred. *The Columbian Exchange: Biological and Cultural Consequences of 1492*. Westport, Conn.: Greenwood Press, 1972.

Cuban Economic Research Project, ed. *A Study on Cuba: The Colonial and Republican Periods, the Socialist Experiment*. Coral Gables: University of Miami Press, 1965.

Curtin, Philip D. *The Rise and Fall of the Plantation Complex*. Oxford: Cambridge University Press, 1990.

de Céspedes, Carlos Manuel. *Escritos*, 2d ed., edited by Fernando Portuondo and Hortensia Pichardo. Havana: Editorial de Ciencias Sociales, 1982.

de la Fuente, Alejandro. *A Nation for All: Race, Inequality, and Politics in Twentieth Century Cuba*. Chapel Hill: University of North Carolina Press, 2001.

de la Torre, Carlos. *Populist Seduction in Latin America: The Ecuadorian Experience*. Athens: Ohio University Press, 2000.

de Paz Sánchez, Manuel, José Fernández Fernández, and Nelson López Novegil. *El bandolerismo en Cuba (1800–1933: Presencia canaria y protesta rural)*, 2 vols. Santa Cruz de Tenerife: Centro de la Cultura Popular Canaria, 1994.

Derby, Lauren. *The Dictator's Seduction: Politics and Popular Imagination in the Era of Trujillo*. Durham: Duke University Press, 2009.

Deutsch, Sandra McGee. *The Argentine Right: Its History and Intellectual Origins, 1910 to the Present*. Landham, Md.: Scholarly Resources, 1993.

———. "Gender and Sociopolitical Change in Twentieth-Century Latin America." *Hispanic American Historical Review* 71, no. 2 (1991): 259–306.

DeWilde, John O. "Sugar: An International Problem." *Foreign Policy Reports* 11, no. 15 (27 September 1933): 162–72.

Di Tella, Torcuato. "Populism and Reform in Latin America." In *Obstacles to Change in Latin America*, edited by Claudio Véliz, 47–74. Oxford: Oxford University Press, 1969.

Dix, Robert H. "Populism: Authoritarian and Democratic." *Latin American Research Review* 20, no. 2 (1985): 29–52.

Domínguez, Jorge. *Cuba: Order and Revolution*. Cambridge, Mass.: Belknap Press, 1978.

Duke, Cathy. "The Idea of Race: The Cultural Impact of American Intervention in Cuba, 1898–1912." In *Politics, Society, and Culture in the Caribbean*, edited by Blanca G. Silvestrini. San Juan: University of Puerto Rico Press, 1983.

Dumoulin, John. *Azúcar y lucha de clases, 1917*. Havana: Editorial de Ciencias Sociales, 1980.

Dye, Alan. *Cuban Sugar in the Age of Mass Production: Technology and the Economics of the Sugar Central, 1899–1929*. Stanford, Calif.: Stanford University Press, 1998.

Estrade, Paul. "Los clubes femeninos en el Partido Revolucionario Cubano." *Anuario de Estudios Martianos* 10 (1987): 175–92.

Ewell, Judith, trans. "Angel Santana Suárez: Cuban Sugar Worker." In *The Human Tradition in Latin America: The Twentieth Century*, edited by William H. Beezley and Judith Ewell, 75–88. Lanham, Md.: Scholarly Resources, 1998.

Farber, Samuel. *The Origins of the Cuban Revolution Reconsidered*. Chapel Hill: University of North Carolina Press, 2006.

Farnsworth-Alvear, Ann. *Dulcinea in the Factory: Myths, Morals, Men, and Women in Colombia's Industrial Experiment, 1905–1960*. Durham: Duke University Press, 2000.

Fernández, Artemio and Antonio, Comisión de Historia Partido Comunista de Cuba Municipal. "Historia del movimiento obrero del Central Antonio Guiteras (antes Delicias)." Typed ms., library, Instituto de Historia, Havana.

Fernández, Frank. *Cuban Anarchism: The History of a Movement*, trans. Charles Bufe. Tucson: Sharp Press, 2001.

Fernández, Pablo Armando. *De memorias y anhelos*. Oriente: Ediciones Unión, 1998.

Fernández Robaina, Tomás. *El negro en Cuba: 1902–1958, apuntes para la historia de la lucha contra la discriminación racial*. Havana: Editorial de Ciencias Sociales, 1990.

Ferrer, Ada. *Insurgent Cuba: Race, Nation, and Revolution, 1868–1898*. Chapel Hill: University of North Carolina Press, 1999.

Fick, Carolyn E. *The Making of Haiti: The Saint Domingue Revolution from Below*. Knoxville: University of Tennessee Press, 1990.

Foner, Philip S. *The Spanish-Cuban-American War and the Birth of American Imperialism*. 2 vols. New York: Monthly Review Press, 1972.

Frankel, Noralee, and Nancy S. Dye, eds. *Gender, Class, Race, and Reform in the Progressive Era*. Lexington: University Press of Kentucky, 1991.

Franqui, Carlos. *Family Portrait with Fidel: A Memoir*, trans. Alfred MacAdam. New York: Vintage, 1985.

French, John D. *The Brazilian Workers' ABC: Class Conflict and Alliances in Modern São Paulo*. Chapel Hill: University of North Carolina Press, 1992.

———. "Workers and the Rise of Adhemarista Populism in São Paulo, Brazil, 1945–1947." *Hispanic American Historical Review* 68, no. 1 (February 1988): 1–43.

French, William E. *A Peaceful and Working People: Manners, Morals, and Class Formation in Northern Mexico*. Albuquerque: University of New Mexico Press, 1996.

Funes Monzote, Reinaldo. *From Rainforest to Cane Field in Cuba: An Environmental History since 1492*, trans. Alex Martin. Chapel Hill: University of North Carolina Press, 2008.

García, Alejandro, and Oscar Zanetti, eds. *United Fruit Company: un caso de dominio imperialista en Cuba*. Havana: Editorial de Ciencias Sociales, 1976.

García Galló, Gaspar Jorge. *Esbozo biográfico de Jesús Menéndez*. Havana: Editora Política, 1978.

García-Pérez, Gladys Marel. *Insurrection and Revolution: Armed Struggle in Cuba, 1952–1959*. Boulder: Lynne Reinner Publishers, 1998.

Geggus, David Patrick. *The Impact of the Haitian Revolution in the Atlantic World*. Columbia: University of South Carolina Press, 2001.

Genovese, Eugene. *From Rebellion to Revolution: Afro-American Slave Revolts in the Making of the New World*. New York: Vintage, 1981.

Germani, Gino. "El rol de los obreros y de los migrantes internos en los orígenes del peronismo," *Desarrollo Económico* 13, no. 51 (1973): 435–88.

Giovannetti-Torres, Jorge Luis. "Black British Subjects in Cuba: Race, Ethnicity, and Empire in the Migration Experience, 1898–1938." Ph.D. diss., University of London, 2001.

Gleijeses, Piero. *Shattered Hope: The Guatemalan Revolution and the United States, 1944–1954*. Princeton: Princeton University Press, 1991.

González Sánchez, Michael. "Del esclavo al colono: notas acerca del colonato azucarero cubano en el siglo XIX." *Catauro: Revista Cubana de Antropología* 6, no. 11 (2005): 57–64.

Gould, Jeffrey L. *To Lead as Equals: Rural Protest and Political Consciousness in Chinandega, Nicaragua, 1912–1979*. Chapel Hill: University of North Carolina Press, 1990.

"Los Grandes Centrales." *Bohemia*, 10 June 1923, 13–15, 17–24.

Grandin, Greg. *The Last Colonial Massacre: Latin America in the Cold War*. Chicago: University of Chicago Press, 2004.

Gudmundson, Lowell. *Costa Rica before Coffee: Society and Economy on the Eve of the Export Boom*. Baton Rouge: Louisiana State University Press, 1986.

Guerra, Lillian. *The Myth of José Martí: Conflicting Nationalisms in Early Twentieth-Century Cuba*. Chapel Hill: University of North Carolina Press, 2005.

Guerra y Sánchez, Ramiro. *La industria azucarera de Cuba*. Havana: Editorial Cultural, 1940.

———. *Sugar and Society in the Caribbean: An Economic History of Cuban Agriculture*. New Haven, Conn.: Yale University Press, 1964.

Guillermoprieto, Alma. *Dancing with Cuba: A Memoir of the Revolution*. New York: Pantheon Books, 2004.

Guridy, Frank A. "Racial Knowledge in Cuba: The Production of a Social Fact, 1912–1944." Ph.D. diss., University of Michigan, Ann Arbor, 2001.

Guy, Donna J. *Sex and Danger in Buenos Aires: Prostitution, Family, and Nation in Argentina*. Lincoln: University of Nebraska Press, 1991.

Hackett, Charles W. "Mexican Constitutional Changes." *Current History* (May 1933): 214.

Hamilton, Nora. *The Limits of State Autonomy: Post-Revolutionary Mexico*. Princeton: Princeton University Press, 1982.

Hannaford, Ivan. *Race: The History of an Idea in the West*. Baltimore: Johns Hopkins University Press, 1996.

Helg, Aline. *Our Rightful Share: The Afro-Cuban Struggle for Equality, 1886–1912*. Chapel Hill: University of North Carolina Press, 1995.

Herring, Hubert. "The Downfall of Machado." *Current History* (October 1933): 17–18.

Hidalgo de Paz, Ibrahim. *Cuba 1895–1898: contradicciones y disoluciones*. Havana: Centro de Estudios Martianos, 1999.

Hobsbawm, Eric. *The Age of Revolution 1789–1848*. New York: Vintage Books, 1996.

Hoernel, Robert. "A Comparison of Sugar and Social Change in Puerto Rico and Oriente, Cuba: 1898–1959." Ph.D. diss., Johns Hopkins University, 1977.

Ibarra Cuesta, Jorge. *Cuba, 1898–1958: Estructura y procesos sociales*. Havana: Editorial de Ciencias Sociales, 1995.

———. *Cuba 1898–1921: Partidos políticos y clases sociales*. Havana: Editorial de Ciencias Sociales, 1992.

———. *Ideología mambisa*. Havana: Instituto del Libro, 1967.

Iglesias García, Fe. *Del ingenio al central*. Havana: Editorial de Ciencias Sociales, 1999.

Impresiones de la República de Cuba en el siglo XX. London: Lloyds Greater Britain Publishing, 1913.

Instituto de Historia de Cuba y del Movimiento Comunista y de la Revolución Socialista de Cuba. *Historia del movimiento obrero cubano*, 2 vols. Havana: Editorial Política, 1985.

James, Daniel. *Doña María's Story: Life History, Memory, and Political Identity*. Durham: Duke University Press, 2000.

———. *Resistance and Integration: Peronism and the Argentine Working Class, 1946–1976*. Cambridge: Cambridge University Press, 1988.

Jenks, Leland H. *Our Cuban Colony*. New York: Vanguard Press, 1928.

Jiménez Pastrana, Juan. *Los chinos en las luchas por la liberación cubana, 1847–1930*. Havana: Instituto de Historia, 1963.

Joseph, Gilbert M., and Daniel Nugent. *Everyday Forms of State Formation: Revolution and the Negotiation of Rule in Modern Mexico*. Durham: Duke University Press, 1994.

Kazin, Michael. *The Populist Persuasion: An American History*. Ithaca, N.Y.: Cornell University Press, 1998.

Klein, Herbert S. *The Atlantic Slave Trade*. Cambridge: Cambridge University Press, 1999.

Klubock, Thomas Miller. *Contested Communities: Class, Gender, and Politics in Chile's El Teniente Copper Mine, 1904–1951*. Durham: Duke University Press, 1998.

Knight, Alan. "Populism and Neo-Populism in Latin America, especially Mexico." *Journal of Latin American Studies* 30 (1998): 223–48.

Knight, Franklin W. "Jamaican Migrants in the Cuban Sugar Industry, 1900–1934."
In *Between Slavery and Free Labor: The Spanish-Speaking Caribbean in the Nine-teenth Century*, edited by Manuel Moreno Fraginals, Frank Moya Pons, and
Stanley L. Engerman, 84–118. Baltimore: Johns Hopkins University Press, 1985.
———. *Slave Society in Cuba during the Nineteenth Century*. Madison: University of
Wisconsin Press, 1970.

Laclau, Ernesto. *On Populist Reason*. London: Verso, 2005.

LaFeber, Walter. *Inevitable Revolutions: The United States in Central America*. New
York: W. W. Norton, 1983.

Langley, Lester. *America in the Age of Revolution*. New Haven, Conn.: Yale University
Press, 1996.

Lauriault, Robert Nairne. "Virgin Soil: The Modernization of Social Relations on a
Cuban Sugar Estate: The Francisco Sugar Company, 1898–1921." Ph.D. diss., University of Florida, Gainesville, 1994.

Lefevre, Edwin. "Soldier and Student Control in Cuba." *Saturday Evening Post* (Philadelphia), 6 January 1934, 36.

LeGrand, Catherine C. "Informal Resistance on a Dominican Sugar Plantation during the Trujillo Dictatorship." *Hispanic American Historical Review* 75, no. 4 (1995):
555–96.

Le Riverand, Julio. *La República: Dependencia y revolución*. Havana: Instituto del
Libro, 1969.

Les années trente à Cuba. Paris: Editions L'Harmattan, 1982.

Levine, Robert M. *Father of the Poor? Vargas and His Era*. Cambridge: Cambridge
University Press, 1998.

López, Kathleen. "'One Brings Another': The Formation of Early-Twentieth-
Century Chinese Migrant Communities in Cuba." In *The Chinese in the Caribbean*,
edited by Andrew R. Wilson, 93–128. Princeton, N.J.: Markus Wiener, 2004.

López Segrera, Fracisco. "La economía y la política en la república neo-colonial
(1902–1933)." In *La república neo-colonial: anuario de estudios cubanos*, 127–64.
Havana: Editorial de Ciencias Sociales, 1975.

Loveman, Brian. *For La Patria: Politics and the Armed Forces in Latin America*.
Lanham, Md.: Scholarly Resources, 1999.

Lynch, John. *Caudillos in Spanish America, 1800–1850*. Oxford: Clarendon Press, 1992.

Maceo, Antonio. *Antonio Maceo: documentos para su vida*. Havana: Archivo Nacional
de Cuba, 1945.

Marconi Braga, Michael. "No Other Law but Supply and Demand: Institutional
Change and the Cuban Sugar Economy, 1917–1934." M.A. thesis, University of
Texas, Austin, 1993.

Marrero Zaldívar, Víctor Manuel. "Dulce amargo de una historia obrera." Typed ms.,
Office of the Historian of the City of Las Tunas, n.d.

Martí, Carlos. *Films cubanos: Oriente y Occidente*. Barcelona: Sociedad General de
Publicaciones, 1915.

Martínez-Alier, Juan. *Haciendas, Plantations, and Collective Farms.* London: Frank Cass, 1977.

Martínez-Alier, Juan, and Verena Martínez-Alier. *Cuba: economía y sociedad.* Paris: Ruedo Ibérico, 1972.

Martínez-Alier, Verena. *Marriage, Class and Color in Nineteenth-Century Cuba: A Study of Racial Attitudes and Sexual Values in a Slave Society,* reprint ed. Ann Arbor: University of Michigan Press, 1989.

Martínez Moles, M. *Epítome de la historia de Sancti Spíritus.* Havana: Imprenta Siglo XX, 1936.

Martínez Ortiz, Rafael. *Cuba: Los primeros años de independencia,* 2 vols. Paris: Le Livre Libre, 1929.

McAvoy, Muriel. "Lion's Tail, Mouse's Head: Manuel Rionda and the Fortunes of Cuba Cane." Typed ms., Special Collections, Smathers Library, University of Florida, Gainesville.

———. *Sugar Baron: Manuel Rionda and the Fortunes of Pre-Castro Cuba.* Gainesville: University Press of Florida, 2003.

McLeod, Marc. "Undesirable Aliens: Race, Ethnicity, and Nationalism in the Comparison of Haitian and British West Indian Immigrant Workers in Cuba, 1912–1939." *Journal of Social History* 31, no. 3 (1998): 599–623.

McNeill, John. *Atlantic Empires of France and Spain: Louisbourg and Havana, 1700–1763.* Chapel Hill: University of North Carolina Press, 1985.

Meade, Teresa A. *Civilizing Rio: Reform and Resistance in a Brazilian City, 1889–1930.* University Park: Pennsylvania State University Press, 1996.

Memoria de la Asociación de Colonos de los Centrales "Chaparra" y "Delicias" Correspondiente a los años 1924 a 1925 y 1925 a 1926. Havana: La Propagandista, 1926.

Milton, Cynthia. *The Many Meanings of Poverty: Colonialism, Social Compacts, and Assistance in Eighteenth-Century Ecuador.* Stanford, Calif.: Stanford University Press, 2007.

Mintz, Sidney W. *Sweetness and Power: The Place of Sugar in Modern History.* New York: Penguin, 1985.

Montgomery, David. *Workers' Control in America.* Cambridge: Cambridge University Press, 1979.

Moreno Fraginals, Manuel. *El ingenio: complejo económico social cubano del azúcar,* 3 vols. Havana: Editorial de Ciencias Sociales, 1978.

———. *The Sugarmill: The Socioeconomic Complex of Sugar in Cuba, 1760–1860,* trans. Cedric Belfrage. New York: Monthly Review Press, 1976.

Moyano Fraga, Bolivar. "Central–Colono Relations within the Cuban Sugar Industry, 1914–1993: Exploring the Local Consequences of Global Changes, the Case of San Vicente from World War I to the Great Depression." M.A. thesis, University of Florida, Gainesville, 1997.

Newman, Philip C. *Cuba before Castro: An Economic Appraisal.* Ridgewood, N. J.: Foreign Studies, 1965.

O'Connor, James. *The Origin of Socialism in Cuba.* Ithaca, N. Y.: Cornell University Press, 1970.

Okihiro, Gary Y. *Cane Fires: The Anti-Japanese Movement in Hawaii, 1865–1945.* Philadelphia: Temple University Press, 1991.

Ortiz, Fernando. *Cuban Counterpoint: Tobacco and Sugar.* New York: Alfred A. Knopf, 1947. (Spanish ed.: *Contrapunteo cubano del tabaco y el azúcar.* Havana: Jesús Montero, 1940.)

Paquette, Robert. *Sugar Is Made with Blood: The Conspiracy of La Escalera and the Conflict between Empires over Slavery in Cuba.* Middletown, Conn.: Wesleyan University Press, 1988.

Paterson, Thomas G. *Contesting Castro: The United States and the Triumph of the Cuban Revolution.* New York: Oxford University Press, 1994.

Pérez, Louis A., Jr. *Army Politics in Cuba, 1898–1958.* Pittsburgh: University of Pittsburgh Press, 1976.

———. *Cuba between Empires, 1878–1902.* Pittsburgh: University of Pittsburgh Press, 1983.

———. *Cuba: Between Reform and Revolution,* 2d ed. New York: Oxford University Press, 1995.

———. *Cuba under the Platt Amendment, 1902–1934.* Pittsburgh: University of Pittsburgh Press, 1986.

———. "Dependency." In *Explaining the History of American Foreign Relations,* edited by Michael Hogan and Thomas G. Paterson, 99–110. New York: Cambridge University Press, 1991.

———. "Insurrection, Intervention, and the Transformation of Land Tenure Systems in Cuba, 1895–1902." *Hispanic American Historical Review* 65, no. 2 (May 1985): 229–54.

———. *Lords of the Mountain: Social Banditry and Peasant Protest in Cuba, 1878–1918.* Pittsburgh: University of Pittsburgh Press, 1989.

———. *On Becoming Cuban: Identity, Nationality and Culture.* Chapel Hill: University of North Carolina Press, 1999.

———. "The Pursuit of Pacification: Banditry and the United States' Occupation of Cuba, 1889–1902." *Journal of Latin American Studies* 18, no. 2 (1986): 313–32.

———. *To Die in Cuba: Suicide and Society.* Chapel Hill: University of North Carolina Press, 2005.

———. *The War of 1898: The United States and Cuba in History and Historiography.* Chapel Hill: University of North Carolina Press, 1998.

Pérez de la Riva, Juan. *El barracón y otros ensayos.* Havana: Editorial de Ciencias Sociales, 1975.

———. "Los recursos humanos de Cuba al comenzar el siglo: inmigración, economía y nacionalidad (1899–1906)." In *La república neo-colonial: anuario de estudios cubanos,* 7–44. Havana: Editorial de Ciencias Sociales, 1975.

Pérez Guzmán, Francisco. *Herida profunda.* Havana: Unión, 1998.

Pérez Guzmán, Francisco, Rolando Zulueta Zulueta, and Yolanda Díaz Martínez. *Guerra de Independencia 1895–1898*. Havana: Editorial de Ciencias Sociales, 1998.

Pérez Stable, Marifeli. *The Cuban Revolution: Origins, Course, and Legacy*, 2d ed. New York: Oxford University Press, 1993.

Pichs Brito, Marina. "Una compañía azucarera, paradigma de las inversiones norte-americanas en Las Tunas." Typed ms., Las Tunas Provincial Archives, January 1999.

Pino Santos, Oscar. *El imperialismo norteamericano en la economía cubana*. Havana: Editorial Lex, 1960.

Pollitt, Brian. "The Cuban Sugar Economy and the Great Depression." *Bulletin of Latin American Research* 3, no. 2 (1984): 3–28.

Portell Vilá, Herminio. *Nueva historia de la República de Cuba*. Miami: La Moderna Poesía, 1986.

Portuondo, Fernando. *Historia de Cuba*. Havana: Editorial Obispo, 1950.

Portuondo Moret, Octaviano. *El soviet de Tacajó: experiencias de un estudiante de los 30*. Santiago de Cuba: Editorial Oriente, 1979.

Primelles, León. *Crónica cubana, 1919–1922*. Havana: Editorial Lex, 1955.

Reid Andrews, George. *Afro-Latin America*. London: Oxford University Press, 2004.

Renato Ibarra, Jorge. *La mediación del '33: Ocaso del machadato*. Havana: Editora Política, 1999.

Richardson, Bonham C. *Igniting the Caribbean's Past: Fire in British West Indian History*. Chapel Hill: University of North Carolina Press, 2004.

Riera Hernández, Mario. *Cuba política, 1899–1955*. Havana: Impresora Modelo, 1955.

Rodríguez García, Judith, and Madelyn Morales Fuentes. "Apuntes para la historia del antiguo central Tuinucú hasta 1959." M.A. thesis, Instituto Superior Pedagógico Silverio Blanco, Sancti Spiritus, 1998.

Rojas, Ursinio. *Las luchas obreras en el central Tacajó*. Havana: Editora Política, 1979.

Román, Reinaldo L. *Governing Spirits: Religion, Miracles, and Spectacles in Cuba and Puerto Rico, 1898–1956*. Chapel Hill: University of North Carolina Press, 2007.

Roseberry, William. "Images of the Peasant in the Consciousness of the Venezuelan Proletariat." In *Proletarians and Protest*, edited by Michael Hanagan and Charles Stephenson, 149–69. Westport, Conn.: Greenwood Press, 1986.

Ruiz, Ramón Eduardo. *Cuba: The Making of a Revolution*. New York: W. W. Norton, 1968.

Sánchez, Serafín. *Héroes humildes; y, los poetas de la guerra*. Havana: Editorial de Ciencias Sociales, 1981.

Santa Cruz y Mallén, Francisco Xavier de. *Historia de Familias Cubanas*, 7 vols. Havana: Editorial Hércules, 1940–50.

Santamaría-García, Antonio. *Sin azúcar, no hay país: la industria azucarera y la economía cubana (1919–1939)*. Seville: University of Seville, 2001.

Santiago Serrano R., Eladio. "Historia del movimiento obrero en el central Melanio Hernández (antes Tuinucú)." Typed ms., photocopy in the author's possession.

———. "La incidencia de un central azucarero en la comunidad 'Tuinucú Ayer y Hoy.'" Typed ms., Sancti Spiritus Public Library Collection, n.d.

Santos, Rosann. "The Peaceful Invasion of 1900: The Harvard University Summer School for Cuban Teachers." Paper presented at the Latin American Studies Association conference, Miami, March 2000.

Sauer, Carl Ortwin. *The Early Spanish Main*. Berkeley: University of California Press, 1966.

Schwartz, Rosalie. *Lawless Liberators: Political Banditry and Cuban Independence*. Durham: Duke University Press, 1989.

Scott, James C. *Domination and the Arts of Resistance: Hidden Transcripts*. New Haven, Conn.: Yale University Press, 1990.

Scott, Rebecca J. *Degrees of Freedom: Louisiana and Cuba after Slavery*. Cambridge, Mass.: Belknap Press, 2005.

———. "Fault Lines, Color Lines, and Party Lines: Race, Labor, and Collective Action in Louisiana and Cuba, 1862–1912." In *Beyond Slavery: Explorations of Race, Labor, and Citizenship in Postemancipation Societies*, edited by Frederick Cooper, Thomas C. Holt, and Rebecca J. Scott, 61–106. Chapel Hill: University of North Carolina Press, 2000.

———. "'The Lower Class of Whites' and 'The Negro Element': Race, Social Identity, and Politics in Central Cuba, 1899–1909." In *La Nación Soñada: Cuba, Puerto Rico y Filipinas ante el 98*, edited by Consuelo Naranjo Orovio, Miguel Angel Puig-Samper, and Luis Miguel García Mora, 179–91. Aranjuez, Spain: Editorial Doce Calle, 1996.

———. *Slave Emancipation in Cuba: The Transition to Free Labor, 1860–1899*. Princeton: Princeton University Press, 1985.

———. "Three Lives, One War: Barbara Pérez, Rafael Iznaga, and Gregoria Quesada between Emancipation and Citizenship." Paper presented at the Latin American and Caribbean Studies Roundtable on War, Race, and Nation in Late Nineteenth-Century Cuba, University of Michigan, Ann Arbor, 7 November 2000.

Secretaría de Agricultura, Comercio y Trabajo. *Industria azucarera de Cuba 1913–1914*. Havana: La Moderna Poesía, 1915.

Shaffer, Kirwin W. *Anarchism and Countercultural Politics in Early Twentieth-Century Cuba*. Gainesville: University Press of Florida, 2005.

Sims, Harold D. "The Cuban Sugar Workers' Progress under the Leadership of a Black Communist, Jesús Menéndez Larrondo, 1941–1948." MACLAS *Latin American Essays* 6 (1993): 9–21.

———. "Cuba's Organized Labor, from Depression to Cold War." MACLAS *Latin American Essays* 11 (1997): 45–62.

Smith, Carol. "Culture and Community: The Languages of Class in Guatemala." In *The Year Left II: Towards a Rainbow Socialism*, edited by Mike Davis, Manning Marable, Fred Pfeil, and Michael Sprinker, 197–217. London: Verso, 1987.

Soler, Rafael. "El Trotskismo en Cuba." Ph.D. diss., Universidad de Oriente, Santiago de Cuba, 1997.

Spalding, Hobart, Jr. *Organized Labor in Latin America: Historical Case Studies of Workers in Dependent Societies*. New York: New York University Press, 1977.

Speck, Mary. "Prosperity, Progress, and Wealth: Cuban Enterprise during the Early Republic, 1902–1927." *Cuban Studies* 36 (2005): 50–86.

Stanley, William. *The Protection Racket State: Elite Politics, Military Extortion, and Civil War in El Salvador*. Philadelphia: Temple University Press, 1996.

Stocking, George. *Race, Culture, and Evolution: Essays in the History of Anthropology*. Chicago: University of Chicago Press, 1982.

Stoner, K. Lynn. *From the House to the Street: The Cuban Women's Movement for Legal Reform*. Durham: Duke University Press, 1991.

———. "Militant Heroines and the Consecration of the Patriarchal State: The Glorification of Loyalty, Combat, and National Suicide in the Making of Cuban National Identity." Paper Presented at the American Historical Association Conference, Chicago, December 2002.

Strode, Hudson. "Behind the Cuban Revolt." *New Republic*, 4 October 1933, 204–7.

Stubbs, Jean. *Tobacco on the Periphery: A Case Study of Cuban Labour History*. Cambridge: Cambridge University Press, 1985.

Suarez Findlay, Eileen J. *Imposing Decency: The Politics of Sexuality and Race in Puerto Rico, 1870–1920*. Durham: Duke University Press, 2000.

Suchlicki, Jaime. *University Students and Revolution in Cuba, 1920–1968*. Coral Gables: University of Miami Press, 1969.

Swanger, Joanna Beth. "Lands of Rebellion: Oriente and Escambray Encountering Cuban State Formation, 1934–1974." Ph.D. diss., University of Texas, Austin, 1999.

Sweig, Julia E. *Inside the Cuban Revolution: Fidel Castro and the Urban Underground*. Cambridge, Mass.: Harvard University Press, 2002.

Tabares del Real, José. *Guiteras*. Havana: Editorial de Ciencias Sociales, 1973.

Thomas, Hugh. *Cuba, the Pursuit of Freedom*. New York: Harper and Row, 1971.

———. *The Cuban Revolution*. New York: Harper and Row, 1971.

Thompson, E. P. *Customs in Common*. New York: New Press, 1993.

———. *The Making of the English Working Class*, reprint ed. London: Pelican Books, 1991.

———. "The Moral Economy of the English Crowd in the Eighteenth Century." *Past and Present* 50 (1971): 76–136.

Thomson, Charles A. "The Cuban Revolution: The Fall of Machado." *Foreign Policy Reports* 11, no. 21 (18 December 1935): 250–60.

———. "The Cuban Revolution: Reform and Reaction." *Foreign Policy Reports* 11, no. 22 (1 January 1936): 265–78.

Tone, John Lawrence. *War and Genocide in Cuba, 1895–1898*. Chapel Hill: University of North Carolina Press, 2006.

Turits, Richard Lee. *Foundations of Despotism: Peasants, the Trujillo Regime, and Modernity in Dominican History*. Stanford, Calif.: Stanford University Press, 2003.

United States. Department of Justice, Spanish Treaty Claims Commission. *Special Report of William E. Fuller, Assistant Attorney General*. Washington, D.C.: Government Printing Office, 1907.

United States. Department of War, Cuban Census Office. *Report on the Census of Cuba, 1899*. Washington, D.C.: Government Printing Office, 1900.

Urbino, Jacobo. "El movimiento obrero y comunista en el territorio de la actual Provincia de Holguín." Typed ms., Provincial Archives of Holguín, n.d.

Urbino Ochoa, Jacobo, Gabriel Milord Ricardo, and Dionisio Estévez Arenas. *Datos para la historia. Movimiento Obrero y Comunista, Holguín 1918–1935*. Holguín: Ediciones Holguín, 1983.

———. "Las primeras luchas obreras en los centrales Chaparra y Delicias." Typed ms., Provincial Archives of Holguín, n.d.

Van Ness, Carl. "Series Directory: The Braga Brothers Collection, 1860–1970." Gainesville: University of Florida, Braga Brothers Collection.

Vega Suñol, José. *Presencia norteamericana en el area nororiental de Cuba*. Holguín: Ediciones Etnicidad y Cultura, 1991.

Villafruela, Omar. *El General de las cañas*. Las Tunas: Editorial Sanlope, 1999.

Viotti da Costa, Emilia. *Crowns of Glory, Tears of Blood: The Demerara Slave Rebellion of 1823*. Oxford: Oxford University Press, 1994.

Walter, Knut. *The Regime of Anastasio Somoza, 1936–1956*. Chapel Hill: University of North Carolina Press, 1993.

Weinstein, Barbara. *For Social Peace in Brazil: Industrialists and the Remaking of the Working Class in São Paulo, Brazil, 1920–1964*. Chapel Hill: University of North Carolina Press, 1996.

Wells, Allen. "Did 1898 Mark a Fundamental Transformation for the Cuban Sugar Industry?" Paper presented at the Latin American and Global Trade Conference, Stanford, Calif., November 2001.

Wells, Allen, and Gilbert M. Joseph. *Summer of Discontent, Seasons of Upheaval: Elite Politics and Rural Insurgency in Yucatán, 1876–1915*. Stanford, Calif.: Stanford University Press, 1996.

Wells, Allen, and Stephen C. Topik, eds. *The Second Conquest of Latin America: Coffee, Henequen, and Oil during the Export Boom, 1900–1930*. Austin: University of Texas Press, 1998.

Whitney, Robert. *State and Revolution in Cuba: Mass Mobilization and Political Change, 1920–1940*. Chapel Hill: University of North Carolina Press, 2001.

Williams, William Applebaum. *The Tragedy of American Diplomacy*. New York: W. W. Norton, 1988.

Winn, Peter. *Weavers of Revolution: The Yarur Workers and Chile's Road to Socialism*. Oxford: Oxford University Press, 1986.

Wolf, Eric, *Europe and the People without History*. Berkeley: University of California Press, 1982.

Wolfe, Joel. *Working Women, Working Men: São Paulo and the Rise of Brazil's Industrial Working Class, 1900–1955*. Durham: Duke University Press, 1993.

Wood, Bryce. *The Making of the Good Neighbor Policy*. New York: W. W. Norton, 1967.

Zanetti, Oscar. "El colonato azucarero cubano en 1959, una aproximación a sus características socioeconómicas." *Revista Bimestre Cubana* 20 (January–June 2004): 64–102.

———. "Historia y azúcar." *Catauro: Revista Cubana de Antropología* 6, no. 11 (2005): 15–25.

———. "The Workers' Movement and Labor Regulation in the Cuban Sugar Industry." *Cuban Studies* 25 (1995): 183–205.

Zanetti, Oscar, and Alejandro García. *Sugar and Railroads: A Cuban History, 1837–1959*, trans. Franklin W. Knight and Mary Todd. Chapel Hill: University of North Carolina Press, 1998.

Zeuske, Michael. "1898. Cuba y el problema de la 'Transición Pactada.' Prolegómeno a una historia de la cultura política en Cuba (1880–1920)." In *La Nación Soñada: Cuba, Puerto Rico y Filipinas ante el 1898*, edited by Consuelo Naranjo Orovio, Miguel Angel Puig-Samper, and Luis Miguel García Mora, 131–47. Aranjuez, Spain: Editorial Doce Calle, 1996.

———. "Clientelas regionales, alianzas interraciales y poder nacional en torno a la 'guerrita de agosto' 1906." *Islas e Imperios* 2 (Spring 1999): 127–56.

———. "'Los negros hicimos la independencia': Aspectos de la movilización afrocubana en un hinterland cubano. Cienfuegos entre colonia y república." In *Espacios, silencios, y los sentidos de la libertad: Cuba, 1878–1912*, edited by Fernando Martínez Heredia, Rebecca Scott, and Orlando García Martínez, 193–234. Havana: Editorial Unión, 2001.

Gillian McGillivray is an assistant professor in the Department of History at Glendon College, York University.

Library of Congress Cataloging-in-Publication Data

McGillivray, Gillian, 1971–
Blazing cane : sugar communities, class, and state formation in Cuba, 1868/1959 / Gillian McGillivray.
p. cm. — (American encounters/global interactions)
Includes bibliographical references and index.
ISBN 978-0-8223-4524-4 (cloth : alk. paper)
ISBN 978-0-8223-4542-8 (pbk. : alk. paper)
1. Cuba—History—1810–1899.
2. Cuba—History—1895–
3. Sugarcane industry—Cuba—History—19th century.
4 . Sugarcane industry—Cuba—History—20th century.
I. Title. II. Series: American encounters/global interactions.
F1783.M397 2009
972.9106—dc22
2009013114